Final Report of the Forty-sixth Antarctic Treaty Consultative Meeting

ANTARCTIC TREATY
CONSULTATIVE MEETING

Final Report of the Forty-sixth Antarctic Treaty Consultative Meeting

Kochi, India
20 - 30 May 2024

Volume I

Secretariat of the Antarctic Treaty
Buenos Aires
2024

Antarctic Treaty Consultative Meeting (46th : 2024 : Kochi)
Final Report of the Forty-sixth Antarctic Treaty Consultative Meeting. Kochi, India, 20 - 30 May 2024.
Buenos Aires : Secretariat of the Antarctic Treaty, 2024.
310 p.

ISBN 978-987-8929-33-0

1. International law – Environmental issues. 2. Antarctic Treaty system.
3. Environmental law – Antarctica. 4. Environmental protection – Antarctica.

DDC 341.762 5

Published by:

Secretariat of the Antarctic Treaty
Secrétariat du Traité sur l'Antarctique
Секретариат Договора об Антарктике
Secretaría del Tratado Antártico

Maipú 757, Piso 4
C1006ACI Ciudad Autónoma Buenos Aires
Argentina
Tel: +54 11 3991 4250
ats@ats.aq

This book is available for free in digital format from www.ats.aq and for purchase in hard copy from https://www.amazon.com/.

ISSN 2346-9897
ISBN 978-987-8929-33-0

Contents

VOLUME I

Acronyms and Abbreviations 9

PART I. FINAL REPORT 11

1. ATCM 46 Final Report 13

2. CEP 26 Report 83

3. Appendices 165

Appendix 1: Preliminary Agenda for ATCM 47, Working Groups and Allocation of Items 167

Appendix 2: Host Country Communiqué 169

PART II. MEASURES, DECISIONS AND RESOLUTIONS 171

1. Measures 173

Measure 1 (2024) Antarctic Specially Protected Area 116 (New College Valley, Caughley Beach, Cape Bird, Ross Island): Revised Management Plan 175

Measure 2 (2024) Antarctic Specially Protected Area 128 (Western shore of Admiralty Bay, King George Island, South Shetland Islands): Revised Management Plan 177

Measure 3 (2024) Antarctic Specially Protected Area No 135 (North-east Bailey Peninsula, Budd Coast, Wilkes Land): Revised Management Plan 179

Measure 4 (2024) Antarctic Specially Protected Area No 136 (Clark Peninsula, Budd Coast, Wilkes Land, East Antarctica): Revised Management Plan 181

Measure 5 (2024) Antarctic Specially Protected Area No 137 (Northwest White Island, McMurdo Sound): Revised Management Plan 183

Measure 6 (2024) Antarctic Specially Protected Area No 141 (Yukidori Valley, Langhovde, Lützow-Holm Bay): Revised Management Plan 185

Measure 7 (2024) Antarctic Specially Protected Area No 142 (Svarthamaren): Revised Management Plan 187

Measure 8 (2024) Antarctic Specially Protected Area No 151 (Lions Rump, King George Island, South Shetland Islands): Revised Management Plan 189

Measure 9 (2024) Antarctic Specially Protected Area No 154 (Botany Bay, Cape Geology, Victoria Land): Revised Management Plan 191

Measure 10 (2024) Antarctic Specially Protected Area No 160 (Frazier Islands, Windmill Islands, Wilkes Land, East Antarctica): Revised Management Plan 193

Measure 11 (2024) Antarctic Specially Protected Area No 161 (Terra Nova Bay, Ross Sea): Revised Management Plan 195

Measure 12 (2024) Antarctic Specially Protected Area No 171 (Narębski Point, Barton Peninsula, King George Island): Revised Management Plan 197

Measure 13 (2024) Antarctic Specially Protected Area No 173 (Cape Washington and Silverfish Bay, Terra Nova Bay, Ross Sea): Revised Management Plan 199

Measure 14 (2024) Antarctic Specially Protected Area No 175 (High Altitude Geothermal sites of the Ross Sea region): Revised Management Plan 201

Measure 15 (2024) Antarctic Specially Protected Area No 180 (Danger Islands Archipelago, North-eastern Antarctic Peninsula): Management Plan 203

Measure 16 (2024) Antarctic Specially Protected Area No 181 (Farrier Col, Horseshoe Island, Marguerite Bay): Management Plan 205

Measure 17 (2024) Antarctic Specially Protected Area No 182 (Western Bransfield Strait and Eastern Dallmann Bay): Management Plan 207

Measure 18 (2024) Revised List of Antarctic Historic Sites and Monuments: new Historic Sites and Monuments No 96 and updating information for Historic Sites and Monuments No 93, 63, 75, and 24 209

2. Decisions **213**

Decision 1 (2024) Notification by the Consultative Parties regarding the list of observers under Article VII of the Antarctic Treaty and Article 14 of the Protocol on Environmental Protection to the Antarctic Treaty through the Secretariat of the Antarctic Treaty 215

Decision 2 (2024) Revised Rules of Procedure for the Antarctic Treaty Consultative Meeting 217

Annex: Revised Rules of Procedure for the Antarctic Treaty Consultative Meeting (2024) 219

Decision 3 (2024) Secretariat Report, Programme and Budget 229

Annex 1: Audited Financial Report for 2022/2023 231

Annex 2: Provisional Financial Report for 2023/2024 241

Annex 3: Secretariat Programme 2024/2025 245

Decision 4 (2024) Multi-year Strategic Work Plan for the Antarctic Treaty Consultative Meeting 255

Annex: ATCM Multi-year Strategic Work Plan 257

Decision 5 (2024) Development of a Framework for the Regulation of Tourism and Other Non-Governmental Activities in Antarctica 265

Annex: List of Topics 267

3. Resolutions **269**

Resolution 1 (2024) Revised Guide to the Preparation of Management Plans for Antarctic Specially Protected Areas 271

Annex: Guide to the Preparation of Management Plans for Antarctic Specially Protected Areas 273

Resolution 2 (2024) General Guidelines for Visitors to the Antarctic 305

Annex: General Guidelines for Visitors to the Antarctic 307

Additional documents derived from this meeting, including opening and closing remarks, reports from Depositaries, Observers and Experts, a list of participants, and other materials, are available in the Final Reports section of the ATS website. Management plans adopted at this meeting are available as attachments in the Antarctic Treaty database.

Acronyms and abbreviations

ACAP	Agreement on the Conservation of Albatrosses and Petrels
ACBR	Antarctic Conservation Biogeographic Region
ASMA	Antarctic Specially Managed Area
ASOC	Antarctic and Southern Ocean Coalition
ASPA	Antarctic Specially Protected Area
ATS	Antarctic Treaty System or Antarctic Treaty Secretariat
ATCM	Antarctic Treaty Consultative Meeting
ATCP	Antarctic Treaty Consultative Party
ATME	Antarctic Treaty Meeting of Experts
BP	Background Paper
CCAMLR	Convention on the Conservation of Antarctic Marine Living Resources and/or Commission for the Conservation of Antarctic Marine Living Resources
CCAS	Convention for the Conservation of Antarctic Seals
CCRWP	Climate Change Response Work Programme
CEE	Comprehensive Environmental Evaluation
CEP	Committee for Environmental Protection
COMNAP	Council of Managers of National Antarctic Programs
EIA	Environmental Impact Assessment
EIES	Electronic Information Exchange System
HCA	Hydrographic Committee on Antarctica
HSM	Historic Site or Monument
IAATO	International Association of Antarctica Tour Operators
IBA	Important Bird Area
ICAO	International Civil Aviation Organization
ICG	Intersessional Contact Group
IEE	Initial Environmental Evaluation
IGP&I Clubs	International Group of Protection and Indemnity Clubs
IHO	International Hydrographic Organization
IMO	International Maritime Organization
IOC	Intergovernmental Oceanographic Commission
IOPC Funds	International Oil Pollution Compensation Funds
IP	Information Paper
IPCC	Intergovernmental Panel on Climate Change
IUCN	International Union for Conservation of Nature
MPA	Marine Protected Area
NCA	National Competent Authority
RCC	Rescue Coordination Centre
SAR	Search and Rescue
SCAR	Scientific Committee on Antarctic Research
SC-CAMLR	Scientific Committee of CCAMLR
SGCCR	Subsidiary Group on Climate Change Response
SGMP	Subsidiary Group on Management Plans
SOLAS	International Convention for the Safety of Life at Sea
SOOS	Southern Ocean Observing System
SP	Secretariat Paper
ToR	Term of Reference
UAV/RPAS	Unmanned Aerial Vehicle / Remotely Piloted Aircraft System
UNEP	United Nations Environment Programme
UNFCCC	United Nations Framework Convention on Climate Change
VSSOS	Vessel-Supported Short Overnight Stay
WMO	World Meteorological Organization
WP	Working Paper
WTO	World Tourism Organization

PART I

Final Report

1. ATCM 46 Final Report

Final Report of the Forty-sixth Antarctic Treaty Consultative Meeting

Kochi, India, 21 – 30 May 2024

(1) Pursuant to Article IX of the Antarctic Treaty, Representatives of the Consultative Parties (Argentina, Australia, Belgium, Brazil, Bulgaria, Chile, China, Czechia, Ecuador, Finland, France, Germany, India, Italy, Japan, the Republic of Korea, the Netherlands, New Zealand, Norway, Peru, Poland, the Russian Federation, South Africa, Spain, Sweden, Ukraine, the United Kingdom of Great Britain and Northern Ireland, the United States of America, and Uruguay) met in Kochi from 21 to 30 May 2024, for the purpose of exchanging information, holding consultations, and considering and recommending to their Governments measures in furtherance of the principles and objectives of the Treaty. The Meeting was held in person with a virtual audience.

(2) The Meeting was also attended by delegations from the following Contracting Parties to the Antarctic Treaty which are not Consultative Parties: Belarus, Canada, Colombia, Estonia, Malaysia, Portugal, Romania, Switzerland, Türkiye and Venezuela.

(3) In accordance with Rules 2 and 31 of the Rules of Procedure, Observers from the Commission for the Conservation of Antarctic Marine Living Resources (CCAMLR), the Scientific Committee on Antarctic Research (SCAR) and the Council of Managers of National Antarctic Programs (COMNAP) attended the meeting.

(4) In accordance with Rule 39 of the Rules of Procedure, Experts from the following international organisations and non-governmental organisations attended the Meeting: the Antarctic and Southern Ocean Coalition (ASOC), the International Association of Antarctica Tour Operators (IAATO), the International Union for the Conservation of Nature (IUCN), the United Nations Environment Programme (UNEP), and the World Meteorological Organization (WMO).

(5) The Host Country, India, fulfilled its information requirements towards the Contracting Parties, Observers and Experts through the Secretariat, Circulars, letters, and a dedicated website.

Item 1: Opening of the Meeting

(6) The Meeting was officially opened on 21 May 2024. On behalf of the Host Government, in accordance with Rules 5 and 6 of the Rules of Procedure, the Head of the Host Government Secretariat, Dr Vijay Kumar, called the Meeting to order and proposed the candidacy of Ambassador Pankaj Saran as Chair of ATCM 46. The proposal was accepted and Ambassador Saran was elected as Chair of the ATCM 46 in accordance with Rule 6.

(7) The Chair warmly welcomed all Parties, Observers and Experts to Kochi. The Chair thanked the Meeting for its trust and expressed his hope that Parties could interact productively for the good of Antarctica and for the Antarctic Treaty. Noting the remoteness and the difficult conditions of the Antarctic winter, the Chair acknowledged the valuable contributions of the people participating in their national Antarctic programmes, supporting and conducting scientific research on the Antarctic continent.

(8) Delegates observed a minute of silence in honour of friends, colleagues, and service members who had been active in the Antarctic community and had passed away in the previous year.

(9) Minister Kiren Rijiju, Union Cabinet Minister, Ministry of Earth Sciences and Ministry of Food Processing Industries, Government of India, welcomed delegates to Kochi and expressed India's honour in hosting an ATCM for the second time. Mr Rijiju recalled the

ancient Sanskrit wisdom *Vasudhaiva Kutumbakam*, meaning "one earth, one family, one future", as a guiding principle to unite Parties under the Antarctic Treaty system, promoting peace, cooperation, and the preservation of Antarctica for humankind. Mr Rijiju underlined that India was proud to contribute to the ongoing dialogue and emphasised that collaboration was essential for stewardship of the most pristine continent in the world. He noted that Antarctica, with its vast icy wilderness expanse, was a critical climate regulator and sentinel of climate change. It held invaluable information about the planet's past and future climate and was a dynamic living laboratory that demanded the highest protection from Parties. He recalled that India's Antarctic connection dated back to 1956 when India advocated Antarctica as the land for peace at the 11th UN General Assembly. He noted that since the first Indian Scientific Expedition to Antarctica in 1981, India had remained committed to the principles of the Antarctic Treaty for the utilisation of Antarctica for peaceful purposes and scientific research. He shared that India's research station Maitri, established in 1989, had been the country's primary workhorse, facilitating numerous scientific endeavours and expeditions, and stood as a beacon of India's enduring commitment to Antarctic research. He further added that in 2012, India expanded its research capabilities with the establishment of Bharati, reiterating its commitment to peace and science. Mr Rijiju announced India's plan to expand its research capabilities by constructing a new station, Maitri-II, and stressed that India's goal was to strengthen global scientific knowledge, especially vital studies on mitigating the impacts of climate change. Mr Rijiju emphasised the critical role Antarctica played in regulating global climate, sea levels and ocean currents, weather patterns and marine life, and underlined that its protection was essential for preserving biodiversity and ecological balance. Mr Rijiju emphasised that by participating in conservation efforts, Parties could ensure that this pristine continent remained a symbol of international collaboration and environmental stewardship. He called on Parties to reaffirm their shared commitments to these principles and work towards preserving Antarctica for future generations, fostering a spirit of collaboration and mutual respect, noting that decisions made during the meeting would echo through time, shaping the destiny of the pristine land. He wished the Parties a successful meeting and iterated working together as a global family for the betterment of the planet and preservation of Antarctica.

(10) Ambassador Pavan Kapoor, Secretary (West) of the Ministry of External Affairs of India, Government of India, thanked the Chair and welcomed all Parties to ATCM 46. He expressed India's honour in hosting an ATCM for the second time. He highlighted the importance of Antarctica as a natural laboratory for understanding ocean systems and climate change and emphasised the need to advance scientific knowledge to find solutions to climate change and global warming, especially in polar ecosystems. He mentioned that India abided by the fundamental principles of the Antarctic Treaty system and asked all Parties to do the same. Referring to Article 2 of the Environmental Protocol, Ambassador Kapoor emphasised that Parties should show their commitment to designating Antarctica as a natural reserve devoted to peace and science. Ambassador Kapoor highlighted that India's 43rd Antarctic expedition underway in Antarctica included scientists from Bangladesh and Mauritius, and noted India stood ready for any possible collaboration with all like-minded Parties to undertake joint scientific research in the Antarctic. Ambassador Kapoor referred to India's Antarctic Act, which was in accordance with India's accession to the Antarctic Treaty, Madrid Protocol, and Convention on the Conservation of Antarctic Marine Living Resources. He added that the Act aimed to provide a stable, transparent and accountable process for regulating India's interest and involvement in activities in the Antarctic, including tourism and fisheries. He concluded by urging all Parties to engage in outcome-oriented discussions for the development of a tourism framework, which was imperative to protect the pristine Antarctic environment and related fragile ecosystems.

(11) Dr Shailesh Nayak, Director of the National Institute of Advanced Studies and Former Secretary of the Ministry of Earth Sciences, Government of India, highlighted that

Antarctica was a unique territory free from sovereign control and international discord and that the region had seen significant advancements in understanding its role in modulating global weather and climate. Dr Nayak underlined that three major issues related to climate change required attention. First, he noted that the rate of polar ice sheet melting had accelerated, contributing to a rise in the global sea level, and that the stability of Antarctic ice shelves and shifting of atmospheric rivers towards Antarctica were a significant concern for the world. Dr Nayak reported that the second issue involved the impact of regional warming, ocean acidification, and sea ice distribution changes on Antarctic species, ecosystems, and resources. He noted that the habitat and food availability for many species were shrinking, certain penguin populations were dwindling and experiencing shifts due to warming, and there was a risk of non-native species becoming invasive. Dr Nayak highlighted that the third issue involved the increasing demand for resources and the potential for exploitation of mineral resources, noting that the Environment Protocol prohibited such activity only for Contracting Parties, which could further be aggravated by unregulated tourism. He emphasised the need for strategies to protect ecologically sensitive areas, the importance of long-term monitoring and baseline data for marine life, and the challenges posed by increased human activities and tourism. Dr Nayak called for improved compliance with environmental laws, scientific information especially climate change forecasts, and decision-making to address these global challenges. He acknowledged the ATCM as the platform for international cooperation to safeguard Antarctica's environment and scientific values. Dr Nayak called for collaboration and mutual respect to ensure Antarctica's preservation for future generations.

Item 2: Election of Officers and Creation of Working Groups

(12) Dr Anna Fioretti, Head of Delegation of Italy, Host Country of ATCM 47, was elected Vice-chair. In accordance with Rule 7 of the Rules of Procedure, Mr Albert Lluberas Bonaba, Executive Secretary of the Antarctic Treaty Secretariat, acted as Secretary to the Meeting. Dr Vijay Kumar, head of the Host Country Secretariat, acted as Deputy Secretary.

(13) The Meeting noted that the meeting of the Committee for Environmental Protection was led by its first Vice-chair Dr Anoop Kumar Tiwari of India, with support from Vice-chair Dr Heike Herata of Germany.

(14) Three Working Groups were established:

- Working Group 1: Policy, Legal and Institutional Issues;
- Working Group 2: Operations, Science and Tourism;
- Special Working Group 3: Development of a Tourism Framework.

(15) The following Chairs of the Working Groups were elected:

- Working Group 1: Mr Theodore Kill from the United States;
- Working Group 2: Ms Sonia Ramos Garcia from Spain and Dr Phillip Tracey from Australia;
- Special Working Group 3: Prof. Dr René Lefeber from the Netherlands.

Item 3: Adoption of the Agenda and Allocation of Items to Working Groups and Consideration of the Multi-year Strategic Work Plan

(16) The following Agenda was adopted:

1. Opening of the Meeting
2. Election of Officers and Creation of Working Groups
3. Adoption of the Agenda and Allocation of Items to Working Groups and Consideration of the Multi-year Strategic Work Plan

4. Operation of the Antarctic Treaty System: Reports by Parties, Observers and Experts
5. Report of the Committee for Environmental Protection
6. Operation of the Antarctic Treaty System
   a. Request from Canada to become a Consultative Party
   b. Request from Belarus to become a Consultative Party
   c. General matters
7. Operation of the Antarctic Treaty System: Matters related to the Secretariat
8. Liability
9. Biological Prospecting in Antarctica
10. Exchange of Information
11. Education Issues
12. Multi-year Strategic Work Plan
    a. Policy, Legal and Institutional priorities
    b. Science, Operations and Tourism priorities
13. Safety and Operations in Antarctica
14. Inspections under the Antarctic Treaty and the Environment Protocol
15. Science issues, future science challenges, scientific cooperation and facilitation
16. Implications of Climate Change for Management of the Antarctic Treaty Area
17. Tourism and Non-Governmental Activities in the Antarctic Treaty Area, including Competent Authorities Issues
18. Development of a Tourism Framework
19. Preparation of the 47th Meeting
20. Any Other Business
21. Adoption of the Final Report
22. Close of the Meeting

(17) The Meeting adopted the following allocation of agenda items:

- Plenary: Items 1, 2, 3, 4, 5, 6a, 6b, 19, 20, 21, 22.
- Working Group 1: Items 6c, 7, 8, 9, 10, 11, 12a.
- Working Group 2: Items 12b, 13, 14, 15, 16, 17.
- Special Working Group 3: Item 18.

(18) The Meeting also decided to allocate draft instruments arising out of the work of the Committee for Environmental Protection and the Working Groups to a legal drafting group for consideration of their legal and institutional aspects.

Item 4: Operation of the Antarctic Treaty System: Reports by Parties, Observers and Experts

(19) Pursuant to Recommendation XIII-2, the Meeting received reports from depositary governments and secretariats.

(20) The United States, in its capacity as Depositary Government of the Antarctic Treaty and its Environmental Protocol, reported on the status of the Antarctic Treaty and the Protocol on Environmental Protection to the Antarctic Treaty (IP 95 rev. 2). Since the last report, there had been one accession to the Antarctic Treaty. The United States noted that the

Kingdom of Saudi Arabia deposited its instrument of accession on 22 May 2024, and the Antarctic Treaty entered into force for the Kingdom of Saudi Arabia on the same date. With respect to Measure 1 (2005) recommending that Annex VI on Liability Arising from Environmental Emergencies form part of the Environmental Protocol, the United States reported that Czechia approved Measure 1 (2005) on 21 May 2024. With respect to Measure 16 (2009) (Amended Annex II), Czechia approved Measure 16 (2009) on 21 May 2024. The United States noted that there were currently 57 Contracting Parties to the Treaty and 42 Parties to the Protocol.

(21) The United States highlighted that the President of the United States had very recently signed a new United States policy on the Antarctic region, noting it was the first update of Presidential Antarctic policy since 1994. The United States also acknowledged the valuable work and significant contributions of Dr Polly Penhale to the ATCM and CEP over the past 21 years.

(22) Australia, in its capacity as Depositary for the Convention on the Conservation of Antarctic Marine Living Resources (CCAMLR), reported that it had not received any requests to accede to the Convention or any instruments of accession since ATCM XLV (IP 50).

(23) The United Kingdom, in its capacity as Depositary of the Convention for the Conservation of Antarctic Seals (CCAS), reported that it had not received any requests to accede to the Convention or any instruments of accession since ATCM XLV (IP 81). The United Kingdom reminded Contracting Parties to CCAS that the Exchange of Information for the reporting period of 1 March 2023 to 28 February 2024 was due by 30 June 2024. The United Kingdom encouraged all Contracting Parties to CCAS to submit their returns on time.

(24) Australia, in its capacity as Depositary for the Agreement on the Conservation of Albatrosses and Petrels (ACAP), reported that there had been no new accessions to the Agreement since ATCM XLV and that there were currently 13 Parties to the Agreement (IP 49).

(25) CCAMLR presented IP 34 rev. 1 *Report by the CCAMLR Observer to the Forty-Sixth Antarctic Treaty Consultative Meeting*, which reported on the 42nd Annual Meeting of the Commission for the Conservation of Antarctic Marine Living Resources (CCAMLR-42) held in Hobart, Australia, from 16 to 27 October 2023. Mr V. Tsymbaliuk (Ukraine) chaired the Meeting. CCAMLR noted that the Standing Committee on Implementation and Compliance (SCIC), the Standing Committee on Administration and Finance (SCAF) and the Scientific Committee met in Hobart the week of 16 to 20 October 2023. In response to the threats associated with Highly Pathogenic Avian Influenza (HPAI), the Commission had requested that the CCAMLR Secretariat cooperate with other organisations to track HPAI outbreaks and develop guidance on HPAI for fishing vessels and scientific observers. CCAMLR reported that modifications to krill-related conservation measures were proposed in relation to the new krill management approach being developed by the Commission, including a proposal for collecting acoustic data from fishing vessels. The Commission had agreed to hold, jointly with the Scientific Committee, a symposium in 2024 which would provide recommendations to CCAMLR on steps to harmonise the implementation of the revised krill fishery management approach and the establishment of a Domain 1 MPA in the Antarctic Peninsula Region. The Commission had adopted revised Conservation Measures relating to toothfish and icefish fisheries. CCAMLR reported that the Third Special Meeting of the Commission (CCAMLR-SM-III) was held in Santiago, Chile, from 19 to 23 June 2023 to consider how to progress MPA design, designation and implementation. The Commission noted that despite not achieving the desired outcome of creating a roadmap to establishing a representative system of MPAs, the meeting had generated a better understanding of the different positions among members, facilitating a clearer vision for a way forward. CCAMLR reported that it would host its next meeting in Hobart from 14 to 25 October 2024.

(26) SCAR presented IP 10 *The Scientific Committee on Antarctic Research Annual Report 2024 to the 46th Antarctic Treaty Consultative Meeting*, which summarised its recent work to advance scientific research and to promote scientific knowledge, understanding and education on the Antarctic region. SCAR informed the Meeting that its flagship Scientific Research Programmes, INStabilities & Thresholds in ANTarctica (INSTANT), AntClimNow, and AntICON, continued to address high-priority topical scientific questions. Group activities within SCAR were also highlighted, including work on the Highly Pathogenic Avian Influenza (HPAI), the RINGS Action Group, the Krill Expert Group, the Antarctic Near-Shore and Terrestrial Observation System (ANTOS) Expert Group, the Astronomy & Astrophysics from Antarctica (AAA) Expert Group, the Plastics Action Group, and the development of a new group: the Antarctic Monitoring and Assessment Programme (AnMAP). SCAR informed the Meeting that it continued to engage with the work of bodies of the United Nations: SCAR had participated in a number of side events at the United Nations Climate Change Conference (COP28) and also noted that it had recently received accreditation from the United Nations Environment Programme. SCAR notified the Meeting that its 11th Open Science Conference would be held in Pucón, Chile, from 19 to 23 August 2024, and the 38th Delegates Meeting would be held in Punta Arenas, Chile, from 26 to 28 August 2024.

(27) COMNAP presented IP 16 *Annual Report 2023/2024 for the Council of Managers of National Antarctic Programs (COMNAP)*, also referring to its Annual General Meeting 2023, the 20th COMNAP Symposium (BP 3) and the 5th COMNAP Antarctic Search & Rescue Workshop (IP 1). COMNAP noted it had 33 member national Antarctic programmes, with Portugal becoming the 33rd Member programme. COMNAP highlighted the preparedness and response to the heightened risk of HPAI in Antarctica which had travelled by way of natural migration of wildlife species to the Antarctic Treaty area for the first time in late December 2023, and noted that the work on addressing HPAI continued (WP 47 and IP 4). The paper showcased examples of international collaboration and noted the range of COMNAP tools produced in support of information exchange and safety. COMNAP also noted its work on improving efficiency in operations, preventing harassment in Antarctica, developing best practice in support of facilitation of science, and education and outreach.

(28) The Meeting thanked COMNAP for its report and acknowledged its important support to the Antarctic Treaty system, noting the value of sustained cooperation between national Antarctic programmes in support of science and safe operations in Antarctica.

(29) In relation to Article III-2 of the Antarctic Treaty, the Meeting received reports from other international organisations.

(30) WMO presented IP 9 rev. 1 *Annual Report of the World Meteorological Organisation (WMO)*. WMO noted that its purpose as documented in its Convention of the World Meteorological Organization covered a range of technological and scientific activities on weather and climate research that were of relevance to the work of the ATCM. WMO reported on various aspects of its Antarctic science activities, world climate and world weather research programmes and Antarctic climate services, including participation in a high-level panel on high mountains and glaciers. WMO took the opportunity to reaffirm its commitment to working in partnership with the Antarctic Treaty system and the other expert bodies in the spirit of Resolution 2 (2014) on oceanographic and cryospheric research.

(31) ASOC presented IP 142 *ASOC Report to the ATCM*. ASOC reported on its activities that were relevant to the work of the ATCM and the protection of the Antarctic environment. These included attendance at meetings of the IMO, the UNFCCC and CCAMLR, and broad support to scientific research and outreach involving krill, baleen whales, penguins,

and other species, as well as their natural habitats. The outreach included engaging with World Penguin Day and World Krill Day. ASOC noted that the continuing impacts of climate change in Antarctica and the Southern Ocean had received growing attention in the past year and thanked the Parties and COMNAP, SCAR and IAATO for their intersessional cooperation. Observing how independent actors had begun to promote geoengineering schemes in the Antarctic, ASOC also stated that it believed these initiatives were misguided and that the most efficient method for mitigating adverse climate change continued to be global emissions reductions.

(32) IAATO presented IP 101 *Report of the International Association of Antarctica Tour Operators 2023-24.* IAATO highlighted its continued collaboration with SCAR and COMNAP to address the anticipated arrival of HPAI in the Antarctic area, including the revision of its guidelines and protocols, actions taken through the season and supporting a scientific expedition. IAATO drew attention to the work it had done around its five-year strategic plan, *Embracing Our Role as Stewards of Antarctica*, and noted that 17 new IAATO Visitor Site Guidelines had been approved at its 2024 Annual General Meeting. IAATO thanked several Parties and Experts for attending its annual meeting and welcomed all Parties to join in the coming year in Portugal. IAATO reaffirmed its continued support of scientific work in Antarctica, including joint early career fellowships with COMNAP and logistical support to the national Antarctic programmes. IAATO also expressed its appreciation for the opportunity to continue to participate in intersessional discussions, including the COMNAP Annual General Meeting and the Workshop on Tourism Monitoring hosted by Germany online in October 2023.

(33) The Meeting thanked WMO, ASOC, and IAATO for their reports and welcomed their continuing contribution to the work of the ATCM and the CEP.

(34) Dr Sheeba Chenoli presented a lecture referring to IP 162 *Decoding the Intricate Link Between the Tropics and Antarctica* (SCAR). Dr Chenoli explained that the scientific understanding of tropical influences on the Antarctic climate had recently improved, with significant implications for understanding and projecting future changes to the Antarctic climate and ice shelves. Dr Chenoli introduced the concept of climate interactions between Antarctica and the tropical latitudes and illustrated them with concrete examples of regional impacts from tropical weather phenomena from the Indian and Atlantic Oceans in Antarctica, as well as the effects of Antarctic climate variability and weather felt in the Indian Ocean and Southern Hemisphere land masses such as South America and Australia, and on the Indian monsoon, due to Antarctic teleconnections. She highlighted SCAR's ongoing work and outreach activities and stressed the need for future research on this important topic.

(35) The Meeting thanked Dr Chenoli for her lecture and recognised the importance of this subject for the Antarctic Treaty system as a whole. Parties emphasised the significance of the findings that helped understand various teleconnections between Antarctic climate conditions and global weather phenomena, including the monsoon and the El Niño. The Meeting commended SCAR for its continuing work, stressed the need for sustained long-term observations and improved climate models, and restated its commitment to supporting Antarctic scientific research through SCAR and the national Antarctic programmes.

Item 5: Report of the Committee for Environmental Protection

(36) Dr Anoop Kumar Tiwari, first Vice-chair of the Committee for Environmental Protection, introduced the report of CEP 26. The CEP had considered 43 Working Papers and 85 Information Papers, noting the consistency in workload from the past few years. Dr Tiwari noted that 38 of 42 Members had attended CEP 26.

(37) Dr Tiwari recalled ATS Circular 4/2024 that had informed Parties about the resignation of CEP Chair Patricia Ortúzar of Argentina. Dr Tiwari explained that in accordance with Rule

17 of the CEP Rules of Procedure, the CEP meeting had been chaired by the first Vice-chair, and he thanked second Vice-chair Dr Heike Herata of Germany for her support.

(38) The Chair of the CEP advised that there had been no new accessions to the Protocol since the last meeting and that the CEP still comprised 42 Members.

(39) The Meeting thanked Dr Tiwari for chairing the CEP at short notice and for both Vice-chairs' efficient shared leadership during CEP 26. It also acknowledged the breadth of work undertaken by the CEP and thanked its Members for their endeavours.

(40) The Meeting underscored the important role of the CEP in providing advice to the Parties in connection with the implementation of the Environmental Protocol. Some Parties highlighted the importance of all CEP Members' actively engaging in intersessional work, noting that some Members had raised concerns and objections only during the CEP meeting after having not participated in intersessional discussions.

(41) Some Parties, recalling that the CEP was an independent body, also suggested that the CEP and ATCM consider amending their meeting schedules to maximise the ATCM's opportunity to fully consider and action the CEP's advice.

Strategic Discussions on the Future Work of the CEP (CEP Agenda Item 3)

(42) The Chair of the CEP reported that the Committee had discussed the outcomes of the Intersessional Contact Group (ICG) established at CEP XXV to develop a draft revised Five-year Work Plan for consideration at CEP 26 and to give advice on practical measures that the CEP might consider in initiating, pursuing, and monitoring progress on Work Plan actions. The Committee had agreed to adopt the Five-year Work Plan. It had also agreed to continue reviewing and updating the Five-year Work Plan to reflect the agreed outcomes of discussions at the CEP and to review the work plan strategically on a regular basis.

(43) The Meeting commended the CEP on the completion of its review of the Five-year Work Plan. It noted that the Five-year Work Plan was a flexible and practical guide for the CEP and an important tool for communicating CEP priorities and actions to the ATCM and a broader audience.

Operation of the CEP (CEP Agenda Item 4)

(44) The Chair of the CEP reported that work had progressed during the intersessional period in 2023/24, along with anticipated outcomes for CEP 27.

(45) Some Parties noted that the ATCM had not received any new advice from the CEP on liability arising from environmental emergencies since 2013. Noting that the ATCM had a pending decision in 2025 to discuss the timeframe for a resumption of liability negotiations, they suggested it would be valuable for the CEP to consider if its 2013 advice remained up to date.

Cooperation with other Organisations (CEP Agenda Item 5)

(46) The Chair of the CEP reported that the Committee had received annual reports from its Observers and had nominated CEP representatives to attend the meetings of other organisations over the coming year.

Climate Change Implications for the Environment: Strategic approach (CEP Agenda Item 7)

Strategic Approach

(47) The Chair of the CEP reported that the Committee had agreed to advise the ATCM that it supported the development of a best practice manual on the use of renewable energy in Antarctica, the increase of renewable energy use in Antarctic operations, and the promotion of innovative applications of new green energy facilities and technologies suitable for the

unique Antarctic environment. In its advice the Committee also noted that COMNAP would discuss the matter of energy efficiency at its meeting in August 2024, and bring back the outcome for ATCM and CEP consideration.

(48) The Meeting expressed support for developing a best practice manual on using renewable energy in Antarctica and the other recommendations of the CEP. The Meeting also welcomed the work COMNAP had agreed to contribute towards this effort.

(49) The Chair of the CEP reported that the Committee had considered a proposal to update the Climate Change Response Work Programme (CCRWP) with new actions relating to sea-ice change based on a request from the joint ATCM-CEP session on climate change at ATCM XLV (2023). The Committee had expressed concern about the rapid and significant sea-ice loss and its consequences and cumulative impacts on Antarctic species and their habitat and had agreed to update the CCRWP. The Committee had emphasised that it was important to respond to requests from the ATCM in a timely manner.

(50) The Committee had agreed to advise the ATCM that it had updated the CCRWP by including a new sea-ice-related action 'Assess vulnerabilities in space and time, exposed by changing sea-ice extent in the Antarctic Peninsula region and on this basis consider potential management implications for this region, noting that it experiences high and increasing levels of human activity' under the climate-related issue #7 (in CCRWP column 1) as requested by ATCM XLV. The Committee had tasked the SGCCR: to consider and suggest how the proposed tasks could be moved forward, and in doing so also provide an overview of ongoing work that may be relevant in informing this action item; and in collaboration with SCAR, to consider options for preparing an annual update on the most recent sea-ice changes for the CEP's attention to support its work in understanding and act on the implication of sea-ice change for management of human activity.

(51) The Meeting underscored the importance of the CCRWP and encouraged the CEP to continue to implement it as a matter of priority. Noting that the CCRWP had not been updated since 2016 and, in light of rapidly changing environmental conditions, some Parties highlighted the need to regularly update the CCRWP as a whole and not just on a case-by-case basis.

(52) The Meeting echoed the CEP's concern about rapid and significant sea-ice loss and its consequences and cumulative impacts on Antarctic species and their habitat. It welcomed the CEP's decision to add this item to the CCRWP, encouraged additional research on sea-ice loss, and looked forward to annual updates on sea-ice changes.

(53) China suggested that Parties consider the development of a definition and operative criteria of vulnerability in the context of the Antarctic environment in the intersessional period. China also highlighted the importance of assessing distribution, population and habitat change dynamics in the context of climate change with the participation of national Antarctic programmes as well as SCAR, with the view to provide scientific data and advice to the CEP and ATCM. China further expressed the concern on the expected outcome in WP 38 *Updating the CCRWP with new actions relating to sea-ice change,* to prohibit or limit access of human activities to marine or terrestrial areas, taking into account the Antarctic Treaty principle of freedom of scientific investigation.

(54) New Zealand thanked the CEP for its work on climate-vulnerable species, and for the ongoing advice on the need to afford special protection to species accordingly. New Zealand noted that the CEP should not wait for common definitions of concepts like vulnerability or a certain standard of science to implement the CCRWP or to give advice to the ATCM to support precautionary decisions in the context of rapidly changing environments.

(55) The Chair of the CEP noted that the Committee also had discussed a paper about the SCAR AntClimNow Antarctic Climate Indicators project, which had identified a range of

Antarctic Climate Indicators (ACIs) with the aim of providing an accessible visualisation of broad aspects of the Antarctic climate system. The Committee had highlighted the value of Antarctic Climate Indicators for identifying and monitoring climate change impacts and informing the Committee's discussion and decision-making on this topic. The Committee had agreed to invite SCAR to provide annual updates on Antarctic Climate Indicators and had suggested that the Environments Portal might be useful for presenting such information. The relevance of the annual updates on Antarctic Climate Change and the Environment (ACCE) had also been noted.

Implementation and Review of the Climate Change Response Work Programme

(56) The Chair of the CEP noted that the Committee had considered a report from the Subsidiary Group on Climate Change Response (SGCCR), which had outlined the work and outputs of the SGCCR during the intersessional period. The Committee had thanked the SGCCR convenor, Dr Heike Herata, and all SGCCR members for their work during the intersessional period. It had also noted that the SGCCR had made steady progress on several priority issues and should maintain its momentum to ensure the full implementation of the CCRWP.

(57) The Committee had agreed to advise the ATCM that it continued work to implement the CCRWP (2016). Following discussion on the six priority activities endorsed by CEP XXV (2023), the CEP had agreed to advise the ATCM that it had made the following recommendations:

- Supporting work to assess the status of climate-vulnerable Antarctic species (Action 6c): The CEP agreed to start work to identify known climate-vulnerable species as a basis for prioritising efforts to advance assessments of climate-vulnerable species.
- Developing guidance on climate change considerations in documents for establishing and managing protected areas (Action 2e): Noting that SGMP members had commenced reviewing existing tools for area protection and management, the CEP recommended no further action at this time.
- Keeping the Non-native Species Manual updated with current developments (Action 1a): Noting that no urgent revisions were needed, the CEP recommended no further action at this time.
- Intensifying coordination on climate change response in the marine realm with SC-CAMLR (Action 3e): Recognising that efforts were underway for a joint CEP/SC-CAMLR workshop scheduled in 2025, the CEP encouraged Members to actively participate in the preparatory work for this workshop.
- Decontamination of past sites of activities in the Antarctic area (Action 5f); and
- Assessing the risk of climate change for existing and projected Antarctic infrastructure and associated environmental consequences and considering the impacts of climate change linked with the EIA guidelines, e.g., ensuring proposed long-term facilities are suitably resilient to climate change (Actions 5a and 5d): The CEP invited Members to actively pursue efforts to address decontamination of past sites and climate change risks to infrastructure. It also acknowledged COMNAP's ongoing work and suggested aligning future discussions with COMNAP's advice to the CEP meetings in 2024 and 2025.

(58) The Chair of the CEP noted that the Committee had also taken note of and discussed the following actions that had been delivered or concerned ongoing research that was regularly provided to the Committee:

- Action 5a: National operators to assess the risk of change in climate (e.g. permafrost) to their infrastructure and environmental consequences (WP 18 and IP 30);

- Action 5b: Assess risk of climate change to HSM/heritage ASPA (IP 88 and IP 120);
- Action 6c: Supporting work to assess the status of climate-vulnerable Antarctic species (WP 34 and WP 48); and
- Action 7: Improved understanding of potential expansion of human presence in Antarctica as a result of changes resulting from climate change through e.g. changes in sea ice distribution; collapse of ice shelves; expansion of ice-free area (WP 37).

(59) The Meeting thanked the SGCCR and its convenor Dr Heike Herata for their extensive and important work in supporting implementation of the CCRWP, noting that the six priority activities identified by the CEP were timely and worthy of focus. Noting that climate change was an important driver of biodiversity loss, several Parties also stressed the importance of assessing the status of climate-vulnerable species.

(60) The Chair of the CEP reported that the Committee had continued its preparation of the next joint CEP/SC-CAMLR Workshop, agreeing to hold a joint CEP/SC-CAMLR workshop focusing on climate change and its impacts in Antarctica in conjunction with CEP 27 in 2025. The Committee had noted that the final dates, location, and format would be examined by the Steering Committee, and would be confirmed in due course by a Circular from the CEP Chair.

(61) The Chair of the CEP reported that the Committee had agreed to: adopt the terms of reference provided by SC-CAMLR; appoint new CEP co-convenors; adopt the revised composition of the workshop steering committee; and provide guidance on the practical arrangements of the workshop. The Committee had also requested the ATCM to allocate a budget for the joint CEP/SC-CAMLR workshop.

(62) Highlighting the need for collaboration with other organisations to address climate change, the Meeting strongly supported the joint CEP/SC-CAMLR workshop on climate change and monitoring. It further agreed to allocate a budget for the workshop.

(63) Some Parties highlighted the work already undertaken to plan for the workshop, and expressed their hope that the steering committee would overcome practical issues so that the workshop could be held in 2025. The United Kingdom expressed the view that an online workshop should not be ruled out if an in-person workshop could not be organised.

(64) The Committee had also considered a paper on COMNAP's work in assessing built infrastructure and potential environmental consequences of a changing Antarctica. The Committee had endorsed the recommendation that Members support their national Antarctic programmes by participating in and continuing to provide their technical and practical expertise to the topical discussions at COMNAP Annual General Meetings and throughout the year.

(65) Noting that the CEP had considered many of the same papers submitted under ATCM Agenda Item 16, the United Kingdom suggested that the Meeting consider if the CEP and ATCM might be presented with this scientific information together in the plenary on the first day of the ATCM.

Environmental Impact Assessment (EIA) (CEP Agenda Item 8)

Other EIA Matters

(66) The Chair of the CEP reported that the Committee had discussed potential improvements to the CEE review procedures. The Committee had underscored the EIA process as a fundamental part of the Environmental Protocol's framework for environmental protection. It had acknowledged the importance of continued review and update of the EIA

process to ensure it remained an effective and contemporary tool. It had also acknowledged the need for further guidance on the application of Annex I, including the circumstances under which a new or revised EIA could be required and the application of the EIA processes in situations where any activity changed.

(67) The Chair of the CEP advised that the Committee would discuss improvements to CEE review procedures through informal intersessional discussions and that the Committee had welcomed the offer from New Zealand and the United Kingdom to jointly lead these informal intersessional discussions.

(68) The Committee had also noted that the ATCM would discuss screening and scoping in the CEE process and agreed to advise the ATCM that it stood ready to consider any requests arising.

(69) The Meeting noted that the CEP would have intersessional discussions on the issue.

(70) The CEP Chair reported that the Committee had considered a paper on cumulative impacts in Antarctica. The Committee had endorsed the recommendation to collate an evaluation of best practice methods and approaches used to assess cumulative impacts. It highlighted the value of considering experience from within and away from Antarctica. The Committee had agreed to advise the ATCM that it would continue discussions to advance guidance on cumulative impact assessment and had included tasks related to this in its Five-year Work Plan.

(71) The Meeting noted the continued importance of better understanding cumulative impacts and supported the CEP's renewed focus on this topic.

(72) The Chair of the CEP advised that the Committee had considered the issue of nested permitting, which involved the issuance of two or more separate permits for a combined visit on a single vessel that travelled to Antarctica. The Committee had also highlighted the need for increased and effective coordination between national competent authorities as the complexity and interconnectedness of activities increased in Antarctica. The Committee had noted the importance of ensuring all activities were appropriately assessed and authorised and encouraged continued discussion on the topic of nested permits in the National Competent Authorities Forum.

(73) The Committee had agreed to advise the ATCM that: the issue of nested permits should continue to be discussed in the Competent Authorities Discussion Forum as one of the five priority issues to ensure that all activities of the multi-number expeditions were assessed appropriately for environmental impacts; and the Electronic Information Exchange System (EIES) should be updated to allow for the identification of separate authorisations for activities that took place as part of a single overall expedition.

(74) The Meeting agreed the issue of nested permits should continue to be discussed through the Competent Authorities Discussion Forum. The Russian Federation noted that the issue should also be considered by the ATCM.

Area Protection and Management Plans (CEP Agenda Item 9)

Management Plans

(75) The CEP Chair reported that the Committee had considered draft management plans for two proposed new ASPAs at Danger Islands Archipelago, North-eastern Antarctic Peninsula and at Farrier Col, Horseshoe Island, Marguerite Bay, which had been reviewed by the Subsidiary Group for Management Plans (SGMP) and had agreed to forward the management plans to the ATCM for adoption by means of a Measure.

(76) The Committee had considered a revised management plan for a proposed new ASPA at Western Bransfield Strait and Eastern Dallmann Bay (comprising a merger of ASPA 152 Western Bransfield Strait and ASPA 153 Eastern Dallmann Bay), which had been

reviewed by CEP XXV and approved at CCAMLR-42 (2023), and had agreed to forward the management plan to the ATCM for approval by means of a Measure.

(77) The CEP Chair stated that the Committee had further considered 16 revised ASPA management plans, which had undergone pre-meeting review by the SGMP in accordance with its term of reference 4. The Committee had noted that for fourteen of these plans, the pre-meeting review had raised minor issues that had been addressed by the proponents before or at the meeting. The Committee had approved these plans. The CEP Chair noted that most Members had supported putting forward the revised management plan for ASPA 139 Biscoe Point, Anvers Island, Palmer Archipelago, to the ATCM for adoption, but consensus was not reached. The views expressed in the discussion were presented in paragraphs 122-131 of the CEP report.

(78) The Meeting thanked the Committee for its work revising management plans and congratulated the proponents of the management plans.

(79) Many Parties expressed their disappointment that a consensus had not been reached in the CEP on forwarding the revised management plan for ASPA 139 for adoption, even though many Members had indicated that the inclusion of the adjacent marine area was appropriate to increase species protection in the area.

(80) China noted the major change of the ASPA size from 0.6 square kilometres to 3.9 square kilometres to include surrounding marine areas with insufficient support of scientific data, and that alternative measures to manage human impacts in the area need to be considered. China suggested that the proposal be sent to CCAMLR for consideration because of the inclusion of adjacent marine areas. It emphasised that while there was currently no fishing in that area, there could potentially be CCAMLR-related activities in the future.

(81) Many Parties recalled the importance of ASPAs in the context of climate change and that ASPAs should be dynamic to respond to change, and commended the proposal to amend the boundaries of ASPA 139 for doing just that. They recalled that any area, including any marine area, may be designated as an ASPA. It was noted that the terms "major change" and "minor change" of a management plan are not defined, nor do these terms have any status in Annex V of the Protocol. Given the strength of the CEP's advice to the ATCM and the scientific basis for the revised management plan, justifying the inclusion of the very small marine area, they called for the ATCM to adopt the revised Management Plan for ASPA 139 by means of a Measure.

(82) Many Parties expressed their view that this proposal did not need to be forwarded to CCAMLR as the marine area was very small and shallow, and that it would be unsafe to conduct fishing in the area due to pinnacle rocks, and so it would not be an area of interest for any future CCAMLR-related activities. Some Parties referred to the SC-CAMLR Chair's comment in the CEP that there was currently no fishing activity within the proposed boundaries of ASPA 139. Many Parties emphasised that Decision 9 (2005) had been agreed between the ATCM and CCAMLR, and should not be applied in a way that delayed progress by tasking CCAMLR to review areas unlikely to be of interest for fishing, such as the proposed new area.

(83) Regarding the CEP's advice that consensus was not reached on this matter, some Parties pointed out Rule 13 of the CEP Rules of Procedure which stated that the Committee should try to reach consensus, and where that was not possible, should set out all views advanced on the matter in question in its report. Those Parties suggested that Rule 13 allowed for the CEP's advice to the ATCM to set out the views expressed, and emphasised that the ATCM can take decisions on how to move forward if presented with such CEP advice.

(84) Following further discussions, Parties did not reach consensus on the adoption of the revised Management Plan for ASPA 139.

(85) ASOC welcomed the new ASPAs but regretted that the CEP had not reached consensus on forwarding ASPA 139 to the ATCM for adoption. ASOC noted that it had been ten years since research had been published that had concluded that Antarctica's protected areas were inadequate, unrepresentative, and at risk and that the situation had largely not changed. Parties had not met their obligation under Annex V of the Environment Protocol to identify ASPAs within a systematic environmental-geographical framework. ASOC stated that the ATCM seemed to be moving backwards if it could not protect very small areas.

(86) The CEP Chair noted that the Committee had agreed to forward the management plan for a proposed new ASPA at Otto-von-Gruber-Gebirge, Dronning Maud Land, East Antarctica, to the SGMP for review in the coming intersessional period.

(87) China noted that, in the CEP, it had welcomed the referral of the draft management plan to the SGMP for intersessional review on the condition that further consideration would be given to its concerns about the size and boundary of the area, and that it looked forward to further discussions in the intersessional period.

(88) Germany thanked the Committee for supporting its proposal for a new ASPA at Otto-von-Gruber-Gebirge, Dronning Maud Land, East Antarctica, jointly proposed by the United States. It stated that it looked forward to discussions in the SGMP to further develop the management plan.

(89) The Committee had requested the Secretariat add a new field to the Protected Area Database for 'Party undertaking management plan review' and had noted that CEP Members would be added to this field for relevant ASPAs and ASMAs, including ASPA 128 (Poland and the United States) and ASMA 5 (the United States and Norway).

(90) The CEP Chair further noted that the Committee had also considered the prior assessment of two proposed new protected areas under this agenda item. The Committee had agreed that the proposed ASPA at Signy Island, South Orkney Islands merited special protection and had endorsed the development of a Management Plan for the area. The CEP had also encouraged interested Members to work with the co-proponents informally during the intersessional period. With respect to the proposed ASPA within the Collins Bay and Graham Coast, Kyiv Peninsula, the Committee had encouraged the proponent to move forward in collaboration with interested Members and to take into account the concerns and questions raised during the meeting, convening informal discussions during the intersessional period.

(91) France noted that it did not see any obstacles to moving ahead with the proposed new ASPA within the Collins Bay and Graham Coast, Kyiv Peninsula, and that the prior assessment for this area was supported by excellent scientific work.

(92) The Meeting adopted the following Measures on Protected Areas:

- Measure 1 (2024) *Antarctic Specially Protected Area No 116 (New College Valley, Caughley Beach, Cape Bird, Ross Island): Revised Management Plan*
- Measure 2 (2024) *Antarctic Specially Protected Area No 128 (Western shore of Admiralty Bay, King George Island, South Shetland Islands): Revised Management Plan*
- Measure 3 (2024) *Antarctic Specially Protected Area No 135 (North-east Bailey Peninsula, Budd Coast, Wilkes Land): Revised Management Plan*
- Measure 4 (2024) *Antarctic Specially Protected Area No 136 (Clark Peninsula, Budd Coast, Wilkes Land, East Antarctica): Revised Management Plan*
- Measure 5 (2024) *Antarctic Specially Protected Area No 137 (Northwest White Island, McMurdo Sound): Revised Management Plan*
- Measure 6 (2024) *Antarctic Specially Protected Area No 141 (Yukidori Valley,*

Langhovde, Lützow-Holm Bay): Revised Management Plan

- Measure 7 (2024) *Antarctic Specially Protected Area No 142 (Svarthamaren): Revised Management Plan*
- Measure 8 (2024) *Antarctic Specially Protected Area No 151 (Lions Rump, King George Island, South Shetland Islands): Revised Management Plan*
- Measure 9 (2024) *Antarctic Specially Protected Area No 154 (Botany Bay, Cape Geology, Victoria Land): Revised Management Plan*
- Measure 10 (2024) *Antarctic Specially Protected Area No 160 (Frazier Islands, Windmill Islands, Wilkes Land, East Antarctica): Revised Management Plan*
- Measure 11 (2024) *Antarctic Specially Protected Area No 161 (Terra Nova Bay, Ross Sea): Revised Management Plan*
- Measure 12 (2024) *Antarctic Specially Protected Area No 171 (Narębski Point, Barton Peninsula, King George Island): Revised Management Plan*
- Measure 13 (2024) *Antarctic Specially Protected Area No 173 (Cape Washington and Silverfish Bay, Terra Nova Bay, Ross Sea): Revised Management Plan*
- Measure 14 (2024) *Antarctic Specially Protected Area No 175 (High Altitude Geothermal sites of the Ross Sea region): Revised Management Plan*)
- Measure 15 (2024) *Antarctic Specially Protected Area No 180 (Danger Islands Archipelago, North-eastern Antarctic Peninsula): Management Plan*
- Measure 16 (2024) *Antarctic Specially Protected Area No 181 (Farrier Col, Horseshoe Island, Marguerite Bay): Management Plan*
- Measure 17 (2024) *Antarctic Specially Protected Area No 182 (Western Bransfield Strait and Eastern Dallmann Bay): Management Plan*

Historic Sites and Monuments

(93) The CEP Chair reported that the Committee had considered a proposal to update information for HSM 93, Wreck of *Endurance*, and a prior assessment for a proposed ASPA encompassing HSM 93. The Committee had acknowledged the Conservation Management Plan for HSM 93 and had agreed to recommend that the ATCM update the 'Description' information field for the HSM. While some Members had not endorsed the development of a management plan for the area for consideration for ASPA designation, many Members had done so.

(94) The United Kingdom emphasised the historical importance of the *Endurance*. It stated that it had already received several inquiries regarding access to the site and expected more international attention in the near future due to an anticipated documentary. The United Kingdom, therefore, intended to continue by developing a draft ASPA management plan for further protection and welcomed interested Parties to engage in this process during the intersessional period.

(95) New Zealand welcomed the ongoing work to develop a management plan for the site.

(96) The CEP Chair noted that the Committee had also considered a proposal to update information for HSM 63 and had agreed to change the 'Description' and 'Physical features of the environment and cultural and local context' information field of HSM 63.

(97) The Committee had further considered a proposal to update HSM 75 to include its two remaining ancillary structures, the geomagnetic Huts G and H. The Committee had agreed to update the designation of HSM 75.

(98) The CEP Chair reported that the Committee had considered a proposal to update coordinates, description, and conservation status for HSM 24 Amundsen's Cairn. The Committee had agreed to modify the coordinates and description of HSM 24 and to make slight changes to the conservation status description.

(99) The Committee had also considered a proposal for the designation of a new HSM at Lake Untersee, commemorating the first visit to this area. The Committee had highlighted the exploration of the Lake Untersee's value to Antarctic science and had approved the designation of the 'Commemorative plaque of the first visit to the Lake Untersee area' as a new HSM.

(100) The Meeting thanked the Committee for its work on HSMs. The Meeting adopted Measure 18 (2024) *Revised List of Antarctic Historic Sites and Monuments: new Historic Sites and Monuments No 96 and updating information for Historic Sites and Monuments No 93, 63, 75, and 24.*

(101) The CEP Chair reported that the Committee had further agreed to update the listings on the Antarctic Protected Area database:

- The Conservation Status of HSM 75 to read: 'Following major conservation work by the New Zealand-based Antarctic Heritage Trust 2016-17, Hut A is structurally sound and weather tight and artefact collection has been conserved. Annual monitoring and maintenance ensures ongoing stability of this building. Conservation works have yet to be carried out on Huts G and H. The buildings are structurally sound and serviceable, showing the wear and tear expected for buildings some 65 years old. The New Zealand-based Antarctic Heritage Trust intend to carry out asbestos removal and conservation works on the buildings in the coming years'.
- The photographs of HSM 75 to include photos of Hut G and H attached to WP 21 (Figures 1 to 4).
- The Conservation Status of HSM 24 to read: 'The cairn remains intact. There is a paraffin tank inside the cairn, which is in good condition. A tin box containing two notes which was originally placed in the cairn by Amundsen, has long since been removed. A plaque commemorating Amundsen's expedition is placed at the base of the cairn.'
- The photographs attached to WP 41 (Figures 2 to 4).
- The Management Tools of HSM 93 to read: 'A Conservation Management Plan is being updated.'

(102) The Meeting noted these updates to the listings on the database.

Site Guidelines

(103) The CEP Chair reported that the Committee had considered a paper on strengthening the usefulness of Site Guidelines for Visitors. The Committee had highlighted the need and timeliness for revising existing Site Guidelines. The Committee had expressed its disappointment that many Site Guidelines had not been updated in the agreed timeline. The Committee had agreed to endorse informal discussions to further develop the issues raised in the paper, aiming to increase the usefulness and effectiveness of Site Guidelines by improving the consistency, completeness, and usefulness of the information contained within the Site Guidelines. The CEP Chair noted that the Committee had agreed to recommend that the ATCM encourage proponent Parties to revise existing Site Guidelines for Visitors using the Checklist adopted through Resolution 4 (2021).

(104) Noting the CEP's advice, the Meeting supported the revision of existing Site Guidelines for Visitors using the Checklist.

(105) The CEP Chair stated that the Committee had also discussed proposed Visitor Site Guidelines for the emperor penguin colony on Snow Hill Island. The Committee had noted the importance of developing Visitor Site Guidelines for this area. The Committee had welcomed Argentina's offer to lead informal discussions on the proposed guidelines and to submit a revised draft to CEP 27.

(106) New Zealand welcomed the advice of the CEP on Site Guidelines. It recalled that the ATCM had just discussed the importance of site considerations, including the sensitivity and protection of sites, in the context of its work on the tourism framework. It encouraged CEP advice on visitor sites, including on the effectiveness of Site Guidelines, and how they relate to EIAs and other tools that could be helpful for further site management.

Other Annex V Matters

(107) The CEP Chair reported that the Committee had considered the report of the work by the Subsidiary Group on Management Plans (SGMP) under its terms of reference 5 and 6. The SGMP had reviewed and revised the Revised Guide to the Preparation of Management Plans for Antarctic Specially Protected Areas (Resolution 2 (2011)) to consider if and how it effectively considered climate change issues. The Committee had endorsed a revised version of the Guidelines and had also adopted the SGMP work plan for 2024-25.

(108) The Committee had advised the ATCM that, to support Parties to consider climate change issues using existing management tools, it had agreed to forward a draft Resolution on the revised Guide to the Preparation of Management Plans for Antarctic Specially Protected Areas for approval; and to request the Secretariat to make Appendix 2 in the amended Guide available.

(109) The Meeting adopted Resolution 1 (2024) *Revised Guide to the Preparation of Management Plans for Antarctic Specially Protected Areas.*

(110) The Committee had also considered a proposal on the development and use of 'Summary Site Requirements' as a non-mandatory, practical aid to understanding and implementing the detailed measures in ASPA management plans. The Committee had considered this a useful and practical idea, which would help permitted visitors better understand and comply with the requirements and restrictions applicable to them when entering protected areas. The Committee had noted the importance of ensuring that in case of conflict between the ASPA Summary Site Requirements and the management plan, the latter would be the authoritative document.

(111) The Committee had agreed to endorse the development of ASPA Summary Site Requirements where relevant and useful to ensure that those entering ASPAs were aware of the requirements of the management plan. The Committee had agreed that ASPA Summary Site Requirements would be included as an Annex to relevant ASPA management plans. The Committee had further agreed to consider revising the Guide to the Preparation of Management Plans for Antarctic Specially Protected Areas (Resolution 2 (2011)) to include the option of preparing ASPA Summary Site Requirements.

Conservation of Antarctic Flora and Fauna (CEP Agenda Item 10)

Quarantine and Non-native Species

(112) The CEP Chair reported that the Committee had considered updates on the status of Highly Pathogenic Avian Influenza (HPAI) in Antarctica after the 2023/24 season. The Committee had expressed deep concern about the risks of HPAI for Antarctic wildlife and human health and had reaffirmed the importance of maintaining efforts to monitor and prevent the spread. The Committee had commended SCAR, COMNAP, IAATO and CCAMLR for their collaboration and had thanked Members for their coordination in monitoring and reporting.

(113) The Chair of the CEP advised the ATCM that the Committee had agreed to recommendations to: ensure the robust implementation of HPAI biosecurity guidelines and procedures to eliminate or mitigate the risk to humans, as well as the risk of spreading the disease within Antarctica through human activities; encourage continued vigilance and

monitoring, as well as sample collection and testing where necessary expertise is available and permitted; and continue to report and share information on suspected and confirmed cases (including through the SCAR Antarctic Wildlife Health Network (AWHN) HPAI Monitoring Project) to support collaboration, inform decision-making, and improve scientific understanding of the spread and impact of the disease.

(114) The Meeting noted that these recommendations had been agreed by the ATCM (Agenda Item 13).

Specially Protected Species

(115) The CEP Chair reported that the Committee had considered an update from SCAR on the status of the emperor penguin based on results from a recently published 10-year circumpolar assessment (2009-18) of emperor penguin colonies, showing a 9.6% decline in the emperor penguin population during this period. The Committee had thanked SCAR for its commitment to continue this work and encouraged interested Members to contribute to this important topic. It had also supported SCAR's recommendation to encourage Parties to support enhanced collaboration across national Antarctic programmes to improve understanding of the species and factors contributing to observed population change.

(116) The CEP Chair reported that the Committee had also considered a paper that highlighted the recent research showing a decline in the emperor penguin population over the period 2009-18 and an increasing failure of emperor penguin colonies due to the break-up of the fast ice upon which they breed, and that proposed the Committee recommend to the ATCM designation of the emperor penguin as a Specially Protected Species.

(117) The CEP Chair noted that the Committee was unable to reach consensus on the need to designate the emperor penguin as a Specially Protected Species. The Committee had agreed that emperor penguins should remain a high priority for the Committee, had encouraged further intersessional discussion on this matter to resolve any outstanding questions in advance of next year's meeting, and had emphasised the importance of comprehensive participation in these discussions.

(118) The CEP Chair reported that the CEP agreed to advise the ATCM that most Members had strongly supported recommending that the ATCM designate the emperor penguin as a Specially Protected Species, but consensus had not been reached. The views expressed in the discussion were presented in paragraphs 230-240 of the CEP report.

(119) Most Parties expressed disappointment that the CEP had not reached consensus on putting forward advice to designate the emperor penguin as a Specially Protected Species. Most Parties emphasised that there was clear scientific evidence to support the designation. They highlighted that the recent research showing a nearly 10% decline in emperor penguin populations over the past decade added to SCAR's earlier advice that the species was vulnerable to ongoing and projected climate change, in particular due to sea-ice decline. Several Parties raised concerns that not designating the emperor penguin as a Specially Protected Species would hinder its protection and emphasised the importance of taking a precautionary approach, involving concrete action to respond to the threat of climate change and protect an important species, while continuing research to better understand the drivers of the population decline.

(120) Several Parties commended SCAR on its expertise and its clear advice on the status of the emperor penguin population.

(121) While acknowledging that designation as a Specially Protected Species could not prevent sea-ice decline, most Parties emphasised that the designation would allow for action to minimise additional pressures on the emperor penguin, for example including from human activities and HPAI, which could maximise the species' ability to adapt and respond to climate change.

(122) Most Parties pointed out that the emperor penguin was an iconic and emblematic Antarctic species, which resulted in heightened public attention on this matter. They reiterated that there was no scientific basis to oppose the designation of the emperor penguin as a Specially Protected Species, and highlighted that such designation would not have negative impacts.

(123) Most Parties called for the designation of the emperor penguin as a Specially Protected Species by means of a Measure at this meeting on the basis of the strength of the advice from the CEP to the ATCM and the science that underpinned that advice.

(124) Most Parties emphasised that it was the ATCM's responsibility to decide on whether to designate the emperor penguin as a Specially Protected Species and expressed strong support for taking that decision immediately.

(125) Some Parties did not support designating the emperor penguin as a Specially Protected Species. The reasons given included: the 9.6% population decline needed further assessment due to the great scientific uncertainty and contradictory information; drivers of such population change not being fully understood; there was little evidence that sea-ice would continue to decline; there is a weak correlation between sea-ice reduction and penguin population decline; there is very low threat from human activities to emperor penguins; and particularly, the emperor penguin was already adequately protected under series of existing measures.

(126) In response, SCAR emphasised that there was clear evidence for a nearly 10% decline in the population of emperor penguins over the past decade. It highlighted the statistically significant correlation between sea-ice decline and emperor penguin numbers and that the importance of sea-ice to emperor penguins was well understood and documented. It further reported that sea-ice continued to decline, with record low sea-ice extents in recent years which were expected to continue as outlined in IP 166. SCAR highlighted that emperor penguins were vulnerable to climate change, that current research was in line with predictions of the species' decline toward extinction by the end of the century, and that the population of this species was not stable. SCAR encouraged Parties to collaborate on international research and noted that Specially Protected Species designation would only help, not hinder, research and monitoring of emperor penguins.

(127) ASOC emphasised that the tools of the Environment Protocol were created for situations such as this one and recalled the precautionary approach. It stated that clear scientific evidence had been provided to support the SPS designation. ASOC reminded Parties that the public was looking for leadership in tackling climate change and that the world was watching the ATCM.

(128) Following further discussions, the Meeting could not reach consensus on the designation of the emperor penguin as a Specially Protected Species.

(129) New Zealand, noting the very strong support in the ATCM for the adoption of ASPA 139 and the designation of the emperor penguin as a specially protected species, encouraged those Parties who were not ready to support the proposals at this meeting to work hard in the intersessional period with a view to progressing them at the next ATCM.

Environmental Monitoring and Reporting (CEP Agenda Item 11)

(130) The CEP Chair reported that the Committee had considered the report of the Intersessional Contact Group (ICG) on an international environmental monitoring framework that had been established at CEP XXV. The Committee had highlighted that environmental monitoring was an obligation under Article 12 of the Environment Protocol and an essential instrument of its work. It had agreed to extend the ICG for a further year and had noted that objective, purpose and scope should be the focus of this next phase.

(131) The Committee had welcomed the offer from Uruguay and the Netherlands to act as ICG convenors.

(132) The Meeting welcomed the CEP's advice on the continuation of the ICG, and looked forward to further advice from the CEP on an international environmental monitoring framework.

(133) The Russian Federation suggested the word 'definition' should be changed to 'proposal' in the terms of reference of the ICG, as the CEP could only deliver advice to the ATCM. In response, New Zealand noted that while it did not disagree with the Russian Federation's proposal, the ATCM could not change the terms of reference as the CEP was an independent body; however, the CEP could take note of comments raised in the ATCM when undertaking its work.

(134) The CEP Chair highlighted that the Committee had also considered work by SCAR's Ant-ICON Scientific Research Programme to develop an example online application to inform elements of 'State of the Antarctic Environment Reporting' (SAER). The Committee had commended SCAR for this useful tool and for its continued input to CEP to support its decision-making. The Committee had agreed that SCAR's online application to inform State of the Antarctic Environment Reporting was regarded as a useful tool, and that it would likely improve the accessibility of data.

(135) The Committee had further considered a draft Resolution presented by the Netherlands on ending plastic pollution and had underscored its concern about the growing presence of plastic pollution in Antarctica and its threat to the Antarctic environment. The Committee had not reached an agreement in the time available during the meeting. The Committee had agreed to forward the draft Resolution to the ATCM for consideration.

(136) Several Parties thanked the Netherlands for bringing forward a draft Resolution on plastic pollution in the CEP, and noted the importance of the topic.

(137) Noting that the draft Resolution had not been attached to a Working Paper, several Parties noted their view that the draft Resolution should not be considered. These Parties requested that Parties adhere to established procedures, and submit substantive decisions through a Working Paper, allowing the draft to be translated into all four official languages. It was also noted that a legally binding instrument regarding plastic pollution was under negotiation in the United Nations and it would not be appropriate for the ATCM to consider without the appropriate expertise.

(138) Several Parties emphasised that the ATCM allowed for flexibility, and that Parties could bring topics forward at any time. Some Parties also mentioned that, while translations were an important part of the procedures of the ATCM, many Parties needed to constantly work in a non-native language, and that it should not prevent Parties from making decisions.

(139) Several Parties suggested that the CEP be requested to bring forward technical, scientific and environmental advice on plastic pollution to inform further discussions on this matter next year.

Inspection Reports (CEP Agenda Item 12)

(140) The CEP Chair noted that the Committee had considered the reports from inspections conducted by Australia and France, respectively, in the 2023/24 season. The Committee had thanked and congratulated Australia and France on their reciprocal inspections, noting the significant effort involved and that these inspections took place at stations that were rarely inspected. Noting the importance of inspections for building trust and transparency in the Antarctic Treaty system, the Committee had welcomed the conclusions presented in the inspection reports that both Parties were operating their Antarctic activities in compliance with the Antarctic Treaty and Environment Protocol.

Election of Officers (CEP Agenda Item 14)

(141) The CEP Chair reported that the Committee had elected Ceisha Poirot of New Zealand as Chair for a two-year term and had congratulated her on her appointment to the role. The CEP Chair also noted that the Committee had re-elected Dr Heike Herata as Vice-chair for a second two-year term and had congratulated her on her reappointment. She had also been reappointed as convenor of the SGCCR. The Committee had also thanked Patricia Ortúzar for her work.

(142) The Meeting congratulated Ceisha Poirot on her appointment and Dr Heike Herata on her reappointment.

Preparation for Next Meeting (CEP Agenda Item 15)

(143) The CEP Chair noted that the Committee had adopted the Preliminary Agenda for CEP 27, reflecting the agenda for CEP 26 (Appendix 3 to the CEP Report).

Item 6a: Operation of the Antarctic Treaty System: Request from Canada to become a Consultative Party

(144) The United States, in its capacity as Depositary Government of the Antarctic Treaty and the Environment Protocol, confirmed that Canada had complied with the guidelines set out in Decision 2 (2017).

(145) The Meeting agreed to give Canada an opportunity to present its IP 7 *Canada's Support for Polar Science and Research* and IP 32 *Overview and Update of Canada's Antarctic Regulatory Framework*, providing an overview of the Canadian Antarctic scientific research programme and its domestic legislation concerning Antarctica. Canada showcased its active promotion of research in Antarctica through its government departments and agencies and through academic funding. It also highlighted activities undertaken through its international network of universities and agencies, including in cooperation with Parties, on scientific issues in the spirit of sustainable international collaboration. Canada reiterated its commitment to the Antarctic Treaty system through its active participation in and support for its various subsidiary bodies, including via participation in the CEP, SCAR, COMNAP, and CCAMLR by its various federal organisations. In conclusion, Canada thanked the Meeting for the opportunity to present its update.

(146) The Consultative Parties thanked Canada for its presentation. Most Parties supported Canada's candidature to be the Consultative Party, meeting the requirement for substantial scientific research activity in accordance with Article IX (2) of the Antarctic Treaty and the requirements set out in Decision 2 (2017), acknowledging the quality and diversity of science demonstrated in Canada's presentation.

(147) Two Parties noted that although Canada demonstrated a commitment and support of science, they did not consider it had met the requirement in Article IX (2) for the need to have conducted substantial scientific research activity in Antarctica with few scientific and national operational activities provided in the EIES or IPs presented.

(148) Parties welcomed consideration of Canada's application at ATCM 47 and encouraged Canada to continue to pursue Consultative Party status. Accordingly, that item has been included on the provisional agenda and there is no need for reapplication.

Item 6b: Operation of the Antarctic Treaty System: Request from Belarus to become a Consultative Party

(149) The United States, in its capacity as Depositary Government of the Antarctic Treaty and the Environment Protocol, observed that Belarus had communicated its request for Consultative Party status by diplomatic note slightly less than 210 days before the current Meeting. Observing that the wording of Decision 2 (2017) uses both the mandatory "shall"

and the permissive "should", and that a short delay was unlikely to prejudice the object and purpose of allowing the Parties to properly assess the application, the United States proposed that the Meeting determine whether to accept Belarus's request.

(150) The Meeting agreed that the Belarus' application could be heard.

(151) Belarus presented IP 45 *Basis for the Request of the Republic of Belarus on granting the status of a Consultative Party of the Antarctic Treaty*. It presented the different aspects of Belarus' participation in Antarctic Treaty bodies, its national Antarctic legislation and implementation of the Antarctic Treaty, the Environmental Protocol and five Annexes, as well as its scientific activities and infrastructure in Antarctica. Belarus showcased its scientific activity in Antarctica and drew attention to the increasingly regular and multidisciplinary nature of its scientific research. Belarus also highlighted the commitment of its National Academy of Sciences to Antarctic research, the establishment of a Belarusian polar research journal, and the positive feedback it received after an inspection by Australia in 2020. Belarus noted that its presentation considered the comments it had received during its previous request for Consultative Party status at ATCM XLV (2023) and thanked the Meeting for the opportunity.

(152) The Consultative Parties thanked Belarus for its presentation. Some Parties supported Belarus' candidature as a Consultative Party on the basis that Belarus' substantial scientific research activities in Antarctica met the requirement in Article IX (2). In this context these Parties appreciated the establishment of the research station, expeditions, research activities in Antarctica, as well as research outcomes reported to the ATCM and CEP.

(153) Other Parties stated they did not consider Belarus had fulfilled the requirements outlined in Article IX (2) of the Antarctic Treaty as well as in Decision 2 (2017), noting that their concerns regarding the quality of its science and diversity of its programme remained.

(154) Many Parties further noted that under current political circumstances, discussed at ATCM XLIV and ATCM XLV, they did not consider that an agreement on this issue could be reached.

(155) Some Parties stressed that such evaluation with respect to Consultative Party status should be based on scientific and consistent criteria rather than political consideration.

(156) Parties welcomed consideration of Belarus' application at ATCM 47 and encouraged Belarus to continue to pursue Consultative Party status. Accordingly, that item has been included on the provisional agenda and there is no need for a re-application.

Item 6c: Operation of the Antarctic Treaty System: General Matters

(157) Whilst noting the inclusion of items 6a and 6b on the provisional agenda for ATCM 47, Parties also underscored that the ATCM remained open to receive requests from other non-Consultative Parties who wish to apply for Consultative Party status, and who consider that they meet the requirements of the Antarctic Treaty.

(158) The United Kingdom introduced WP 40 *Agreement under the United Nations Convention on the Law of the Sea on the Conservation and Sustainable Use of Marine Biological Diversity of Areas beyond National Jurisdiction ("BBNJ Agreement")*, prepared jointly with Australia, Norway and New Zealand. It drew the Meeting's attention to the adoption of an agreement under the United Nations Convention on the Law of the Sea on the Conservation and Sustainable Use of Marine Biological Diversity of Areas Beyond National Jurisdiction ('BBNJ Agreement') at the United Nations on 19 June 2023. It recommended that the ATCM adopt a Resolution to recognise and welcome the BBNJ Agreement's adoption and to reaffirm the competence of the Antarctic Treaty system over matters relating to the Antarctic.

(159) Most Parties supported the adoption by the Meeting of a Resolution welcoming the BBNJ

Agreement, reaffirming that the Antarctic Treaty system had competence over matters relating to the Antarctic and supporting cooperation and collaboration between the Antarctic Treaty system and the BBNJ Agreement.

(160) The Russian Federation stated its disagreement with the proposal to recognise the significance of the BBNJ Agreement as a global milestone consistent with the role of the Antarctic Treaty system in Antarctica. It pointed out the Working Paper to be silent about dissociation of the Russian Federation from the consensus on the text as reflected in the report of the conference to the UNGA by expressing its position that provisions of UNCLOS were undermined and that norms of the BBNJ Agreement would allow for intrusion into the mandate and competence of relevant sectoral and regional organisations.

(161) With regard to the first recommendation presented in the Paper, the Russian Federation noted lack of basis for the ATCM to "apply" or "interpret" the 2023 Agreement. It supported the recommendation to confirm the competence of the Antarctic Treaty system on issues related to Antarctica, including issues of rational use of marine living resources. Besides, the Russian Federation reiterated that in a general analysis of the relationship between the ATS and other relevant international legal frameworks, including UNCLOS and the BBNJ process, conducted in the ICG on Relevant Issues, Trends and Challenges to the ATS, and reflected in the ATCM XLIII Final Report (para. 89), there was "consensus that the ATS should maintain its specificity when considering other international legal frameworks and global processes". According to the Russian Federation consideration of instruments in force, in particular UNCLOS, should be prioritized by the ATCM. The Russian Federation considered adoption of the resolution irrelevant since Resolution 1 (2006) and Resolution 9 (2009) provided for "the prime responsibilities of the Antarctic Treaty Consultative Parties for the protection and preservation of the Antarctic environment" and "that the Antarctic Treaty System is the appropriate framework for managing the collection of biological material in the Antarctic Treaty area and for considering its use".

(162) Many Parties welcomed the fact that the BBNJ Agreement was now open for signature and considered that action by the Meeting during ATCM 47 would be timely as the BBNJ Agreement would not enter into force for at least another year.

(163) Argentina introduced WP 59 *Communication of the start and end dates of observer activities for inspections*, prepared jointly with Chile. Argentina noted that many notifications shared by Parties indicating the appointment of observers do not indicate the end date of their terms and that, in some cases, the duration of appointment was imprecise. To achieve greater clarity regarding observers authorised to carry out inspections at Antarctic bases, Argentina suggested that the Meeting adopt a Decision:

- instructing Parties to include both the start date and the end date of an observer's appointment in their communications;
- setting forth that where an end date was not provided, an observer's appointment would end on the 30 April after the start date of activities; and
- indicating that where a designated observer ceased their duties prior to the date notified to other Parties, the responsible Party must communicate this to the Secretariat to keep the list up to date.

(164) The Meeting thanked Argentina and Chile for their useful proposal and acknowledged the possible uncertainties arising from the matter. The Meeting supported the adoption of a Decision. The Meeting observed that in the current notification procedure, a method was already in place to state the end date of an appointment. Several Parties also observed that nothing would prevent Parties from appointing observers for several years or more, so as to maintain the possibility of conducting inspections without prior notification to the inspected Party.

(165) Following further discussion, the Meeting adopted Decision 1 (2024) *Notification by the Consultative Parties regarding the list of observers under Article VII of the Antarctic Treaty and Article 14 of the Protocol on Environmental Protection to the Antarctic Treaty through the Secretariat of the Antarctic Treaty.*

(166) The Russian Federation introduced WP 62 *The contribution of the ATS to strengthening the principles of a multipolar world order*, noting its continuing efforts to address systemic issues of the Antarctic Treaty. It noted that it considered that the values of the Antarctic Treaty system were important for strengthening the multipolar world order. It expressed its aim to confirm the role of each Party in the effective development of international cooperation in the Antarctic Treaty system, and search for further ways to strengthen multilateral principles within the ATCM. The Russian Federation considered that the main goals and principles of the Antarctic Treaty were aimed at preserving Antarctica as a zone of peace, freedom of scientific research and international cooperation, which had led to the establishment of a mini-model of a multipolar world order. It stated that equal multilateral cooperation required the preservation of the multipolar features of the Antarctic Treaty system, such as openness to new participants. The Russian Federation noted that there were no mandatory requirements to maintain a substantial research programme to join the Antarctic Treaty. It reflected that, in its view, the requirement arose for those receiving the status of Consultative Parties, since these Parties played a decisive role in the process of developing measures that promote the implementation of the goals and principles of the Antarctic Treaty. It highlighted that consensus-based decision-making was the key factor in taking into account the positions of all Parties. The Russian Federation suggested that the Meeting:

- record the understanding that the Antarctic Treaty system made an important contribution to strengthening the foundations of a multipolar world and that the Antarctic community was a value of the Antarctic Treaty system and related to all staff of national Antarctic programmes;
- reaffirm the fundamental importance of the goals and principles of the Antarctic Treaty;
- exchange views on the following issues: how could the Consultative Parties contribute to the development of effective mechanisms for multilateral cooperation within the Antarctic Treaty and what issues, in the opinion of the Consultative Parties, required priority attention in order to ensure the sustainability of the Antarctic Treaty system, and including these issues for reflection in the Multi-year Strategic Work Plan; and
- provide for the possibility of continuing work on the issues of multipolarity and multilateral cooperation and priorities on this topic during the intersessional period.

(167) The Meeting thanked the Russian Federation for WP 62.

(168) Many Parties did not support conducting informal intersessional discussions concerning the theory of a multipolar world order, or any connection between the Antarctic Treaty and this concept. These Parties reaffirmed their commitment to the principle of consensus at the ATCM, which most Parties understood to entail not only rights to affect joint decisions but also a positive obligation to work in good faith towards common solutions. These Parties noted the pursuit of peace and international cooperation should not be restrained to the Antarctic Treaty area, and that where the rules-based order of the world was weakened, so was the Antarctic Treaty system.

(169) China expressed appreciation for recommendations contained in WP 62 and stressed the need for continued discussion on this issue manifested by the divergent views expressed. China further highlighted that consensus was a useful tool aimed at reaching common ground for the benefit of all Parties at the ATCM.

(170) ASOC agreed that consensus was a key feature of the ATCM, but also noted that consensus

should not be a mechanism to block progress. ASOC considered that the ATCM had recently been unable to reach consensus on a wide range of environmental protection issues, despite acknowledgement that the planet was experiencing a global environmental crisis. ASOC also recalled that many of the ATCM's achievements, such as the mining ban, were only possible because Parties worked to overcome their significant initial differences rather than simply blocking consensus.

(171) The Russian Federation expressed appreciation for the positive comments from Parties. In response to comments, the Russian Federation clarified that by multipolar order it expressed there were more poles than one or two, with a large number of actors interacting on an equal basis, as well as the need to respect their different views. The Russian Federation also noted its adherence to international law and its view that international law was primarily weakened by the so called "rules-based order".

(172) India presented IP 61 *The Indian Antarctic Environmental Protection Rules, 2023: A step towards enforcement of Indian Antarctic Act 2022,* providing a follow-up on ATCM XLV - IP 141. It summarised the measures adopted through the promulgation of new rules to the Indian Antarctic Act. It noted the availability of the legislation and its recently published EIA report on the National Centre for Polar and Ocean Research website for review.

(173) Peru presented IP 134 *XXXIV Reunión de Administradores de Programas Antárticos Latinoamericanos-RAPAL (Perú, 2023).* It reported on the 34th Latin American Antarctic Programme Administrators (RAPAL) meeting in Lima in 2023. Argentina, Brazil, Chile, Uruguay, Ecuador and Peru participated as consultative members, and Colombia and Venezuela, as observer members. Peru referred to RAPAL's aims to promote scientific, technical, logistical, and environmental cooperation among Latin American Antarctic programmes.

(174) The United States presented IP 185 rev. 1 *Updated United States Policy on the Antarctic Region,* which informed the Meeting of the recent signing of the National Security Memorandum on United States Policy on the Antarctic Region by the President of the United States. It explained that under this policy, the United States would continue its cooperative international efforts through the Antarctic Treaty system, seeking to maintain the Antarctic region for peaceful purposes, to protect its environment and ecosystems, and to conduct scientific research with a greater collective commitment of the Parties.

(175) The Secretariat introduced SP 14 *Report of current ATCM measures (1961–2023),* which reported on all 562 Recommendations, Measures, Decisions, and Resolutions in the Antarctic Treaty Database currently in force. The report presented all measures grouped by categories and in chronological order. The Secretariat noted that it had started refining the categories and topics presently used to classify ATCM measures in the Antarctic Treaty Database to facilitate the search and filtering of measures. The Secretariat suggested that the ATCM might wish to review which texts could be considered no longer current.

(176) The Meeting thanked the Secretariat for its work and expressed appreciation and support for the development of the tool.

(177) The Executive Secretary presented SP 3 *List of Measures with status "not yet effective",* which provided a list of Measures that were not yet effective according to the information provided by the Depositary Government. These included three Measures adopted at ATCM XXVII (Cape Town, 2004), ATCM XXVIII (Stockholm, 2005) and ATCM XXXII (Baltimore, 2009), respectively. The Executive Secretary noted that Measure 1 (2005) *Annex VI to the Protocol on Environmental Protection to the Antarctic Treaty: Liability Arising from Environmental Emergencies* had not yet been approved by Argentina, Belgium, Brazil, Bulgaria, China, India, Japan, the Republic of Korea, or the United States. It was also noted that Measure 4 (2004) *Insurance and Contingency Planning for Tourism*

and Non Governmental Activities in the Antarctic Treaty Area had not yet been approved by Brazil, Bulgaria, China, Germany, India, Italy, the Republic of Korea, Peru, Sweden, or the United States. The Executive Secretary further noted that Measure 15 (2009) *Landing of Persons from Passenger Vessels in the Antarctic Treaty Area* had not yet been approved by Brazil, Bulgaria, China, Germany, India, Italy, the Republic of Korea, Norway, Peru, Poland, South Africa, Sweden, or the United States.

(178) The Meeting observed that the entry into force of Annex VI of the Environmental Protocol still required domestic implementation by nine of the original signatory Consultative Parties in 2005. The Parties provided updated information on the status of their approval of Annex VI and its implementation in domestic legislation. India reported that it had completed the domestic implementation of Annex VI with the *Indian Antarctic Act* (2022). Czechia reported that it had completed all internal procedures for the implementation of Annex VI and submitted its notice of approval to the depositary government. Several Parties reported that they were in the process of implementing Annex VI in domestic legislation. The Meeting encouraged all Parties to implement the remaining Measures domestically to bring them into force.

(179) Spain introduced WP 42 *Procedure for the establishment and operation of intersessional activities of the ATCM.* Spain proposed that the ATCM adopt a formal procedure for the establishment and operation of activities that took place during the intersessional period on the online forum of the Antarctic Treaty Secretariat's website. Spain mentioned the importance and the valuable contribution of the intersessional activities in examining specific issues of concern to the ATCM for over 20 years. It noted that although the ATCM had formalised the existence of some intersessional activities, it had not yet developed many specific provisions in this regard. As a first step, Spain proposed to request the Antarctic Treaty Secretariat analyse the various intersessional activities so that the Parties could have sufficient information to discuss the matter properly.

(180) The Meeting thanked Spain and offered broad support for the proposal. The Meeting expressed its interest in the possibility of establishing a unified procedure for the opening and functioning of ATCM Forum groups which could lead to a better understanding of Parties on procedures to be followed regarding activities of the Forum. The Meeting noted that intersessional work could assist, but does not replace, discussions at the ATCM.

(181) The Meeting agreed to request the Secretariat to compile a list of the different activities under the online forum of the Secretariat website during the intersessional periods. The list would include a brief description of each type of activity including the topics and the procedural basis. It would address activities during the last eight years.

(182) The Executive Secretary expressed readiness to assist the Meeting with its request and reported that it would provide the requested information at ATCM 47.

(183) The Secretariat introduced SP 8 *Review of gender-neutral language in ATCM and CEP documents*, which provided the ATCM with options for potential adoption to ensure the use of gender-neutral language in Antarctic Treaty documents, following the United Nations (UN) Guidelines for gender-inclusive language as suggested by the Russian Federation at ATCM XLV. The Secretariat presented information about the commissioning of an editorial review of four documents from the Antarctic Treaty. It was proposed that the Secretariat: incorporate the agreed UN Guidelines for gender-inclusive language into its standard editorial procedures to ensure that future ATCM and CEP documents reflect the specificities and unique features of the four Treaty languages and, at the same time, comply with the principle of parity among the official languages established by the Treaty and the Protocol; and include a link to the UN guidelines in the preparation of documents of the next meeting's webpage each year, as a resource for delegates.

(184) The Meeting thanked the Secretariat for its comprehensive review, highlighted the

importance of using a gender-neutral approach to language in ATCM documents and supported the proposals. Many Parties emphasised the usefulness of referring to the UN Guidelines for assuring the use of gender-inclusive language when elaborating documents, noting it was an excellent tool. Parties underlined that gender equality was an overarching objective that should be pursued and that ensuring gender-neutral and inclusive language was an important step forward. Several Parties commented on their actions to promote inclusiveness and diversity within their national Antarctic programmes. Parties suggested that a Decision be adopted to update the ATCM Rules of Procedure and a Resolution to update the General Guidelines for Visitors to the Antarctic in accordance with the suggestions made by the Secretariat.

(185) Several Parties noted that the introduction of gender-neutral language should not result in unintentional changes to the substance of the Rules of Procedure, noting that this could potentially lead to discrepancies between the versions in different languages; in particular, concerns were raised with regard to the proposals in the Russian text. Several Parties called for particular caution when editing to avoid discrepancies in different languages.

(186) The Meeting agreed to adopt a revised English version of its Rules of Procedure and General Guidelines for Visitors to the Antarctic to include gender-neutral, inclusive language. The versions in French, Spanish and Russian would be revised by proofreaders during the intersessional period and submitted for approval at ATCM 47.

(187) The Meeting adopted Decision 2 (2024) *Revised Rules of Procedure for the Antarctic Treaty Consultative Meeting.*

(188) The Meeting adopted Resolution 2 (2024) *General Guidelines for Visitors to the Antarctic.*

(189) The following papers were also submitted under this agenda item:

- BP 21 *Diplomatic Participation to the Eighth Turkish Antarctic Expedition* (Türkiye).
- BP 35 *Programa de celebración por el XXXV Aniversario de la constitución del Perú como Parte Consultiva del Tratado Antártico* (Peru).

Item 7: Operation of the Antarctic Treaty System: Matters related to the Secretariat

(190) The Executive Secretary introduced SP 4 *Secretariat Report 2023/24*, which provided details on the Secretariat's activities in the Financial Year 2023/24 (1 April 2023 to 31 March 2024), including the organisation of the ATCM XLV and CEP XXV meeting in Finland and the preparation for ATCM 46 and CEP 26 in India. The Executive Secretary drew the Meeting's attention to the intersessional activities it had supported during this period, including: hosting ATCM online discussions and contact groups established by ATCM XLV and later at Parties' request; the National Competent Authority Forums; intersessional Forum activities established by CEP XXV; diverse website and web-based services, maps and databases; EIES training and training of representatives on the functioning of the ATCM; coordination and contact including visits to the Secretariat; and the preparation of the Secretariat Papers that were submitted to ATCM 46 and CEP 26. The Executive Secretary reported that the Finance Officer had retired and had been replaced by a new recruit in an Accountant position. Concerning financial matters, the Executive Secretary provided an overview of contributions the Secretariat had received and presented its externally audited financial report for the financial year 2022/23. The Executive Secretary presented the provisional Financial Report 2023/24, remarking that appropriations were in line with the budget except for Financing, which was affected by the strong devaluation of the Argentine Peso against the United States Dollar (USD), and translation and interpretation which included the cost of additional translation requests. The period ended with a provisional deficit for 2023/24 of USD 99,370, outstanding contributions amounted to USD 178,672, and the Cash Surplus amounted to USD 812,657.

(191) The Executive Secretary introduced SP 5 *Secretariat Programme 2024/2025*, which outlined the activities proposed for the Secretariat in the Financial Year 2024/25 (1 April 2024 to 31 March 2025). The Executive Secretary summarised the Secretariat's regular activities such as the preparation of ATCM 47, the publication of reports, and other tasks assigned to the Secretariat under Measure 1 (2003). The Executive Secretary noted no personnel changes foreseen in the upcoming period. With regard to financial matters, the Executive Secretary drew the Meeting's attention to continuing inflation and the rising cost of living in Argentina, which was only partially compensated by the USD's rise against the Argentine Peso. The Executive Secretary proposed to increase the Secretariat's salaries by 2.9%. The Executive Secretary reported that despite the impact of local and global inflation, due to conservative and precautionary management, the budget estimated a deficit of only USD 89,922, which would be covered by the existing surplus in the General Fund, and that the contributions for the financial year 2024/25 would not rise. In terms of intersessional activities, he announced continued work with several website and information systems developments and improvements. The Executive Secretary also advised that Parties might decide on an updated procedure for the Call for Selection of a new Executive Secretary to be carried out during ATCM 46 in 2024 and ATCM 47 in 2025.

(192) The Executive Secretary introduced SP 6 *Five Year Forward Budget Profile 2025/2026 – 2029/30*, which provided the Secretariat's budget profile for the period 2025-30. He estimated that despite local and global inflation, the accumulated surplus in the General Fund still allowed for a prediction of zero nominal increase in contributions until 2029-30. He nevertheless advised that future changes in local and global conditions might still create the need to discuss ways to offset possible deficits through adjustments in contributions or otherwise.

(193) The Meeting expressed its gratitude to the Secretariat for the invaluable support it had provided and continued to provide to the ATCM. It also commended the Executive Secretary for his leadership and availability. The Meeting thanked the Secretariat for maintaining zero nominal growth, which allowed contributions to remain unchanged until 2029/30. Many Parties commended the Secretariat for the EIES virtual training sessions and, reflecting on their positive experience, encouraged other Parties to utilise this opportunity. Several Parties welcomed the Secretariat's readiness to assume new tasks and activities as requested by the ATCM. Some Parties reported that their nationals had been warmly received by the Secretariat in Buenos Aires and were very grateful. Some Parties cautioned on the need to consider a balance and consistency between the budget allocated to the Secretariat and the work it was requested to do.

(194) Some Parties highlighted the importance of submitting financial contributions in due time to ensure the Secretariat had enough funds to maintain its activities and provide adequate assistance. Parties that had not yet provided their contributions were encouraged to do so. Some Parties also cautioned against working with deficit budgets.

(195) India thanked the Secretariat for the great support it had provided during the preparation of the Meeting and acknowledged that its successful organisation was due to the excellent coordination and collaboration between the Host Country Secretariat and the Antarctic Treaty Secretariat.

(196) In responding to queries from Parties, the Executive Secretary highlighted that despite current unpredictable conditions and the increase in expenses and inflation, the Secretariat had been running on the same budget since 2014 and was expected to do so until 2029. The Executive Secretary highlighted that the Secretariat had not considered requesting Parties increase contributions and that it had evaluated several alternatives to address changing scenarios.

(197) The Meeting requested the Secretariat to open a new topic in the ATCM Forum for informal discussion for Consultative Parties, moderated by Germany and Belgium, with the support of the Secretariat, to evaluate options for income to the Secretariat such as:

- The categories of contributions selected by each Party at the time of establishment of the Secretariat and the possible intention of some Parties to move to higher categories, which under Measure 1 (2003) Article 4 (3) are "based on the extent of their national Antarctic activities, taking into account their capacity to pay". For the purposes of facilitating Parties' assessment of the extent of their national Antarctic activities the moderators may include in the forum publicly available COMNAP data.
- The feasibility of voluntary contributions to be received from Consultative Parties, Non-Consultative Parties (especially those that are CEP members) and other organisations.
- Any other alternative for income.

(198) The Meeting, at the request of the Netherlands, authorised the establishment of a Special Fund by the Secretariat to be used to fund activities in support of the development of a consistent and comprehensive framework for the regulation of tourism and other non-governmental activities in Antarctica. The Netherlands would provide a voluntary contribution to this Special Fund and any other Party could also provide voluntary contributions. The estimated value of this Special Fund was USD 55,000.

(199) The Meeting, at the request of the CEP, authorised the establishment of a Special Fund by the Secretariat to be used to defray the cost of a joint CEP/SC-CAMLR Workshop to be conducted in the week before the CEP 27 meeting in 2025. The Parties would provide voluntary contributions to this Special Fund, but, if necessary, the use of the surplus in the General Fund of the Secretariat up to USD 20,000 was authorised. The estimated value of this Special Fund was USD 65,000.

(200) Following further discussion, the Meeting adopted Decision 3 (2024) *Secretariat Report, Programme and Budget.*

(201) The Executive Secretary introduced SP 12 *The Antarctic Treaty Secretariat: twenty years after its establishment*, which gave a detailed history of the activities, tasks, and outputs of the Secretariat, focused on five main areas: meeting organisation, information repositories, tools and resources for delegates, exchange of information, and institutional and ATCM/CEP memory. The Executive Secretary noted that the paper provided a timeline of products, services and reports. It also noted that images had been added to the document to make its reading more enjoyable. The Executive Secretary highlighted that the document serves as a historical memory of its work over the past 20 years, acknowledged that there was still much to be done, and expressed great pleasure in assisting Parties.

(202) The Meeting thanked the Executive Secretary for presenting this paper and congratulated the Secretariat for its 20th anniversary. Several Parties recognised the critical, increasing and important work it had done throughout the years while maintaining a constant budget.

(203) The Executive Secretary thanked the Parties for their comments, and expressed that the Secretariat was proud to have met the Parties' expectations. The Secretariat remained open to receiving feedback on improving its work further.

(204) Argentina introduced WP 17 *Revised Procedure for Selection and Appointment of the Executive Secretary of the Secretariat of the Antarctic Treaty*, prepared jointly with the United States. It proposed new selection and appointment procedures for adoption at ATCM 46 by a Decision, to permit the ATCM to appoint a new Executive Secretary at ATCM 47 in 2025 in accordance with Article III (1) of Measure 1 (2003) and Secretariat Staff Regulation 6.1. Argentina and the United States proposed that candidates be invited to apply via their national competent authorities no later than 180 days before ATCM 47,

after which a shortlist of candidates would be invited to attend an interview at the ATCM. Argentina noted that WP 17 included a proposed Decision on a revised procedure for the selection and appointment of the Executive Secretary of the Secretariat of the Antarctic Treaty, attached as Annex A, and suggested wording of an advertisement for use by Consultative Parties for the forthcoming appointment, attached as Annex B.

(205) The Meeting thanked Argentina and the United States for their proposal. In relation to the selection criteria, several Parties stressed the importance of promoting diversity and equal opportunities in the selection process and proposed options to address this adequately. Proposals included: including a requirement for candidates to demonstrate a solid commitment to inclusion and diversity values; specifically encouraging female candidates to apply, without prioritising candidates by gender; eliminating the burden on the Depositary Government to carry out initial assessment of the candidates; and holding virtual interviews to allow those who did not have the means to cover their travel expenses to be considered.

(206) The Meeting did not reach consensus regarding the revised procedure for selecting and appointing the new Executive Secretary. The Meeting noted that Decision 4 (2016) remained operative and set forth the procedure for the advertisement, selection and appointment of the new Executive Secretary. Parties were reminded of the need to revise the text of the draft advertisement in Annex 1 of Decision 4 (2016) to reflect the correct dates.

Item 8: Liability

(207) Australia presented IP 48 *Summary Report on an Informal Intersessional Process to Share Information on Domestic Implementation of Annex VI to the Protocol on Environmental Protection to the Antarctic Treaty*. It summarised the activities of the informal intersessional process established in ATCM XLV (2023) to share information between Parties on the domestic implementation of Annex VI to the Environmental Protocol. Australia thanked all participants in the discussions and reported that all participants had reaffirmed their support for the principles underlying Annex VI. Australia informed the Meeting that while some participants had found the domestic implementation of Annex VI somewhat complex and lengthy, no insurmountable impediments had been reported in the discussions.

Item 9: Biological Prospecting in Antarctica

(208) The following paper was submitted under this agenda item and taken as presented:

- IP 59 *Contribution towards Study of Psychrophilic organisms in the Antarctic by India* (India).

Item 10: Exchange of Information

(209) Spain introduced WP 54 *Redesign of the Electronic Information Exchange System (EIES)*, prepared jointly with Argentina. Spain proposed a comprehensive review of the EIES, considering the updated requirements for information exchange provided in Decision 4 (2023). Spain noted that significant debate had taken place over the past decade on how to improve the use and effectiveness of the EIES and that the presentation of this document responded to the decreasing trend in its use. It highlighted that the use and usefulness of the large amount of information exchanged offered to the Parties was not clear. To simplify the process and to enhance the EIES's overall effectiveness, the co-proponents suggested instructing the Antarctic Treaty Secretariat to conduct a detailed analysis of the EIES to identify obsolete, unnecessary, or duplicated requirements and report its findings to ATCM 47. Spain noted that this analysis could then assist the ATCM in conducting a comprehensive review of the EIES process and identify possible steps to improve

information exchange and ensure greater use. It suggested that following the Secretariat's analysis, Parties could: identify outdated, unnecessary and repeated requirements; ensure that information was exchanged simply and efficiently; simplify the information exchanged as much as possible; and recognise the usefulness of the information exchanged.

(210) The Meeting thanked Spain and Argentina for their proposal and agreed on the need to conduct a comprehensive review of the EIES. The Meeting recalled the obligation to exchange information and reaffirmed that information sharing and transparency were fundamental aspects of the Antarctic Treaty system. Several Parties agreed that considerable improvements could be made to make the EIES more user-friendly and clear. Parties agreed that simplifying the EIES was desirable and that providing information was fundamental to the Antarctic Treaty. Several Parties expressed concern about the low level of information being exchanged through the EIES, noting that several inconsistencies made it difficult to analyse data comparatively and effectively. The Meeting recalled that Parties had obligations to exchange information under the Antarctic Treaty and its Environmental Protocol, which had been reflected in the updated requirements for information exchange given in the Annex to Decision 4 (2023).

(211) Many Parties considered the issue of nested permits, which occurred when an expedition permitted by one national competent authority was carrying passengers permitted for activities permitted by another national competent authority. Several Parties noted that in these cases recording data on the EIES could be challenging and could result in an inaccurate number of expeditions being recorded as travelling to Antarctica.

(212) While supporting the improvement of the EIES, the Russian Federation presented its view that updated requirements for information exchange given in the annex to Decision 4 (2023) were clear and comprehensive. It stated that analysis of the requirements was a matter of substance and implied interpretation of relevant obligations and as such should be provided by the Parties but not by the Secretariat.

(213) The Meeting agreed to initiate a comprehensive review of the requirements for the exchange of information given in the Annex to Decision 4 (2023), with support of the Secretariat, which would include: the possibility of processing the data received through the EIES; the clarity of each requirement; the possible duplication with information provided through other bodies such as SCAR and COMNAP; possible inconsistencies between categories of information; and the proportion of users that were complying with each requirement.

Item 11: Education Issues

(214) Bulgaria introduced WP 29 *Seventh report of the Intersessional Contact Group on Education and Outreach,* prepared jointly with ASOC, Australia, Belgium, Brazil, Chile, COMNAP, Estonia, Finland, France, IAATO, India, Italy, the Republic of Korea, Poland, Portugal, Romania, Türkiye, SCAR, Spain, the United Kingdom, the United States, Uruguay, Venezuela, and the WMO. Bulgaria recalled that ATCM XLV had supported the continuation of the ICG on Education and Outreach and reported on the discussions within the ICG over the past year via the ATCM Discussion Forum. Bulgaria noted that the forum had attracted 51 posts and over 1105 views from 24 Parties, Observers and Experts discussing education and outreach activities they had carried out. Bulgaria reported on examples of education concerning EDI and the future development of the ICG. The reported activities highlighted included lectures and seminars, webinars, public visits to Antarctic ships, film and music festivals, outreach museum events, national and international science conferences, educational materials, publications and social media campaigns. The co-proponents recommended that the ATCM recognise the usefulness of the Forum on Education and Outreach; support the work of the ICG during another intersessional period; and promote the usage of the forum. They also proposed that the ATCM plan to organise a second workshop on education and outreach.

(215) Portugal supported Bulgaria's presentation and highlighted that there had been a considerable increase in the engagement of Parties in the ATCM Discussion Forum. Portugal called on Parties to update their contact details on the website. It noted that the increased participation in the forum resulted in information-sharing and identifying key issues to further address, including EDI and Climate Change. Portugal reflected that education and outreach were among the most unifying themes in the ATCM and encouraged Parties to continue this close collaboration.

(216) The Meeting thanked Bulgaria for the report and commended Bulgaria and Portugal for their leadership in the ICG on Education and Outreach. Many Parties emphasised the importance of education and outreach activities as an essential element of cooperation enshrined in the Antarctic Treaty and the Environmental Protocol. Many Parties highlighted the importance of showing the ATCM's work to the wider public and building the public's understanding of its objectives and accomplishments and the risks Antarctica faced. Parties acknowledged that education and outreach were crucial to raising awareness and inspiring future scientists. The United Kingdom underlined the importance of adapting and updating materials, considering social media formats, for example, to engage a new and broader audience. Belgium noted it was celebrating the 125th anniversary of the Belgian Antarctic Expedition of 1897–1899, which was the first expedition to winter in the Antarctic region and highlighted that members from five different nations were on the vessel, making it a symbolic precursor of the Antarctic spirit.

(217) The Meeting supported the recommendations of WP 29 and agreed to continue the work of the ICG during another intersessional period. The Meeting also supported the organisation of a second workshop on education and outreach.

(218) The Meeting agreed to continue the ICG on Education and Outreach for another intersessional period with the aim of:

- fostering collaboration at both the national and international level, on Education and Outreach;
- identifying key international activities/events related to education and outreach for possible engagement by the Antarctic Treaty Parties;
- sharing results of education and outreach initiatives that demonstrate the work of Antarctic Treaty Parties in managing the Antarctic Treaty area;
- emphasising ongoing environmental protection initiatives that had been informed by scientific observations and results, in order to reinforce the importance of the Antarctic Treaty and its Protocol on Environmental Protection;
- promoting related education and outreach activities by Experts and Observers, and encouraging cooperation with these groups;
- sharing best practices and encouraging, enhancing and promoting diversity and inclusion across the global Antarctic community, including among scientists, logisticians, policy-makers and all others engaged in Antarctic matters, in order to lower any barrier to the engagement of all the talents needed to tackle the challenges of the future of Antarctica;
- encouraging Parties to provide the Secretariat with link(s) to their webpage(s) with educational and outreach resources (the Secretariat would include these links in its "Educational Resources" section of the Secretariat webpage); and
- inviting Parties, Observers and Experts to review, during the intersessional period on the ATCM Education and Outreach Forum, the work carried out by the ICG, discussing its future development and the possibility to organise and plan for the second Workshop on Education and Outreach.

(219) It was further agreed that:

- Observers and Experts participating in the ATCM would be invited to provide input;
- the Executive Secretary would open the ATCM Forum for the ICG and provide assistance to the ICG; and
- Bulgaria would act as convenor and report to the next ATCM on the progress made in the ICG.

(220) The United States presented IP 92 *Polar Science Early Career Community Office (PSECCO): An Initiative to Increase Accessibility and Inclusion in Antarctic Research.* It stated that providing direct support for professional development and cohort building to early career polar scientists through different initiatives and programmes was one way to ensure that future generations were ready to lead polar research and field teams in Antarctica's challenging international collaboration spaces. The United States expressed its commitment to advance the careers of polar scientists, with a particular focus on early career scientists, with the aim to maintain a vibrant and diverse community with the engagement of researchers at all career stages.

(221) Brazil presented IP 17 *Education & Outreach activities of Brazil in 2023/2024*, which outlined the education and outreach activities undertaken by the Brazilian Antarctic Program (PROANTAR) during the 2023/24 season. These activities included, among others, the first Brazilian Polar Film Festival, an Antarctica Day event, a virtual trip to Antarctica, and several exhibitions and presentations.

(222) Peru presented IP 137 *Educación y Difusión de la Temática Antártica*, which reported on various Peruvian activities to raise awareness of Antarctic issues at the national level. Peru proposed to strengthen the inclusion of Antarctic topics in basic education to foster informed citizenship regarding Antarctica's scientific and historical relevance and significance for nature. It also reaffirmed its commitment to research and international cooperation in the region.

(223) Türkiye presented IP 96 *Education & Outreach Activities of Türkiye in 2023-2024*, which summarised Turkish education and outreach activities to raise awareness of polar regions for young generations and increase young people's interest in polar research. It noted that the activities included festivals, contests, the publication of a polar encyclopaedia and a painting contest. It reported that since the early initiatives related to polar regions, Türkiye had attached great importance to education and awareness-raising activities for polar research and global climate change and remained committed to increasing its efforts in the future.

(224) IAATO presented IP 110 *IAATO Antarctic Ambassador Expedition Program* which highlighted IAATO's Education and outreach initiatives. IAATO reported that its Antarctic Ambassadorship Committee began developing the Antarctic Ambassador Expedition Program foundation pack in 2023 with the intent to create ready-to-use materials which could be easily interpreted, modified to suit specific circumstances, and delivered by polar field staff to their guests. IAATO noted that the resulting materials were given a soft launch at the start of the 2023/24 Antarctic season, which enabled field staff to test the materials and provide feedback and ideas to broaden the programme in 2024-25. These materials included a programme presentation, expedition challenge, and Certificate of Antarctic Ambassadorship.

(225) India presented IP 56 *From Poles to Public: Communicating Indian Polar Research through Science Communication and Outreach*, which described India's key polar

education and outreach activities and highlighted India's commitment to fulfilling its social responsibility and enhancing public understanding of the polar regions. India highlighted that its activities included the International Yoga Day Celebration at India's Antarctic stations and its live streaming to Indian Schools and the general public; virtual interaction with around 8000 school students with expedition members at Antarctic stations to generate scientific curiosity among students in polar studies; laboratory visits of students and general public to the National Centre for Polar and Ocean Research and organisation of exhibitions, science talks, and social media campaigns on Antarctic Day celebrations. India also highlighted that it was building a Polar Museum in Goa to promote Antarctic education and outreach.

(226) Colombia presented IP 159 *XXIV Encuentro Historiadores Antárticos Latinoamericanos y IX Foro de Educación Antártica*, which noted that Colombia would host the 24th Meeting of Latin-American Antarctic Historians and the 9th Antarctic Education Forum in September 2024. It reported on the objectives for these meetings, which included: optimising the exchange of historical research; strengthening national Antarctic historical research; and encouraging Antarctic education at all levels. Colombia invited all Parties to join these meetings.

(227) The Russian Federation presented IP 177 *Outreach and Education Activities Review*, summarising different Russian outreach and education activities concerning information about Antarctica, its environment, its role in global climate processes, Antarctic research and the Antarctic Treaty system. The Russian Federation highlighted that it had conducted exhibitions, conferences, social media initiatives, school lectures, online seminars, video content, and art projects to promote Antarctic education and outreach.

(228) The following paper was also submitted under this agenda item and taken as presented:

- IP 154 *Romanian Antarctic Education and Outreach activities 2023-2024* (Romania).

(229) The following papers were also submitted under this agenda item:

- BP 12 *Fostering Education & Outreach Initiatives* (COMNAP).
- BP 13 *Celebración del X Simposio Español de Estudios Polares* (Spain).
- BP 14 *Educación Antártica, desde Punta Arenas para el mundo* (Chile).
- BP 19 *Divulgación y Educación en Venezuela 2023-2024* (Venezuela).
- BP 20 *Digital Technology Making Antarctic Heritage Globally Accessible* (New Zealand).
- BP 30 *Ibero-American postgraduate course "Introduction to cetacean research in the open waters of the Southern Hemisphere"* (Uruguay, Spain).
- BP 31 *Outreach project "Antarctica: The continent of all"* (Uruguay).
- BP 32 *Uruguay's educational and outreach activities in 2023* (Uruguay).
- BP 33 *Education & Outreach Activities of Ukraine in 2022-2024* (Ukraine).
- BP 43 *Data base of those who died in Antarctica* (Russian Federation).
- BP 50 *Education & Outreach Activities of Malaysia in 2023* (Malaysia).

Item 12a: Multi-year Strategic Work Plan: Policy, Legal and Institutional priorities

(230) The Meeting considered the Multi-year Strategic Work Plan adopted at ATCM XLV (Decision 5 (2023)) relating to policy, legal and institutional priorities. It considered how

to take each priority item forward in the coming years and whether to delete current priorities and add new priorities.

(231) Australia introduced WP 22 *Report on the Intersessional Contact Group (ICG) to review the use* and *functioning of the Multi-Year Strategic Work Plan (MYSWP)*. Australia recalled that it had convened the ICG from January to April 2024 and reported that six participants had been involved in the ICG. It noted that the participants in the ICG had determined that the Multi-year Strategic Work Plan helped focus their attention on ATCM priorities, had seen value in its continued use and had broadly supported the suggestions put forward by the Secretariat at ATCM XLV. Based on comments provided by participants, Australia advised the ATCM that the Multi-year Strategic Work Plan remained a valuable tool for Parties and could be improved by revising the Meeting's procedure for discussing priorities and developing further guidance for the content of the Multi-year Strategic Work Plan itself. On behalf of the ICG Australia recommended that the ATCM:

1. Establish a periodic review procedure for every third ATCM, for example, a more detailed discussion in the ATCM supported by margins work. Support for that review procedure could include a guidance document for ATCM Chairs, a Secretariat-supported procedure, and/or using the Meeting report to identify Multi-year Strategic Work Plan items more explicitly;
2. Invite host governments from 2025 to, if desired, identify a Multi-year Strategic Work Plan issue that will be a focus for their hosting year;
3. Support the monitoring and implementation of priorities, for example, by requesting ATCM Chairs to summarise in the ATCM report any action on priority items;
4. Adopt a guideline of no more than 5 to 10 priorities over a five-year term;
5. Set a maximum five-year term for a priority issue, consistent with the five-year horizon of the Multi-year Strategic Work Plan;
6. Develop guidance to assist the ATCM in drafting priorities, producing time-bound, action-oriented priorities, and
7. Encourage cross-referencing of Multi-year Strategic Work Plan priorities in papers submitted to the ATCM, including requesting the Secretariat to update the paper template to allow authors to reference a Multi-year Strategic Work Plan priority.

(232) The Meeting thanked Australia for its work and emphasised the importance of the Multi-year Strategic Work Plan as a tool for the ATCM. Many Parties agreed that limiting the number of priorities adopted over a five-year term was beneficial but noted the need for flexibility as new issues emerged or as some issues are of a more lasting nature.

(233) The Meeting reached consensus on recommendations 4 through 7.

(234) Norway introduced WP 36 *Assessing the need for a more developed scoping approach as an element of the CEE process*, jointly prepared with New Zealand and the United Kingdom. Norway recalled that in 2016, the CEP had reviewed the environmental impact assessment procedures in the Environmental Protocol and its Annex I. In its advice to the ATCM that year, the CEP had requested the extent to which it should begin work on the potential application for Antarctica of 'screening and scoping' processes, commonly applied as part of the EIA process for large projects in other parts of the world. Norway proposed that the ATCM request the CEP to: start work on assessing the potential application of a scoping process for CEE-level EIAs; consider whether the CEE process could be strengthened and be more transparent and efficient; and consider how Parties and stakeholders could or should be engaged in a potential scoping process. Norway underlined that the proposal was intended to apply to major activities likely to have more than a minor or transitory impact on the Antarctic environment, that would require a CEE under Article 3 of Annex I to the Environment Protocol.

(235) The Meeting thanked the proponents for WP 36.

(236) Several Parties supported the proposal to request advice from the CEP and noted that scoping and early involvement of stakeholders, as characterised in WP 36, were widespread international practices that the ATCM should consider adopting. These Parties suggested that it may be useful to look to, and share experiences from the use of scoping processes in national non-Antarctic legislation in this process.

(237) Several Parties expressed other views, including: that the present procedures for environmental impact assessment were well settled in the Environmental Protocol and its Annex I and that Parties were implementing these procedures through their national legislation and procedures; that the Meeting should agree on more specific terms before requesting the CEP for advice; and that the fact that scoping practices were standard in external fora did not suffice as a reason for their adoption within the Antarctic Treaty system. These Parties noted that the procedure already established through Annex I to the Environmental Protocol was enough, and were not in favour of adding new stages to the CEE process.

Item 12b: Multi-year Strategic Work Plan: Science, Operations and Tourism priorities

(238) The Meeting considered the Multi-year Strategic Work Plan adopted at ATCM XLV (Decision 5 (2023)) relating to science, operations and tourism priorities. It considered how to take each priority item forward in the coming years, and whether to delete current priorities and add new priorities.

(239) Following discussion, the Meeting agreed to add Priority 14: Continue work on addressing the heightened risks highly pathogenic avian influenza presents in Antarctica.

(240) The Meeting adopted Decision 4 (2024) *Multi-year Strategic Work Plan for the Antarctic Treaty Consultative Meeting.*

Item 13: Safety and Operations in Antarctica

(241) The Co-chair of Working Group 2, Sonia Ramos Garcia (Spain) noted that a large amount of Information Papers had been submitted to the Meeting and many of them referred to information required to be reported through the EIES.

(242) Following a proposal from the Co-chair, the Meeting agreed that, in future ATCMs, papers containing information that was to be circulated through the EIES should be submitted to the Meeting as Background Papers rather than Information Papers.

(243) The Co-chair also reminded the Meeting that all papers submitted should contain an adequate and clear summary to facilitate the work of delegates and the Chairs. The Co-chair directed Parties to the helpful guidance on how to prepare papers provided by the Secretariat on its website.

Modernisation of Antarctic Stations

(244) COMNAP introduced WP 18 *Assessing Built Infrastructure and Potential Environmental Consequences from a Changing Antarctica.* COMNAP provided information on its work to aid understanding and support the assessment of built infrastructure in a changing Antarctica and the potential environmental consequences of any impact on that infrastructure from those changed conditions. It highlighted that national Antarctic programmes were considering how a changing Antarctica may impact their built infrastructure, to ensure continuing support to research and safety objectives, and to meet their environmental obligations related to their Antarctic activities. COMNAP noted that

through national Antarctic programmes, it was working to understand how local and regional changes in their areas of operations might create new impacts on existing Antarctic infrastructure. COMNAP recommended that Parties support their national Antarctic programmes to participate in discussions and continue to provide their technical and practical expertise on the assessment of infrastructures in a changing Antarctica at the COMNAP Annual General Meetings and throughout the year. Finally, COMNAP reported that it would provide further information and advice on the subject at future ATCM.

(245) The Meeting agreed to COMNAP's recommendation that Parties continue supporting their national Antarctic programmes to participate in ongoing discussions on the issue. Parties acknowledged the importance of understanding and addressing the implications of a changing environment on existing and new infrastructure in Antarctica. In noting their activities related to the modernisation and construction of stations, Parties highlighted the importance of sharing experiences, exchanging information and looking systematically at the risks to which stations were subject.

(246) The Secretariat presented SP 9 *Summary of documents submitted to the ATCM on the modernisation of Antarctic stations from 2016 to 2023* in response to the request made by ATCM XLV (Helsinki, 2023) with the aim of assessing this topic in the Multi-year Strategic Work Plan. It highlighted that between 2016–2023, 22 papers were submitted by Parties to the ATCM on issues related to the modernisation of Antarctic stations in the context of climate change. The Secretariat noted that another 41 papers submitted to the ATCM and CEP meetings during the period described modernisation activities but did not directly refer to climate change as a primary reason. Finally, five papers informed the Meeting about plans to build new stations in Antarctica. The Secretariat observed that the number of papers submitted to the ATCM since this issue was included in the Multi-year Strategic Work Plan correlated well with what was reported by COMNAP. The Secretariat noted that the number of papers on climate change constituted approximately a third of all papers submitted on the modernisation of stations. It expressed its readiness to prepare additional material or clarify any questions for Parties to make informed decisions on this issue.

(247) The Meeting congratulated the Secretariat for its excellent work and appreciated its comprehensive analysis. Several Parties noted that many stations had been undertaking modernisation work, highlighted the importance of exchanging up-to-date information and underlined the usefulness of this kind of information to help assess priority issues contained in the Multi-year Strategic Work Plan.

(248) United Kingdom presented IP 52 *An Update on British Antarctic Survey's Antarctic Infrastructure Modernisation Programme (AIMP)*. The paper updated Parties on the United Kingdom's ongoing work on modernising its infrastructure in Antarctica. The United Kingdom noted that the construction of the Discovery Building and Site Wide Services began in 2019, and completion was expected by 2025. The United Kingdom highlighted that work on their runway was completed, fully operational, and open to transit. It thanked Parties for their flexibility and assistance during the past season.

(249) India presented IP 57 *Maitri-II: Redevelopment of the Indian Research Station Maitri in Antarctica*. The paper highlighted that the redevelopment of its Maitri research station was necessary due to the ageing of its old station and the need to address the existing challenges to enhance its capabilities for scientific research and environmental sustainability. India noted that it was developing a detailed CEE and would report on its progress at ATCM 47.

(250) The United States presented IP 71 *An overview of the South Pole Station Master Plan*, which reported on the final stages of completing a master plan for redeveloping its South Pole station. The United States reported that its Antarctic programme was at risk of losing science capabilities annually as facilities, utilities, equipment, and vehicle fleet degraded. It noted that it would summarise current conditions, constraints, and opportunities for the

South Pole Station and a site plan for redeveloping infrastructure requiring replacement. The United States invited interested Parties to query the particulars of the process.

(251) Peru presented IP 135 *Proyecto de la nueva Estación Científica Antártica Machu Picchu (ECAMP)*, which reported its plan to renovate its Machu Picchu Antarctic Scientific Station. It highlighted that the objective was to have an appropriate scientific station that covered its technical and scientific needs. It noted it had completed the second phase out of the four that comprise Peru's public investment cycle. Peru reported that its objective was to have a scientific station adapted to current technical and environmental requirements while also strengthening Peru's presence in Antarctica.

(252) The following paper was also submitted under this agenda item:

- BP 28 *Update of Information on the Progress of the Renovation of the Henryk Arctowski Polish Antarctic Station on King George Island, South Shetland Islands* (Poland)

Energy management and efficiency in Antarctic operations

(253) The United Kingdom introduced WP 35 *Use of Alternative Fuels in Antarctic Operations to Reduce Carbon Emissions*. The United Kingdom reported that the British Antarctic Survey (BAS) had an ambitious target to reach net zero carbon emissions by 2040 and that to meet the interim targets, BAS had been investigating the role of alternative fuels as part of the short and long-term decarbonisation roadmap. The United Kingdom outlined the experience of BAS in using Hydrotreated Vegetable Oil (HVO) in their polar research vessel and on station to support construction projects and plans to use Sustainable Aviation Fuel (SAF) in aircraft (and potentially vehicles and on station) as a short-term method to reduce carbon emissions. It described the trials in progress and outlined the results obtained and the benefits and challenges of alternative fuel use. The United Kingdom recommended that:

- Parties note the benefit of using sustainably sourced alternative fuels to reduce carbon emissions and consider trialling alternative fuel use in their operations;
- Parties share the results of their experience in alternative fuel trial or use; and
- operators of gateway ports consider improving the availability and traceability of alternative fuels and increasing their accessibility for Antarctic operations.

(254) The Meeting emphasised the importance of sharing best practices in using sustainably sourced alternative fuels to mitigate the impacts of climate change in Antarctica and reduce emissions. Many Parties highlighted the usefulness of learning from other experiences and exchanging experiences on this subject. Several Parties noted challenges related to using alternative fuels in Antarctica, including higher costs, identifying how they were sourced, and availability, particularly in gateway cities. Several Parties stressed the need to work toward decarbonisation and reducing emissions in Antarctica. Chile expressed its readiness to jointly work on the issue of availability of alternative fuels at gateway cities. Noting its wide experience on biofuels, Brazil welcomed the exchange of best practices on alternative fuels, while cautioning against creating obligations regarding specific technologies.

(255) IAATO reported that it annually surveyed its members on actions they were implementing to reduce emissions and that its members were working towards this goal. COMNAP and IAATO noted that their communities had highlighted the need to address supply and availability issues. COMNAP invited the British Antarctic Survey to present its work in the upcoming COMNAP Annual General Meeting and suggested creating a taskforce to search for ways of improving the availability of alternative fuels. ASOC encouraged Parties to continue strengthening efforts towards implementing renewable energies and sharing knowledge.

(256) Although most Parties expressed general support for the recommendations of the paper,

the Russian Federation considered it premature to conclude on the need for using alternative fuels in Antarctica, suggesting it required further research and assessment. The Russian Federation suggested there was insufficient scientific justification for the use of specific types of fuels in Antarctica. Parties agreed on the need for continued research and collaboration to identify sustainable solutions and reduce emissions in Antarctica.

(257) Chile presented IP 30 *Hybrid generation pilot project at the Chilean Antarctic Naval Base "Arturo Prat"*, which reported on its effort to have the first Chilean Net Zero Antarctic base by 2030. It noted that the project was part of the national and global effort to reduce the sources of pollution that caused environmental damage due to the emission of greenhouse gases and the consequent increase in global temperature.

(258) The United Kingdom presented IP 89 *Using Artificial Intelligence (AI) to Support Decision Making in Marine Operations to Reduce Carbon Emissions*, which reported on the initial steps the AI Lab at the British Antarctic Survey (BAS) was taking to better understand the potential use of AI to support Antarctic activities. It reported that BAS had developed a fully automated system for planning the annual logistics and science itineraries for a fleet of research vessels and that, given a collection of science requests, including science surveys to be done at particular locations within particular time windows, this shore-based system would plan how to task the ships in the fleet with the different requests to minimise the overall carbon emissions involved in a field season. The United Kingdom noted that the system could look ahead over three or more years, planning how best to schedule tasks to maximise science delivery as efficiently as possible within each field season.

(259) Norway presented IP 115 *High Greenhouse Gas Reduction Ambitions at Troll Research Station*, which reported that it had initiated a process towards modernisation and renewal of its Troll Research Station. Norway highlighted that it had set high ambitions for greening the operations and aimed for a 50% reduction in greenhouse emissions associated with station operations. Norway noted it would continue sharing information on its modernisation process and submit a draft Comprehensive Environmental Evaluation in due course.

Safety issues related to Antarctic operations

(260) COMNAP introduced WP 1 *Air Safety in Antarctica - Importance of ATCM XLIV Resolution 3 (2022) Provisions*. It reminded Parties of the importance of Resolution 3 (2022), which had been adopted following COMNAP advice to improve air safety in Antarctica. COMNAP reminded Parties of the importance of transponders being installed and turned on in all aircraft while in flight to enhance real-time situational awareness. COMNAP also highlighted that the agreed Traffic Information Broadcast by Aircraft (TIBA) frequency was 129.7 MHz. COMNAP noted that TIBA and the agreed TIBA frequency for use in Antarctica remained an essential tool for information exchange, even with technological improvements that allowed for automatic reporting of positions. COMNAP recommended that Parties ensure that their governmental and non-governmental operators were implementing the provisions of Resolution 3 (2022) to contribute to the safety of air operations in the Antarctic Treaty area.

(261) The Meeting welcomed the reminders in WP 1. Recalling Resolution 3 (2022) and ATCM XLV - WP 44, the Parties and IAATO restated their sustained commitment to improving the safety of aerial operations in Antarctica. Several Parties and IAATO informed the Meeting about the newest guidelines adopted by their national Antarctic programmes and operators. The Meeting encouraged all Parties to keep adopting and enforcing high safety standards in their aerial operators, and agreed to follow up on the issue in future meetings.

(262) COMNAP presented IP 1 *Report from the COMNAP Antarctic Search and Rescue (SAR) Workshop 5*. The report contained key messages about Antarctic search and rescue of relevance to Parties. COMNAP thanked all participants for their active cooperation.

(263) New Zealand presented IP 6 *Safety Risks at Cape Adare, North Victoria Land, Ross Sea region*. It drew the Meeting's attention to historic ammunition, explosives, and flares that might be buried near the historic hut at Cape Adare. New Zealand planned to send experts to the site in the next summer season to assess the risk and, if necessary, prepare for disposal. New Zealand stated it would keep the other Parties informed of the situation.

(264) Colombia presented IP 157 *Identification and characterization of dangerous meteorological phenomena for air navigation in Antarctica* and IP 158 *Identificación de los factores de riesgo técnico en operaciones aéreas*. Colombia described how Colombian and Argentinian researchers had developed improved weather forecasting models and procedures after conducting surveys and studies at the Marambio Aerodrome. It noted that the new tools would contribute positively to the efficiency and safety of future operations in the area.

(265) ASOC presented IP 141 *Harmonised implementation of the Polar Code and related shipping issues*. It provided an overview of the discussions and outcome of last year's special session on the harmonised implementation of the Polar Code hosted by Argentina and Finland. ASOC also provided information on potential lessons learned from two vessel fire incidents in the Southern Ocean and reported on new IMO guidance on reducing underwater noise from ships. ASOC underlined that there had not been much progress on this issue, and urged Parties to provide further information on their experiences of implementing the Polar Code in the coming year to assess progress due at ATCM 47 in 2025.

(266) The Meeting reconfirmed its commitment to the proper implementation of the Polar Code and acknowledged its intent to continue to discuss the matter.

(267) ASOC presented IP 144 rev. 1 *Unregulated discharges in the Antarctic Treaty Area: gray water from ships*, which drew Parties' attention to the unregulated discharge of greywater from ships in the Antarctic Treaty area. ASOC noted that despite the known toxicity of many greywater constituents, its disposal was not regulated globally and was not being considered by the International Maritime Organization (IMO). ASOC encouraged Parties to consider the matter of greywater disposal for inclusion in the ATCM work plan and suggested that stakeholders share information about current greywater practices to inform further work on this issue.

(268) Parties welcomed initiatives to share best practices, definitions and recommendations regarding greywater management in the coming meetings.

(269) The following paper was also submitted under this agenda item and taken as presented:

- IP 46 *Report on the 26th edition of the Joint Antarctic Naval Patrol – 2023/2024* (Argentina, Chile).

(270) The following papers were also submitted under this agenda item:

- BP 37 *Soporte Logístico Aéreo y las Operaciones Aéreas de Búsqueda y Rescate (SAR) en la Isla Rey Jorge de la Fuerza Aérea del Perú en la Campaña Científicas del Perú a la Antártida – ANTAR XXX* (Peru).
- BP 47 *Accident at Mirny station* (Russian Federation).
- BP 48 *Search and Rescue operation involving vessel in distress "El Doblon" at Drake Passage, accomplished by Bulgarian RSV 421* (Bulgaria, Chile).

Biosecurity issues

(271) Chile introduced WP 56 *Prevention, control and management of avian influenza in Antarctica: Need to unify biosafety criteria*. Chile proposed establishing an ICG to analyse the various protocols being applied in Antarctica by the Parties concerning HPAI and, generally, in biosecurity matters. Chile proposed that the ICG should be instructed to gather

the relevant information and promote the unification of biosecurity criteria among the Consultative Parties, either through a Measure agreed upon at a future ATCM or by suggesting common guidelines for implementation through domestic legislation. Chile noted that the proposal was based on the results of monitoring conducted in different areas of Antarctica by scientific groups from various national Antarctic programmes following the guidelines and procedures previously devised by COMNAP, IAATO, SCAR and CCAMLR.

(272) SCAR introduced WP 47 rev. 1 *Update on High Pathogenicity Avian Influenza in Antarctica*, prepared jointly with COMNAP, IAATO, and CCAMLR. It provided an update on the current status, known impacts, and community actions in response to HPAI in Antarctica. The paper reported the first confirmed cases in the Antarctic Treaty Area had been recorded in February 2024, and that seven sites of confirmed infection and seven sites of suspected infection had been identified to date. There were clear indications that HPAI was brought to the Antarctic through natural migration and not through direct human activity or interactions with wildlife. With HPAI confirmed in the northern Antarctic Peninsula region, there remained a high risk for intra-regional spread, infection to multiple species, and continuing impact on Antarctic wildlife.

(273) SCAR, COMNAP, and IAATO recommended that the Parties:

- ensure that biosecurity guidelines and procedures are robustly implemented to eliminate or mitigate the risk to humans, as well as the risk of spreading the disease within Antarctica through human activities;
- encourage continued vigilance and monitoring, as well as sample collection and testing where necessary expertise is available and permitted; and
- continue to report and share information on suspected and confirmed cases (including through the SCAR Antarctic Wildlife Health Network (AWHN) HPAI Monitoring Project) to support collaboration, inform decision-making, and improve scientific understanding of the spread and impact of the disease.

(274) The Meeting thanked the co-proponents for addressing the urgent matter through the two Working Papers. The Meeting agreed to establish an intersessional contact group (ICG) on the prevention, control and management of HPAI in Antarctica with the following terms of reference:

- reviewing and reporting on national practices and protocols associated with the prevention, control, management, measurement and monitoring of HPAI in Antarctica;
- discussing possible recommendations for consideration at ATCM 47; and
- reporting back to ATCM 47.

(275) It was further agreed that:

- Observers and Experts participating in the ATCM would be invited to provide input;
- the Executive Secretary would open the ATCM forum for the ICG and provide assistance to it; and
- Chile would act as convenor and report to the next ATCM on the progress made in the ICG.

(276) Many Parties acknowledged COMNAP, SCAR, IAATO and CCAMLR for their timely and dedicated work in the previous seasons in designing and distributing useful guidelines for detecting and preventing HPAI in Antarctica. Stressing the importance of acting without unnecessary delay, the Meeting endorsed the recommendations proposed in the paper. However, some Parties cautioned the Meeting against the preparation of unified protocols on this issue.

(277) The Meeting also decided to include addressing the risks of HPAI as a priority issue in the ATCM Multi-year Strategic Work Plan.

(278) Argentina presented IP 39 *Avian Influenza: Situation in Argentine Antarctic Bases*, which summarised the measures taken in Argentine bases to detect and prevent the spread of HPAI. Argentina informed that samples collected at Primavera Station, after being tested jointly with the Spanish Antarctic programme, resulted in the confirmation of HPAI cases. The same happened in samples from brown skuas collected from the northern Weddell Sea and Esperanza station. Argentina noted that it would continue coordinating with COMNAP, SCAR and IAATO during the following season, and urged national Antarctic programmes to continue monitoring and establishing controls and biosafety measures.

(279) The Republic of Korea presented IP 127 *Practices to prevent the highly pathogenic Avian Influenza in Antarctica (HPAI)*. It presented the actions the Korean Antarctic programme had undertaken and implemented to prevent the spread of HPAI in the past season. The Republic of Korea expressed gratitude to SCAR, COMNAP, and IAATO for providing an update on HPAI in Antarctica and recalled the joint efforts taken between national Antarctic programmes on King George Island.

(280) COMNAP presented IP 4 *Actions in response to heightened risk of highly pathogenic Avian influenza (HPAI) in Antarctica*. It showcased the range of actions taken by COMNAP and by COMNAP members to contribute to the understanding of HPAI in the Antarctic, to protect human life, and to enhance biosecurity protocols to ensure that the natural spread of the disease was not assisted through direct human activities. COMNAP noted that the work of the joint COMNAP/SCAR Expert Group on Human Biology & Medicine contributed significantly to the development of COMNAP guidance on the subject. In addition to the development of protocols specific to their Antarctic operations, COMNAP highlighted that national Antarctic programmes were actively leading and contributing to surveillance, monitoring, sample collection and testing. COMNAP noted that national Antarctic programmes had reported collecting approximately 1000 samples in Antarctica during the 2023/24 Antarctic season. Education, training and heightened vigilance for signs of HPAI in wildlife near areas of operations would continue for the 2024/25 season and the COMNAP guidance would be updated as the situation evolved.

(281) Spain presented IP 42 *Measures taken to guarantee the safety of activities carried out during the Spanish Antarctic campaign in the face of the threat of highly pathogenic avian influenza*. It summarised the protocols the Spanish national Antarctic programme followed in the previous season to attempt minimising risks and ensuring safety of researchers working around fauna susceptible to being infected by HPAI; and to prevent transferring this disease among colonies. Spain highlighted its diagnostic laboratory, which, in collaboration with the Argentinian Antarctic programme, confirmed by molecular analysis and *in situ* sequencing the first case of HPAI in Antarctica.

(282) Chile presented IP 28 *Monitoring and detection of Highly Pathogenic Avian Influenza (HPAI) in the South Shetland Islands and Antarctic Peninsula*. It presented the monitoring activities carried out by Chile in the South Shetland Islands and the Antarctic Peninsula for the detection of HPAI. Chile joined the other Parties to acknowledge the need for more studies to genetically characterise the virus and better understand the role of skuas in its spreading in Antarctica.

(283) IAATO presented IP 105 *IAATO operator response to high pathogenicity Avian influenza*, which provided an update on IAATO's response to the evolving HPAI situation in Antarctica. It included details of enhanced biosecurity procedures, outlining new and enhanced materials and tools that IAATO provided to its members to assist in developing operator-specific standard operating procedures to help educate visitors and those in the field. It recalled the strong collaboration between IAATO, SCAR and COMNAP on HPAI in 2022/23 and its continuation in the 2023/24 season, as well as between its operators and national Antarctic programmes. IAATO also noted that its joint reporting procedures had

allowed operators in the field to report suspected infections and temporarily close sites for the duration of verification following assessment by SCAR. It also summarised its planned actions for the upcoming season including: continuing to hone protocols and tools; hosting town halls and webinars; supporting meaningful science where appropriate; and continuing to share IAATO's HPAI Protocols with national competent authorities prior to the season.

(284) Portugal presented IP 12 *Impacts of the COVID-19 pandemic on Antarctic researchers*, jointly prepared with Belgium, Chile, the Republic of Korea, the Netherlands, New Zealand and SCAR. It reported on the findings of a post-pandemic survey of more than 400 Antarctic researchers. The findings suggested that the pandemic had affected women more adversely than men, in particular in mental health, and that early-career researchers had felt their research particularly affected by the pandemic. The proponents encouraged Parties to address these structural inequalities accentuated by the pandemic.

(285) The following papers were also submitted under this agenda item and taken as presented:

- IP 41 *Australia's Preparedness and Response for Avian Influenza* (Australia).
- IP 139 *Actions taken by the Peruvian Antarctic Programme to tackle Highly Pathogenic Avian Influenza (HPAI) in the surroundings of the ECAMP – Antarctic Peninsula* (Peru).

Management of natural hazards

(286) Argentina presented IP 117 *Consolidation of the Argentine-Spanish Permanent Instrumental Volcano Monitoring Network on Deception Island volcano*, prepared jointly with Spain. It reported on the collaboration in establishing technologies and protocols that enabled joint real-time monitoring of volcanic activity on Deception Island. The proponents invited the Meeting to recognise the usefulness of these studies in assessing risks associated with volcanic activity in the region.

(287) The Meeting welcomed the collaboration between Argentina and Spain. It recognised the value of developing the real-time monitoring mechanism, which could also potentially enhance the management of the nearby Antarctic Specially Managed Area (ASMA) 4.

(288) The following paper was submitted under this agenda item and taken as presented:

- IP 65 *Study of the geochemistry of fluids of the volcanic-hydrothermal system of Deception Island* (Argentina).

Operation of national Antarctic programmes: results and resources

(289) Chile presented IP 27 *Air Capacities on King George Island Landing strip maintenance at the "Teniente Rodolfo Marsh M." Airfield* and IP 29 *Air Capacities on King George Island "Búfalo" Aircraft Hangar Maintenance*, which drew attention to the ongoing airfield renovation works on King George Island. Chile noted that the work would not impede the research taking place at the station.

(290) The United States presented IP 43 *The Use of Wheeled Vehicles for Science Support on the East Antarctica Plateau*. It reported on the positive initial results from using Arctic Truck vehicles to support research activities on the Antarctic plateau.

(291) The United Kingdom presented IP 66 *Report on Low Earth Orbit communication systems trials*. It highlighted the promising results of the United Kingdom in experimenting with offering private high-speed internet connections in its Antarctic bases by using commercial satellite constellations operating in low Earth orbit.

(292) The United Kingdom presented IP 68 *Operations and Scientific use of Remotely Piloted Aircraft Systems (RPAS) in Antarctica: a review*. It provided the Parties with a summary of the United Kingdom's experiences and lessons learned in utilising Remotely Piloted Aircraft Systems (RPAS). It reported on recent trials of operating larger, more capable

RPAS platforms that operated beyond visual line of sight, which could lead to new research capacities and overall savings in fuel and emissions.

(293) Spain presented IP 51 *Optimizing Antarctic National Programs Assets on the Antarctic Peninsula,* prepared jointly with the Republic of Korea, Poland, Türkiye and COMNAP. The proponents reported on their experiences in organising a joint task force within the auspices of COMNAP, which had led to enhanced capacities and mutual savings through the coordinated sharing of logistical assets under a barter (point valued) system. The co-proponents jointly commended each other for their collaboration and expressed to the Parties their willingness to further collaborate to build up this experience into a collaboration scheme that could serve as a system that could be adapted to the wider community of national Antarctic programmes.

(294) Bulgaria presented IP 164 *The discovery of the remains of the Neptune 2-p-103 aircraft of the Argentinian navy by members of the 32nd Bulgarian Antarctic expedition*, prepared jointly with Argentina and Chile. Bulgaria reported on the discovery of the remains of the Argentinian Neptune 2-P-103 aircraft, which had been lost in 1976. Bulgaria summarised the story behind the wreckage and noted that a commemorative ceremony had been held at the location.

(295) Argentina expressed gratitude for the respectful manner in which Bulgaria had dealt with the remains.

(296) Chile presented IP 5 *Theoretical and practical training for the crews of the Chilean Bases covered by the Antarctic Defence Operators*. It informed the Meeting about a new multidisciplinary training programme offered to Chilean personnel before their deployment to bases in Antarctica.

(297) The following papers were also submitted under this agenda item and taken as presented:

- IP 69 *The Antarctic Infrastructure Recapitalization (AIR) Program: 2024-2028 Aviation Safety Initiatives* (United States)
- IP 72 *Overview of the McMurdo Offload Infrastructure Project* (United States)
- IP 93 *Palmer Station pier replacement: environmental monitoring update* (United States)

(298) The following papers were also submitted under this agenda item:

- BP 9 *42nd Brazilian Antarctic Operation (OPERANTAR XLII) – 2023/2024* (Brazil).
- BP 10 *Incorporación de unidades antárticas a la Armada de Chile* (Chile).
- BP 23 *The Eighth Turkish Antarctic Expedition (TAE-VIII)* (Türkiye).
- BP 34 *Resumen de la Campaña Antártica de Verano 2023-2024 del Programa Nacional Antártico de Uruguay* (Uruguay).
- BP 36 *Trigésima Expedición Científica del Perú a la Antártida (ANTAR XXX)* (Peru).
- BP 38 *Operaciones del B.A.P. "Carrasco"* (Peru).
- BP 39 *Ejecución de la XXVII Expedición Antártica Ecuatoriana (2022-2023)* (Ecuador).
- BP 41 *10° Expedición Antártica de Colombia* (Colombia).
- BP 44 *Progress of work on the assembly of the new wintering building at Vostok station in the 2023/2024 season* (Russian Federation).
- BP 52 *Sistema de Posicionamiento Dinámico del B.A.P. Carrasco* (Peru).

- BP 53 *Plan de eliminación de residuos orgánicos e inorgánicos en el B.A.P. Carrasco* (Peru).
- BP 54 *Operación del equipo Bell-412 en las Expediciones Antárticas de Colombia* (Colombia)
- BP 55 *ARC "Simón Bolívar", Colombian Marine Scientific Research Vessel, contributes to scientific knowledge and international cooperation in Antarctica* (Colombia).

Item 14: Inspections under the Antarctic Treaty and the Environment Protocol

(299) Australia presented IP 40 *Australian Antarctic Treaty and Environmental Protocol inspections: December 2023*, which provided a summary of inspections conducted by Australia in December 2023 of Dumont d'Urville station (France), Robert Guillard station (France and Italy) and the vessel L'Astrolabe (France). Australia informed the Meeting that the inspection had been part of reciprocal inspections between Australia and France. Each Party had provided operational support for the other's observers; however, the inspections were undertaken independently and the inspection reports were prepared independently. Australia reported that its observers had been given full access to all areas of the visited facilities, and had observed strong commitment to Antarctic research and environmental protection. The inspection team had observed full compliance with the Antarctic Treaty and a high level of compliance with the Environmental Protocol. The inspection report presented the inspection team's recommendations for consideration by France and Italy. Australia thanked France for the close collaboration on the successful initiative, and also for the warm hospitality and support provided to the inspection team.

(300) France presented IP 86 *French inspection pursuant to Article VII of the Antarctic Treaty and Article 14 of the Protocol on Environmental Protection: February 2024*, which provided a summary of the reciprocal inspection conducted by French observers in February 2024 of Australia's Casey station, the abandoned Wilkes station and the Wilkins aerodrome. France noted that this was part of an unprecedented cooperation with Australia and emphasised that the inspection was conducted independently. France reported that the inspection team had full access to all infrastructure and sites of interest. It stated that infrastructure and activities in the sites had fully complied with the provisions of the Antarctic Treaty and the Environmental Protocol. It identified a number of points of caution and possible areas for improvement, which were shared with Australia for its consideration.

(301) Australia and France thanked each other for their successful cooperation and facilitation during the inspections and their recommendations. France underscored that reciprocal inspections offered a valuable opportunity to share experiences and best practices to improve the management of activities in Antarctica. France highlighted its plans to renovate the Dumont d'Urville station in the coming years. Australia informed the Meeting of its ongoing work to develop a robust cleanup strategy for Australian stations and sites in Antarctica, including the abandoned Wilkes station, as reported in IP 54 presented to the CEP meeting in 2022. Australia also highlighted its commitment to exploring opportunities to increase renewable energy use, and to collaborating with other national Antarctic programmes on the operation and modernisation of Antarctic infrastructure.

(302) The Meeting thanked Australia and France for their inspection reports and welcomed the findings of high compliance in all inspected facilities. It noted with interest the unprecedented, successful manner in which these two cross-inspections had been reciprocally organised. Noting that inspection activities did not need to be previously agreed, Parties reaffirmed the importance of providing complete freedom of access to all duly designated observers as originally provided in the Antarctic Treaty and the Environmental Protocol.

Item 15: Science Issues, Future Science Challenges, Scientific Cooperation and Facilitation

Opportunities for scientific international cooperation

(303) COMNAP introduced WP 61 *International Collaboration*, which suggested that the Meeting consider ways to expand how COMNAP provided advice to better showcase the depth and breadth of international collaboration across Antarctica in science support, operations, and logistics. COMNAP expressed its willingness to provide regular presentations to the ATCM in an engaging and informative manner, if the ATCM schedule would allow, on topics that demonstrated international collaboration. It suggested that showcasing these activities would lead to understanding where gaps in management or information exchange may be addressed or improved and may assist the Parties in their decision-making. COMNAP noted that it also stood ready to continue to provide this information in the usual manner, that is, through the continuation of submission of papers to the ATCM.

(304) The Meeting welcomed COMNAP's willingness to provide further advice to the ATCM. Parties stressed COMNAP's importance to all Antarctic operations, and many Parties supported hosting a COMNAP lecture or presentation at the ATCM. After discussing the details of the proposal, Parties suggested that COMNAP follow up with a more detailed proposal about the specific contents, frequency, format and location within the agenda of the ATCM for the presentation.

(305) The Russian Federation stressed the importance of data sharing on collaboration in national Antarctic programmes in order to regularly assess the implementation of the principle of international cooperation. The Russian Federation pointed out the systemic and institutional nature of this issue and therefore the need of the involvement of Working Group 1. It noted the need for the active participation of all Parties in the discussion, not only COMNAP.

(306) COMNAP thanked the Meeting for the discussion and agreed to prepare a fuller proposal on its suggestion to the next ATCM after further consultation with its members.

(307) Germany presented IP 91 *Update 2024: International Science & Infrastructure for Synchronous Observation (Antarctica InSync)*, prepared jointly with Australia, Brazil, France, India, Italy, New Zealand, Norway, the Republic of Korea, Sweden, Switzerland, the United Kingdom and the United States. The proponents reported on current progress with the Antarctica InSync research programme, which aimed to bring together large-scale international collaboration across several important fields of Antarctic research. Highlights included establishing a new steering committee, an endorsement by the United Nations Educational, Scientific and Cultural Organization as a regional Oceans Decade programme, and participation in the joint planning of the forthcoming 5th International Polar Year 2032–33. The co-proponents invited all Parties and their research institutions to collaborate.

(308) Germany presented IP 97 *POLARIN – Polar Research Infrastructure Network*, prepared jointly with Bulgaria, Finland, France, Italy, Norway, Poland, Portugal, Spain and Sweden. It announced a new large-scale international polar research programme funded by the European Union, which aimed at tackling several Arctic and Antarctic scientific challenges. Germany stated that the network offered fully funded access to over 60 polar research stations, including 11 installations in Antarctica, vessels and ice breakers operating at both poles, observatories (on land and at sea), data infrastructure and ice and sediment core repositories. The proponents underlined that these opportunities were open to calls from researchers and projects from any nationality.

(309) India presented IP 55 *Geological Exploration of Amery Ice Shelf (GeoEAIS)-Looking at*

rocks beneath the ice, which provided information on the geological observatory program designed to improve understanding of sub-ice geology in the East Antarctic Ice Sheet. India welcomed all interested Parties to participate in future scientific activities.

(310) The United States presented IP 70 *The Value of Low-Powered Geospace Instrumentation in Antarctica*, and IP 73 *IceCube Neutrino Observatory and International Collaboration*, showcasing some of the latest groundbreaking research results in Antarctica. This year's highlights included the observation of steady-state neutrinos at the South Pole and near-Earth space weather measurements using ground-based magnetometers. Both papers stressed the importance of international collaboration.

(311) Peru presented IP 147 *Grupo de Trabajo Regional sobre el Krill*. It informed Parties about the creation of a regional working group on krill to study population dynamics and the links to climate change with a regional approach among the Latin American Antarctic Program Administrators (RAPAL). Peru invited Parties interested in the study of krill, as well as in the analysis of historical data on krill in the Antarctic Peninsula, to join this initiative.

(312) SCAR presented IP 121 *Update on the Southern Ocean contribution to the United Nations Decade of Ocean Science for Sustainable Development*. It reported that in June 2023 the UN Ocean Decade approved the Decade Collaborative Centre for the Southern Ocean Region (DCC-SOR) coordinated by SCAR with the Southern Ocean Task Force as its advisory body. The DCC-SOR aimed to connect Southern Ocean science with global ocean science, reinforcing scientific cooperation between the Antarctic region and other regions globally and supporting the objectives of Article III of the Antarctic Treaty.

(313) SCAR presented IP 122 *Plans for a fifth International Polar Year 2032/33*, prepared jointly with WMO. It provided an update on initial plans for the 5th International Polar Year (IPY) to be held in 2032–33, 25 years after the previous IPY in 2007–08. The proponents highlighted that initial planning had been led by SCAR and the International Arctic Science Committee (IASC) working closely with partners, including representatives of Indigenous Peoples in the Arctic. A focus of the coming year would be to expand stakeholder engagement. In the absence of a funded IPY Secretariat, the Secretariats for SCAR and IASC were temporarily fulfilling the role of an interim IPY Secretariat. The proponents offered to provide further information to any interested Parties, Observers or Experts.

(314) WMO presented IP 123 *Recommendations on the contribution of the World Meteorological Organization (WMO) on the coordination of meteorological programmes in Antarctica, as operated by WMO Members, and in support of evolving global needs*, jointly prepared with India, New Zealand and Norway. It summarised the WMO recommendations made by the Panel on Polar and High Mountains Observations, Research, and Services. WMO invited the Meeting to take note of these consultations and stated that it planned to provide specific recommendations to the Parties for consultation during ATCM 47.

(315) New Zealand recalled the importance of the Antarctic Treaty system being aware of, drawing on and contributing its experience to the work of the WMO. New Zealand highlighted the Panel's observations on the global importance of improved and sustained data from Antarctica to support global climate models and thanked Parties for the important collaborative science which was contributing to this work.

(316) The Meeting thanked the WMO for its commitment to providing relevant climate and cryosphere information to the ATCM, and looked forward to discussing its recommendations at ATCM 47.

(317) Brazil presented IP 20 *Ten-Year Plan for Antarctic Science in Brazil 2023-2032*, reporting the scientific guidelines for Brazilian research on the Antarctic continent over the next decade through its ten-year plan for Antarctic science in Brazil 2023-32. Brazil noted that

the plan provided reference information for scientific cooperation and coordination with other Parties to the Antarctic Treaty. It highlighted that the strategic document guided research areas through seven thematic research programmes, including issues like biodiversity, climate change, geodynamics and geospace, among others. Brazil invited Parties to identify any opportunities for strengthening cooperation in its ten-year plan.

(318) Australia presented IP 76 *Update on the Australian Antarctic Strategy and 20 Year Action Plan and major initiatives*, which highlighted new measures and initiatives for Antarctica for the next 20 years. Australia reported on the progress of major initiatives associated with the Australian Antarctic Strategy and 20 Year Action Plan update of 2022, initially released in 2016, including: the state-of-the-art icebreaker RSV *Nuyina*; Australia's traverse capability to support drilling for a million-year ice core; and krill research. Australia noted that the updated Strategy and Action Plan identified several activities to further strengthen opportunities for Antarctic science and expressed openness to discuss these initiatives with interested Parties.

(319) Türkiye presented IP 98 *Turkish Polar Science Strategy 2023-2035*, which summarised the new polar research strategy document of Türkiye covering the time frame between 2023-35. It included information on mission and vision, priority scientific themes, core values, and strategic aims defined within the strategy. Türkiye concluded that this strategy provided a roadmap for all national stakeholders in Antarctic science. Türkiye aimed to strengthen the existing ties between researchers and decision-makers and gain differentiating competitive power in the scientific field.

(320) Portugal presented IP 167 *Marine Spatial Planning for a sustainable and climate-resilient Antarctic Ocean*, prepared jointly with Canada, France, Italy and IUCN. It provided information on how sustainable "climate-smart" marine spatial planning could be a valuable tool for Parties to facilitate the development of policies and decision-making in Antarctic Treaty waters by analysing and allocating the spatial and temporal distribution of human activities in the Southern Ocean. The co-authors encouraged Parties to plan in a climate-smart way and implement key components to increase the resilience of Antarctica's vital ecosystems.

(321) IUCN emphasised that sustainable "climate-smart" marine spatial planning was an excellent tool to better manage Antarctic resources, ensure that suitable activities were taking place in the right places, and identify which activities should be avoided. It noted that effective marine spatial planning was only possible by genuine international collective efforts. IUCN encouraged Parties to collaborate on this topic and implement the proposed tool.

(322) SCAR presented IP 163 *Observing systems in Antarctica*, which provided an overview and examples of current long-term observation efforts to inform further work to assess gaps and establish sustained and coordinated observing systems. SCAR noted that long-term monitoring of the physical and living environment was essential to understand ongoing environmental changes in Antarctica and to obtain data needed as the basis for analyses and modelling. SCAR reiterated the need for international agreement, coordination, and collaboration to determine the priority observations to be collected and for data management and delivery to be internationally coordinated. SCAR concluded this was necessary to deliver sustained and coordinated observing and data delivery systems.

(323) SCAR also referred to IP 168 *Status of Observational Coverage and Gaps in the Southern Ocean*, which presented preliminary maps of observational coverage of the Southern Ocean, developed by the Southern Ocean Observing System (SOOS) and invited all interested parties to give feedback on these maps to ensure they captured all observation efforts and community needs. SCAR highlighted that large-scale international collaboration would provide opportunities for further advancements in effectively developing observation systems in Antarctica.

(324) New Zealand thanked SCAR for IP 163, noting that it responded directly to a request from the ATCM following its agreement on the importance of long-term monitoring to facilitate better understanding of climate change impacts.

(325) Belarus presented IP 2 *First results on the content of microplastic in soils and freshwater of East Antarctica.* Belarus stated that although many microplastic studies had been conducted in Antarctica, most of the studies had been carried out in West Antarctica, and mainly in marine areas. Noting that there had been minimal investigations of microplastics in East Antarctica, and its terrestrial areas, Belarus highlighted that it considered that its report on microplastics in the freshwater of Thala Hills, East Antarctica, that had been published in peer-reviewed journals, was important. Belarus reported that the detected levels of microplastic content were high, which may have been the result of the highly impacted levels of microplastics, and noted it would continue its investigations. Belarus stressed the importance of further study and research collaborations into the emerging issue of microplastic pollution in Antarctica.

(326) Peru presented IP 148 *Contaminación por plásticos en Antártida, revisión del estado actual del conocimiento*, which provided a literature review on plastic pollution in Antarctica to identify existing gaps. Peru highlighted a lack of standardisation in collection and analysis, especially regarding microplastics. Peru recommended that future work on microplastics should implement quality control measures for collection, transportation and monitoring of solid waste generated at bases. Peru noted that knowing how much pollution originated from scientific bases or human activities was crucial.

(327) Argentina presented IP 15 *Information on the implementation of the Nutec Plastics Initiative in the Argentine Antarctic Programme*, which reported on a project to study microplastic pollution in the Antarctic environment that was being developed at Carlini Base and aboard the icebreaker *ARA Almirante Irízar* in cooperation with the International Atomic Energy Agency (IAEA). Argentina highlighted the need to standardise microplastic monitoring procedures in Antarctica and offered the practice and knowledge acquired in the Nutec Plastics Initiative to Parties looking to adopt similar initiatives.

(328) ASOC presented IP 140 *Microplastic pollution in Antarctica: a complex challenge*, which, drawing on the provisions contained in Resolution 5 (2019), recommended the ATCM to take further action to address the problem of plastic pollution in the Antarctic Treaty Area, including: considering the development of an action plan, considering a review of provisions related to the management of plastic pollution in the Environmental Protocol, encouraging cooperation to reduce the use of plastic in Antarctica, and supporting global initiatives to address this problem. ASOC reported that microplastics could be ingested by living organisms, such as Antarctic krill, and, once ingested, they could have toxicological effects on keystone species, with impacts that affected entire marine ecosystems, including through bioaccumulation and biomagnification. ASOC reported that local operations, such as research stations, tourism, fishing and research vessels, were the most significant sources of microplastic pollution in Antarctica, and stated current practices in Antarctica to reduce plastic pollution.

(329) The Netherlands noted that it had introduced a draft resolution on the issue of microplastics for consideration by the CEP and encouraged Parties to work towards eradicating plastic pollution in Antarctica.

(330) The following papers were also submitted under this agenda item and taken as presented:

- IP 3 *First assessment of cumulative impact of scientific stations on the ambient air of an Antarctic oasis* (Belarus).
- IP 7 *Canada's Support for Polar Science and Research* (Canada).
- IP 8 *120 years of Argentine scientific research in Antarctica* (Argentina).

- IP 11 *Portugal and the Antarctic Treaty: review since 2010* (Portugal).
- IP 18 *Public Calls for PROANTAR Research Projects 2022/2023* (Brazil).
- IP 19 *Scientific production of the Brazilian Antarctic Program (PROANTAR)* (Brazil).
- IP 35 *Report by WMO on the implementation of the International Year of Glaciers' Preservation 2025 and the World Glaciers Day* (WMO).
- IP 58 *Preliminary studies on microplastics from the Indian sector of the Southern Ocean* (India).
- IP 59 *Contribution towards Study of Psychrophilic organisms in Antarctic by India* (India).
- IP 60 *Teleconnections between Antarctica, the Southern Ocean, and the Indian Summer Monsoon Rainfall* (India).
- IP 62 *Unravelling the Mysteries of Antarctic Lakes: International Collaboration on Scientific Exploration (India - Japan - Belgium)* (India, Japan, Belgium).
- IP 83 *Australian Antarctic Science Program Highlights 2023-24* (Australia).
- IP 113 *Fimbulisen Ice-shelf Observatory – contributing to sea-level change research* (Norway, United Kingdom).
- IP 128 *Report on 20 Years of Asian Forum for Polar Sciences* (AFoPS) (China, India, Japan, Republic of Korea, Malaysia).
- IP 129 *Scientific and Science-related Cooperation with the Antarctic Community* (Republic of Korea).
- IP 130 *The international cooperation and support of Ukraine's National Antarctic Program* (Ukraine).
- IP 132 *Research Vessel Noosfera: three years of operational experienc*e (Ukraine, Poland).
- IP 153 *Programa Técnico Científico de la XXVII Expedición Antártica Ecuatoriana y la cooperación para fines de investigación* (Ecuador).
- IP 156 *Determination of the Contribution of Atmospheric Pressure to Sea Level Variations in Antarctica in Austral Summer* (Colombia).
- IP *157 Identification and characterization of dangerous meteorological phenomena for air navigation in Antarctica* (Colombia).
- IP 161 *Colombian Antarctic Science. Highlights of the last 10 years of activities in Antarctica* (Colombia).
- IP 175 *Progress of glaciological research activities at the Dome Fuji Observation Camp II* (Japan).
- IP 178 *Indian-Norwegian Scientific Co-operation in Antarctica* (Norway, India).
- IP 180 *An update on the regional RINGS survey in Dronning Maud Land and Enderby Land* (Norway, China, Germany).

(331) The following papers were also submitted under this agenda item:

- BP 3 20th *COMNAP Symposium: "Antarctic Innovations and Collaborations"* (COMNAP).
- BP 4 *Resultado de la operación en la Estación Polar Científica Conjunta "Glaciar Unión" 2023* (Chile).
- BP 7 *Memorandums of Understanding and cooperation protocols between Portugal and other Parties of the Antarctic Treaty: a review* (Portugal).

- BP 8 *Portugal in Antarctica History* (Portugal).
- BP 11 *Romania Strengthening Global Partnerships: Extends Collaboration Agreements with South Korea and Oriental Republic of Uruguay* (Romania).
- BP 15 *Distribución de microplásticos en sitios de playa de Península Fildes (Isla Rey Jorge/25 de Mayo) y Glaciar Nelson (Isla Nelson): resultados preliminaries* (Venezuela).
- BP 16 *Correlación fisicoquímica espacio-temporal del agua de deshielo a lo largo de las costas de las islas Nelson y Rey Jorge/25 de Mayo, Antártida* (Venezuela).
- BP 17 *Quimiotaxonomía basada en pigmentos de microalgas bentónicas en la isla Greenwich, Antártida. Aislamiento y cultivo de los principales taxones de algas* (Venezuela).
- BP 18 *Variación de la reflectancia espectral solar con la distribución de impurezas ópticas y el área específica de la nieve en sitios de interés en Península Fildes, Isla Rey Jorge/25 de Mayo* (Venezuela).
- BP 22 *Scientific Contributions of Türkiye to Antarctic Research (2023/2024 Update)* (Türkiye).
- BP 24 *Turkish Polar Science Symposium (2023/2024 Update)* (Türkiye).
- BP 25 *Colombia-Türkiye Scientific and Logistical Collaboration in Antarctica* (Colombia, Türkiye).
- BP 26 *Ecuador-Türkiye Scientific Collaboration* (Ecuador, Türkiye).
- BP 27 *Spain-Türkiye Scientific & Logistic Cooperation* (Spain, Türkiye).
- BP 29 *Malaysia's activities and achievements in Antarctic research and diplomacy* (Malaysia).
- BP 40 *Investigación de la Dinámica de la Tierra Sólida y Atmosférica en la región Antártica a partir de observaciones geodésicas* (Colombia).
- BP 45 *Russian scientific research in Antarctica 2022–2023* (Russian Federation).
- BP 49 *"40 años de la primera misión oficial antártica uruguaya"* (Uruguay).
- BP 55 *ARC "Simón Bolívar", Colombian Marine Scientific Research Vessel, contributes to scientific knowledge and international cooperation in Antarctica* (Colombia).
- BP 56 *Türkiye-Switzerland Scientific Collaboration on Mapping and Absolute Dating of Stepped Coastal Terraces at Horseshoe Island, Marguerite Bay, West Antarctic Peninsula* (Türkiye, Switzerland).
- BP 57 *Japan's Antarctic Research Highlights 2023 – 24* (Japan).
- BP 58 *Proposal of cooperation of Romania with Uruguay in Antarctica* (Romania).

Diversity issues in Antarctic science

(332) COMNAP introduced WP 7 *The COMNAP Working Group Project to Support Understanding of EDI and to Prevent Harassment in Antarctica.* COMNAP reported the aim of the project was to support improving individuals' understanding of equity, diversity and inclusivity (EDI), and to continue to incorporate EDI principles in the organisational structure of COMNAP. The project was established to assist COMNAP as an organisation and national Antarctic programme members to understand EDI issues and improve practices especially to prevent harassment in Antarctica. COMNAP noted the project would create a hub that would include: a Community of Practice to act as a forum; a COMNAP Resource Library that programmes could use; and an online invited speaker series in which individuals with expertise in EDI and harassment prevention would share their knowledge with the COMNAP community. COMNAP encouraged all Parties to support their national Antarctic programmes in taking part and sharing expertise and best practices to this project.

(333) The Russian Federation recalled a paper submitted by a Consultative Party at the last ATCM and reiterated that common understanding of "inclusiveness and diversity" was not achieved. The Russian Federation advocated for the diversification of research areas, increasing the diversity of operators carrying out such work and subsequently presenting data at Antarctic fora.

(334) The Meeting thanked COMNAP for WP 7.

(335) Many Parties acknowledged COMNAP for promoting safe and equitable work environments in Antarctica. Several Parties and Observers shared their experiences promoting and implementing EDI in their national programmes. Several Parties underlined the need to ensure that the Antarctic was a region free of harassment and discrimination. Many Parties expressed strong support for COMNAP and the recommendations in the paper.

(336) Regarding the COMNAP proposal outlined in the paper, the Russian Federation advised to avoid the reference to the COMNAP project but elaborate on possible ATCM contributions including through the call on Parties to support national Antarctic programmes in the exchange of experience and practices aimed at ensuring equality among participants in all national Antarctic expeditions, thus diversifying Antarctic science and inclusiveness of scientific projects in Antarctica.

(337) The United Kingdom referred to IP 67 *'Safety together culture' using a holistic approach to expeditioner's safety and wellbeing,* which shared information on how the British Antarctic Survey had developed a new safety campaign to integrate physical, mental and social wellbeing of individuals deployed in Antarctica. The United Kingdom underscored its strong support for the COMNAP actions as presented in WP 7.

(338) Australia highlighted IP 75 *Diversity and inclusion in the Australian Antarctic program*, noting that it sought to ensure diversity and inclusion in its Antarctic programme.

(339) SCAR presented IP 124 *The SCAR Equality, Diversity and Inclusion Action Group*, which provided information on SCAR's Equality, Diversity and Inclusion (EDI) Action Group and on its recent activities, which included the development of a Code of Conduct on EDI issues, the review of existing external diversity and inclusion resources, and work with other organisations to share experience and best practices. SCAR noted that the Action Group, established in 2021, now had over 150 members and that activities had included: a webinar for the International Science Council Standing Committee on Gender Equality in Science (SCGES); a report on the results of a demographic survey of the SCAR community; and that the upcoming 2024 SCAR Open Science Conference would include a number of events dedicated to discussions on EDI.

(340) Chile presented IP 26 *Gender, diversity and inclusion policy of the Chilean Antarctic Institute*, which gave an overview of the actions implemented by the Chilean Antarctic Institute (INACH) regarding gender, diversity, and inclusion. It highlighted the growing number of women in its Antarctic science and operations and the establishment of a protocol for the reporting, investigation and sanctioning of mistreatment, workplace sexual harassment and sexist or discriminatory practices. It also highlighted that around 55% of employees at INACH were trained in gender issues. Chile also underlined that it had created a document with its gender, diversity, and inclusion policy to eliminate the obstacles impeding the advancement of women in Antarctica, which yielded positive results.

(341) Peru presented IP 136 *Avances en materia de género en las Expediciones Científicas del Perú a la Antártida (ANTAR)*. Peru reported that it had been promoting gender equality in its scientific expeditions to Antarctica, and there was increased participation of women in various roles, including general operations. It highlighted the ministerial resolution that would set rules of conduct in relation to equality, respect and integrity issues.

(342) Uruguay presented IP 183 *Protocolo de prevención y tratamiento de Acoso Laboral y Sexual del Programa Nacional Antártico Uruguayo, aplicable a las Bases, Estaciones y Expediciones en el Área del Tratado Antártico*. It informed the Meeting of a protocol it had developed to prevent sexual harassment in its national Antarctic programmes. Uruguay noted the difficulty of implementing relevant national legislation in its Antarctic stations and protecting victims of sexual offences and gender harassment in the workplace. Uruguay had focused on undertaking preventive actions and training programmes beyond deployment in their Antarctic programmes. It informed the Meeting of its concrete reporting mechanisms, including an independent commissioner, medical personnel, and legal experts to handle harassment issues. The matter had been sent to the Ministry to develop a course of action.

(343) The Meeting thanked the Parties, Observers and the Experts who presented the papers on this topic and expressed the need for continued discussion on EDI issues in Antarctic scientific research.

(344) The following paper was also submitted under this agenda item and taken as presented:

- IP 53 *Gender Equity Practices in Indian Antarctic Program* (India).

Item 16: Implications of Climate Change for Management of the Antarctic Treaty Area

(345) China introduced WP 16 *Promote the Share of Best Practices of the Use of Renewable Energy in Antarctica*, which outlined the advantages of reducing the use of fossil fuels in Antarctica and provided information on domestic experiences on Net Zero emissions facilities. China recalled that the ATCM had adopted Resolution 2 (2023) *Helsinki Declaration on Climate Change and the Antarctic*, which recognised the objectives and principles of the UNFCCC and the ongoing work to tackle climate change, and also noted the endorsement of the concept of the Green Expedition in Resolution 4 (2017). China highlighted that using renewable energy in Antarctica had potential benefits for mitigating the impact of climate change through emission reduction and reducing the environmental risk of incidents and accidents related to fuel transportation, spills and fires. China highlighted that with the progress of 'green' science and technology, increasing use of renewable energy systems to sustain the operation of Antarctic research stations to achieve net zero emission was becoming more feasible and affordable during the summer, but it further noted that providing renewable energy during wintertime was still challenging. China reported that its summer camp, Taishan, had achieved net zero operations during the 2018-19 Antarctic summer and that it had adopted both high energy efficient equipment to lower the use of energy and a renewable energy system, and further reported that it had followed the COMNAP guidance principles on best practice for the use of energy adopted by the CEP. Encouraged by those positive results, China informed the Meeting that it had established a team to study, develop and maintain renewable energy systems to make further contributions to address the impact of climate change on Antarctic operations.

(346) China recommended that the Meeting encourage Parties to:

- collaborate to develop a manual that outlined the practical best practices in the operation of the renewable energy systems used in Antarctic operations, taking into account COMNAP expertise and experience;
- increase the use of renewable energy in Antarctic operations, with a view to reduce the green gas emissions from human activities in Antarctica; and
- promote the innovation, application and sharing of new green energy facilities and technologies suitable for the unique Antarctic environment.

(347) The Meeting thanked China for sharing its valuable experience and acknowledged the successful implementation of the renewable energy system at Taishan. The Meeting noted

that it was a good example of the feasibility and implementation of reducing emissions and achieving a net zero goal in Antarctica. The Meeting highlighted the importance and timeliness of promoting green energy, technologies and facilities in Antarctica, as well as improved energy efficiency, and underlined the usefulness of information exchange and sharing best practices among Parties.

(348) Noting the key role of COMNAP in sharing best practice on national Antarctic programmes, several Parties suggested that COMNAP be requested to develop a best practices manual to continue reducing carbon footprint and investigate pathways to move towards net zero operations.

(349) The Russian Federation thanked China for a comprehensive approach based on scientific and practical aspects of activities. It stated that an exchange of views between a broader number of Parties on the topic would be beneficial and recommended the enhancing of the sustainable work of Antarctic stations taking into account specific needs and differences for seasonal and wintering stations.

(350) Norway referred to IP 115, which reported on its process towards modernising and renewing its Troll Research Station. This project aimed for a 50% reduction of emissions associated with station operations. Belgium mentioned the pioneering role of its Princess Elisabeth Antarctica research station, which was powered by wind and solar energy and resulted in increased autonomy and reduced environmental footprint. The United Kingdom noted that it had significant experience in this field and could offer help to adequately assess the consequences of novel technologies on local wildlife. Brazil noted its new polar vessel would be energy efficient, as part of its overall efforts to reduce emissions and advance towards energy efficiency. Australia recalled that it had inspected China's station in 2019 and had been very pleased with the findings in relation to its use of renewable energy.

(351) While supporting efforts to reduce carbon emissions, the Russian Federation reminded Parties that it constituted only one of several strategic goals for the Antarctic community and that the ATCM should aim to advance in all areas. The Russian Federation welcomed COMNAP's contribution but noted that further research was required to assess how specific energy sources impacted the environment and that evaluation of effectiveness of each alternative in different scenarios was needed and that innovation should be promoted.

(352) COMNAP noted that the CEP had encouraged it to collaborate with Parties through their national Antarctic programmes to explore best practices on safe, renewable energy use in the Antarctic. COMNAP reported that it would continue to support the work of national Antarctic programmes on this topic, primarily through the COMNAP Advancing Critical Technologies Expert Group. COMNAP also invited the Polar Research Institute of China to present its work on Taishan Station at the upcoming COMNAP annual general meeting. COMNAP confirmed that it stood ready to bring back advice from its meeting on how renewable energy information could be compiled and made available to the Parties.

(353) China welcomed COMNAP's suggestion to prepare a presentation for its annual general meeting and encouraged all Parties to continue sharing information and work together on this important issue.

(354) The Meeting supported the recommendations proposed by China in WP 16 and looked forward to receiving further advice from COMNAP on information on best-practice renewable energy. The Meeting highlighted the need to continue collectively making progress on advancing the goals set in Resolution 2 (2023) *Helsinki Declaration on Climate Change and the Antarctic*.

(355) SCAR introduced WP 49 *SCAR AntClimNow Antarctic Climate Indicators project*, prepared jointly with WMO. The SCAR AntClimNow group had been working together

with partners including the World Climate Research Programme (WCRP) Climate and Cryosphere (CliC) project to identify a range of Antarctic Climate Indicators with the aim of providing an accessible visualisation of broad aspects of the Antarctic climate system. A new webpage displayed key climate variables relevant to Antarctica and the Southern Ocean, filling a gap in the provision of this type of accessible information. SCAR and WMO encouraged the ATCM to: consider the relevance of Antarctic Climate Indicators to inform their discussions on climate change; provide feedback on specific indicators that could be considered for further development and inclusion as Antarctic Climate Indicators; and consider whether and how Antarctic Climate Indicators might be routinely presented to provide context for both CEP and ATCM discussions.

(356) The Meeting thanked SCAR and WMO for their efforts to keep Parties updated on the latest available information in the context of a rapidly changing climate. The Meeting noted the usefulness of having clear visual indicators to identify ongoing changes related to climate in Antarctica, noting it was an important contribution to the broader monitoring framework. Several Parties highlighted the need for scientific information to be presented in a clear and simplified way to make it accessible and understandable to non-scientists. Parties encouraged SCAR and WMO to consider working on the presentation of data to make it more accessible to non-scientists. Some Parties suggested including additional indicators related to ocean data, sea ice (including extent and thickness), indicators that demonstrated the interrelated link between climate and biodiversity, and teleconnections. Several Parties supported the inclusion of the indicators in the Antarctic Environments Portal, hosted by SCAR, highlighting the utility of the Portal for presenting peer-reviewed summaries of science for policymakers.

(357) Several additional points were raised, including: the possibility of SCAR and WMO engaging with Antarctica InSync to contribute to the further development of Antarctic climate indicators; the relevance of considering SCAR's ACCE update and the possibility of including the indicators as an annex to these updates; the fact that the indicators depended on the methods of the interpretation and on the specific area where they were obtained, as changes in Antarctica were variable and not homogenous; and the importance of taking into account the CEP's advice on this issue.

(358) The United Kingdom recalled that the International Tribunal for the Law of the Sea (ITLOS) had reminded Parties to the United Nations Convention on the Law of the Sea of their obligations to prevent, control and reduce marine pollution from anthropogenic greenhouse gas emissions and called on Antarctic Treaty Parties to reflect on whether they were both individually and collectively doing enough to address the effects of climate change in Antarctica. The United Kingdom proposed requesting SCAR to provide an update on climate change during the opening Plenary of the ATCM to ensure that the awareness of this issue underpinned considerations in discussions in both ATCM and CEP.

(359) The Meeting agreed to consider the matter further under agenda item 20.

(360) SCAR thanked Parties for their positive feedback and noted that it would duly consider comments about making information accessible and user-friendly. It also welcomed suggestions for additional indicators and their potential inclusion in the Antarctic Environments Portal. SCAR noted its readiness to engage with Antarctica InSync and looked forward to providing further updates.

(361) The Meeting supported the recommendations, encouraged SCAR and WMO to continue working on this issue and highlighted the need to contribute data and information in a simple and accessible manner. The Meeting also supported the recommendation to consider inclusion of Antarctic Climate Indicators in the Antarctic Environments Portal.

(362) COMNAP presented IP 184 *Understanding Future Sea-level Change Around Antarctica*, prepared jointly with SCAR and WMO. COMNAP updated key information presented at

ATCM XLV. It reiterated COMNAP, SCAR and WMO advice for consideration by the ATCM on the importance of closing knowledge gaps in support of the development of robust management and policy-making decisions in the future. It advised Parties to support their national Antarctic programmes to carry out certain research and operational activities to face sea-level rise consequences in Antarctica. The proponents specifically recommended that Parties should extend observational infrastructure; facilitate research to improve projections of Antarctic ice mass loss and its regional variability; monitor local sea-level and land elevation near identified coastal hazards; identify risk and adapt with urgency to impacts that were now unavoidable; and adopt a dynamic decision-making approach that could be updated and modified as new information evolved.

(363) ASOC presented IP 143 *Southern Ocean acidification*, which outlined the causes and negative effects of increasing rates of acidification of the Southern Ocean. ASOC stressed the severe impacts to the Southern Ocean from ocean acidification under intermediate or high emissions scenarios unless immediate action was taken to reduce global emissions to the very low emission scenarios in line with the 1.5°C goal. ASOC recommended that, in line with Resolution 8 (2021), Parties take action through the UNFCCC to immediately and rapidly reduce global CO_2 emissions and therefore the threat of ocean acidification in the Southern Ocean.

(364) WMO presented IP 116 *Understanding the rapid changes in the frozen parts of our planet and the related global impacts - A knowledge base compiled at a high-level event in Oslo, Norway*, prepared jointly with Norway. It provided key messages from an event attended by cryosphere experts, politicians and decision-makers to raise awareness about the ongoing changes in the cryosphere and their significant, long-term impacts. The WMO emphasised the importance of collaboration between the Parties, SCAR, and WMO in tackling the changes in Antarctica that affect global communities, particularly vulnerable areas and small islands.

(365) Norway expressed its gratitude to WMO for bringing this knowledge to the Parties through the Meeting and encouraged the Parties to draw on the expert information provided by WMO to identify actions, in response to climate change challenges in Antarctica. Norway highlighted the importance of management and protection, *ie*, adaptation to ongoing and projected future climate changes and changing sea ice conditions. Norway further stressed the importance of joint initiatives within ATCM to spread knowledge and awareness of consequences and risks, particularly with regard to global consequences.

(366) SCAR presented IP 166 *Antarctic Climate Change and the Environment update*, which provided information on recent climate change-related research and observations that were relevant to the discussions and priorities of the CEP and ATCM and complemented SCAR's regular ACCE reports. Key research and observational updates comprised, among others, that global ocean temperatures reached record highs in 2022 and 2023; Antarctic sea ice extent dropped below 2 million sq. km in 2024 for the third year in a row; and Antarctica was likely warming at almost twice the rate of the rest of the world, and that this warming could be attributed to human activities.

(367) SCAR presented IP 169 *Southern Ocean Observing System (SOOS) Symposium 2023*, which informed Parties of the inaugural SOOS Symposium and stressed the importance of the Southern Ocean in the operation of the Earth System. The Report of the SOOS Symposium recalled the critical changes in the Southern Ocean, from record low sea ice levels to catastrophic breeding failure of emperor penguins and highlighted the urgent need for sustained and coordinated observations of the Southern Ocean. SCAR reported that a community statement had been released after the SOOS Symposium, which gained international media attention and put the importance of Southern Ocean research into focus.

(368) Chile presented IP 25 *Advances in the climate change sensor network on the Antarctic Peninsula*, which reported on the progress of installing the Network of Multiparametric Stations in Antarctica. Chile explained that the network was an integrated environmental monitoring system that allowed studying environmental variations at different time scales. The network aimed to install stations at 21 points and thus provide data from Antarctica to the rest of the world with relevant and real-time information. As Antarctica had the greatest potential for research and recording environmental parameters to study global climate change, Chile highlighted the significance of the network and the possibility of future international collaborations in this area.

(369) India presented IP 54 *Antarctic Sea Ice Dynamics in a Changing Climate: Insights from Long-Term Observations*. The paper reported the observed changes in Antarctic sea ice and the processes driving these changes. India stressed that sea ice extent was receding significantly with regional and local differences. It emphasised the importance of continued research and collaborative efforts on a global scale to understand and address the complex dynamics of Antarctic sea ice. India noted that the current sea ice dynamics represented a crucial turning point in understanding Earth's polar regions and the effects of climate change. India emphasised the importance of continued research and collaborative efforts on a global scale to understand and address the complex dynamics of Antarctic sea ice and its future.

(370) The Meeting expressed its gratitude to Parties, Observers and Experts for the presentation of their papers.

(371) The following paper was also submitted under this agenda item:

- BP 6 *Fifteen years (2008/09 – 2022/23) of New Zealand carbon emission measurements and reduction initiatives* (New Zealand).

Item 17: Tourism and Non-Governmental Activities in the Antarctic Treaty Area, including Competent Authorities Issues

Policy and Management

(372) The United Kingdom introduced WP 15 *Nested Permitting*. It discussed the increasing trend in Antarctica, where scientific and non-government expeditions relied on tourist operators for logistical support, raising challenges for national competent authorities in assessing the total environmental impact of activities when making permitting decisions. The United Kingdom drew the Parties' attention to situations involving two or more separate permits being issued for a combined visit on a single vessel travelling to Antarctica. It recalled Article 8(4) of the Environment Protocol, which stated that where activities were planned jointly by more than one Party, the Parties involved should nominate one of their number to coordinate the implementation of the relevant environmental impact assessment procedures. It suggested that this requirement was not necessarily being met. The United Kingdom also highlighted that permits obtained from different national competent authorities could have different requirements, which could make managing expeditions involving nested permits more difficult. In addition, it noted that the EIES did not allow Parties to report accurately an activity that was occurring on a separately authorised expedition, which could result in inaccurate information in the EIES. The United Kingdom recommended that Parties:

- continue to discuss this issue in the Competent Authorities Discussion Forum as one of the five priority issues to determine how best to ensure the assessment of all activities in multi-member expeditions for environmental impacts in the context of Article 8(4) of the Environmental Protocol; and
- request that the Antarctic Treaty Secretariat change the EIES to allow Parties to identify better which other Parties are authorising activities taking place on their

authorised vessels or operations and enable those Parties to record the activities on the EIES as part of a single overall expedition.

(373) Spain introduced WP 33 *Scientific activities on board tourist vessels*, which reported a significant increase in the participation of its scientific community in activities aboard tourist ships during the austral summer of 2023/24. Spain noted that those activities had been sporadic and had practically gone unnoticed as they had occurred within scientific projects carried out aboard tourist ships authorised by other Parties. Spain recommended that Parties deepen their knowledge and management of scientific activities aboard tourist ships and enhance the exchange of detailed information about these activities, including through the EIES.

(374) The Meeting thanked the United Kingdom and Spain, and noted that the papers covered similar and related issues. Parties recalled previous proposals, information and discussions on related questions, and also noted that these issues were important in the context of the development of a tourism framework. The Meeting noted the importance of ensuring that EIA requirements were applied for all activities, and of understanding the combined impacts of separate activities occurring on one vessel or expedition. Parties identified a range of issues that arose in the administration and reporting of these types of activities, and outlined the approaches used by their national competent authorities, noting that these varied in accordance with national arrangements. There were differing views on approaches to considering and authorising nested activities jointly or separately. Some Parties noted the importance of ensuring that the relevant organiser retained legal control and responsibility for each activity, through the application of authorisation and permit requirements to the responsible person. The Meeting confirmed the importance of cooperation and communication among national competent authorities in considering these activities.

(375) Some Parties noted that there might be differing interpretations of Article 8(4) of the Environment Protocol in regard to these activities.

(376) In response to WP 15, the Meeting encouraged further discussion of these issues in the convened Competent Authorities Discussion Forum, acknowledging the informal nature of that forum, and noting that the ATCM was the appropriate place for any formal considerations.

(377) Many Parties expressed their support for the recommendations in WP 15.

(378) The Russian Federation noted its disagreement with the interpretation of a multimember expedition and Article 8(4) of the Protocol as presented in the paper and called on Parties to elaborate a common understanding of this provision as a priority. It also pointed out that issues of interpretation were beyond the mandate of the Competent Authorities Discussion Forum and were outside the scope of the EIES. The Russian Federation stressed that the use of a single vessel by different operators and for purposes of different activities did not constitute by itself a ground for a single authorisation and should not be considered as a reason to enable a Party to record the activities on the EIES.

(379) The Meeting supported the recommendation of WP 33 for the Parties to extend their knowledge and management of scientific activities onboard tourist vessels and exchange relevant information in a formal and detailed manner.

(380) The Meeting noted the ATCM's undertaking to work on a comprehensive review of information exchange requirements and the EIES, and agreed that these issues relating to information exchange requirements and the EIES could be taken up in the context of that work. Interested Parties agreed to discuss what specific changes to the EIES might be needed, and consider bringing forward any proposals for changes to the ATCM.

(381) The United States introduced WP 52 *Strengthening the usefulness of Site Guidelines for*

Visitors, prepared jointly with IAATO. The United States recalled that the ATCM had recently taken steps to enhance the site-specific guidelines for visitors to Antarctica, including revising its checklist for updating them in Resolution 4 (2021). However, most existing site guidelines had not yet been updated using the checklist. The co-proponents recommended that the Meeting encourage Parties to revise existing site guidelines for visitors using the checklist, and establish an ICG to discuss potential further improvements to the consistency, completeness, and usefulness of the information contained within the site guidelines.

(382) The Meeting thanked the United States and IAATO for WP 52. Parties noted the importance of the site guidelines, and welcomed the work of the CEP in this regard. The Meeting noted the importance of both updating existing guidelines in keeping with the flexible nature of the tool, and adopting new guidelines for additional sites, in both cases using the checklist adopted through Resolution 4 (2021). The Meeting also encouraged IAATO to advise the Parties and the ATCM regarding sites where updates would be warranted. The Meeting noted that the CEP had also addressed the matter and had advised the ATCM that informal intersessional discussions would take place within the CEP in order to further develop the proposals in WP 52.

(383) The Co-chair of Working Group 2, Dr Phil Tracey, as convener of the discussion forum, presented IP 74 *Competent authorities discussion forum on tourism regulatory activities: report by the convener*, submitted by Australia. The convenor noted that IP 74 summarised work conducted in the permanent web-based forum for competent authorities since 2019, noting that the forum was an informal group for discussion and cooperation among competent authority representatives, open to participation by all competent authorities, with no role in policy or decision making, which were functions of the ATCM. The forum had provided valuable opportunities for identifying and discussing key issues faced by national competent authorities, with wide and active participation. It was noted that the discussions had developed a statement of scope and purpose for the work, identified issues of interest, and agreed on priority issues for discussion and opportunities for enhanced cooperation. The convenor noted that IP 74 provided details on an informal online workshop to discuss one of the priority issues, on science activities associated with tourism activities, hosted by Germany in the intersessional period and participated in by many competent authority representatives. The paper included suggestions by the convenor for further work in the forum.

(384) The Meeting thanked the Co-chair for IP 74, and acknowledged the value of the discussions for their national competent authorities. Engagement in the forum, direct communication between national competent authorities, and further informal online workshops were encouraged.

(385) The Russian Federation noted that IP 74 had not met the requirements of the Rules of Procedure for translation in four official languages so that a document could be discussed at the Meeting. The Co-chair noted that Information Papers were not translated into the four official languages, and that this and other Information Papers did not contain substantive proposals that required decisions of the Meeting. The United Kingdom noted that the Meeting had a well-established practice of discussing Information Papers on important topics, including where the authors were not able to submit Working Papers.

(386) SCAR presented IP 172 rev. 1 *Antarctic tourism diversification: current state and issues previously discussed by the ATCM*, which outlined a peer-reviewed publication identifying seven dimensions of diversification in Antarctic tourism. The study also compiled information on over 75 issues previously discussed by the ATCM in relation to tourism diversification. SCAR highlighted that this information was relevant to tourism discussions, especially in light of Decision 6 (2023) and the development of a tourism framework. The paper provided up-to-date policy-relevant knowledge on tourism diversification that could inform decision-making by the ATCM.

(387) The Meeting thanked SCAR for its contribution and welcomed the information. Several Parties noted that the study had contributed to their understanding of the overall picture of current activities in Antarctica and that the findings would help them better monitor and evaluate Antarctic tourism. Concerns were expressed in relation to the process of diversification and several Parties noted that the analysis presented by SCAR was of importance for the work on a framework for the regulation of tourism and other non-governmental activities in Antarctica. IAATO noted there was an opportunity to further update Table 1 of IP 172 rev. 1 to reflect IAATO operational procedures for items such as wildlife watching, found in the IAATO Field Operations Manual, detailed in IP 106.

(388) ASOC presented IP 150 *Tourism and the growth of air-cruising in the Antarctic Peninsula*, which drew the Meeting's attention to increasing air-cruise operations centred on King George Island, and noted that this increased human pressure on surrounding land and marine areas. ASOC reported that research had shown how the rise in air-cruise operations was changing the uses and dynamics of King George Island, and the paper raised questions about the environmental implications of this growth. ASOC recommended that the desirability of the air cruise modality, and its associated environmental, logistical, safety, and regulatory implications be considered in the development of the tourism framework.

(389) Several Parties agreed with the recommendation to give focus to air cruise tourism activities. IUCN noted that it shared the concerns and recommendations expressed and encouraged further research. IAATO noted that air cruise activities by its members were appropriately authorised, following submission of EIAs, to relevant national competent authorities. IAATO noted that some data reported in the paper did not reflect its own understanding, and encouraged reference to the most recent air-cruise IAATO data and statistics in Appendix 1 of IP 102 rev. 1.

(390) IUCN presented IP 173 *Scientific research supporting the development of a comprehensive and consistent framework for Antarctic tourism management*, prepared jointly with SCAR. It showcased several relevant scientific publications identified by SCAR Tourism Action Group members. The compiled publications were organised by the five cross-cutting building blocks of growth, diversification, monitoring, compliance/enforcement, and overall governance. The proponents restated their commitment to offering expert advice and invited the ATCM to take note of the significant body of scholarly research to inform their actions and decisions.

(391) The Meeting thanked SCAR, IUCN and ASOC for their papers, noting their relevance to the Meeting's work on the regulation and management of Antarctic tourism and non-governmental activities.

Information, activities and trends

(392) Argentina presented IP 47 *Report on Antarctic tourist flows and cruise ships operating in Ushuaia during the 2023/2024 Austral summer season*, providing information on the movement of passengers and vessels that visited Antarctica during the 2023/24 season using the port of Ushuaia. Argentina reported relevant statistics including the number of trips, vessels, passengers, and nationalities. The information showed an increase in the number of vessels, voyages and passengers compared with the previous season. Argentina noted that the study offered an alternative and complementary source to evaluate tourism in the Antarctic region.

(393) IAATO thanked Argentina for the information and welcomed the cooperation with Argentina and other Parties with gateway cities.

(394) New Zealand presented IP 82 *On-board Observation of Tourist Vessels during the 2023 / 2024 Season*, jointly prepared with the United States and France. Observation of four

tourist voyages was carried out during the 2023/24 Antarctic season, under the framework adopted by Resolution 9 (2021). New Zealand noted that the observers had reported a high standard of compliance and commended the benefits of on-board observation. The proponents encouraged further use of observers to support a strategic approach to the management of Antarctic tourism and ensure it was conducted in a safe and environmentally responsible way. New Zealand noted its willingness to share its experiences with interested authorities, as New Zealand had been operating its observer programme since 1996.

(395) France thanked New Zealand for this cooperation which enabled the implementation of Resolution 9 (2021). France, in collaboration with IAATO, had also conducted on-board observations which would be presented in an Information Paper at the next ATCM. France stated that it stood ready to share its experience further with other authorities and encouraged the implementation of Resolution 9 (2021). IAATO thanked the proponents of the paper and detailed its own experiences with its observer programme.

(396) The United Kingdom presented IP 84 rev. 1 *Data Collection and Reporting on Yachting Activity in Antarctica in 2023-24*, jointly prepared with Argentina, Chile, Spain, the United States and IAATO. It consolidated information from the proponents relating to yachts sighted in Antarctica or indicating an intention to travel to Antarctica during the 2023/24 season. The Meeting noted the small but persistent occurrence of unauthorised yacht visits reported through this and previous papers, and encouraged attention to this issue.

(397) IAATO presented IP102 rev. 1 *IAATO Vessel Overview of Antarctic Tourism: The 2023-24 Season, and Preliminary Estimates for 2024-25*, which presented statistics compiled from ATCM post-visit reports for the 2023/24 season for those travelling with IAATO operator companies. The overall number of visitors in 2023/24 was 122,027. Estimates for 2024/-25 indicated that passenger numbers would stay steady, with approximately 78,910 making landings, and 28,360 passengers travelling on cruise-only vessels.

(398) The Meeting thanked IAATO for IP 102 rev. 1 and supported the efforts of IAATO to provide verified data on current and estimated numbers of visitors and the activities of member operators. Parties noted the value of the information provided by IAATO, including for the ATCM's work to develop a tourism framework. Some Parties expressed interest in longer-term estimates from IAATO member operators to support the work of the Parties.

(399) IAATO presented IP 107 *A Catalogue of IAATO Operator Activities*. IAATO provided information on the range of activities conducted by its member operators and reiterated that all activities undertaken were duly permitted or authorised by national competent authorities. The paper included a catalogue of the activities conducted by its operators, reflecting the IAATO database for deep field and marine activities, with a brief explanation of each activity. IAATO had expanded its reporting categories to provide clearer information and noted that changes and updates were reported annually to the ATCM to help Parties update their own database.

(400) IAATO presented IP 108 *IAATO Site Management Methods*, which described IAATO's work on operator guidance for activities and for management of sites, as well as the ongoing development of tools and support documents. IAATO described 18 new IAATO site guidelines, both terrestrial and marine, and noted that it would welcome the opportunity to work with Parties should there be interest in adopting them as ATCM visitor site guidelines. IAATO provided information on its ship scheduler used to coordinate ship visits to landing sites and its new live ship scheduler, used to re-schedule landings in real time. It also provided information on its Site Stewardship Program, which drew on the field personnel community's experience and local expert knowledge to collect site information. IAATO underlined that it remained committed to reporting information on site guidelines and IAATO operator activities to the CEP and ATCM.

(401) The United Kingdom thanked IAATO for its presentations, and noted that priority should be given to updating and developing new site guidelines by the ATCM to sites used by multiple actors, not only IAATO operators.

(402) IAATO presented IP 109 *IAATO Observer & Compliance Program*. IAATO provided information specifically around its Compliance & Dispute Resolution mechanism. This programme, in place since 2013, received reports through IAATO's website, operators and observer programme. Items were reviewed and determined to be either a level one issue - minor or unintentional – or level two - serious, repeated, or intentional. Level two issues may result in reprimand, probation or expulsion. IAATO communicated sanctions to the appropriate national competent authority. IAATO thanked Treaty Parties for holding open discussions with its operators when questions had arisen in relation to the IAATO observer and compliance programmes.

(403) Spain thanked IAATO for its presentation and its commitment to ensuring transparency when assessing if its operators were complying with the provisions of the Antarctic Treaty and the Environment Protocol.

(404) The following papers were also submitted under this agenda item and taken as read:

- IP 80 *Tourism monitoring in Antarctica – status and preliminary findings on developing a concept for the analysis of the impacts of tourism on the assets to be protected in the Antarctic* (Germany).
- IP 103 *IAATO Deep Field and Air Overview of Antarctic Tourism: 2023-24 Season and Preliminary Estimates for 2024-25 Season* (IAATO).
- IP 104 *A Five-Year Overview and 2023-24 Season Report on IAATO Operator Use of Antarctic Peninsula Landing Sites and ATCM Visitor Site Guidelines* (IAATO).
- IP 106 *IAATO Field Operations Manual (FOM)* (IAATO).

Item 18: Development of a Tourism Framework

(405) The Chair of Working Group 3, Prof. Dr René Lefeber (the Netherlands), recalled that the mandate for the discussions to develop a framework for Antarctic tourism and other non-governmental activities was agreed to in Decision 6 (2023) *Dedicated process for the development of a comprehensive and consistent framework for Antarctic tourism and other non-governmental activities*.

(406) The United Kingdom introduced WP 3 *Comprehensive and Consistent Framework for the Regulation of Tourism and Other Non-Governmental Activities in the Antarctic Treaty Area - Suggestions for a Framework Structure*, and WP 4 *Comprehensive and Consistent Framework for the Regulation of Tourism and Other Non-Governmental Activities in the Antarctic Treaty area - Suggestions for Additional Elements to be Included in a Tourism Framework*, prepared jointly with Finland, France, Germany, India, and the Netherlands. The United Kingdom presented an example of what such a tourism framework could look like (WP 3). The United Kingdom also outlined a range of policy options and suggestions on additional elements that might be inserted into the framework structure document (WP 4). Noting the broad and overarching scope of the task, the proponents offered their contributions as a starting point for an open discussion. The United Kingdom suggested that throughout its work, the Meeting might first seek to identify the essential substantive questions that would need to be addressed to achieve a holistic framework and, second, agree on an appropriate procedure for discussions and actions required to address and resolve those relevant matters. Taking stock of topics discussed at recent workshops and ATCMs, the proponents suggested that Parties had a broad selection of the necessary ingredients already at hand and that their priority should be to select which elements Parties needed to develop a framework they could all accept.

(407) Australia introduced WP 24 *Matters for consideration in the development of a*

comprehensive and consistent framework for Antarctic tourism and non-governmental activities, which proposed a number of matters warranting consideration by the Parties in the development of the tourism framework. Given the observed and likely future growth in Antarctic tourism, Australia stressed the timeliness of the process and its strong support for the development of the framework. Australia drew attention to the importance of attention to site management, and consideration of different modes of operation within the tourism industry, different circumstances in different regions of Antarctica, and differences between commercial tourism and private non-governmental activities. Australia also noted that the framework would need to consider provisions to manage and constrain growth which might involve constraints overall, spatially, temporally, regionally or by category of activity. Australia supported further work in the context of an ATCM Working Group, and noted that intersessional work was also likely to be necessary.

(408) The United States introduced WP 58 *Proposal for Beginning the Development of a Framework for the Regulation of Tourism and Other Non-Governmental Activities in Antarctica*, which proposed a Resolution through which the Parties could articulate the concepts and considerations that should be addressed in any effective tourism framework. The United States suggested that such a Resolution would offer a blueprint for developing the framework, providing direction on information gathered and issues addressed. It suggested that, after adopting a Resolution, the Consultative Parties could begin to consider the form an effective tourism framework should take. The United States welcomed all discussions regarding the Resolution. It proposed that the Meeting take a methodical approach, by first identifying the key problems to be solved and then seeking to develop an approach that would best enable it to address them.

(409) Argentina introduced WP 60 *Considerations on the Work of ATCM WG3*, which raised a series of questions, considerations and proposals for the special ATCM Working Group to develop a tourism framework. These questions included the Working Group's terms of reference, which topics it would discuss and take action on, and its mechanisms and schedules. Topics highlighted by Argentina included the duty of care and protection of the Antarctic environment, the safety of human life and operations, and addressing the continuing precedence of scientific activities over tourism and other non-governmental activities in Antarctica. It also stressed the need to manage tourism's environmental impact in Antarctica and address the cumulative impacts of activities in Antarctica. It suggested that the Meeting might wish to consider recognising zones of special scientific interest to manage the adverse impact of tourism on scientific priorities. Argentina also observed that the Meeting would have to eventually reach an agreement on the type of regulatory tools it wished to adopt in its framework and to come to an understanding about the appropriate mechanisms and schedule for the focused continuation of its work in upcoming ATCMs.

(410) The Russian Federation introduced WP 63 *Key elements in a comprehensive uniform system for Antarctic tourism*. The Russian Federation observed that tourist activities did not contradict the principles and purposes of the Antarctic Treaty while scientific activities were prioritised, and remained permissible within the meaning of the Environmental Protocol. It noted that there was a need for a holistic and strategic approach for the effective management of tourism in the long term. Recalling the importance of Decision 6 (2023), the Russian Federation suggested that a unified process could facilitate the step-by-step development of both mandatory and advisory standards. The Russian Federation recommended: 1) the leadership role of the ATCM in the control and management of Antarctic tourism; 2) the importance of data collection and reporting; 3) ensuring effective protection of the Antarctic environment and non-interference in the activities of national Antarctic programmes; 4) the precautionary approach for the regulation of both extreme and adventure tourism or other extensive land-based activities; and 5) ensuring liability of tour operators for non-compliance with the requirements of the Antarctic Treaty system and the exchange of information on the national legislation of the Parties on issues of

liability of tour operators and tourists. It also recommended the harmonisation of approaches between the Parties.

(411) New Zealand presented IP 77 *Tourism and other Non-Governmental Activities in the Antarctic Treaty Area: Information to support the development of the framework.* New Zealand expressed its support for a binding and ambitious framework, consistent with Antarctica's status as a natural reserve, and consistent with the high level of ambition that is a hallmark of the Antarctic Treaty system. The paper provided principles to support the development of the framework, including that: the Parties should draw on, give effect to, and go further than existing obligations, principles and guidelines including, *inter alia*;

- limiting adverse impacts on the environment, and prior assessment of cumulative impacts and impacts on values (Environment Protocol);
- avoiding or mitigating non-climatic stresses to the Antarctic terrestrial and marine environment: Resolution 8 (2021);
- preventing permanent facilities for tourism and NGO activities in Antarctica: Resolution 5 (2022);
- Voluntary on-board observer operational framework for vessel-based tourism in the Antarctic Treaty Area: Resolution 9 (2021);
- agreed recommendations of the CEP Tourism Study (ATCM XXXV-WP 22 and ATCM XXXV-IP 33), including to develop a centrally managed database of tourism activities, to develop an appropriate method of assessing site sensitivity, and to consider the vulnerability of sites to non-native species establishment; and
- managing human activities in the context of Antarctica's biogeographic regions (Resolution 3 (2017)).

(412) IAATO presented IP 111 *IAATO Considerations During the Development of a Tourism Framework.* IAATO welcomed the work of the ATCM pursuant to Decision 6 (2023) and noted its special capacities and constraints arising from its role as a trade association. To contribute to the work of the ATCM, IAATO highlighted challenges and potential actions from Parties including: aligning their domestic permitting and authorisation processes to avoid permit shopping and confusion amongst operators; ratifying new tourism-related instruments at the earliest opportunity and avoiding long implementation periods; and how the Parties could support their competent authorities in pursuing non-compliant operators and increasing compliance through accountability. IAATO recalled its long experience in the practical management of Antarctic tourism and suggested opportunities to build upon, which included: expanding participation of Parties in its voluntary on-board observer programme (Resolution 9 (2021)); building upon existing collaboration to further enhance the current framework provided by IAATO; and identifying opportunities to leverage the expert knowledge of IAATO field personnel to assist in understanding the needs and changes related to specific areas in Antarctica. IAATO also drew the Meeting's attention to the information provided in its previously presented Information Papers.

(413) ASOC presented IP 149 *ASOC perspectives on the development of a comprehensive and consistent framework for Antarctic tourism and non-governmental activities*, expressing some initial responses on selected aspects of the relevant Working Papers submitted by Parties to ATCM 46. ASOC indicated that these responses were not intended to be exhaustive and did not highlight every issue of importance. ASOC encouraged the development of a framework based on the precautionary approach that: prioritised environmental protection; created a system that was effective at multiple spatial scales and for multiple modes of tourism; and that instituted a robust monitoring programme for tourism and its environmental impacts.

(414) ASOC presented IP 152 *Developing a systematic approach to addressing the footprint of*

tourism, which highlighted that the growing footprint of tourism in the Antarctic Peninsula was much larger than the area protected in ASPAs. To manage this growing footprint, ASOC recommended that the ATCM undertake among others a systematic conservation planning process and implement a target of 30% protection of terrestrial, coastal, and marine areas by 2030.

(415) IUCN presented IP 173 *Scientific research supporting the development of a comprehensive and consistent framework for Antarctic tourism management*, prepared jointly with SCAR, which provided a summary of relevant scientific publications on Antarctic tourism suggested by SCAR Tourism Action Group members, some of whom were also members of the IUCN World Commission on Protected Areas. The IUCN emphasised that tourism in the Antarctic should only be supported if it did not generate more than a minor or transitory impact on the environment. The IUCN encouraged Parties to discuss the information, bearing in mind the protection of Antarctica.

(416) The Meeting welcomed the papers submitted under this agenda item and acknowledged their usefulness for preparing and feeding discussions on the development of a framework for Antarctic tourism and other non-governmental activities. The Meeting noted significant alignments and commonalities between the issues addressed in the papers. The Meeting reaffirmed its strong support for the development of a comprehensive and consistent framework for the regulation of tourism and other non-governmental activities in Antarctica. The Meeting also took note of the growth and diversification of tourist activities.

(417) Concerning the nature of the framework, the Meeting considered that the form should follow function and that function should not be limited only to environmental aspects. The Meeting also noted that the framework could include other issues related to tourism and other non-governmental activities. The Meeting acknowledged the leading role of the ATCM in creating the framework and underscored the importance of avoiding duplication of work with the CEP. The Meeting noted that the framework should be enduring, ambitious, comprehensive, flexible, dynamic, and without prejudice as to whether it was legally binding in nature.

(418) When considering the development of the framework, several Parties pointed to the need to focus on the following key priority issues: tourism and its impact on the environment; the relationship between tourism and science; and tourism and human safety. Several Parties expressed their high level of ambition for the development of the framework and the importance of advancing a shared vision for Antarctic tourism.

(419) Several Parties suggested that when considering the development of the framework, the first aspect to consider was the protection of the Antarctic environment, and the impacts and consequences tourism had on that environment. Several Parties noted the priority of ensuring that tourism in Antarctica had no more than a minor or transitory impact and preserving its environment for future generations. Several Parties underlined the need to develop the framework following the precautionary approach to ensure tourism was conducted in a sustainable, safe and sound manner. Several Parties noted the importance of understanding and addressing the cumulative impacts of tourist and all other activities on the Antarctic environment.

(420) Some Parties noted that the tourism and non-governmental activities discussion at hand was a systemic issue, concerning the core of the Antarctic Treaty. Some of these Parties noted that with numerous non-national players it is essential that the Antarctic Treaty system is robust and able to capture such ongoing changes while enshrining the mechanisms that were put in place to operationalise the objectives of Article 2 when the Treaty was signed. Recognising that a large part of the tourism and non-governmental discussions relate to the Protocol, these Parties noted that the questions at hand go beyond the scope of the Protocol and that the framework discussions rightly belong in the realm of the ATCM.

(421) When considering the scope of the framework, several Parties highlighted that the framework should regulate all activities related to Antarctic tourism, including permitting procedures, reporting, monitoring, and potential new activities. Some Parties suggested mechanisms to manage the potential for disputes between operators and national Antarctic programmes. Several Parties suggested: the need to consider human safety aspects; a conservative approach to allowing for tourism while limiting its growth; a specific tool for addressing adventure tourism and extreme tourism; the need to properly define scientific activities and ensure an effective permitting procedure with clear criteria and information to avoid nested permits and independent activities; and introducing a fee mechanism.

(422) Several Parties noted the significant regulations already in place under the Antarctic Treaty system that applied to tourism, and that there would be value in identifying which elements were adequately addressed and which additional aspects required consideration.

(423) Many Parties acknowledged IAATO's commitment to safe and environmentally responsible tourism, and its efforts to respond to the growth of the industry, as well as the potential educational value of tourism.

(424) Reflecting the discussion held during the meeting, the Meeting agreed to adopt Decision 5 (2024) *Development of a Framework for the Regulation of Tourism and Other Non-Governmental Activities in Antarctica.*

(425) To proceed with the work on the framework, the Meeting expressed the wish of convening six sessions of the Special Working Group at ATCM 47, insofar as was practicable regarding the duration and structure of the meeting, and insofar as was practicable with no more than two sessions concurring with other ATCM Working Groups or the CEP.

(426) The Meeting also agreed to establish an ICG on the Development of a Comprehensive and Consistent Framework for Tourism and Other Non-governmental Activities for the intersessional period 2024/25 with the aim of progressing discussions foreseen by the Decision.

(427) It was further agreed that:

- Observers and Experts participating in the ATCM would be invited to provide input;
- The Executive Secretary would open the ATCM Forum for the ICG and provide assistance to the ICG; and
- Prof. Dr René Lefeber (the Netherlands) would act as convenor and report to the next ATCM on the progress made in the ICG.

(428) The Netherlands offered to finance and organise a workshop immediately prior to and in conjunction with ATCM 47 at or in the proximity of the venue of ATCM 47. The Meeting welcomed the offer and considered that it could assist in progressing discussions, but noted that the organisation of such a workshop should be coordinated with the organisation of any other workshop.

(429) The Meeting agreed to reflect in the Multi-year Strategic Work Plan the specific components of the sessional work and the intersessional work through to ATCM 47.

(430) The following papers were also submitted under this agenda item and taken as presented:

a. IP 106 *IAATO Field Operations Manual (FOM)* (IAATO).
b. IP 107 *A Catalogue of IAATO Operator Activities* (IAATO).
c. IP 109 *IAATO Observer and Compliance Programs* (IAATO).
d. IP 172 rev. 1 *Antarctic tourism diversification: current state and issues previously discussed by the ATCM* (SCAR).

Item 19: Preparation of the 47th Meeting

a. Date and place

(431) The Meeting welcomed the kind invitation of the Government of Italy to host ATCM 47 and CEP 27 in Milan, not before May 2025.

(432) For future planning, the Meeting took note of the following likely timetable of upcoming ATCMs:

- 2026 Japan
- 2027 Republic of Korea

(433) The following paper was submitted under this agenda item:

- IP 90 *Preparation of the 47th Meeting – 2025* (Italy).

b. Invitation of International and Non-governmental Organisations

(434) In accordance with established practice, the Meeting agreed that the following organisations having scientific or technical interest in Antarctica should be invited to send experts to attend ATCM 47: the ACAP Secretariat, ASOC, IPCC, IAATO, the International Civil Aviation Organization (ICAO), IHO, IMO, IOC, IOPC Funds, IUCN, UNEP, UNFCCC, WMO and the World Tourism Organization (WTO).

c. Preparation of the Agenda for ATCM 47

(435) The Meeting approved the Preliminary Agenda for ATCM 47 (see Appendix 1).

d. Organisation of ATCM 47

(436) In accordance with Rule 11 of the Rules of Procedure, the Meeting decided to propose the same Working Groups for ATCM 47 as observed in this meeting. According to the Rules of Procedure, Chairs for these groups should be appointed before the close of the meeting and, in the absence of any nomination, Chairs would be appointed at the start of the next ATCM. There were no nominations for Chairs of WG 1 and WG 2 during the meeting. Parties are expected to nominate Chairs for these groups in the intersessional period. The Meeting agreed to appoint Prof. Dr René Lefeber from the Netherlands as Chair of WG 3 in 2025.

(437) The Meeting expressed its thanks to outgoing Working Group Chairs, Mr Theodore Kill from the United States, Ms Sonia Ramos Garcia from Spain and Dr Phillip Tracey from Australia for their valued contributions over the last four years.

(438) The Meeting also agreed to invite SCAR to include a presentation to update the opening Plenary on the state of climate change effects in Antarctica as part of its annual report submitted under agenda item 4.

e. The SCAR Lecture

(439) Taking into account the valuable series of lectures given by SCAR at a number of ATCMs, the Meeting decided to invite SCAR to give another lecture on scientific issues relevant to ATCM 47.

Item 20: Any Other Business

(440) Canada thanked the Chair and the Host Country for the successful meeting and thanked the Consultative Parties for the strong support it had received for its request for Consultative Party status. Canada noted the importance of being provided with clear indications of any further improvements needed regarding its application and

hopes that it can clear up remaining questions and misunderstanding of Canada's Antarctic activities and legislation in the intersessional period. It reiterated its strong support and continued engagement in the Antarctic Treaty system.

Item 21: Adoption of the Final Report

(441) The Meeting adopted the Final Report of the 46th Antarctic Treaty Consultative Meeting. The Chair of the Meeting, Ambassador Pankaj Saran, made closing remarks.

Item 22: Close of the Meeting

(442) The Meeting was closed on Thursday, 30 May at 18:55.

2. CEP 26 Report

Report of the Twenty-sixth Meeting of the Committee for Environmental Protection (CEP 26)

Kochi, India, 20 – 24 May 2024

(1) Pursuant to Article 11 of the Protocol on Environmental Protection to the Antarctic Treaty, Representatives from 38 of the 42 Parties to the Protocol (Argentina, Australia, Belarus, Belgium, Brazil, Bulgaria, Canada, Chile, China, Colombia, Czechia, Ecuador, Finland, France, Germany, India, Italy, Japan, Malaysia, the Netherlands, New Zealand, Norway, Peru, Poland, Portugal, Republic of Korea, Romania, the Russian Federation, South Africa, Spain, Sweden, Switzerland, Türkiye, Ukraine, the United Kingdom, the United States, Uruguay, and Venezuela) met in Kochi, India, from 20 to 24 May 2024, for the purpose of providing advice and formulating recommendations to the Parties in connection with the implementation of the Protocol.

(2) In accordance with Rule 4 of the CEP Rules of Procedure, the meeting was also attended by representatives of the following Observers:

- the Scientific Committee on Antarctic Research (SCAR), the Scientific Committee for the Conservation of Antarctic Marine Living Resources (SC-CAMLR), and the Council of Managers of National Antarctic Programs (COMNAP); and
- scientific, environmental and technical organisations: the Antarctic and Southern Ocean Coalition (ASOC), the International Association of Antarctica Tour Operators (IAATO), the International Union for the Conservation of Nature (IUCN), and the World Meteorological Organization (WMO).

Item 1: Opening of the Meeting

(3) CEP first Vice-chair, Dr Anoop Kumar Tiwari (India), opened the meeting on Monday 20 May 2024 and thanked India for arranging and hosting the meeting.

(4) The first Vice-chair recalled CEP Circular 1/2024 and ATS Circular 4/2024 that informed Members about the resignation of CEP Chair Patricia Ortúzar (Argentina). The first Vice-chair explained that, in accordance with Rule 17 of the CEP Rules of Procedure, the Committee would be chaired by the first and second Vice-chairs. The first Vice-chair welcomed the support of the second Vice-chair, Dr Heike Herata (Germany) for this arrangement, and also highlighted that the Committee would need to elect a new CEP Chair to commence in the role at the conclusion of the meeting.

(5) The Committee thanked the Vice-chairs for their preparations, and for chairing the meeting in unexpected circumstances.

Item 2: Adoption of the Agenda

(6) The Committee adopted the following agenda and confirmed the allocation of 43 Working Papers (WP), 85 Information Papers (IP), 5 Secretariat Papers (SP) and 10 Background Papers (BP) to the agenda items:

1. Opening of the Meeting
2. Adoption of the Agenda
3. Strategic Discussions on the Future Work of the CEP
4. Operation of the CEP
5. Cooperation with other Organisations
6. Repair and Remediation of Environment Damage
7. Climate Change Implications for the Environment
    a. Strategic Approach

    b. Implementation and Review of the Climate Change Response Work Programme
8. Environmental Impact Assessment (EIA)
    a. Draft Comprehensive Environmental Evaluations
    b. Other EIA Matters
9. Area Protection and Management Plans
    a. Management Plans
    b. Historic Sites and Monuments
    c. Site Guidelines
    d. Marine Spatial Protection and Management
    e. Other Annex V Matters
10. Conservation of Antarctic Flora and Fauna
    a. Quarantine and Non-native Species
    b. Specially Protected Species
    c. Other Annex II Matters
11. Environmental Monitoring and Reporting
12. Inspection Reports
13. General Matters
14. Election of Officers
15. Preparation for the Next Meeting
16. Adoption of the Report
17. Closing of the Meeting

Item 3: Strategic Discussions on the Future Work of the CEP

CEP Five-year Work Plan

(7) Norway introduced WP 37 *Outcomes and Proposals from the ICG on CEP strategic priorities and the 5-year work plan.* Norway reported on the outcomes of the Intersessional Contact Group (ICG) established at CEP XXV to develop a draft revised Five-year Work Plan for consideration at CEP 26, prepare advice on practical measures that the CEP might consider in initiating, pursuing, and monitoring progress on Work Plan actions, and then report to CEP 26. Norway presented a revised Five-year Work Plan for consideration, stating that the plan was built around a set of suggested priority topics. Norway noted that for each priority, the plan included a description of context, interlinkages, objectives, priority actions, and regular actions. Norway highlighted that the engagement in the ICG had been broad, with a significant number of Members and Observers participating. Norway recommended that the CEP:

- consider, adjust as appropriate, and adopt the revised Five-year Work Plan and use it to frame its future work;
- request that the Secretariat ensure the Five-year Work Plan was available on the CEP webpage in its most updated form at all times;
- consider the use of icons in the Five-year Work Plan and agree to a process of incorporating them as appropriate;
- consider and agree to a format for a summary matrix attached as a front cover to the Five-year Work Plan; and
- agree to a list of modalities for actioning priority actions and request that the Secretariat make this list available as a "Toolbox" on the CEP webpage.

(8) The Committee commended Norway for convening and leading the intersessional work. The Committee expressed broad support for the ICG process and the outcomes and noted that discussions in the ICG had been very positive and productive. Members noted that the revised Five-year Work Plan was clear and well-structured and could be a valuable tool for framing the work of the CEP in the future, enhancing the understanding of Members and communicating its advancements to the broader public.

(9) In responding to a question on how frequently the Five-year Plan should be updated, many Members underlined that the Five-year Work Plan was a flexible and living document. Members noted that the Five-year Work Plan should be updated frequently as new issues emerge in light of the rapidly changing environment.

(10) In the discussion it was noted that the Five-year Work Plan is a non-binding document guiding Members in their work. The importance of keeping an eye on whether all priorities were followed up by actions was emphasised. Members were encouraged to take leadership to facilitate work on issues across the Five-year Work Plan where they have the expertise and capacity, to promote wider engagement.

(11) Members supported incorporating icons into the plan, as well as attaching a summary matrix tracking progress, and making a toolbox of modalities available on the CEP webpage. Members also highlighted the importance of participation to activate the tools in the toolbox and stressed the need to engage new Members. Some Members noted only icons that added clarity should be used and proposed further work on icons before adding them to the Five-year Work Plan.

(12) The Committee agreed to adopt the Five-year Work Plan as attached and to use this for framing its work in the years to come. It further agreed that:

- the Five-year Work Plan would continue to be reviewed and updated to reflect the agreed outcomes of discussions at the CEP and be reviewed strategically on a regular basis; and
- the Secretariat should ensure that the Five-year Work Plan was available on the CEP webpage in its most updated form at all times.

(13) The Committee agreed to continue informal work on developing icons and to ask the Secretariat to assist with the design of icons based on those provided in the attachment to SP 13, with the aim to provide a proposal at CEP 27.

(14) The Committee agreed to the format of the summary matrix to be attached as a front cover to the Five-year Work Plan. The Secretariat was tasked to update the summary matrix so that it reflects the content of the agreed Five-year Work Plan.

(15) The Committee agreed that the list of modalities for actioning priority actions provided a useful toolbox for the CEP and its Members to refer to when initiating and moving actions forward and requested the Secretariat to make this list available on the CEP webpage.

Item 4: Operation of the CEP

(16) The Chair presented IP 145 *Committee for Environmental Protection (CEP): summary of activities during the 2023/24 intersessional period.* The Chair highlighted the work undertaken during this period and noted that many actions arising from CEP XXV, with outcomes anticipated for CEP 26, had been addressed.

Item 5: Cooperation with other Organisations

(17) SC-CAMLR presented IP 33 *Report by the SC-CAMLR Observer to CEP*, which reported on activities conducted during the 2023/24 period that related to the six identified issues of continued common interest, including outcomes from the 42nd SC-

CAMLR meeting held in October 2023 and an extraordinary meeting of the Commission on managing marine protected areas held in Santiago, Chile in June 2023. SC-CAMLR reported the Scientific Committee had discussed, and the Commission had endorsed, the proposal to merge the management plans for Antarctic Specially Protected Areas (ASPA) 152 and 153. SC-CAMLR highlighted an upcoming Harmonisation Symposium in the Republic of Korea from 16-20 July 2024, to discuss how spatial management in the Antarctic Peninsula could accommodate further development of the krill fishery, ecosystem monitoring, climate change monitoring, and spatial protection. SC-CAMLR also explained how its Marine Debris Monitoring Program used three sources of data: reports from national Antarctic programmes and IAATO; reports from observers on-board fishing vessels in the Convention area; and lost fishing gear reported from long-line vessels in the Convention area. SC-CAMLR noted it would welcome efforts to coordinate, verify, standardise, and integrate data collected across programmes to ensure a comprehensive view of marine debris in the Antarctic area.

(18) COMNAP presented IP 16 *Annual Report 2023/2024 for the Council of Managers of National Antarctic Programs (COMNAP).* COMNAP reported on discussions at its 35th Annual General Meeting in June 2023, including the heightened risk of Highly Pathogenic Avian Influenza (HPAI) in Antarctica; the environmental protection aspects of station activity including modernisation projects, the management implications of a changing Antarctica including risk to built infrastructure; and increasing efficiency, decarbonising and offsetting carbon emissions from Antarctic activities. COMNAP highlighted that the COMNAP Antarctic Forest concept to support national Antarctic programmes to offset their emission had received general support from the COMNAP Membership. Regarding HPAI, COMNAP noted that national Antarctic programmes would continue their leadership in observation, collection of samples, testing, reporting, information exchange and enhanced biosecurity measures. COMNAP also highlighted the 20th COMNAP Symposium Proceedings (BP 3) and its continued support to early-career persons through the COMNAP Antarctic Awards.

(19) SCAR presented IP 10 *The Scientific Committee on Antarctic Research Annual Report 2024 to the 46th Antarctic Treaty Consultative Meeting.* SCAR reported on recent activities relevant to the work of the CEP, including its three flagship scientific research programmes on near-term climate prediction (AntClimNOW), conservation (Ant-ICON), and quantification of Antarctica's contribution to global sea level rise (INSTANT - INStabilities & Thresholds in ANTarctica). SCAR highlighted the Antarctic Wildlife Health Network, which helped stakeholders prepare for the likely arrival of HPAI in Antarctica, and the new Antarctic Monitoring and Assessment Programme (AnMAP). SCAR also stated that it continued to engage with the work of bodies in the United Nations (UN), including the United Nations Framework Convention on Climate Change (UNFCCC), and that it had received accreditation from the UN Environment Programme (UNEP), which it would use to connect with international organisations working across the field of environmental matters. Other highlights included initial planning for the Fifth International Polar Year (IPY) and the next SCAR Open Science Conference, which would be held in Pucón, Chile in August 2024.

(20) IAATO presented IP 101 *Report of the International Association of Antarctica Tour Operators 2023-24.* IAATO noted issues of particular interest to the work of the CEP. IAATO highlighted its collaboration with SCAR and COMNAP to address the anticipated arrival of HPAI in the Antarctic area, including the revision of its guidelines, protocols and action taken throughout the season and supporting a scientific expedition. IAATO drew attention to the work it had done around its 5-year strategic plan, Embracing Our Role as Stewards of Antarctica, and noted that 17 new IAATO Visitor Site Guidelines had been approved at its 24th Annual General Meeting, which included marine locations for the first time. IAATO reaffirmed its continued support of scientific

work in Antarctica, including the Antarctic Site Inventory – Oceanites and Penguin Watch, and reported that many of its operators continued to provide logistical support to national Antarctic programmes. IAATO also expressed its appreciation for the opportunity to continue to participate in Antarctic discussions, including the COMNAP Annual General Meeting and the Workshop on Tourism Monitoring hosted by Germany online in October 2023.

(21) ASOC presented IP 142 *ASOC report to the ATCM* . ASOC reported on its activities relevant to the conservation of Antarctica and to the CEP over the past year. These activities included participation in meetings of other organisations, such as the International Maritime Organization (IMO) and UNFCCC; support for science on important topics such as the status of the emperor penguin and cetacean populations; participation as a stakeholder in research programmes; and contributions to the intersessional work of the CEP.

(22) WMO presented IP 9 rev. 1 *Annual Report of the World Meteorological Organization (WMO)*, which outlined its recent activities in Antarctic observations, infrastructure, and science, the latter conducted through its co-sponsored World Climate Research Programme (WCRP) and the World Weather Research Programme. WMO highlighted its coordination of the WCRP's Climate and Cryosphere Core Project, the Antarctic Coordinated Regional Downscaling Experiment project, and the World Weather Research Programme's Polar Coupled Analysis and Prediction for Services Project. WMO reaffirmed its commitment to working in partnership with the ATCM.

(23) WMO presented IP 35 *Report by WMO on the implementation of the International Year of Glaciers' Preservation 2025 and the World Glaciers Day*, which provided information on the planning for the International Year of Glaciers' Preservation (IYGP 2025) and the World Glaciers Day. The WMO encouraged Members to actively engage in various initiatives associated with these two events in the lead-up to 2025.

(24) WMO presented IP 123 *Recommendations on the contribution of the World Meteorological Organization (WMO) on the coordination of meteorological programmes in Antarctica, as operated by WMO Members, and in support of evolving global needs*, prepared jointly with India, New Zealand and Norway. The WMO reported on recommendations on its role in coordinating meteorological programmes in Antarctica, as made by the Panel on Polar and High Mountains Observations, Research, and Services (PHORS) of the Executive Council of the WMO. The WMO noted that Members should take note of the potential for engaging and contributing to the actions arising from the Panel's recommendations. The recommendations included:

- the organisation of consultations with WMO Members representing Parties for gathering and sharing of observations, taking into account the Antarctic environment;
- exploring mutually beneficial contributions through WMO towards advancing its operational and scientific goals in the Antarctic, and facilitating access to sound scientific information for countries affected by the consequences of changes to the Antarctic;
- fostering a framework of coordinated engagements between WMO Members' national meteorological services with responsibilities for Antarctic activities and other agencies with responsibilities undertaken through the ATCM, including SCAR, COMNAP and the informal Working Group of Antarctica Meteorology and Climate (WAMC); and
- noting Resolution 2 (2014), for Members to initiate a roadmap for a WMO climate and weather service strategy for Antarctica.

(25) The Committee thanked the Observers for their contributions and work, and welcomed the progress reported in the several areas of continuing interest for the CEP. The Committee welcomed the actions taken by WMO for stronger collaboration with the CEP, and on working towards establishing climate and cryosphere services for the Antarctic.

Nomination of CEP Representatives to other organisations

(26) The Committee nominated:

- Ceisha Poirot (New Zealand) to represent the CEP at the 36th COMNAP Annual General Meeting to be held in Buenos Aires, Argentina, from 14 to 16 August 2024;
- Dr Yan Ropert-Coudert (France) to represent the CEP at the 38th SCAR Delegate Meeting to be held in Punta Arenas, Chile, from 26 to 28 August 2024; and
- Dr Andrew Titmus (United States) to represent the CEP at the 43rd SC-CAMLR meeting to be held in Hobart, Australia, from 14 to 18 October 2024.

Item 6: Repair and Remediation of Environment Damage

(27) The Committee noted the following Information Paper submitted under this agenda item:

- IP 31 *Development of actions to detect, survey and remedy environmental liabilities due to hydrocarbons in Argentine Antarctic Bases* (Argentina).

(28) The Committee noted the following Background Paper submitted under this agenda item:

- BP 46 *Preparation for cleanup work in the Molodezhnaya station area* (Russian Federation).

(29) Referring to BP 46, the Chair noted that Molodezhnaya station had been reported by the Russian Federation to the inventory of locations of past activities in the EIES, and highlighted that maintaining an inventory of past activities was required by Article 8(3) of Annex III to the Environmental Protocol. The Chair invited Members who had not reported in the EIES the location of their past activities (such as traverses, field depots, field bases, and crashed aircraft) to do so before the information was lost.

Item 7: Climate Change Implications for the Environment

7a) Strategic Approach

(30) China introduced WP 16 *Promote the Share of Best Practices of the Use of Renewable Energy in Antarctica,* which noted that the use of renewable energy in Antarctica had great potential benefits in mitigating the impact of climate change through emission reduction, as well as reducing the environmental risk of incidents and accidents related to fuel transportation, spills, and fires. China recalled that, in recent years, Parties reaffirmed their commitment to address the impact of climate change and protect the Antarctic environment through all available methods, including reducing their carbon footprints. China noted that technological progress had increased the feasibility of net zero emissions stations in Antarctica and shared that it had achieved net zero emissions at the Taishan Summer Camp in the 2018-19 season. China reported that recent tests of similar renewable technologies at Qinling Station in the Ross Sea Region had yielded positive results and that it had established a team to study renewable energy systems in the Antarctic. It recommended that the ATCM and CEP encourage Parties to work with COMNAP to develop a manual outlining best practices for renewable energy systems in Antarctica, increase the use of renewable energy in Antarctic operations to reduce anthropogenic greenhouse gas emissions and promote the innovation of new green energy technologies suitable for the Antarctic environment.

(31) The Committee expressed support for the recommendations in the paper. Members noted that they had already aligned with Resolution 2 (2023) *Helsinki Declaration on Climate Change and the Antarctic*, as well as Resolution 4 (2017) *Green Expedition in the Antarctic*. The Meeting also encouraged the development of a best practice manual and referenced existing documents that could be relevant to its development, including COMNAP's Best Practice for Energy Management (2007). Members agreed on the importance of utilising renewable energy technologies to decarbonise Antarctic operations and the usefulness of exchanging information about experiences. Members emphasised the important role COMNAP had played and would continue to play in this area. Some Members reported that their national Antarctic programmes had previously achieved, or had been working towards, net zero emissions stations, such as Belgium's Princess Elisabeth Station.

(32) Some Members highlighted that the choice of an approach to renewable energy technologies depended heavily on the site characteristics. Members also emphasised that, in addition to implementing renewable energies, energy efficiency must also be considered when reducing greenhouse gas emissions.

(33) COMNAP reported that it had worked with its members to increase energy efficiency and share best practices through the Advancing Critical Technology and the Environmental Protection Expert Groups. COMNAP agreed to work with Members to support their work on this topic, and noted that the issue of energy efficiency would be discussed at the COMNAP Annual General Meeting in August in Buenos Aires, Argentina.

(34) The Committee encouraged Members to increase the use of renewable energy in Antarctic operations, and promote the innovation, application and sharing of new green energy facilities and technologies suitable for the unique Antarctic environment.

CEP advice to the ATCM on sharing Best Practices on the Use of Renewable Energy in Antarctica

(35) The Committee agreed to advise the ATCM that it supported the development of a best practice manual on the use of renewable energy in Antarctica, the increase of renewable energy use in Antarctic operations, and the promotion of innovation and application of new green energy facilities and technologies suitable for the unique Antarctic environment, and that COMNAP would discuss the matter of energy efficiency at its meeting in August 2024 and bring back the outcome for ATCM and CEP consideration.

---

(36) Norway introduced WP 38 *Updating the CCRWP with new actions relating to sea-ice change*, prepared jointly with the United Kingdom. Recalling the joint CEP/ATCM climate session at ATCM XLV, Norway reminded Members of the Meeting's request to the CEP to provide, with the support of SCAR, advice on how human activity could avoid or mitigate unintended or unforeseen negative impacts on vulnerable species or habitats affected by local or regional sea-ice loss. Norway noted that ATCM XLV had invited SCAR to provide a first-level assessment of vulnerabilities in space and time, exposed by changing sea-ice extent in the Antarctic Peninsula region, and had asked the CEP to consider potential management implications for the Antarctic Peninsula region. Norway noted that the minimum sea-ice extent in 2024 tied with 2022 for the second lowest in the satellite data record. It further noted that the minimum sea-ice extent of the last three years were the three lowest in the 46-year record, and the first three years that minimum sea-ice extent had reached below two million square kilometres. Norway stressed that the Climate Change Response Work Programme (CCRWP) provided a mechanism for identifying and revising goals and specific actions by the CEP to support efforts within the Antarctic Treaty System to prepare for and build resilience to the

environmental impacts of a changing climate and the associated implications for the governance and management of Antarctica. Noting that the ATCM had requested that the CEP keep the CCRWP under regular review, with the understanding that the Committee discuss and consider additional climate change impact issues to include in the CCRWP, Norway and the United Kingdom recommended that the CEP:

- agree to update the CCRWP by including the sea-ice-related actions requested by ATCM XLV;
- discuss and identify potential specific tasks to implement to respond to this action, including considering the tasks suggested in this paper;
- task the Subsidiary Group on Climate Change Response (SGCCR) to consider and suggest how the proposed tasks could be moved forward and, in doing so, also provide an overview of ongoing work that may be relevant in informing this action item; and
- task the SGCCR, in collaboration with SCAR, to prepare an annual update on the most recent sea-ice changes for the CEP's attention to support its work in understanding and acting on the implication of sea-ice change for management of human activity.

(37) The Committee thanked Norway and the United Kingdom for their paper and expressed concern about the rapid and significant sea-ice loss and its consequences and cumulative impacts on Antarctic species and their habitat. Many Members highlighted that the consequences of sea-ice loss provided an example of the vulnerability of Antarctic biodiversity and ecosystems to climate change and that the Committee should take a precautionary approach to protect any vulnerable species or ecosystems where appropriate. Recognising the important role of SCAR in providing independent and objective scientific advice and information, the Committee emphasised that it was important to respond to requests from the ATCM in a timely manner.

(38) The Committee, therefore, agreed to update the CCRWP by including a new sea-ice-related action "c. Assess vulnerabilities in space and time, exposed by changing sea-ice extent in the Antarctic Peninsula region and on this basis consider potential management implications for this region, noting that it experiences high and increasing levels of human activity." under the climate-related issue #7 (in CCRWP column 1) as proposed, and to task the SGCCR to consider and suggest how they could be moved forward. The Committee asked the SGCCR to consult with SCAR on options for providing an annual update on the most recent sea-ice changes.

(39) China emphasised the importance of science-based decision-making, noting the necessity of assessing the dynamics of distribution, population, and habitat change of important birds and vegetation in the context of climate change, and expressed concerns about expected management actions to prohibit or limit access to marine or terrestrial areas at this stage.

(40) SCAR reiterated that sea-ice change was a significant concern, and was a key factor in species vulnerability. SCAR referred to the Antarctic Environments Portal, which contained several Information Summaries on Antarctic sea ice, and that noted its Expert Group on Antarctic Sea Ice Processes & Climate (ASPeCt) that was working on improving understanding of the sea-ice zone. The SCAR AntClimNow Antarctic Climate Indicators Project (WP 49) may also provide relevant information, and SCAR noted it was ready to support the SGCCR in providing regular updates on sea-ice change.

CEP advice to the ATCM on updates to the CCRWP with new actions relating to sea-ice change

(41) The Committee agreed to advise the ATCM that it had updated the CCRWP by including a new sea-ice-related action 'c. Assess vulnerabilities in space and time, exposed by changing sea-ice extent in the Antarctic Peninsula region and on this basis consider potential management implications for this region, noting that it experiences high and increasing levels of human activity.' under the climate-related issue #7 (in CCRWP column 1) as requested by ATCM XLV; and tasked the SGCCR:

- to consider and suggest how the proposed tasks could be moved forward, and in doing so also provide an overview of ongoing work that may be relevant in informing this action item; and
- in collaboration with SCAR, to consider options for preparing an annual update on the most recent sea-ice changes for the CEP's attention to support its work in understanding and acting on the implication of sea-ice change for management of human activity.

---

(42) SCAR introduced WP 49 *SCAR AntClimNow Antarctic Climate Indicators project*, prepared jointly with WMO. The SCAR AntClimNow Scientific Research Programme, together with partners including the World Climate Research Programme (WCRP) Climate and Cryosphere (CliC) project, had identified a range of Antarctic Climate Indicators (ACIs) with the aim of providing an accessible visualisation of broad aspects of the Antarctic climate system. SCAR stated that the Antarctic Climate Indicators would help users keep track of ongoing changes in Antarctica, with visualisations that could be used for communication and to facilitate collaboration and further studies. SCAR noted that the indicators could be expanded to focus on specific aspects of the climate systems through discussions with scientists and other stakeholders to determine further relevant variables. The proponents encouraged the CEP to:

- consider the relevance of Antarctic Climate Indicators to inform discussions on climate change;
- provide feedback on specific indicators that could be considered for further development and inclusion as Antarctic Climate Indicators; and
- consider whether and how these indicators might be routinely presented to provide context for CEP discussions.

(43) The Committee thanked SCAR and WMO for their paper and commended the AntClimNow Scientific Research Programme for its excellent work. The Committee expressed strong support for the recommendations in WP 49, highlighting the value of Antarctic Climate Indicators for identifying and monitoring climate change impacts and informing the Committee's discussion and decision-making on this topic.

(44) Members provided suggestions for consideration in the further development of the Antarctic Climate Indicators:

- including sea-ice change and ice-shelf loss as potential indicators for further development;
- including indicators on the role of fast ice and polynyas at the nexus between atmosphere, ocean, and land ice in coastal zones;
- including indicators demonstrating the interrelated nature of Antarctic climate and biodiversity loss; and
- presenting these indicators through visualisations that were accessible to various users, including non-scientists.

(45) The Committee agreed to invite SCAR to provide annual updates on Antarctic Climate Indicators and suggested that the Environments Portal might be useful for presenting such information. The relevance of the annual updates on Antarctic Climate Change and the Environment (ACCE) was also noted.

(46) SCAR thanked the Committee for its comments. SCAR noted that it would forward the comments to the AntClimNow Scientific Research Programme and looked forward to providing future updates to the CEP.

(47) SCAR presented IP 166 *Antarctic Climate Change and the Environment update*, which provided information on recent climate change-related research and observations relevant to the discussions and priorities of the CEP. The information complemented the SCAR ACCE Reports, initially published in 2009, subsequently updated through annual submissions to the CEP/ATCM, and most recently with the ACCE Decadal Synopsis Report. SCAR noted that it was working to address some of the specific recommendations arising from the 2023 SC-CAMLR workshop on climate change and that this work might also be relevant to the upcoming Joint CEP/SC-CAMLR workshop on climate change and monitoring.

(48) SCAR presented IP 184 *Understanding Future Sea-level Change Around Antarctica,* prepared jointly with COMNAP and WMO, which provided updated information about understanding future sea-level change around Antarctica. Recalling ATCM XLV - IP 95, the co-proponents reiterated their advice that Parties should support their national Antarctic programmes to extend observational coverage, facilitate research and monitoring, and adopt dynamic decision-making approaches that could provide resilience in response to unavoidable impacts. SCAR noted that it would provide the Committee with further updates at CEP 27.

(49) The Committee noted the following Information Papers submitted under this agenda item:

- IP 116 *Understanding the rapid changes in the frozen parts of our planet and the related global impacts - A knowledge base compiled at a high-level event in Oslo, Norway* (Norway, WMO).
- IP 169 *Southern Ocean Observing System (SOOS) Symposium* (SCAR).

(50) The Committee noted the following Background Paper submitted under this agenda item:

- BP 6 *Fifteen years (2008/09 – 2022/23) of New Zealand carbon emission measurements and reduction initiatives* (New Zealand).

7b) Implementation and Review of the Climate Change Response Work Programme

(51) The convenor of the SGCCR, Dr Heike Herata (Germany), introduced WP 6 *Report of the Subsidiary Group on Climate Change Response (SGCCR) 2023-2024*, which outlined the work and outputs of the SGCCR during the intersessional period. The convenor noted that the SGCCR prioritised activities outlined in the Climate Change Response Work Programme (CCRWP) and made recommendations on key areas of focus, including: assessing the status of climate-vulnerable Antarctic species; developing guidance for establishing and managing protected areas; keeping the Non-Native Species (NNS) Manual updated; and progressing decontamination of past activity sites. Additionally, the convenor noted that efforts were made to assess climate change risks to infrastructure, with COMNAP indicating ongoing work on infrastructure vulnerability.

(52) The Committee thanked Dr Herata and all SGCCR members for their work during the intersessional period and endorsed the SGCCR's recommendations. It noted that the

SGCCR had made steady progress on several priority issues and should maintain its momentum to ensure the full implementation of the CCRWP.

(53) Many Members emphasised the importance of the SGCCR's recommendation relating to the identification of known climate-vulnerable species. Some suggested that ATCM XLV - IP 45 could offer a good starting point and that engaging SCAR in the process would be helpful. Some Members stressed the importance of including not only iconic species but also less charismatic species and microbiological communities.

(54) Several Members also highlighted the importance of decontamination of past sites and of assessing climate change risks to infrastructure, encouraging close cooperation with COMNAP to prevent potential hazards posed by changing environments. Argentina referred to IP 31 relating to its work to detect, survey and remedy environmental liabilities caused by hydrocarbons at Argentine Antarctic bases.

(55) Acknowledging the need to strengthen coordination on climate change response with other organisations, Members also encouraged strong participation at the upcoming joint CEP/SC-CAMLR workshop.

(56) SCAR expressed its willingness to work with the SGCCR to provide information relevant to status assessments for climate-vulnerable species and to identify species or species groups that require consideration, to continue its work to address recommendations arising from the 2023 SC-CAMLR workshop on climate change, and to actively participate in the upcoming joint CEP/SC-CAMLR workshop.

CEP advice to the ATCM on implementation of the Climate Change Response Work Programme (CCRWP)

(57) The Committee agreed to advise the ATCM that it continued work to implement the CCRWP (2016). Following discussion on the six priority activities endorsed by CEP XXV, the CEP agreed to advise the ATCM that it made the following recommendations:

(1) Supporting work to assess the status of climate-vulnerable Antarctic species (Action 6c): The CEP agreed to start work to identify known climate-vulnerable species as a basis for prioritising efforts to advance assessments of climate-vulnerable species.

(2) Developing guidance on climate change considerations in documents for establishing and managing protected areas (Action 2e): Noting that SGMP members had commenced reviewing existing tools for area protection and management, the CEP recommended no further action at this time.

(3) Keeping the Non-native Species Manual updated with current developments (Action 1a): Noting that no urgent revisions were needed, the CEP recommended no further action at this time.

(4) Intensifying coordination on climate change response in the marine realm with SC-CAMLR (Action 3e): Recognising that efforts were underway for a joint CEP/SC-CAMLR workshop scheduled in 2025, the CEP encouraged Members to actively participate in the preparatory work for this workshop.

(5) De-contamination of past sites of activities in the Antarctic area (Action 5f); and

(6) Assessing the risk of climate change for existing and projected Antarctic infrastructure and associated environmental consequences and considering the impacts of climate change linked with the EIA guidelines, e.g., ensuring proposed long-term facilities are suitably resilient to climate change (Action 5a and 5d): The CEP invited Members to actively pursue efforts to address decontamination of past sites and climate change risks to infrastructure. It also acknowledged COMNAP's

ongoing work in this regard and suggested aligning future discussions with COMNAP's advice to the CEP meetings in 2024 and 2025.

(58) The Committee also took note of and discussed the following actions that had been delivered or concerned ongoing research that was regularly provided to the Committee:

- Action 5a: National operators to assess risk of change in climate (e.g. permafrost) to their infrastructure and environmental consequences (WP 18 and IP 30).
- Action 5b: Assess risk of climate change to HSM/heritage ASPA (IP 88 and IP 120).
- Action 6c: Supporting work to assess the status of climate-vulnerable Antarctic species (WP 34 and WP 48).
- Action 7: Improved understanding of potential expansion of human presence in Antarctica as a result of changes resulting from climate change through e.g. changes in sea ice distribution; collapse of ice shelves; expansion of ice-free area (WP 37).

---

(59) France introduced WP 14 *Preparation of the next Joint CEP/SC-CAMLR climate change and monitoring workshop*, which provided an update on the organisation of the next joint CEP/SC-CAMLR workshop on climate change and monitoring, including suggested Terms of Reference and other recommendations to facilitate the organisation of the joint workshop. Noting that Maude Jolly (France) was unable to continue in the role of co-convenor, France proposed that Dr Heike Herata (Germany) and Dr Rachel Cavanagh (United Kingdom) be appointed as the new co-convenors. It also suggested that the composition of the Steering Committee be slightly revised to include co-convenors of the workshop, CEP and SC-CAMLR Chairs and Vice-Chairs, experts, and the Antarctic Treaty and CCAMLR Secretariats. France further noted SC-CAMLR's recommendation that the workshop be held for 2-3 days in 2025, ideally in conjunction with CEP 27.

(60) The Committee thanked France for the paper and supported the recommendations. It expressed appreciation to Maude Jolly for her valuable work in planning the workshop over the past two years and welcomed Dr Heike Herata and Dr Rachel Cavanagh as co-convenors.

(61) The Committee agreed to adopt the amended Terms of Reference for the workshop in WP 14, noting that the outcomes from the 2023 SC-CAMLR climate change workshop would be a valuable reference for the coming joint workshop: "Building on the 2009 and 2016 joint workshops and the 2023 SC-CAMLR climate change workshop:

- Examine how to progress on matters of mutual interest in the marine realm in the context of climate change (including the five joint priority areas identified in the 2009 joint workshop);
- Identify common research, monitoring and information needs;
- Examine the need to enhance existing monitoring programmes to assess the impacts of climate change; and
- Propose improvements to strengthen cooperation and coordination between the CEP and SC-CAMLR."

(62) Italy noted that, as ATCM 47-CEP 27 host, due to the ongoing tender process for the ATCM, it was not yet able to commit to organising the joint CEP-CCAMLR workshop until the tender was concluded. Italy excluded the possibility of organising the workshop before CEP 27 and suggested considering the possibility of integrating the workshop into the timeframe of the regular ATCM-CEP agenda, possibly using the CEP room, once the respective sessions were concluded.

(63) Members expressed support for a 2- to 3-day workshop in conjunction with CEP 27 provided that Italy could accommodate this request. Many Members highlighted the value of holding the workshop in person, to provide the best opportunity for productive discussions on the complex issues under consideration, while some Members expressed a preference to also allow for virtual participation. Other Members preferred that the workshop be held without delay, noting that the last joint CEP/SC-CAMLR workshop was held in 2016 and that there was an agreement to hold such a workshop every five years.

(64) France nominated Dr Marc Eléaume, CCAMLR Scientific Committee representative for France, to join the Steering Committee as an expert.

(65) The Committee noted final dates, location and format would be examined by the Steering Committee and confirmed in due course by Circular from the CEP Chair. The Committee identified a need for support from the Antarctic Treaty Secretariat in holding the workshop.

(66) Noting that ATCM XLI had agreed to consider requests for budget on a case-by-case basis, the Committee agreed to request the allocation of budget for the joint CEP/SC-CAMLR workshop from the ATCM. The Committee noted that it would welcome voluntary contributions from Members, Non-Consultative Parties, and Observers.

CEP advice to the ATCM on the next Joint CEP/SC-CAMLR climate change and monitoring workshop

(67) The Committee agreed to advise the ATCM that it had agreed to recommendations in WP 14 relating to a Joint CEP/SC-CAMLR workshop on climate change and monitoring, including:

- adopting Terms of Reference as revised by SC-CAMLR;
- appointing new CEP co-convenors (Dr Rachel Cavanagh, the United Kingdom and Dr Heike Herata, Germany);
- adopting a revised composition of the workshop Steering Committee, and nominating experts to join; and
- providing guidance on the practical arrangements of the workshop in relation to location, dates, format, outputs, attendance and support.

(68) The Committee requested that the ATCM allocate budget for the joint CEP/SC-CAMLR workshop.

---

(69) COMNAP introduced WP 18 *Assessing Built Infrastructure and Potential Environmental Consequences from a Changing Antarctica.* COMNAP advised that the assessment of built infrastructure in a changing Antarctic was important and ongoing work for national Antarctic programmes. COMNAP recognised that the issue was broader than environmental alone. It noted that improving efficiencies in operations and safely decarbonising activities while introducing innovative technologies will carry with it requirements for changes to current infrastructure and, in some instances, installation of new infrastructures.

(70) The Committee endorsed the recommendation of WP 18 that Members support their national Antarctic programmes by participating in and continuing to provide their technical and practical expertise to the topical discussions at COMNAP Annual General Meetings and throughout the year.

(71) The Committee noted the following Information Papers submitted under this agenda item:

- IP 30 *Hybrid generation pilot project at the Chilean Antarctic Naval Base "Arturo Prat"* (Chile).
- IP 88 *Assessing the risk of climate change impacts on Antarctic heritage values: an update on progress* (United Kingdom, Australia).
- IP 120 *Vulnerability of polar heritage remains in context of climate change - experiences and research from Norway* (Norway).

(72) The Committee noted the following Background Paper submitted under this agenda item:

- BP 58 *Proposal of cooperation of Romania with Uruguay in Antarctica* (Romania).

Item 8: Environmental Impact Assessment (EIA)

8a) Draft Comprehensive Environmental Evaluations

(73) No papers were submitted under this agenda item.

8b) Other EIA Matters

(74) The Secretariat presented SP 10 *Review of how comments and responses were reflected in final CEEs (2003-2023)*, which provided an analysis of how feedback to draft CEEs was reflected in final CEEs from 2003 to 2023. This analysis was conducted in response to a request from CEP XXV. The review showed that comments on draft CEEs were communicated through various channels and that CEE proponents responded to comments in various ways, at times responding to individual comments and, at other times, grouping similar comments and providing single answers per group. During the review, the Secretariat developed a new tool to link the EIA database page showing each CEE with other documents, such as the report of the ICG that reviewed the CEE and the initial response to those comments submitted by the CEE proponent to the Committee.

(75) The Committee thanked the Secretariat for this paper and noted that reviewing responses to draft CEEs, as required under Annex I to the Environmental Protocol, was laborious but valuable. It also expressed appreciation for the new tool developed by the Secretariat and requested that the Secretariat enable this feature for future CEEs and link the documents already existing in the EIA database.

(76) With regards to the Secretariat's finding that proponents responded to comments on draft CEEs in various ways and to varying degrees of specificity, Members expressed the view that it was not sufficient to simply state that comments had been taken into account to comply with Article 3(6) of Annex I. It was noted that the variation in responses might arise from the different interpretations of the wording of Article 3(6), that a final CEE 'shall include or summarise' comments received on the draft CEE.

(77) Several Members shared their recent experiences as CEE proponents, explaining how they addressed comments from multiple sources and presented them publicly. They noted that, when responding to all comments, it was practical to group similar comments made by several Members. The Committee highlighted the importance of ensuring transparency in how comments were addressed in the final CEE, while acknowledging the extensive work involved.

(78) New Zealand introduced WP 20 *Improvement to the CEE review procedures*, prepared jointly with Norway, the United Kingdom, and the United States. It recalled that the EIA process was set out in Annex I to the Environmental Protocol, supported by the Guidelines for EIA in Antarctica in Resolution 1 (2016), and noted that discussions on

the continual improvement of the effectiveness of the EIA system were ongoing. New Zealand suggested potential improvements to the CEE review procedures using examples from recent construction projects and noted that national competent authorities did not have a common approach to handling changes within the CEE process after approval. New Zealand stated that this may become an issue given the many multi-year construction-related CEEs dealt with by the CEP. The proponents recommended that the CEP:

- consider and discuss if an interim process could be useful to support CEE reviews in addition to the requirements outlined in Annex I of the Protocol. This might include consideration of a CEP EIA Expert Group or interim shortened process to support robust reviews of CEEs when the scope of the activity changed;
- discuss whether there were any examples of processes or activities that would trigger a CEE update, including re-writing a CEE, updating the CEE, post-CEE tiering of IEEs or other variations; and
- reinforce the need for post-activity reporting on CEE-level activities as set out in Resolution 2 (1997) and consider if developing a reporting template and procedure would be useful and identifying if further improvements were needed.

(79) The Committee thanked New Zealand, Norway and the United Kingdom for the paper and underscored the EIA process as a fundamental part of the Environmental Protocol's framework for environmental protection. It acknowledged the importance of continually reviewing and updating the EIA process to ensure it remained an effective and contemporary tool. It also acknowledged the need for further guidance on the application of Annex I, including on the circumstances under which a new or revised EIA may be required and the application of the EIA processes in situations where any activity changed.

(80) ASOC noted that WP 20 highlighted a weakness in the EIA process that was not apparent when Annex I was drafted, relating to changes to an original proposal, and supported the proposals to ensure the EIA process is carried out in accordance with any changes to the proposed activity.

(81) The Committee welcomed efforts to strengthen the EIA process. Members cautioned against the adoption of a one-size-fits-all approach, and noted that a CEP EIA Expert Group might create an extra burden for a small handful of Members. Members expressed a willingness to further discuss the issues raised in WP 20 through informal intersessional discussions. The Committee welcomed the offer from New Zealand and the United Kingdom to jointly lead these discussions.

CEP advice to the ATCM on improvement to the CEE review procedures

(82) The Committee agreed to advise the ATCM that it would discuss improvements to CEE review procedures through informal intersessional discussions, and that the Committee had welcomed the offer from New Zealand and the United Kingdom to jointly lead these informal intersessional discussions.

(83) The Committee also noted that the ATCM would consider a Working Paper on the topic of screening and scoping in the CEE process, and agreed to advise the ATCM that it stood ready to consider any requests arising.

---

(84) The Secretariat presented SP 11 *Summary of CEP discussions on assessing cumulative impacts (2013-2023),* which provided a summary of the CEP discussions on assessing cumulative impacts during the last decade, prepared in response to a request by CEP

XXV. It also provided a table with links to all documents referenced in its main body that are publicly available on the Secretariat website. The Secretariat suggested that Members might also want to consider the summarised report and the map of locations of past activities, which was based on data submitted by Parties through the Inventory of Past Activities section of the EIES.

(85) The United Kingdom introduced WP 10 *Cumulative Impacts in Antarctica*, recalling that the CEP had considered the issue of cumulative impacts in previous years. Considering that the topic required more attention, the United Kingdom informed the CEP that it had commissioned a consultant (Dr Neil Gilbert) to explore cumulative impacts further and that their report was appended to WP 10. The report described the legal requirements for assessing cumulative impacts in Antarctic EIAs and provided a brief overview of discussions on this topic within CEP Meetings. The report referenced the definition provided in the CEP's *Guidelines for Environmental Impact Assessment in the Antarctic* (Resolution 1 (2016)) and other global EIA regimes, noting the general consistency in definitions. The report provided a conceptual model of cumulative impacts, stating that they could occur because of different aspects arising from within an activity and other elements arising from multiple past, present or reasonably foreseeable activities. The United Kingdom recommended that the CEP consider:

- collating an evaluation of best practice methods and approaches used to assess cumulative impacts away from Antarctica and consider how these could apply to Antarctica;
- the development of enhanced guidelines on undertaking cumulative impact assessments, which could be standalone or accommodated within the CEP's *Guidelines for Environmental Impact Assessment in the Antarctic*;
- reaffirming the importance of conducting high-quality environmental impact assessments as well as the need to continue to develop Antarctic environmental impact assessment processes following best practice; and
- seeking scientific advice on the development of thresholds for a selection of ecological and environmental values in Antarctica.

(86) The United Kingdom further recommended that Parties consider:

- undertaking EIAs or cumulative impact assessments that are independent of any one particular activity but instead focussed on key values over broader temporal and spatial scales;
- sharing any experience of undertaking strategic environmental assessments or joint environmental impact assessments with a view to informing the potential development of new or enhancement of existing guidelines;
- undertaking cumulative impact assessments jointly among multiple operators with an interest in particular regions of Antarctica; and
- undertaking assessments that are focussed on understanding the cumulative impacts of multiple activities on key Antarctic values.

(87) The Committee thanked the Secretariat for SP 11, which provided a helpful overview to support its discussion on cumulative impacts. It also thanked the United Kingdom for WP 10 and the accompanying report, which would inform the CEP's ongoing work to support understanding and effective assessment of cumulative impacts. The Committee noted that this was a complex and challenging topic that the CEP had discussed for many years.

(88) Many Members noted the need to develop enhanced guidelines for assessing cumulative impacts, especially given the increasing pressure on the Antarctic environment due to the growing scale and diversity of activities.

(89) The Committee endorsed the recommendation to collate an evaluation of best practice methods and approaches used to assess cumulative impacts, highlighting the value of considering experience from both within and away from Antarctica. Many Members noted that effective assessment of cumulative impacts could only be achieved with cooperation, such as through data sharing, the development of shared databases, inventories of past and present activities, and regional cooperation. Some Members noted the need to assess cumulative impacts under the framework provided by the Protocol and its Annex I.

(90) While acknowledging the merit in further discussions on how to approach methodologically the larger scale questions related to cumulative impact assessment, some Members also recalled that the Committee had a range of existing tools at its disposal, such as ASPAs, ASMAs, Site Guidelines for Visitors, and Specially Protected Species. Members noted such tools also served as a good approach to limiting cumulative impacts when used well.

(91) Some Members suggested that it could be useful to conduct a regional assessment of cumulative impacts across temporal scales to advance the topic in a practical and concrete manner. Several locations for such an assessment were suggested, including ASPA 126 Byers Peninsula, Livingston Island, or areas such as King George Island or McMurdo Sound, where multiple operators undertook multiple activities.

(92) Belarus noted that, as it would be unreasonable to expect that a universal practice on cumulative impacts assessment would be developed in a short time, it was advisable to focus, in the first instance, on important activities such as tourism and air impacts.

(93) Belarus referred to its IP 3 *First assessment of cumulative impact of scientific stations on the ambient air of an Antarctic oasis*, which noted research on the assessment of the cumulative air impact from different operators. The study estimated pollutant emission and ambient air pollutant concentrations from diesel generators of all research stations located in the Larsemann Hills, East Antarctica. Belarus believed that this research would be useful to CEP for creating methods to measure cumulative impacts.

(94) IAATO stated that it supported the sharing of information among competent authorities to assist with the management of cumulative impacts and encouraged its operators to maintain close contact with their competent authorities, before, after and during the season, to help all stakeholders with the sharing of information. IAATO noted that it was open to discussions about how it could provide information to support improving cumulative impact assessments or the EIA process more generally.

(95) ASOC highlighted the paper's recommendation that Parties conduct EIAs focused on key values affected by multiple individual activities. It noted that this could be applied to the Antarctic Peninsula where activity levels were comparatively higher and could also contribute to discussion on a tourism framework. ASOC supported the idea outlined in WP 10 of conducting a retrospective and prospective study in a specific location to better understand cumulative impacts.

(96) Following further discussion on this topic, the Committee agreed on the need to continue advancing guidance on cumulative impact assessment and to reflect this by including tasks in its Five-year Work Plan.

CEP advice to the ATCM on cumulative impacts in Antarctica

(97) The Committee agreed to advise the ATCM that it had agreed to continue discussions to advance guidance on cumulative impact assessment and had included tasks related to this in its Five-year Work Plan.

(98) Peru presented IP 135 *Proyecto de la nueva Estación Científica Antártica Machu Picchu (ECAMP)*, which reported on Peru's plans to modernise the Machu Picchu Antarctic Scientific Station (ECAMP) infrastructure. Peru noted that it aimed to ensure its scientific platform met current technical and environmental requirements, and was moving towards the preparation of an environmental impact assessment following the requirements of the Protocol on Environmental Protection to the Antarctic Treaty.

(99) Colombia presented IP 160 *Actualización del procedimiento para el desarrollo de Evaluaciones de Impacto Ambiental en Antártica*, and reported on Colombia's commitment to improving and updating its environmental impact assessment procedures. Colombia noted that its procedures had been updated based on discussions in the CEP and according to guidance provided by environmental institutions in Colombia.

(100) The United Kingdom introduced WP 15 *Nested Permitting,* drawing Members' attention to the issue of nested permitting, which involved issuing two or more separate permits for a combined visit on a single vessel travelling to Antarctica. Recalling Article 13.4 to the Environmental Protocol, the United Kingdom considered that this issue affected the implementation of the objectives of the Protocol. It noted the increasing trend in Antarctica, where non-government-related expeditions relied on tourist operators for logistical support. The United Kingdom stated that while this could provide opportunities for researchers to conduct activities in Antarctica, it also raised challenges for national competent authorities in assessing the total environmental impact of these activities and issuing permits. The United Kingdom noted that nested permits could occur, for instance, when filmmakers travelled alongside scientists and tourists on the same vessel with permits from different national competent authorities. The United Kingdom recalled Article 8.4 of the Protocol, which provided that where activities are planned jointly by more than one Party, one Party should coordinate environmental impact assessment procedures. It was noted that in practice, often multiple EIAs, sometimes from different national competent authorities, were being submitted through the practice of nested permitting, and the requirement of Article 8.4 was not necessarily being met. The United Kingdom further stated that recording data on the Electronic Information Exchange System (EIES) could be challenging with multiple expeditions on a single vessel, as each individual permit had to be recorded separately despite being on the same vessel. The situation could result in an inaccurate number of expeditions being recorded as travelling to Antarctica. To address the issue of 'nested permits', the United Kingdom recommended that:

- Parties continue to discuss this issue in the Competent Authorities Discussion Forum as one of its five priority issues to determine how best to ensure that all activity in multi-member expeditions is assessed for environmental impacts in the context of Article 8.4 of the Environmental Protocol; and
- The Secretariat change the EIES to allow Parties who request separate authorisation be sought for activities taking place on their authorised vessels/operations, to identify which other Parties are authorising those activities, and enable those Parties to record the activities on the EIES as part of a single overall expedition.

(101) The Committee welcomed WP 15 and highlighted that, as the complexity and interconnectedness of activities increased in Antarctica, there was an increasing need for effective coordination between national competent authorities and continued information sharing. The Committee noted the importance of ensuring all activities were

appropriately assessed and authorised and encouraged continued discussion on the topic of nested permits via the National Competent Authorities Forum. The Committee also thanked Germany for organising an informal virtual workshop in the past intersessional period, that had allowed for fruitful exchange between national competent authorities. Some Members noted the relevance of the issue of nested permits for discussions in ATCM Special Working Group 3 and suggested the CEP should note that in its advice to the ATCM.

(102) Noting differences in domestic legislation, many Members noted that they could not issue a single permit for different activities (such as tourism and scientific activities) on one vessel due to different requirements for different types of activities. Some Members pointed to their experiences in nested permitting approaches, including through IP 61 and IP 62 at ATCM 44 (2022). Some Members stated that, in some instances, it would be inappropriate to issue a single authorisation/permit, including to ensure operators retain effective control and legal responsibility for their respective activities.

(103) Some Members stated that they had a different interpretation of the EIA requirements for jointly planned activities under Article 8.4 of the Environmental Protocol, including questions on the types of activities that are covered, and that the wider permitting of activities under the Environmental Protocol is not covered by Article 8.4.

(104) In response to a question on the second recommendation in WP 15, the United Kingdom noted that it would work with the Secretariat and other interested Members over the intersessional period to identify what specific changes to the EIES would be required. The Secretariat stated that it would be available to discuss the technical aspects of implementing a modification to the EIES with interested Members. Some Members noted that it could be relevant for the ATCM to consider this issue in light of the proposed review of the EIES as put forward in WP 54 to the ATCM.

CEP advice to the ATCM on nested permitting

(105) The Committee agreed to advise the ATCM that it had agreed that:

- The issue of nested permits should continue to be discussed in the Competent Authorities Discussion Forum as one of the five priority issues to determine how best to ensure that all activity in multimember expeditions is appropriately assessed for environmental impacts; and
- The EIES should be updated to allow for the identification of separate authorisations for activities taking place as part of a single overall expedition.

---

(106) The Committee noted the following Secretariat Paper submitted under this agenda item:

- SP 7 *Annual list of Initial Environmental Evaluations (IEE) and Comprehensive Environmental Evaluations (CEE) prepared between 1 April 2023 and 31 March 2024* (ATS).

(107) The Committee noted the following Information Papers submitted under this agenda item:

- IP 118 *Initial Environmental Evaluation for the Exploration of Subglacial Lake Qilin (Snow Eagle) in Antarctica* (China).
- IP 133 *Report on the Presentation of the Final Comprehensive Environmental Evaluation for the Renovation of Petrel Base, Dundee Island, Antarctica* (Argentina).
- IP 138 *Pautas para la Evaluación Ambiental Preliminar del Perú en la Antártida (EVAPA)* (Peru).
- IP 176 *Waste Treatment at the Syowa Station Waste Landfill* (Japan).

Item 9: Area Protection and Management Plans

9a) Management Plans

i) Draft Management Plans which have been reviewed by the Subsidiary Group on Management Plans

(108) The convenor of the Subsidiary Group on Management Plans (SGMP), Dr Anoop Kumar Tiwari (India) introduced WP 43 *Subsidiary Group on Management Plans Report of activities during the intersessional period 2023-2024* on behalf of the SGMP. He thanked Dr Polly Penhale (United States) for moderating the pre-meeting review of management plans that were not submitted to the SGMP review process, Ewan McIvor (Australia) for coordinating the review of the new management plan for the Danger Islands Archipelago, and Prof. Antonio Quesada (Spain) for coordinating the review of the new management plan for Farrier Col, Horseshoe Island, Marguerite Bay. The SGMP convenor also thanked all active participants in the SGMP for their work and reminded the Committee that all Members were welcome to join the SGMP.

(109) In accordance with Terms of Reference #1 to #3, the convenor observed that the SGMP had reviewed draft Management Plans for two new Antarctic Specially Protected Areas (ASPAs) referred by CEP XXV for intersessional review.

(110) Regarding the revised management plan for a new ASPA on Danger Islands Archipelago (North-Eastern Antarctic Peninsula), jointly proposed by Germany and the United States, the SGMP advised the Committee that the updated draft management plan was well-written and of high quality and consistent with relevant CEP guidelines. It was further noted that proponents had closely considered the SGMP's advice and addressed most of the SGMP's suggestions. Accordingly, the SGMP recommended that the Committee approve the revised management plan for the ASPA.

(111) Argentina informed the Committee that, since the drafting of the management plan for this ASPA, Petrel Station had changed from a summer-only to a year-round station. The proponents agreed to amend the text in the management plan to reflect this change.

(112) Regarding the revised management plan for a new ASPA at Farrier Col, Horseshoe Island, Marguerite Bay, jointly proposed by Belgium, Türkiye and the United Kingdom, the SGMP advised the Committee that the updated draft management plan was well written, of high quality, consistent with relevant CEP guidelines, and adequately addressed the key points raised in advice to its proponents. Accordingly, the SGMP recommended that the Committee approve the revised management plan for the ASPA.

(113) The co-proponents of the new ASPAs expressed their gratitude to the convenor of the SGMP and the Members who had participated in the SGMP. They highlighted the valuable feedback and the effective coordination between Members in developing and revising the draft management plans.

(114) The Committee welcomed the proposals and thanked the SGMP for its careful review and helpful suggestions to improve the management plans over the intersessional period. The Committee endorsed the SGMP's recommendations and agreed to forward the revised management plans to the ATCM for adoption.

(115) The SGMP called attention to the revised management plan which had been reviewed by the SGMP in 2023, Western Bransfield Strait and Eastern Dallmann Bay (United States). In accordance with Decision 9 (2005), the proposal had been submitted to CCAMLR-41 (2022) for approval. The management plan was approved at CCAMLR-42 (2023) and thus the Committee agreed to forward the management plan to the ATCM for approval by means of a Measure.

(116) The convenor of the SGMP noted Chile's IP 22 *Proposed Measures to Upgrade the Management Plan of ASPA N° 150, Ardley Island, Maxwell Bay, King George Island (25 de mayo),* prepared jointly with Argentina, China, the Republic of Korea, the Russian Federation and Uruguay and IP 23 *Proposed Measures to Upgrade the Management Plan of ASPA N° 125, Fildes Peninsula, King George Island (25 de Mayo)* regarding proposed measures to upgrade the Management Plans of ASPAs 150 and 125. The convenor advised the Committee that the management plans for the following three ASPAs had remained under review by Chile during the intersessional period:

- ASPA 125: Fildes Peninsula, King George (25 de Mayo) Island (Chile)
- ASPA 146: South Bay, Doumer Island, Palmer Archipelago (Chile)
- ASPA 150: Ardey Island (Ardey Peninsula), Maxwell Bay, King George Island (Chile)

ii) Revised draft Management Plans which have not been reviewed by the Subsidiary Group on Management Plans

(117) The United States presented IP 146 rev. 1 *Report of the 2024 Pre-CEP meeting review of ASPA and ASMA Management Plans*. The paper noted that 19 new or revised ASPA management plans had been available for comment prior to CEP 26 and that no new or revised ASMA management plans were submitted this year. The United States emphasised the quality of the management plans. The United States stated that seven Members (Australia, China, France, Germany, Italy, the United Kingdom, and the United States) had commented on eight of the new or revised management plans. It noted that three of the management plans had been reviewed by the SGMP and then revised, and noted one of these plans was approved by CCAMLR at its 2023 meeting. The United States reported that fifteen of the management plans were considered as having minor revisions, and one new management plan had been submitted.

(118) The Committee thanked the convenor of the pre-meeting review, Dr Polly Penhale (United States), for the excellent work undertaken during the intersessional review period and the clear report on the status of draft management plans.

(119) The Committee further thanked the proponents for their efforts in submitting high-quality draft management plans.

(120) With respect to ASPA 128 (WP 2 rev. 1), ASPA 141 (WP 5), ASPA 175 (WP 12 rev. 1), ASPA 154 (WP 23), ASPA 116 (WP 25), ASPA 135 (WP 26), ASPA 136 (WP 27), ASPA 160 (WP 28), ASPA 171 (WP 30), ASPA 161 (WP 32), ASPA 142 (WP 39), ASPA 173 (WP 53), ASPA 151 (WP 64), the Committee noted that the pre-meeting review had raised minor issues with two of these revised management plans (ASPAs 128 and 175), which had already been addressed by the proponents. The Committee approved these plans.

(121) Regarding ASPA 137 (WP 51), the United States had proposed an update to the helicopter air access provisions in the Management Plan to maintain ongoing practical scientific work while ensuring continued protection of a genetically isolated Weddell Seal colony within the ASPA. Noting a minor revision to the text and map in response to requests, the United States revised the Management Plan to refer to an 'air access restricted zone'. With this minor revision, the Committee approved the plan.

(122) Regarding ASPA 139 (WP 19), the United States proposed expanding the boundaries of ASPA 139 to include the surrounding marine area due to significant environmental change. The United States reported much ice retreat in the area, including the loss of an ice bridge, which resulted in significant changes to the seabird populations within the ASPA. This ice retreat was observed via long-term monitoring the United States had conducted in the area over many decades. The United States stated that the area

experienced an increase in human impacts, including helicopter access and zodiac cruising by tourists and noted environmental stewardship concerns as seabirds used both the terrestrial and the marine environment. Related to the proposed increase in size of the ASPA, the United States emphasised that the proposed ASPA 139 was still small at 3.9 square kilometres and only had a water depth of approximately 50 metres.

(123) Many Members welcomed the proposal to modify the boundary of ASPA 139 to include adjacent marine areas and ice margins. Some Members also commended the expertise and scientific research involved.

(124) China noted that the original intention of ASPA 139 was to protect terrestrial values. China raised concerns about the level of scientific data involved in the proposal with regard to the proposed marine environment to be included in the ASPA, and suggested to consider alternative measures to manage the human impact in the surrounding marine environment, taking into account the bird vigilance distance from human activities and the sea (CEP XXIV - IP 122).

(125) In response to these comments, the United States highlighted the inextricable link between terrestrial and marine environments for seabirds and its 30 plus years of data on the seabird populations in ASPA 139. The United States referred to ASPA 178, which was similar in that it also contained a marine area to protect transiting seabirds.

(126) China and the Russian Federation suggested that the proposal be sent to CCAMLR for review due to the inclusion of a marine area. In response, many Members referred to Decision 9 (2005) and highlighted its intent to avoid delaying progress by tasking CCAMLR to review areas of unlikely interest for fishing, such as the proposed boundaries for ASPA 139.

(127) In noting Decision 9 (2005), the SC-CAMLR Chair stated that there was currently no fishing activity within the proposed boundaries of ASPA 139, and offered to continue discussions on clarifying the process between the CEP and CCAMLR.

(128) ASOC recalled that Article 3.1 of Annex V to the Environmental Protocol stated that 'any area, including any marine area, may be designated as an Antarctic Specially Protected Area', and urged Members to continue implementing this requirement.

(129) IAATO, stating its support for the proposal, reported that it limited operator activities in the vicinity of ASPA 139 to only during approved Palmer Station visits and would be implementing a new georeferenced fence so operators would be able to avoid the Area if required.

(130) While most Members supported the revised management plan for ASPA 139, China stated that it was unable to endorse the revised management plan at CEP 26.

(131) Some Members expressed disappointment that the CEP was unable to reach agreement on ASPA 139 and underscored that ASPA 139 encompassed an important area which had been extensively researched and required improved protection due to glacier retreat and ecological changes.

(132) In response to a question from the United States, the Secretariat noted that it could work intersessionally to add the field "Party undertaking management plan review" to the Protected Area Database in addition to the existing "Original Proposing Party" field, as was already done with Historical Sites and Monuments. The Parties that were already listed as original proponents would by default be listed as both "Original Proposing Party" and "Party undertaking management plan review".

(133) The Committee requested that the Secretariat add the suggested field to the Protected Area Database, and noted that Members would be added to "Party undertaking management plan review" of the relevant ASPAs and ASMAs, including ASPA 128

(Poland and the United States) and ASMA 5 (United States and Norway).

iii) New draft management plans for protected/managed areas

(134) The Committee considered draft management plans for two proposed new ASPAs:

- WP 8 *Report on the informal ICG to develop an ASPA Draft Management Plan for the Otto-von-Gruber-Gebirge (Dronning Maud Land, East Antarctica)* (Germany, United States).
- WP 55 *Management Plan Antarctic Specially Protected Area No. XX, Western Bransfield Strait and Eastern Dallmann Bay* (United States).

(135) With respect to WP 8, the Committee noted that the draft management plan had been considered by the pre-meeting review of Management Plans (IP 146), which had recommended that the draft management plan be referred to the SGMP for further consideration.

(136) The Committee thanked Germany and the United States for their work on the proposed new ASPA and draft management plan and commended the informal ICG participants for collaborating with the proponents toward the draft management plan.

(137) India noted that its scientists had been actively researching and mapping the area around the Gruber Mountains since 1985, including monitoring ice dynamics of Lednik Anuchna glacier, and requested that information about the contribution of India's national Antarctic programme to research in this area be included in the management plan.

(138) The proponents supported making changes to the draft management plan to include this information and encouraged India to participate in the SGMP.

(139) While expressing general support for the proposal, China expressed its view that the size of the proposed ASPA was too large. China noted that it supported the protection of northern parts of the proposed ASPA including lakes and snow petrel breeding habitat but that in its opinion, other parts lacked sufficient scientific evidence to justify ASPA protection. China agreed that the draft management plan could be forwarded to the SGMP for review, where discussions regarding the size of the ASPA would be held.

(140) Following further discussion, the Committee agreed to forward the management plan for the proposed new ASPA to the SGMP for review in the coming intersessional period.

(141) With respect to WP 55, the Committee noted the draft management plan had been considered by the CEP and forwarded to CCAMLR for approval. Following approval by CCAMLR at its 2023 meeting, the CEP recommended the management plan for ASPA No. 182, Western Bransfield Strait and Eastern Dallmann Bay be approved without further discussion. The Committee endorsed the proposal.

CEP advice to the ATCM on draft management plans for protected/managed areas

(142) The Committee agreed to forward the following new and revised management plans to the ATCM for adoption by means of a Measure:

- ASPA 116, New College Valley, Cape Bird, Ross Island
- ASPA 128, Western Shore of Admiralty Bay, King George Island, South Shetland Islands
- ASPA 135, North-east Bailey Peninsula, Budd Coast, Wilkes Land
- ASPA 136, Clark Peninsula, Budd Coast, Wilkes Land, East Antarctica
- ASPA 137, Northwest White Island, McMurdo Sound

- ASPA 141, Yukidori Valley, Langhovde, Lützow-Holm Bay
- ASPA 142, Svarthamaren
- ASPA 151, Lions Rump, King George Island, South Shetland Islands
- ASPA 154, Botany Bay, Cape Geology, Victoria Land
- ASPA 160, Frazier Islands, Windmill Islands, Wilkes Land, East Antarctica
- ASPA 161, Terra Nova Bay, Ross Sea
- ASPA 171, Narębski Point, Barton Peninsula, King George Island
- ASPA 173, Cape Washington and Silverfish Bay, Terra Nova Bay, Ross Sea
- ASPA 175, High Altitude Geothermal Sites of the Ross Sea Region (including parts of the summits of Mount Erebus, Ross Island and Mount Melbourne and Mount Rittmann, northern Victoria Land)
- ASPA 180, Danger Islands Archipelago, North-eastern Antarctic Peninsula
- ASPA 181, Farrier Col, Horseshoe Island, Marguerite Bay
- ASPA 182, Western Bransfield Strait and Eastern Dallmann Bay

(143) The Committee agreed to advise the ATCM that most Members supported putting forward the revised management plan for ASPA 139, Biscoe Point, Anvers Island, Palmer Archipelago to the ATCM for adoption, but consensus was not reached. The views expressed in the discussion are presented in paragraphs 122-131.

(144) The Committee agreed to advise the ATCM that it had decided to forward the following draft management plan for a protected area to the SGMP for review:

- Proposal for a new ASPA in the Otto-von-Gruber-Gebirge (Dronning Maud Land, East Antarctica).

---

iv) Papers relating to prior assessment of proposed new protected areas

(145) The Committee considered two Working Papers relating to the prior assessment of proposed new protected areas, in accordance with the *Guidelines: A prior assessment process for the designation of ASPAs and ASMAs*:

- WP 13 *Prior assessment of a proposed Antarctic Specially Protected Area on Signy Island, South Orkney Islands* (Italy, Netherlands, United Kingdom).
- WP 31 *Revised prior assessment of a proposed multi-site Antarctic Specially Protected Area within the Collins Bay and Graham Coast (Kyiv Peninsula)* (Ukraine).

(146) With respect to WP 13, the Committee thanked the proponents for their work in preparing the prior assessment. It agreed with the proponents' assessment that the proposed ASPA merited special protection and endorsed the development of a Management Plan for the area. It also encouraged interested Members to work with the co-proponents informally during the intersessional period in the development of a Management Plan for the ASPA.

(147) With respect to WP 31, the Committee thanked Ukraine for its work in preparing the prior assessment, noting that this was a revised proposal which built on a proposal submitted by Ukraine to CEP XXV (CEP XXV - WP 58) and comments provided by Members at that meeting.

(148) China raised concerns about the large number of unrelated sites included in the ASPA, and the level of supporting scientific data, noting that in this case, the protected sites should be considered one-by-one with enhanced scientific evidence.

(149) In responding to China's concerns, Members noted that the number of sites in the proposed ASPA had decreased from the previous proposal from 30 to five, that the sites were within close proximity to one another, and that Ukraine's prior assessment form provided detailed information on the values of each site and why they merited protection. Members also pointed out that there were many existing multi-site ASPAs, including recently established ASPAs such as ASPA 179.

(150) Following further discussion, the Committee encouraged the proponent to move forward in collaboration with interested Members, and to take into account the concerns and questions raised during the meeting. Ukraine agreed to convene informal discussions during the intersessional period and report back to CEP 27.

v) Other matters relating to management plans for protected/managed areas

(151) The United Kingdom presented IP 63 *Initial informal discussions concerning a potential new Antarctic Specially Managed Area (ASMA) in the vicinity of Marguerite Bay, Antarctic Peninsula.* It reported details of initial informal intersessional discussions about the usefulness of proposing the designation of an area in the vicinity of Marguerite Bay as a new Antarctic Specially Managed Area (ASMA). Having observed the rising levels of tourism activities and national Antarctic programmes in the region and the multitude of ASPAs, IBAs and HSMs in the area, the United Kingdom proposed further discussions to consider whether a preliminary assessment for a new ASMA might be appropriate.

(152) The Committee thanked the United Kingdom for presenting the Information Paper. Spain expressed support for enhanced management of the area and highlighted the importance of addressing the increased activity.

(153) The Committee noted the following Information Papers submitted under this agenda item:

- IP 36 *Initiation of review of Management Plans for Antarctic Specially Protected Area No. 143 and Antarctic Specially Protected Area No. 162* (Australia).
- IP 181 *Initiation of review of Management Plan for Antarctic Specially Protected Area (ASPA) No. 169 Amanda Bay, Ingrid Christensen Coast, Princess Elizabeth Land, East Antarctica* (Australia, China).
- IP 182 *Do we need management groups for ASPAs and handling cumulative impacts?* (Uruguay).

9b) Historic Sites and Monuments

(154) The United Kingdom introduced WP 9 *The Wreck of Endurance – updating information for HSM 93 and Prior Assessment of a proposed Antarctic Specially Protected Area in the Weddell Sea*, prepared jointly with Chile, New Zealand, South Africa, and the United States. The paper provided an update on the preparation of the Conservation Management Plan for HSM 93, the wreck of Endurance, following its discovery on 5 March 2022. The United Kingdom reported that a recent study had shown that the Endurance was in stable condition and that the debris from the wreck extended farther than initially assumed. The United Kingdom stated that the wreck served as an artificial reef that hosted multiple marine organisms, including some considered Vulnerable Marine Ecosystem (VME) organisms by CCAMLR, and therefore was of scientific interest. The United Kingdom expressed a desire to consider the location for ASPA designation for additional site protection due to its outstanding scientific values, unique

historical significance, and vulnerability to risks from human activity and climate change. It also emphasised that, although no ASPAs have been designated to protect an HSM in the marine environment, this was an extraordinary case, and ASPA designation would help manage science opportunities. The proponents recommended that the Committee:

- acknowledge the Conservation Management Plan for HSM 93;
- recommend that the ATCM adopt a Measure to update the 'Description' information field of HSM 93 to extend the area encompassing HSM 93 to a 1500 metre radius; and
- consider the prior assessment for a proposed ASPA for the wreck of *Endurance* and agree that the values within the proposed ASPA merit special protection, endorse the development of a Management Plan for the area, and encourage interested Members to work with the proponents informally during the intersessional period in the development of a Management Plan for potential submission at CEP 27.

(155) Many Members supported the recommendations to acknowledge the Conservation Management Plan for HSM 93, update the description of the information field of HSM 93 to extend the area encompassing HSM 93 to a 1500 metre radius; and endorse the development of a Management Plan for the area for consideration for ASPA designation. Norway, in supporting the proposal to designate HSM 93 as an ASPA noted that the wreck of the *Endurance* was a very special case with extraordinary historic values and such a designation should not be interpreted to create a precedent.

(156) IAATO reported that the wreck's depth at over 3000 metres was currently out of reach of any submersibles carried by IAATO operators, and that the site's environmental conditions made regular visitation unlikely. IAATO supported the ongoing protection of the *Endurance* through an ASPA.

(157) In responding to questions on the size of the area, the United Kingdom noted that it had consulted experts and a 1,500 metre limit was recommended as the best way to capture all debris from the site, that extended much further than was previously understood.

(158) In response to a question about carbon dating the timber of the *Endurance*, the United Kingdom noted that no samples had been taken from the *Endurance*.

(159) China and Argentina did not consider that an ASPA designation was necessary noting that the site was already protected as an HSM. China further expressed that the ocean provided enough protection for the *Endurance* due to its location on the seabed.

(160) In response, the United Kingdom emphasised the scientific community's high interest in the site. It stated that ASPA designation would allow carefully managed research of the area through permitting and that Conservation Management Plans alone for HSMs were not binding on Members. It also highlighted that the precise location of the *Endurance* was only recently discovered in 2022 and that the natural ocean was no longer sufficient protection.

(161) The Committee acknowledged the Conservation Management Plan for HSM 93 and agreed to recommend that the ATCM adopt a Measure to update the 'Description' information field of HSM 93 to extend the area encompassing HSM 93 to a 1500 metre radius. While some Members did not endorse the development of a Management Plan for the area for consideration for ASPA designation, many Members did do so.

(162) The United Kingdom introduced WP 11 rev. 1 *Base Y, Horseshoe Island, Marguerite Bay – updating information for HSM 63*, which proposed an update to the description of HSM 63 following new survey data captured in 2023 on the location of the refuge hut on nearby Blaiklock Island. The United Kingdom reported that during the 2022-23 season, the United Kingdom Antarctic Heritage Trust had surveyed Blaiklock Island to

inspect the refuge hut and undertake any emergency repairs. During that visit, the location coordinates taken using a handheld GPS showed values that deviated from the previously documented coordinates. The United Kingdom informed the Meeting that subsequent analysis of satellite data by the British Antarctic Survey in March 2024, provided an accurate set of coordinates for the refuge hut. It stated that whilst the refuge was a subsidiary structure within HSM 63, its location was on a different island some 20 miles north of the main site on Horseshoe Island. To ensure that the published information about the HSM was accurate and up to date, the United Kingdom recommended that the CEP endorse the updated 'Description' information field of HSM 63.

(163) Following a comment from Argentina, the United Kingdom updated the 'Physical features of the environment' and 'Cultural and local context' information fields to include information missing from the proposal.

(164) The Committee thanked the United Kingdom for its update on the location of the refuge and agreed to change the 'Description' and 'Physical features of the environment and cultural and local context' information fields of HSM 63.

(165) New Zealand introduced WP 21 *Proposed update to HSM 75*, which proposed that the designation of HSM 75, Hut A at Scott Base, be updated to include its two remaining ancillary structures, the geomagnetic Huts G and H. It noted that Huts G and H dated from the 1957 IGY and Commonwealth Transantarctic Expedition and remained structurally unaltered on their original 1957 sites to the northwest of Hut A. Their physical positions were inextricably linked to a continuous record of scientific observations of the earth's magnetism, unbroken between 1957 and 2023.

(166) The Committee agreed to update the designation of HSM 75.

(167) Norway introduced WP 41 *Proposal for modifications to the coordinates, description and conservation status for HSM No. 24 Amundsen's Cairn*. In the 2017/18 austral summer, a private South Pole skiing expedition found that Amundsen's cairn was located at different coordinates than those provided in the HSM 24 listing. It also found that a plaque, which had been placed on the cairn to commemorate the Amundsen expedition, had been placed on the wrong cairn but at the correct location according to the HSM list. Norway recommended that the coordinates and description of HSM 24 be modified and slight adjustments be made to the conservation status description.

(168) The Committee agreed to modify the coordinates and description of HSM 24 and to make slight changes to the conservation status description.

(169) The Russian Federation introduced WP 44 *Proposal for the designation of a new Historic Site or Monument "Commemorative plaque commemorating the first visit to the Lake Untersee area"*. The paper proposed HSM designation for a brass plaque listing the names of five members of the 14th Soviet Antarctic Expedition. The Russian Federation noted that Lake Untersee was discovered by a German air expedition in 1939. In 1969 Lake Untersee was first visited by members of the geological and geophysical detachment of the 14th Soviet Antarctic Expedition (14 SAE), during which physical and geographical studies were carried out, including glaciological, geomorphological and hydrological observations, depth measurements and water sampling, collection of materials on moraine deposits and seabed sediments. The Russian Federation described the brass plaque with the participants' engraved names commemorating the expedition. Recalling Resolution 3 (2009) and highlighting the increasing scientific interest in the Lake Untersee area and frequent visits, the Russian Federation recommended that the CEP approve the registration of the 'Commemorative plaque of the first visit to the Lake Untersee area' as a new HSM.

(170) The Committee thanked the Russian Federation for its submission and highlighted the exploration's value to Antarctic science, especially concerning Lake Untersee. It approved the designation of the 'Commemorative plaque of the first visit to the Lake Untersee area' as a new HSM.

CEP advice to the ATCM on modifications and additions to the List of Historic Sites and Monuments

(171) The Committee agreed to forward four proposals for modifications to the List of Historic Sites and Monuments and one proposal for an addition to the List to the ATCM for approval by means of a Measure:

- HSM 24 Amundsen's Cairn
- HSM 63 Base Y, Horseshoe Island
- HSM 75 Hillary's TAE/IGY Hut 'A', Scott Base, Ross Island
- HSM 93 Wreck of *Endurance*
- HSM 96 Commemorative plaque of the first visit to the Lake Untersee area

(172) The Committee further agreed to update the listings on the Antarctic Protected Area database as follows:

- The Conservation Status of HSM 75 to read: "Following major conservation work by the New Zealand-based Antarctic Heritage Trust 2016-17, Hut A is structurally sound and weather tight and artefact collection has been conserved. Annual monitoring and maintenance ensure ongoing stability of this building. Conservation works have yet to be carried out on Huts G and H. The buildings are structurally sound and serviceable, showing the wear and tear expected for buildings some 65 years old. The New Zealand-based Antarctic Heritage Trust intend to carry out asbestos removal and conservation works on the buildings in the coming years."
- The photographs of HSM 75 to include photos of Hut G and H attached to WP 21 (Figure 1 to 4).
- The Conservation Status of HSM 24 to read: "The cairn remains intact. There is a paraffin tank inside the cairn, which is in good condition. A tin box containing two notes which was originally placed in the cairn by Amundsen, has long since been removed. A plaque commemorating Amundsen's expedition is placed at the base of the cairn."
- The photographs attached to WP 41 (Figure 2 to 4).
- The Management Tools of HSM 93 to read: "A Conservation Management Plan is being updated."

---

(173) The Committee noted the following Information Papers submitted under this agenda item:

- IP 37 *Report on the work carried out at the "Swedish Hut" on Snow Hill Island (HSM No. 38)* (Argentina).
- IP 38 *State of conservation of the Casa Moneta Museum (HSM No. 42)* (Argentina).
- IP 112 *Overview of Norwegian historic remains in Antarctica – and their priority* (Norway).
- IP 164 *The discovery of the remains of the Neptune 2-p-103 aircraft of the Argentinian navy by members of the 32nd Bulgarian Antarctic expedition* (Bulgaria, Argentina, Chile).

(174) The Committee noted the following Background Paper submitted under this agenda item:

- BP 20 *Digital Technology Making Antarctic Heritage Globally Accessible* (New Zealand).

9c) Site Guidelines

(175) The United States introduced WP 52 *Strengthening the usefulness of Site Guidelines for Visitors*, prepared jointly with IAATO. It noted how the CEP and ATCM had taken steps to strengthen the site-specific guidelines for visitors to Antarctica, including the most recent update to the Site Guidelines for Visitors Checklist through Resolution 4 (2021) at ATCM XLII. Previously, Resolution 3 (2019) at ATCM XLII recognised the need for a consistent approach to Site Guidelines for new and revised sites and established the Site Guidelines for Visitors Checklist to aid in this consistent approach. Following an analysis of the existing Site Guidelines for Visitors, the United States reported that out of 44 Site Guidelines, 40 (91%) of the existing Site Guidelines had not been updated using either the 2019 or 2021 guidance. Additionally, 29 (or 66%) of the existing Site Guidelines had been established or last updated more than ten years ago. The United States pointed out that revisions to the existing Site Guidelines would provide the information necessary to potentially improve site protection and effectively evaluate environmental impacts at these visitor sites and ensure that all Site Guidelines were in a consistent format. The United States further noted that the information in the Site Guidelines for Visitors could be further improved by providing additional contextual information about the site and the flora and fauna present. It recommended that Members: encourage proponent Members to revise existing Site Guidelines for Visitors using the Checklist adopted through Resolution 4 (2021) and continue through informal intersessional discussions to consider changes to the Site Guidelines for Visitors Checklist that would improve the consistency, completeness and usefulness of the information contained within the Site Guidelines.

(176) The Committee thanked the United States for its proposals and highlighted the need for and timeliness of revising existing Site Guidelines. The Committee expressed its disappointment that many Site Guidelines had not been updated in the agreed timeline.

(177) Some Members cautioned that there needed to be a balance between revising existing Site Guidelines and creating new Site Guidelines, given the increase in visitation to the Antarctic area. Some Members also suggested that sites with high visitation should be prioritised. Some Members noted the need to evaluate the obstacles that may exist to updating the Site Guidelines that had not been updated before proposing changes to the Site Guidelines for Visitors Checklist.

(178) The Committee agreed to endorse informal discussions to further develop the proposals in WP 52.

CEP advice to the ATCM on Site Guidelines

(179) The Committee agreed to recommend that the ATCM encourage proponent Parties to revise existing Site Guidelines for Visitors using the Checklist adopted through Resolution 4 (2021).

---

(180) Argentina introduced WP 57 *Proposed Guideline for Visitors to the Emperor Penguin Colony on Snow Hill Island*, which presented proposed Visitor Site Guidelines for the emperor penguin colony on Snow Hill Island. Argentina noted that the proposed Visitor Site Guidelines also established a code of conduct, identifying the possible impacts that visitors might generate and listing the requirements for disembarkation. Noting that the emperor penguin had not been designated as a Specially Protected Species, Argentina

stated there was a need to draw on other management tools to protect the emperor penguin colony and avoid additional stress factors. Argentina reported that it had already received valuable comments on its draft guidelines and hoped to continue refining the draft during the intersessional period through informal discussions.

(181) The Committee thanked Argentina for its paper and work over many years in developing guidance to manage the emperor penguin colony and the visitor site at Snow Hill. It noted the importance of developing Visitor Site Guidelines for this area, and some Members expressed their willingness to continue working with Argentina on their development.

(182) The Netherlands advised the Committee that it had previously permitted helicopter visits to the emperor penguin colony at Snow Hill Island but would cease permitting all recreational helicopter flights in line with Resolution 4 (2023) from the 2025-26 season. Recalling Resolution 4 (2023), the Netherlands indicated that it considered the use of helicopters to transport tourists to and from sites such as Snow Hill Island to fall within the scope of that Resolution, and stated that it hoped the helicopter guidelines included in the proposed Visitor Site Guidelines for Snow Hill Island would be temporary and that helicopter visits would eventually not be allowed.

(183) The Committee welcomed Argentina's offer to lead informal discussions on the proposed guidelines with a view to submitting a revised draft to CEP 27.

(184) The Committee noted the following Information Papers submitted under this agenda item:

- IP 104 *A Five-Year Overview and 2023-24 Season Report on IAATO Operator Use of Antarctic Peninsula Landing Sites and ATCM Visitor Site Guidelines* (IAATO).
- IP 108 *IAATO Site Management Methods* (IAATO).

9d) Marine Spatial Protection and Management

(185) No papers were submitted under this agenda item.

9e) Other Annex V Matters

(186) Dr Kevin Hughes (United Kingdom) introduced the second part of WP 43 *Subsidiary Group on Management Plans Report of activities during the intersessional period 2023-24.* The SGMP had the task under ToR 6 to review and revise, where necessary, existing management tools for the protection and subsequent management of environments and habitats at risk from climate change and to consider if and how they effectively considered climate change issues. The SGMP had discussed this task through two rounds of discussions and had concluded that it might be appropriate to prioritise, in the first round, the (Revised) Guide to the Preparation of Management Plans for Antarctic Specially Protected Areas (Resolution 2 (2011)). The SGMP had planned to initiate this work in the next intersessional period and report back to CEP 26 on progress. Dr Hughes noted that Members from Norway and the United Kingdom had led the review and the subsequent revision of the (Revised) Guide to the Preparation of Management Plans for Antarctic Specially Protected Areas (Resolution 2 (2011)). While the primary aim of the review had been to consider how effectively the Guide considered climate change issues, efforts had also been made to update other elements of the Guide since its last revision in 2011. Dr Hughes reported that the draft revised Guide had been submitted to the SGMP for consideration in February 2024, and the resulting proposed amendments had been incorporated into the draft revised Guide.

(187) Following further discussion and consultation, the Committee endorsed the SGMP's recommendations.

CEP advice to the ATCM on the revised Guide to the Preparation of Management Plans for Antarctic Specially Protected Areas

(188) The Committee agreed to advise the ATCM that, to support Parties to take climate change issues into consideration using existing management tools, it had agreed to:

- forward a draft Resolution on the revised Guide to the Preparation of Management Plans for Antarctic Specially Protected Areas for approval;
- request the Secretariat to make Appendix 2 in the amended Guide available.

---

(189) The SGMP also proposed a work plan for the 2024-25 intersessional period.

(190) The Committee thanked the SGMP for its advice and agreed to adopt the SGMP's proposed work plan for 2024-25:

Terms of Reference	Suggested tasks
ToRs 1 to 3	Review draft management plans referred by CEP for intersessional review and provide advice to proponents (including the three pending plans from the previous intersessional period)
	Submit Working Paper to CEP 27 on SGMP ToRs 1 to 3
ToRs 4 to 6	Work with relevant Parties to ensure progress on the review of management plans overdue for five-year review
	Pre-meeting review of all new and revised Management Plans and submit a summary of recommendations to CEP during the discussion of revised Management Plans.
	Review and update the SGMP work plan (additional task of SGMP considering SGCCR Report): To continue work on CCRWP action 2(e) "Review and revise where necessary existing management tools for protection and subsequent management of environments and habitats at risk from climate change," consider if and how they effectively take climate change issues into consideration and submit a progress report to CEP 27. Revise the ToRs and report back to CEP 27.

(191) The United States introduced WP 50 *Antarctic Specially Protected Area (ASPA) Summary Site Requirements*, prepared jointly with Australia and New Zealand. The United States noted that many visitors found that the level of detail and complexity of management plans made it difficult to understand their requirements. The proponents suggested providing permitted visitors with 'Summary Site Requirements' as a practical aid to understanding and implementing the detailed measures in the site management plan. The United States emphasised that the Summary Site Requirements would be entirely consistent with, supplement and not in any way replace the full management plan. It also noted that the summaries would not be mandatory and might only be valuable for a small number of sites that experienced high visitation. The proponents recommended that the Committee:

- note the importance of ensuring that those entering ASPAs were aware of the requirements of the Management Plan;

- consider the attached template model 'ASPA Summary Site Requirements' for endorsement as a recommendation to the ATCM;
- agree that 'ASPA Summary Site Requirements', if prepared, be included as an Annex to the relevant ASPA Management Plans; and
- consider revising the Guide to the Preparation of Management Plans for Antarctic Specially Protected Areas (Resolution 2 (2011)) to include the option of preparing 'ASPA Summary Site Requirements' as an aid for those working in ASPAs.

(192) The Committee thanked the proponents for this useful and practical idea, which would help permitted visitors better understand and comply with the requirements and restrictions applicable to them when entering protected areas.

(193) Some Members suggested enhancing the summaries, including translating them into the languages spoken by those who most frequently visited the site and including icons in the summaries to clarify specific requirements and restrictions. It was also noted that the summary site requirements could be useful for ASMA management plans, including indicating where ASPAs are located within an ASMA.

(194) Several Members emphasised the importance of ensuring that ASPA Summary Site Requirements remained voluntary, noting that they offered little value for seldomly visited ASPAs.

(195) The United Kingdom noted that if a visitor violated a restriction not mentioned in the Summary Site Requirements, it might be difficult to take action against them if they had not also been instructed to read the accompanying management plan. Some Members highlighted that the summary would form part of the management plan and that visitors would still need to formally comply with all the requirements of the management plan. They noted that this concern might be addressed by ensuring that the SGMP and CEP reviewed all ASPA Summary Site Requirements to ensure they captured every prohibited activity listed in the associated management plan.

(196) Following further discussion, the Committee agreed to add a sentence to the header of the ASPA Summary Site Requirements in the section 'Important'. The sentence would state that in the case of a conflict between the ASPA Summary Site Requirements and the management plan, the latter would be the authoritative document, and the provision of a summary did not relieve Parties of their obligations under Annex V, Article 7 of the Environmental Protocol, or of visitors to comply with the management plan.

(197) With these amendments, the Committee agreed to the recommendations in WP 50.

CEP advice to the ATCM on ASPA Summary Site Requirements

(198) The Committee advised the ATCM that it had agreed to endorse the development of ASPA Summary Site Requirements where relevant and useful to ensure that those entering ASPAs were aware of the requirements of the management plan. The Committee agreed that ASPA Summary Site Requirements would be included as an Annex to relevant ASPA management plans.

(199) The Committee noted that it would consider revising the Guide to the Preparation of Management Plans for Antarctic Specially Protected Areas (Resolution 2 (2011)) to include the option of preparing ASPA Summary Site Requirements.

---

(200) ASOC presented IP 151 *Spatial protection supports scientific research*. Referring to its analysis of all ASPA prior assessments submitted to the CEP between 2017 and 2024, ASOC noted that scientific research was part of the rationale and priorities for all proposed ASPAs. ASOC concluded that spatial protection helped to protect

environmental values and scientific research. ASOC also noted that protected areas in Antarctica contributed to global protection objectives, such as the at least 30% marine and land protection target of the 2022 Kunming-Montreal Global Biodiversity Framework, which was supported by most Parties.

(201) ASOC presented IP 152 *Developing a systematic approach to addressing the footprint of tourism*, which noted that the footprint of tourism activity in the Antarctic Peninsula was estimated to be larger than the area protected in ASPAs. ASOC recommended that:

- tourism be managed through additional methods, including systematic conservation planning, to determine which areas need additional protection and which are suitable for visitation;
- setting conservation targets, such as protecting at least 30% of terrestrial, coastal, and marine areas by 2030; and
- creating larger regional ASMAs focused on managing tourism.

(202) The Committee noted the following Information Papers submitted under this agenda item:

- IP 117 *Consolidation of the Argentine-Spanish Permanent Instrumental Volcano Monitoring Network on Deception Island volcano* (Argentina, Spain).
- IP 179 *Report from the management group for Antarctic Specially Managed Area (ASMA) No. 4 Deception Island for the period 2023/24* (Norway, Argentina, Chile, Spain, United Kingdom, United States, ASOC, IAATO).

Item 10: Conservation of Antarctic Flora and Fauna

10a) Quarantine and Non-native Species

(203) SCAR introduced WP 47 rev. 1 *Update on High Pathogenicity Avian Influenza in Antarctica*, prepared jointly with COMNAP, IAATO and CCAMLR. It provided an update on the current status of, known impacts of, and community actions in response to HPAI in Antarctica. SCAR noted that the first confirmed case of HPAI in the Antarctic Treaty area was reported in February 2024 and that confirmed cases have now been recorded at a total of seven sites, with suspected cases at an additional seven sites. Skuas appeared to be the most affected species, with kelp gulls, gentoo penguins, Adélie penguins and Antarctic fur seals having also shown signs of infection. SCAR noted that there was limited information about the mechanisms of virus transmission. There were clear indications that natural migration brought the virus to the Antarctic, and not direct human activity or interactions with wildlife. SCAR highlighted that its Antarctic Wildlife Health Network (AWHN) had established a central reporting database to collate detailed information on suspected and confirmed outbreaks throughout the sub-Antarctic and Antarctica, based on reports submitted by the community (IP 165 *SCAR response to risk of High Pathogenicity Avian Influenza in Antarctica*). SCAR emphasised that continued monitoring and reporting of suspected and confirmed cases was critical to further understanding the impact of HPAI on Antarctic wildlife. SCAR cautioned that there was a high likelihood that HPAI would remain present through the winter in areas where confirmed cases had been recorded, and the risk of high mortality would persist when species returned to breed in the 2024-2025 season. To address the ongoing risks of HPAI in Antarctica, SCAR, COMNAP and IAATO provided recommendations for the Committee to consider.

(204) The Committee commended the co-proponents for their collaboration and thanked Members for their coordination in monitoring and reporting. Many Members expressed their gratitude for the SCAR Antarctic Wildlife Health Network (AWHN) HPAI Database. The Committee expressed deep concern about the risks of HPAI for Antarctic

wildlife and human health and reaffirmed the importance of maintaining efforts to monitor and prevent the spread. Many Members shared information about the HPAI biosecurity measures implemented by their national Antarctic programmes, having incorporated suggestions from SCAR and COMNAP. Some Members suggested further streamlining communication on suspected cases of HPAI even more efficiently, especially for the Committee and for national competent authorities.

(205) Noting its implementation of biosecurity measures using the AHWN HPAI Practical Guide and COMNAP guidance, the Republic of Korea referred to IP 126 *Joint Efforts in the Rapid Detection of Avian Influenza Virus in Antarctic Wildlife on King George Island, South Shetland Islands*, prepared jointly with Chile, the Republic of Korea, and Uruguay, and IP 127 *Practices of the Korean Program to Prevent Highly Pathogenic Avian Influenza in Antarctica.*

(206) Regarding monitoring near research stations, some Members reported that they had detected suspected positive cases of HPAI, while other Members reported that they detected no positive cases but remained vigilant. Some Members noted that monitoring presented many logistical challenges in the field but remained of paramount importance. Looking forward, Members emphasised the utility of taking a precautionary approach, maintaining robust biosecurity measures for national Antarctic programmes and tour operators, and continuing open lines of communication amongst Members.

(207) The Netherlands called for a harmonised approach to HPAI monitoring and proposed a recently developed monitoring protocol as input for such harmonisation. The Netherlands further proposed two recommendations in addition to those already proposed in WP 47 rev. 1, noting that although contamination by human activities would likely not be the most important contamination pathway, the occurrence of HPAI called for a precautionary approach:

- To call on governments and non-governmental organisations to refrain from non-essential visits (only allowing essential science including on HPAI) to isolated bird and mammal populations in the upcoming years, awaiting further refinement of biosecurity protocols; and
- Once HPAI was confirmed on a specific site, to close that site for the remainder of the season for non-essential visits (only allowing essential science), to prevent human-induced transport.

(208) Many Members supported the additional recommendations put forward by the Netherlands, but some Members were unable to support these recommendations until having had the opportunity to consider whether these were based on the best available science.

(209) IAATO reported that its collaborative efforts to address HPAI and reporting procedures began prior to the 2022-23 season and were enhanced for the 2023-24 season. It highlighted the development of a communication and HPAI Wildlife Assessment Protocol in collaboration with SCAR and COMNAP. IAATO's protocols included a pre-landing assessment and 48-hour closures of sites when deemed necessary while SCAR performed a further assessment. IAATO noted that three sites had been closed this season as a result of the Protocol due to suspected HPAI.

(210) SC-CAMLR stated that it had consulted with experts to develop an HPAI response for observers and crews on fishing vessels and that it would continue collaborations with SCAR, COMNAP, IAATO and national Antarctic programmes to manage the risks associated with HPAI.

(211) ASOC encouraged continued collaboration and coordination on HPAI and stressed the need for a highly precautionary approach to ensure that human activities would not worsen the situation. ASOC recommended that Antarctic Treaty Parties be prepared to

take immediate precautionary action, including guidance on when to suspend scientific research and tourism.

(212) The Committee supported the recommendations in WP 47 rev. 1. Members also noted the relevance of WP 56 *Prevention, control and management of avian influenza in Antarctica: Need to unify biosafety criteria* (Chile) submitted to the ATCM on the topic, and considered that a number of issues discussed would be relevant for Parties to consider further in considering this paper.

CEP advice to the ATCM on HPAI in Antarctica

(213) The Committee agreed to advise the ATCM that it had agreed to the following recommendations:

- ensure the robust implementation of HPAI biosecurity guidelines and procedures to eliminate or mitigate the risk to humans, as well as the risk of spreading the disease within Antarctica through human activities;
- encourage continued vigilance and monitoring, as well as sample collection and testing where necessary expertise is available and permitted; and
- continue to report and share information on suspected and confirmed cases (including through the SCAR Antarctic Wildlife Health Network (AWHN) HPAI Monitoring Project) to support collaboration, inform decision-making, and improve scientific understanding of the spread and impact of the disease.

---

(214) IAATO presented IP 105 *IAATO Operator Response to High Pathogenicity Avian Influenza.* It emphasised that its biosecurity procedures had always been at the heart of the operations of its member operators and that robust procedures were already in place to protect Antarctica from introducing or spreading pathogens and non-native species. IAATO reported on its enhanced procedures for the 2023-2024 season, and highlighted tools they had provided for members to assist with the identification and control of HPAI. IAATO reported that it had also prepared explanations for its guests to help explain why stringent HPAI protocols were in place. Noting other papers from Parties about the need for further research to be done around HPAI, and how it may affect the Antarctic environment, IAATO noted the HPAI Australis Expedition, which had been funded by IAATO, the European Union Horizon Europe project Kappa-Flu, and the Spanish National Research Council (CSIC). IAATO noted that the team had investigated the presence and impact of HPAI infections in the region of the Trinity Peninsula and the Northern Weddell Sea. IAATO reported that anticipated actions for the upcoming season included improving protocols and tools, hosting Town Halls and webinars, and supporting meaningful science where appropriate.

(215) COMNAP presented IP 4 *Actions in Response to Heightened Risk of High Pathogenicity Avian Influenza (HPAI) in Antarctica.* COMNAP stated that preparing for and understanding HPAI was a highly collaborative and community effort. COMNAP emphasised that protocols had been developed and implemented so that human actions should not assist the spread of HPAI and that national Antarctic programmes, especially those in the Antarctic Peninsula, had biosecurity protocols based on COMNAP guidance and included HPAI information in pre-deployment and on-site training. COMNAP reported that national Antarctic programmes had collected over 1000 HPAI-related Antarctic samples to date. COMNAP would continue to discuss HPAI at its upcoming meeting in August 2024.

(216) The Republic of Korea presented IP 125 *Eradicating the Non-native Fly, Trichocera maculipennis, at the King Sejong Station: Outcomes and Insights*, which reported on its successful eradication of *Trichocera maculipennis* from King Sejong Station.

(217) Poland presented IP 99 *Monitoring of the presence of a non-native fly, Trichocera maculipennis, in ASPA No. 128* and IP 100 *Monitoring and eradication of a non-native grass, Poa annua, from the Western Shore of Admiralty Bay, King George Island, South Shetland Islands - 2023/2024 update*. Poland stated that from December 2023 to March 2024, 35 eradication events were carried out, which resulted in the removal of 4,149 grasses. It also reported that monitoring of the fly began in the summer of 2023 and that approximately 1000 individuals were observed in ASPA 128, while another five were observed within the station infrastructure. Poland noted that eradicating these two species was difficult, but efforts were ongoing. It also emphasised the usefulness of the British Antarctic Survey (BAS) Mini Guide to Antarctic Invasive Species and encouraged Members to read it.

(218) The Committee thanked Poland for its ongoing non-native species monitoring and eradication efforts and encouraged Poland to continue this important work and report back to the Committee.

(219) The Committee noted the following Information Papers submitted under this agenda item:

- IP 21 *New findings on the presence of non-native insects on the South Shetland Islands* (Chile).
- IP 28 *Monitoring and detection of Highly Pathogenic Avian Influenza (HPAI) in the South Shetland Islands and Antarctic Peninsula* (Chile).
- IP 39 *Avian Influenza: Situation in Argentine Antarctic Bases* (Argentina).
- IP 41 *Australia's Preparedness and Response for Avian Influenza* (Australia).
- IP 139 *Actions taken by the Peruvian Antarctic Programme to tackle Highly Pathogenic Avian Influenza (HPAI) in the surroundings of the ECAMP - Antarctic Peninsula* (Peru).
- IP 165 *SCAR response to risk of High Pathogenicity Avian Influenza in Antarctica* (SCAR).

10b) Specially Protected Species

(220) SCAR introduced WP 48 *Update on the status of emperor penguins in a variable and changing environment,* which presented the results of a recently published 10-year circumpolar assessment (2009-18) of emperor penguin colonies, based on satellite imagery, field validation surveys, and a Bayesian modelling framework, to assess the population size and trajectory of adult emperor penguins across their entire population range. SCAR noted that the paper provided context to a previous SCAR assessment that the emperor penguin might be vulnerable to the ongoing and projected efforts of climate change (ATCM XLIII - WP 37). It reported that the recent study showed a probable 9.6% decline over the study period, and noted that the probability of population decline was greater in regions where fast-ice trends were negative. The drivers of this change were not yet fully understood and SCAR therefore highlighted the importance of further internationally collaborative research. It further referred to a new Information Summary on emperor penguins that was published in the Antarctic Environments Portal. SCAR noted that previous decisions in the CEP emphasised the importance of continuing to report information on population assessments and monitoring for this species.

(221) The Committee thanked SCAR for WP 48 and its research on the emperor penguin.

(222) Many Members noted that the paper presented research data that supported earlier SCAR advice for Specially Protected Species designation. Members highlighted that researchers had observed a decline in emperor penguins and that the species' dependence on declining sea ice as a breeding location meant that the population decline was likely to continue.

(223) China suggested that WP 48 raised questions that related to the proposal in WP 34. China highlighted the large uncertainty in this assessment and the conclusion of WP 48 that drivers of the decline in penguin numbers were not yet fully understood, and the need for more extensive research and monitoring. China further noted that the assessment in WP 48 indicated a weak correlation (Spearman rank $r^2 = -0.52$) between regional fast-ice trends and population numbers. China also pointed out that the 2009 emperor penguin population had been adjusted in WP 48 and suggested that this adjustment accounted for the observed 9.6% decline.

(224) China supported the suggestions made in WP 48 to enhance collaboration across national Antarctic programmes on research to improve understanding about the factors that may be driving observed population change. China recalled its recommendations to develop a targeted research and monitoring plan for emperor penguins (ATCM XLIV - WP 35) and SCAR's previous conclusion that it may be appropriate to establish monitoring schemes for those species evaluated as Near Threatened (ATCM XXVIII - WP 34).

(225) SCAR clarified that while the assessment in WP 48 showed a limited correlation between trends in the population abundance index and regional fast-ice trends, this was still a statistically significant correlation. In addition, the assessment period of this study (2009-18) did not include the recent period of very low sea ice extent. SCAR added that recent research showed that early sea ice break-up had affected the breeding success of emperor penguins.

(226) SCAR further confirmed that the recently published analysis had updated a previous population estimate for 2009, noting that the new index of abundance was more conservative. The observed 9.6% population decline was not due to the population estimate having been updated, and in fact would have been greater without the adjustment.

(227) SCAR underscored the complexity of the drivers of change in emperor penguin populations, but reiterated that the population decline was clear. It further noted that uncertainty was an inherent feature of developing scientific understanding, and that the Committee had a long history of implementing a precautionary approach to protecting the Antarctic environment. SCAR noted that the future research required to better understand the causes of the observed population decline would benefit greatly from international collaboration across the scientific community, and encouraged all Members to consider participating in SCAR's Expert Group on Birds and Marine Mammals. Finally, SCAR noted that, in its opinion, the draft Specially Protected Species Action Plan proposed in WP 34 would help to support such research.

(228) IUCN reminded the Committee that the IUCN Red List 'Near Threatened' status did not indicate a stable population. IUCN noted that the publications cited in WP 34 could change the Red List status for emperor penguins when it would be next reviewed. IUCN stressed that the CEP did not need to wait and could utilise its own scientific expertise in making management decisions.

(229) The Committee thanked SCAR for its commitment to continue this work and encouraged interested Members to contribute to this important topic. It also supported SCAR's recommendation to encourage Parties to support enhanced collaboration across national Antarctic programmes to improve understanding about the species, and factors contributing to observed population change.

(230) The United Kingdom introduced WP 34 *Proposed designation of the emperor penguin as an Antarctic Specially Protected Species*, prepared jointly with Australia, France, Germany, Monaco, New Zealand, Norway, and the United States. The paper highlighted recent research showing a decline in the emperor penguin population over the period 2009-18 and the increasing failure of emperor penguin colonies due to the break-up of the fast ice upon which they breed. The United Kingdom noted that total fast-ice break-up prior to fledging would result in total or partial breeding failure. It further reported that the extent and concentration of spring and summer sea ice in all seasons around Antarctica had fallen significantly since 2016. Four of the lowest sea-ice extent minima occurred since 2016, and both 2022 and 2023 had record low summer sea-ice extents. In relation to IPCC models that predicted that sea ice would continue to decline under current levels of greenhouse gas emissions, the United Kingdom noted that this was predicted to result in further dramatic declines in emperor penguin breeding success and possible near-extinction by the end of the century. The United Kingdom concluded that this research indicated the challenges the species would face in future decades and provided a justification for designation of the emperor penguin as a Specially Protected Species.

(231) Considering these findings and earlier advice from SCAR, the co-authors recommended that the Committee:

- recognise the detrimental impact of climate change on emperor penguin population numbers and breeding success;
- forward the draft Specially Protected Species Action Plan for the emperor penguin (ATCM XLIV - WP 34) and SCAR's assessment of the conservation status of the emperor penguin as vulnerable to the ongoing and projected effects of climate change (ATCM XLIII - WP 37) to the ATCM for its consideration; and
- recommend to the ATCM (i) the designation of the emperor penguin as a Specially Protected Species under Annex II to the Protocol through adoption of the draft Measure in Appendix A, and (ii) that it encouraged Members to undertake the timely implementation of the Specially Protected Species Action Plan.

(232) The Committee thanked the co-proponents of WP 34 for their paper. Many Members expressed their concern about the conservation status of the emperor penguin, and highlighted that the research presented in WP 34 and WP 48 complemented, and did not detract from, SCAR's advice that the emperor penguin was vulnerable to ongoing and projected climate change. These Members supported decisive action utilising all the tools available to the Committee.

(233) Many Members strongly recommended that the Committee adopt a precautionary approach and designate the emperor penguin as a Specially Protected Species. They underlined that any remaining uncertainties about the drivers of the decline of emperor penguin populations should not prevent the ATCM from taking action, as uncertainty was inherent to scientific research. They also highlighted the importance of reducing the impact of additional human activities on the species, noting that HPAI was a new and high-risk threat. Many Members described emperor penguin research undertaken by their researchers and reported declines in penguin numbers at specific colonies.

(234) IUCN strongly endorsed the designation of the emperor penguin as a Specially Protected Species. IUCN noted that two-thirds of Members were also members of IUCN, and that uncertainty was not a reason to justify not designating the emperor penguin as a Specially Protected Species. The IUCN noted that the Committee did not have to wait to understand why populations were declining to move to protect the species and should instead act on the best available science. IUCN offered to work with the Committee to enhance protection of the emperor penguin.

(235) Many Members recommended progressing the draft Specially Protected Species Action Plan and stated that they would continue to apply and progress the draft Action Plan to their own activities.

(236) The Russian Federation raised concerns regarding its position on scientific uncertainty about the drivers of emperor penguin population decline. It also stated that the designation of the emperor penguin as a Specially Protected Species could lead to a reduction in scientific research on the species, citing the Ross seal Specially Protected Species designation as a hindrance to scientific research.

(237) In response, the United Kingdom noted that the Ross seal was designated as a Specially Protected Species in 1966 as a precaution as knowledge of its conservation status was lacking and higher protection would reduce human interference until necessary research was undertaken. Therefore, Specially Protected Species designation should enhance opportunities for research necessary to inform conservation action.

(238) China noted the consideration of WP 34 that Specially Protected Species designation for the emperor penguin would have little impact on changes in sea-ice extent and duration recorded in recent years that had resulted in emperor penguin colony failure, while Specially Protected Species designation would provide an opportunity to manage human activities in Antarctica to minimise additional impacts on the species. China further noted the conclusion of the draft Specially Protected Species Action Plan for the emperor penguin (ATCM XLIV - WP 34 Appendix) that other known and emerging terrestrial and marine threats affecting emperor penguins, except climate change, were considered as relatively small if not negligible. China further stressed that the draft Action Plan also summarised almost 10 types of management measures protecting the emperor penguin which already existed in the Antarctic Treaty System. As a result, China expressed its doubt that there was a sufficient scientific and management basis to designate the emperor penguin as a Specially Protected Species.

(239) The Committee was unable to reach consensus on the need to designate the emperor penguin as a Specially Protected Species and noted that the different views of the Committee should be communicated to the ATCM.

(240) It further agreed that protection of emperor penguins should remain a high priority for the Committee. Many Members highlighted that the CEP should continue encouraging the use of the draft Action Plan for the emperor penguin as guidance to support protection and management actions as well as research and monitoring. The Committee encouraged further intersessional discussion on this matter to resolve any outstanding questions in advance of next year's meeting and emphasised the importance of comprehensive participation in these discussions.

CEP advice to the ATCM on the proposed designation of the emperor penguin as an Antarctic Specially Protected Species

(241) The Committee agreed to advise the ATCM that most Members strongly supported recommending that the ATCM designate the emperor penguin as a Specially Protected Species, but consensus was not reached. The views expressed in the discussion are presented in paragraphs 230-240.

10c) Other Annex II Matters

(242) Spain presented IP 42 *Measures taken to guarantee the safety of activities carried out during the Spanish Antarctic campaign in the face of the threat of highly pathogenic avian influenza.* It emphasised the risk of HPAI to humans and reported that it now had an in situ biosecure molecular diagnostics laboratory at the Spanish Antarctic base

Gabriel de Castilla on Deception Island for early detection of the virus. Spain also reported that it had now developed its 'Procedure for landing in areas where animals are present and where infection with avian influenza is possible' aimed at scientific and technical staff on board ships.

(243) Spain presented IP 131 *terrANTALife: increasing the availability of terrestrial and freshwater biodiversity data checklists to inform CEP decision-making*, prepared jointly with SCAR and Australia. It stated that this was a curated biodiversity data checklist comprising a broad catalogue of known eukaryotic and prokaryotic life forms in Antarctic terrestrial ecosystems. Spain reported that this was the largest database on non-marine Antarctic biodiversity to date and supported Priority 2 'Biodiversity knowledge' in the CEP Five-year Work Plan.

(244) Belgium thanked Spain, SCAR and Australia, as well as SCAR's ANT-ICON Scientific Research Programme members, for their work and highlighted that the database included information on often neglected microorganisms. It further expressed appreciation that the database from the onset was designed to benefit both science and management.

(245) The Committee noted the following Information Paper submitted under this agenda item:

- IP 64 *Considerations for conducting and reporting on remotely piloted aircraft system (RPAS) surveys of penguin colonies* (United Kingdom, United States).

Item 11: Environmental Monitoring and Reporting

(246) Uruguay introduced WP 45 *Report of the Intersessional Contact Group (ICG) on an international environmental monitoring framework* which recalled that at CEP XXV, the CEP had agreed to establish an ICG tasked to develop a proposal for an overall framework for environmental impact monitoring. It noted that Parties had recognised the need to monitor, identify and assess the environmental impacts of human activities in the Antarctic Treaty area since the early 1970s. Uruguay reported that environmental monitoring had been on the agenda of most ATCMs since then. However, it stated that an agreed approach to monitoring was still lacking. Uruguay reminded Members that the Committee had identified monitoring and state of the environment reporting as a Priority 2 issue in its Five-year Work Plan. Uruguay stated that after the first round of consultations, several Members had expressed concerns about the viability of advancing as much as expected in just one year. Following the second round of discussions, many Members still emphasised the importance of establishing a common understanding of the purpose and scope of the monitoring framework, as well as the need to consider the SCAR-COMNAP Practical Guidelines for Developing and Designing Environmental Monitoring Programmes in Antarctica (2005) when designing the framework.

(247) As convenor of the ICG, Uruguay recommended that the CEP:

- extend the work of the ICG for two years;
- request the ICG to produce a report for CEP 27 providing agreed definitions of: what is an international environmental monitoring framework in the context of the Protocol, its purpose, and its scope;
- agree on specific parameters for the design of the framework;
- endorse an in-person workshop to be held before the ATCM 48 (2026) to establish explicit objectives for an international environmental monitoring framework, define criteria for its design, and agree on a roadmap for its implementation;
- commission a catalogue from COMNAP of ongoing environmental monitoring programmes undertaken by national Antarctic programmes to be presented to CEP 27; and

- commission a report from SCAR summarising ongoing continent or regional-wide monitoring schemes in Antarctica and the Southern Ocean conducted by other relevant bodies, such as SC-CAMLR and ACAP, which have designed and implemented integrated approaches to monitoring key attributes of conservation significance to Antarctica to be presented to CEP 27.

(248) The Committee thanked Uruguay for its report and commended Uruguay for its leadership in the ICG in developing a proposal for an overall framework for environmental monitoring. It emphasised the importance and complexity of environmental monitoring, which required further collaborative work. The Committee highlighted that environmental monitoring was an obligation under Article 12 of the Environment Protocol and an essential instrument of its work. In going forward, Members noted that it was fundamental to reach a common understanding on the environmental monitoring framework's objectives, purpose and scope. Many Members noted the desirability of receiving advice and information from SCAR and COMNAP, but also the scale of the task and the need to consider the burden it would entail for these organisations. Members noted several other elements that would be important to consider including: the need for international collaboration; the sharing of information and data; addressing the issue of cumulative impacts; utilising prior work on environmental monitoring; and acknowledging the differences in monitoring needs and methodologies across regions.

(249) SCAR stated that it was unlikely it could deliver a full report to CEP 27 but would continue providing the CEP with information, including extending the work described in IP 163 on Antarctic observing systems.

(250) COMNAP reported that it was not in a position to provide a report at CEP 27, but noted it would consider adding this to its work plan, and if required, asked Members to clarify what was expected in such a report.

(251) Members suggested deferring consideration of future steps, such as a possible in-person workshop until the ICG had defined the objectives, purpose and scope of the monitoring framework.

(252) The Committee agreed to extend the ICG for a further year and noted it should focus on a report that outlined its objectives, purpose and scope.

CEP advice to ATCM on an international framework for environmental monitoring

(253) The Committee agreed to advise the ATCM that it had extended the ICG tasked with discussing the development of an international framework for environmental monitoring for a further year, with the following Terms of Reference:

- Prepare a report for CEP 27, preparing agreed definitions of: (1) what an international environmental monitoring framework was in the context of the Environmental Protocol, (2) its purpose (i.e. a brief explanation of its objectives), and (3) its scope (i.e. a brief description of what the framework was intended to monitor), taking into account the relevant provisions of the Environmental Protocol as contained in WP 45 of CEP 26;

- Review existing continent-wide observation and monitoring initiatives with the aim of preparing an initial set of parameters and indicators that might be included in the framework;

- The ICG would work intersessionally and report back to CEP 27. Observers were welcome to participate in the ICG.

---

(254) The Committee welcomed the offer from Uruguay and the Netherlands to act as ICG convenors.

(255) SCAR introduced WP 46 *An example SCAR online application to inform State of the Antarctic Environment Reporting (SAER),* which described the outcomes of work by SCAR's Ant-ICON Scientific Research Programme to develop an example online application to inform elements of 'State of the Antarctic Environment Reporting' (SAER). It recalled that the CEP had identified state of the environment reporting as a priority issue. SCAR noted that if considered useful by the CEP, it could consider the delivery of further environmental datasets relevant to SAER using the same online application approach with different topics available in a centrally hosted location. It also suggested that the SCAR Antarctic Environments Portal provided an existing platform for delivering policy-relevant information to decision-makers and could prove an effective and updatable mechanism for centralised delivery of information relevant to SAER in the future. SCAR shared a video demonstrating how to use the example online application for non-native species data and visualisation.

(256) SCAR recommended that the CEP consider the example online application developed by SCAR as a mechanism for providing information relevant to SAER to the CEP. SCAR requested the views of Members about: the usefulness of this online tool; what further topics would be most usefully examined to support the Committee in their provision of advice to the ATCM on the state of the Antarctic environment; and whether and how information relevant to SAER might be routinely presented to provide context for CEP discussions.

(257) The Committee commended SCAR for this useful tool and for its continued input to CEP that guided policy and decision-making.

(258) Members suggested adding additional data layers about sites of scientific studies, incidences of HPAI, research station locations, human activity, pollution sources, and other topics related to priority issues identified by the CCRWP and Five-year Work Plan. Many Members also confirmed the SCAR Antarctic Environments Portal as a useful platform to consider for presenting information relevant to SAER. Several Members suggested an annual report of relevant information from SAER to the CEP, such as with the climate change indicators in WP 49. Some Members emphasised the need for current data and asked if the application could be regularly updated to reflect the most recent science.

(259) In response, SCAR welcomed the suggestions and acknowledged that it would be important to keep the data updated regularly and agreed to investigate options to achieve this. SCAR encouraged Members to share any information of relevance for the online application.

(260) The Committee agreed that SCAR's online application to inform State of the Antarctic Environment Reporting (WP 46) was regarded as a useful tool, and that it would likely improve the accessibility of data. SCAR encouraged Members to share information and data to increase the utility of the application.

(261) Portugal presented IP 13 *Changes in Antarctic microalgae may impact seals, penguins, whales and other higher predators,* prepared jointly with Brazil, France, and the United Kingdom. It reported on scientific evidence that the abundance of groups of microalgae was changing and noted that research based on an 11-year (2008–18) *in situ* dataset showed that environmental conditions were favouring a type of microalgae (cryptophyte) in coastal regions of the western Antarctic Peninsula. Portugal noted this had led to an increase in their overall abundance and biomass. Portugal highlighted that these results could have significant future implications at various Antarctic marine food web levels, as Antarctic krill preferred feeding on diatoms and Antarctic krill top

predators may be impacted. Portugal reinforced the importance of long-term Antarctic flora and fauna monitoring programmes to inform management actions.

(262) Portugal presented IP 14 *Consistency in animal spatial tracking for monitoring Antarctic top predators,* prepared jointly with Canada, France, Japan, the Republic of Korea, New Zealand, the United Kingdom and the United States. It highlighted that tracking information helped Members monitor Antarctic animal populations to support policies on conservation. Portugal noted that although animal tracking provided valuable data on the distribution of animals, it could be costly and logistically demanding for national Antarctic programmes. Portugal noted that scientific evidence using tracking data from seabird species (including Antarctic species) collected between 2002 and 2020 showed that collecting tracking data from one year could be sufficient to understand their distribution across years. It also stated that such scientific information could be relevant to aid monitoring programmes involving tracking Antarctic species, specifically allowing the identification of important sites for seabirds on feeding areas and threats at sea, and would be a step towards an effective network of marine protected areas.

(263) Portugal presented IP 167 *Marine Spatial Planning for a sustainable and climate-resilient Antarctic Ocean*, prepared jointly with Canada, France, Italy and IUCN. Portugal noted that the benefits of developing marine spatial planning were globally recognised and it was a vital instrument to support sustainable ocean management and governance. Portugal provided information on how marine spatial planning could be a valuable tool for Members to facilitate the development of policies and decision-making in Antarctic Treaty waters through analysing and allocating the spatial and temporal distribution of human activities in the Southern Ocean. Portugal encouraged Members to note the relevance of climate-smart marine spatial planning to support sustainable ocean use and conservation of Antarctic Treaty waters. It also aimed to use marine spatial planning in the future to accelerate and improve policies related to the Antarctic Treaty System.

(264) ASOC expressed support for IP 167, noting that marine spatial planning, together with existing tools such as ASPAs, ASMAs and marine protected areas, could lead to enhanced environmental protection outcomes.

(265) Germany presented IP 91 *Update 2024: International Science & Infrastructure for Synchronous Observation (Antarctica InSync)*, prepared jointly with Australia, Brazil, France, India, Italy, the Republic of Korea, New Zealand, Norway, Sweden, Switzerland, the United Kingdom and the United States. The paper reported on the progress with Antarctica InSync, first introduced to ATCM XLV in 2023, and noted that in November 2023, UNESCO had endorsed Antarctica InSync as a regional Ocean Decade programme aimed at better understanding, protecting, and sustainably managing the Southern Ocean and Antarctica in a year-round and circumpolar observational effort. Germany reported that the preparatory phase from 2024 to 2026 sought to organise synchronous scientific observation between 2027 and 2030 as a stepping stone to SCAR and International Arctic Science Committee joint plans for the International Polar Year 2032-33. It also noted that Antarctica InSync would organise a circumpolar assessment of the connections between ice, ocean, atmosphere, climate, environment, and life and that it contributed to SCAR's UN Decade Collaborative Centre for the Southern Ocean. Germany highlighted that the ATCM and CEP were key hubs to consult to understand policy and research needs and that the paper provided an update on the planning steps and opportunities to join the effort.

(266) SCAR presented IP 119 *Antarctic Environments Portal,* which provided an update on the publications, management, and operation of the Antarctic Environments Portal in support of issues of priority interest for the CEP. SCAR emphasised that the Antarctic Environments Portal continued to be an important vehicle for SCAR to provide impartial

and up-to-date information based on the best available science, to support informed engagement and discussion on issues of relevance to the work of the CEP and that it was recognised as an important contribution to the delivery of strategic science support in the SCAR Strategic Plan (2023-28). SCAR encouraged the CEP to continue to support the Antarctic Environments Portal and invited Members to consider mechanisms to support its ongoing provision of independent and objective information to the Antarctic Treaty System.

(267) ASOC presented IP 140 *Microplastic pollution in Antarctica: a complex challenge*. It noted that the Protocol on Environmental Protection to the Antarctic Treaty contained relatively limited provisions related to the prevention of microplastic pollution and recalled Resolution 5 (2019) on Reducing Plastic Pollution in Antarctica and the Southern Ocean, noting it represented a positive development and that it could be expanded upon to address the growing environmental problem of microplastic pollution in Antarctica. ASOC highlighted that microplastic pollution posed a serious, emerging threat to Antarctic and Southern Ocean ecosystems, particularly through the poorly understood pathways of ingestion, bioaccumulation, and biomagnification. It noted that more information was needed to understand the real impact of microplastic pollution in Antarctica and its sources and suggested that precautionary action could be required. ASOC recommended that the ATCM take further action to address the problem of microplastic pollution in the Antarctic Treaty Area, including considering the development of an action plan on microplastic pollution, considering a review of provisions related to the management of microplastic pollution in the Environmental Protocol, encouraging cooperation to reduce the use of microplastic in Antarctica, and supporting global initiatives to address the problem of microplastic pollution.

(268) SCAR presented IP 163 *Observing systems in Antarctica*, which provided an overview and examples of current long-term observation efforts to inform further work to assess gaps and establish sustained and coordinated observing systems. SCAR emphasised that well-supported, long-term monitoring of the physical and living environment was essential to understanding ongoing environmental changes in Antarctica and that collecting long-term observations was critical for detecting and understanding change and obtaining data needed for analyses and modelling. SCAR highlighted some of the investigations and programmes established at both regional and circumpolar scales, and those planned for further development. It stated that it was more pressing than ever to have an integrated, sustained and coordinated observing system to provide an understanding of the current Southern Ocean and Antarctic conditions, inform predictions of future states, and support policies and regulations for the benefit of society. SCAR also noted that it dedicated this paper to Prof. Craig Cary (1954-2024), a distinguished Antarctic ecologist, teacher, mentor, and long-standing SCAR expert.

(269) Norway thanked SCAR for providing the Committee with an overview and examples of current long-term observation efforts, appreciating this as a response to a request from the 2023 ATCM-CEP joint session on climate change. Noting the value of this overview, Norway suggested that it could be useful to maintain a live list for the reference of CEP Members in its ongoing work, in particular with respect to monitoring, as well as for those looking to initiate observation programmes. It also noted that it looked forward to information on identified observation gaps being brought back to the Committee at future meetings.

(270) SCAR presented IP 168 *Status of Observational Coverage and Gaps in the Southern Ocean*, which presented preliminary maps of observational coverage of the Southern Ocean, developed by the Southern Ocean Observing System (SOOS). SCAR and SOOS welcomed feedback from interested Members and programmes on those maps.

(271) SCAR presented IP 171 *Incorporation of Antarctica into the Global Monitoring Plan for Persistent Organic Pollutants through co-development of harmonised monitoring frameworks between National Antarctic Programmes and relevant national environmental agencies*, which reported on the Antarctic Monitoring and Assessment Programme (AnMAP), a joint initiative between SCAR, the Arctic Monitoring and Assessment Programme (AMAP), the United Nations Educational, Scientific, and Cultural Organization (UNESCO), and Griffith University, Australia. It noted that it aimed to facilitate sufficient and reliable chemical observation data from the Antarctic region to advise international chemical policy. SCAR outlined the Global Monitoring Plan (GMP) for Persistent Organic Pollutants (POPs). It highlighted the importance of incorporating Antarctica into the GMP by co-developing harmonised monitoring frameworks between national Antarctic programmes and relevant national environmental agencies.

(272) The Netherlands noted that several important papers on plastic pollution had been submitted to CEP 26. The papers highlighted that plastic pollution is a growing problem in Antarctica and that sources outside the Antarctic Treaty area generate most of this pollution. The Netherlands remarked that it was important that Parties enhance efforts to combat plastic pollution through their Antarctic activities but also through action outside the Antarctic Treaty area. Noting that the fifth session of the Intergovernmental Negotiating Committee on Plastic Pollution (INC-5), established under UNEA Resolution 5/14, would be meeting in November 2024, the Netherlands called on Members to send a strong message to INC-5, encouraging it to adopt an ambitious international legally binding instrument to end plastic pollution. The Netherlands presented a draft Resolution on ending plastic pollution, which it recommended the CEP forward to the ATCM for adoption.

(273) The Committee thanked the Netherlands for its proposal, underscoring its concern about the growing presence of plastic pollution in Antarctica and its threat to the Antarctic environment. Several Members shared examples of their research to detect and monitor plastic pollution in Antarctica, as well as efforts by their governments to phase out plastic pollution and to contribute to INC negotiations.

(274) Most Members expressed in-principle support for the Netherlands' proposal while noting that the draft Resolution had been produced and circulated during CEP 26, leaving them little time to consider it in depth or to consult with their plastics experts.

(275) The United Kingdom noted that it might not be practical to aim for a total end to plastic pollution, citing the example of aircraft tyres, which shed plastic and for which there was currently no viable alternative. Some Members, while supporting the intent of the proposal, suggested that it may be outside the remit of the CEP as a technical, scientific and environmental body to consider Parties' engagement with other intergovernmental processes, and that this aspect of the proposal may better be left to the ATCM's consideration. China stated that it had neither the authorisation nor the expertise to meaningfully participate in the discussion of the draft Resolution text at CEP 26 and suggested that the proponents bring back a formal proposal to CEP 27.

(276) The Netherlands thanked Members for allowing this important discussion and considering its proposal at short notice. The Netherlands believed there was a clear consensus on the need for urgent action to address plastic pollution in Antarctica. It thanked Members for their useful suggestions, which the Netherlands was ready to accommodate. In response to concerns about the legal aspects of the Resolution text, the Netherlands noted that this was not the first time the ATCM had called on another international body to conduct successful negotiations, citing the IMO's Polar Code negotiations as one example. The Netherlands also affirmed that the draft Resolution

contained already agreed text from UN Resolutions, which the CEP and ATCM would simply reaffirm.

---

(277) The CEP agreed to advise the ATCM that:

- it had discussed a draft Resolution on Towards Ending Plastic Pollution, but could not reach agreement in the time available during the meeting; and
- Members agreed that the draft Resolution should be brought to the attention of the ATCM.

---

(278) The Committee noted the following Information Papers submitted under this agenda item:

- IP 15 *Information on the implementation of the Nutec Plastics Initiative in the Argentine Antarctic Programme* (Argentina).
- IP 24 *Environmental Bioremediation "Recovering an environmental liability of more than 8 decades"* (Chile).
- IP 25 *Advances in the climate change sensor network on the Antarctic Peninsula* (Chile).
- IP 44 *Microplastic Pollution in the Weddell Sea and Dronning Maud Land Region* (Switzerland).
- IP 58 *Preliminary studies on microplastics from the Indian sector of the Southern Ocean* (India).
- IP 78 *Harmonizing environmental research and monitoring of chemical pollution in the Antarctic and the Southern Ocean - the POLEMP Project* (Germany, Australia, France, Italy, Republic of Korea, Portugal, United Kingdom, United States).
- IP 79 *Discharge of wastewater by ships in polar regions - Scope, impact & regulatory options* (Germany).
- IP 80 *Tourism monitoring in Antarctica – status and preliminary findings on developing a concept for the analysis of the impacts of tourism on the assets to be protected in the Antarctic* (Germany).
- IP 85 *Vagrant and visitor bird species in the Fildes Region, King George Island, between 1980 and 2023* (Germany).
- IP 87 *Report on the results of a population size survey on snow petrels supporting the designation of the proposed ASPA Otto-von-Gruber-Gebirge* (Germany).
- IP 94 *Updated progress on environmental monitoring of McMurdo Station infrastructure modernization activities* (United States).
- IP 148 *Contaminación por plásticos en Antártida, revisión del estado actual del conocimiento* (Peru).
- IP 170 *Plastic and Microplastic pollution in marine and coastal areas of Fildes Peninsula: a comprehensive diagnosis for one of the main and most accessible logistic hubs for Antarctica* (Uruguay).

(279) The Committee noted the following Background Papers submitted under this agenda item:

- BP 1 *Environmental monitoring system at the Belarusian Antarctic station* (Belarus).
- BP 28 *Update of Information on the Progress of the Renovation of the Henryk Arctowski Polish Antarctic Station on King George Island, South Shetland Islands* (Poland).
- BP 42 *Anthropogenic noise in Antarctic terrestrial environments: an update* (Uruguay).
- BP 51 *Assessment of marine litter on the Fildes Peninsula, King George Island in the summer seasons 2022–2023* (Russian Federation).

Item 12: Inspection Reports

(280) Australia presented IP 40 *Australian Antarctic Treaty and Environmental Protocol inspections: December 2023,* which provided a summary of inspections conducted by Australian observers in December 2023 of Dumont d'Urville station (France), Robert Guillard station (France and Italy) and the vessel *L'Astrolabe* (France). Noting that this was part of a reciprocal inspection programme, Australia emphasised that while France had provided the operational support for the Australian inspection team, the inspections and drafting of the inspection report had been carried out independently. Australia reported that the inspection team was given full access to all areas of the facilities visited and the vessel. Australia noted that it observed a strong commitment to Antarctic research and environmental protection in all discussions and interactions with personnel. The inspection team observed that the facilities and vessel were operating in full compliance with the Antarctic Treaty and that there was a high level of compliance with the Environmental Protocol. Australia noted that the inspection report attached to IP 40 contained the inspection team's recommendations, for consideration by France and Italy.

(281) France thanked Australia for its cooperation during the reciprocal inspections and for its useful report. It underscored that reciprocal inspections offered a valuable opportunity to share experiences and best practices to improve the management of activities in Antarctica. In response to some of the inspection team's key comments, France noted that it was: working to upgrade its existing facilities, especially in relation to wastewater management, energy production facilities, and waste management and transport; developing measures aimed at preventing the risks of spreading pathogens as well as a biosecurity strategy; and planning for the reconstruction of Dumont d'Urville station by 2050 with the aim of achieving carbon neutrality, using renewable energies, and limiting the impact of the station on the environment.

(282) France presented IP 86 *French inspection pursuant to Article VII of the Antarctic Treaty and Article 14 of the Protocol on Environmental Protection: February 2024,* which provided a summary of an inspection conducted by French observers in February 2024 of Australia's Casey station, the abandoned Wilkes station and the Wilkins aerodrome. France noted that this was part of an unprecedented cooperation with Australia and emphasised that the inspection was conducted independently. France reported that the inspection team was given full access to all infrastructure and sites of interest and found that infrastructure and activities complied with the provisions of the Antarctic Treaty and the Environmental Protocol. It identified a number of points of caution and possible areas for improvement, which were included in the inspection report for Australia's consideration.

(283) Australia thanked France for its inspection report, noting that it welcomed the inspection and the opportunity to provide operational support for France's inspection team. Australia also made remarks in response to some of the inspection team's recommendations. Regarding the former Wilkes station, Australia highlighted its

ongoing Cleaner Antarctica science program, which aimed to develop an actionable clean-up strategy for Australian stations and sites, (outlined in ATCM XLIV - IP 54), and noted that it would continue to report to the CEP on the initiative. Regarding the hydroponics facility at Casey station, Australia noted that it had previously shared its experience in operating hydroponics facilities with the CEP, and had developed, together with France, the *Guidelines to minimise the risks of non-native species and diseases associated with Antarctic hydroponics facilities* that were endorsed by the CEP and incorporated in the Antarctic Non-native Species Manual. Regarding the evacuation of historical waste, Australia noted that it had undertaken a dedicated project to document and quantify disused materials and was progressively returning such materials to Australia as resources and capacity allowed. Regarding the encouragement to implement additional preventive measures to prevent oil spills, Australia remarked that in addition to the Standard Operating Procedures and Operations Manuals in place for its Antarctic stations, master planning for Casey station was considering opportunities to enhance fuel transport, handling and storage arrangements.

(284) The Committee thanked and congratulated Australia and France on their reciprocal inspections, noting the significant effort involved and that these inspections took place at stations that were rarely inspected. Noting the importance of inspections for building trust and transparency in the Antarctic Treaty System, the Committee welcomed the conclusions presented in the inspection reports that both Parties were operating their Antarctic activities in compliance with the Antarctic Treaty and Environmental Protocol. Members welcomed Australia and France's efforts to take action to address the inspection team's recommendations and looked forward to receiving further updates from Australia and France in the future.

Item 13: General Matters

(285) India presented IP 57 *Maitri-II: Redevelopment of the Indian Research Station Maitri in Antarctica*. It stated that the redevelopment of Maitri research station was necessary due to the ageing of the original station built in 1988. India recalled that several Parties had performed inspections on the station over the years, and that it had taken subsequent recommendations into account. India reported that the National Centre for Polar and Ocean Research, an autonomous institute under the Ministry of Earth Sciences, Government of India was working on preparing a detailed Comprehensive Environmental Evaluation (CEE) as per the Revised Guidelines for Environmental Impact Assessment in Antarctica (2016) for presentation at a future ATCM.

(286) Spain thanked India for its plan to modernise its base and reduce environmental impact and expressed concern about the relocation affecting an environment that is not already impacted, specifically related to permafrost and hydrology. Spain offered to assist India to find a solution to reduce impact on the source of fresh water and waste treatment. In response, India confirmed that it had taken these concerns into consideration and that the water source would remain the same with only a small displacement from the existing area. India advised that it would consult with interested Parties during the development of the draft CEE.

(287) The Czech Republic reported that it had amended its law to implement Annex VI and the amended version of Annex II of the Protocol and that it was ratified on 4 April 2024.

(288) The Committee noted the following Secretariat Paper submitted under this agenda item:

- SP 8 *Review of gender-neutral language in ATCM and CEP documents*.

(289) In response to a query from Japan, the Secretariat confirmed that the work reported in SP 8 did not have any budget implications.

(290) The Committee noted the following Information Papers submitted under this agenda item:

- IP 97 *POLARIN – Polar Research Infrastructure Network* (Germany, Bulgaria, Finland, France, Italy, Norway, Poland, Portugal, Spain, Sweden).
- IP 121 *Update on the Southern Ocean contribution to the United Nations Decade of Ocean Science for Sustainable Development* (SCAR).
- IP 122 *Plans for a fifth International Polar Year 2032/33* (SCAR, WMO).
- IP 144 rev.1 *Unregulated discharges in the Antarctic Treaty Area: gray water from ships* (ASOC).

(291) The Committee noted the following Background Papers submitted under this agenda item:

- BP 2 *Addressing the science knowledge and information needs of the CEP – a New Zealand perspective* (New Zealand).
- BP 5 *"Optimización de la salud ambiental para las instalaciones antárticas en el Islote Isabel Riquelme"* (Chile).
- BP 53 *Plan de eliminación de residuos orgánicos e inorgánicos en el B.A.P. Carrasco* (Peru).

Item 14: Election Officers

(292) The Committee elected Ceisha Poirot from New Zealand as Chair for a two-year term and congratulated her on her appointment to the role.

(293) The Committee re-elected Dr Heike Herata from Germany as Vice-Chair for a second two-year term and congratulated her on her reappointment. She was also reappointed as convenor of the SGCCR.

(294) The Committee warmly thanked Dr Heike Herata and Dr Anoop Kumar Tiwari from India for their excellent leadership in CEP 26. It also warmly thanked Patricia Ortúzar from Argentina for her work, noting that she had stepped down from the position of Chair prior to the meeting.

Item 15: Preparation for the Next Meeting

(295) The Committee adopted the Preliminary Agenda for CEP 27 (Appendix 3).

Item 16: Adoption of the Report

(296) The Committee adopted its Report.

Item 17: Closing of the Meeting

(297) The Chair closed the Meeting on Friday, 24 May 2024.

Appendix 1

Summary of 5-year work plan for overview and progress tracking

		Action initiated	Action well advance	Action completed	CEP desires action completed
1. Environmental Pressure Priorities					
1a.	Introduction of non-native species & wildlife disease				
1a-1	Develop rapid response mechanisms and strategy for use in the instance of NNS and wildlife disease outbreaks.				
1a-2	Identify areas at high risk of wildlife disease and develop a monitoring program for such areas.				
1a-3	Identify biosecurity measures to prevent intra-continental species introductions.				
1b.	Impacts of Tourism and NGO activities and implications of growth and diversification				
1b-1	Develop mechanism enabling rapid considerations of and changes to existing Visitor Site Guidelines when immediate action is required for site management due to particular and urgent environmental concerns.				
1b-2	Develop tools and guidance – in addition to Visitor Site Guidelines – to avoid or minimize environmental impacts of tourism and NGO activities.				
1b-3	Discuss and prepare a framework for an environmental monitoring programme to assess the impacts of tourism and NGO activities that will also consider the potential for using sensitivity and carrying capacity to reduce impacts (relevant to action 2a-1).				
1b-4	Develop a framework for pre-assessment of new, novel or particularly concerning activities (also listed as action 2d-4).				
1b-5	Advance recommendations from ship-borne tourism ATME (2010) and the CEP tourism study (2012).				
1c.	Climate Change Implications for the Environment				
1c-1	Implement the Climate Change Response Work Programme, keep it updated and review and revise in light of relevant input and discussions.				
1d.	Long-range and local Pollution				
1d-1	Develop a framework for systematic, standardised and comparable sampling and data collection of pollution in the Antarctic as per Resolution 5 (2019).				

		Action initiated	Action well advance	Action completed	CEP desires action completed
1d-2	Identify appropriate mechanisms for updates on status and trends of pollutants in Antarctica, including a database to share and store information.				
1d-3	Assess the need for guidance /regional plan on avoiding pollution.				
2.	**Management Response Priorities**				
2a.	Facilitating monitoring and state of the environment reporting				
2a-1	Consider objectives for environmental monitoring needed to fulfil the requirement of the Environmental Protocol and develop an initial framework of parameters that based on environmental values and cumulative impact, would require monitoring to meet those objectives.				
2a-2	Identify existing monitoring activities and data available to undertake and report on an initial gap analysis between the existing monitoring portfolio and what is required.				
2a-3	Consider and facilitate the development of possible mechanisms to facilitate access to monitoring data in collaboration with SCAR, COMNAP, CCAMLR (CEMP) and other relevant expert organisations.				
2a-4	Develop a dashboard system or other appropriate mechanism enabling future periodic summary of monitoring activities in order to derive effective measures.				
2b.	Contributing to marine spatial protection and management				
2b-1	Identify needs for spatial marine protection and management measures.				
2b -2	Consider connectivity between land and ocean, and complementary actions that could be taken by Parties with respect to MPAs, incl. providing advice relating to Resolution 5 (2017).				
2b-3	Consider approaches to managing threats to the marine environment (e.g. pollution, wastewater discharge, etc.).				
2b-4	Consider how the protected areas system could be used to address the protection of terrestrial and marine environments from activities not covered by CCAMLR.				
2c.	Systematic approach to the protected areas system				
2c-1	Undertake work to advance actions agreed by the Committee from discussions on the protected areas workshop (2019) as presented in the final report of CEP XXII (para 182).				

		Action initiated	Action well advance	Action completed	CEP desires action completed
2c-2	Develop criteria for assessing the suitability of bird colonies for ASPA designation, including to identify what constitutes 'major colonies of breeding birds' as set out in Article 3.2(c) of Annex V to the Environmental Protocol, and identify IBAs that meet those criteria. (CEP XX (2017) para 157).				
2c-3	Assess the extent to which type locality of species are or should be represented within the series of ASPAs (CEP XXIX (2022) para 160).				
2c-4	Consider criteria for prioritising areas requiring protection based on risk.				
2c-5	Consider further mechanisms for protection of outstanding geological values.				
2d.	Implementing and improving the EIA provisions of Annex I				
2d-1	Develop guidelines for assessing cumulative impacts.				
2d-2	Develop guidance on how to undertake an environmental baseline condition survey.				
2d-3	Progress recommendations from the EIA assessment of effectiveness report (CEP XXIV, para 73).				
2d-4	Develop a framework for pre-assessment relating to new, novel or particularly concerning activities (also listed as action 1b-3).				
2e.	Increasing the understanding of and protecting Antarctic biodiversity				
2e-1	Consider status and threats to Antarctic biodiversity to inform management/protection of Antarctic biodiversity.				
2e-2	CEP to review further scientific advice on anthropogenic impacts on wildlife, and on basis of this consider any need for further management actions or measures.				
2e-3	Consider the risks for disease when developing biodiversity protocols or tools.				
2f.	Repair and Remediation of Environmental Damage				
2f-1	Develop an inventory of past sites of activities.				
2f-2	Develop an action plan with guidance and priority ranking to implement remediation where needed.				
2f-3	Develop a rapid response mechanism to respond to new or emerging issues.				
2g.	Designating and managing Historic Sites and Monuments				

		Action initiated	Action well advance	Action completed	CEP desires action completed
2g-1	Develop criteria for maintenance and management of HSMs, especially in the context of climate change and its impact on the environment, structure and/or objects.				
2g-2	Implement a regular review process of HSMs for effectiveness of management/conservation plans (if relevant) with regard to climate change and its impacts on the special values and potential clean-up.				
2g-3	Further develop criteria for Conservation Management Plans for historic sites, structure and/or objects.				
3. Operational Priorities					
3a.	Effective Operation of the CEP and Strategic Planning				
3a-1	Use the 5YWP actively to frame the CEP meetings.				
3a-2	Consider opportunities for enhancing the working relationship between the CEP and the ATCM.				
3a-3	Consider opportunities for enhancing broader participation by Members in the work of the Committee.				
3a-4	Implement a regular review of priorities based on ATCM requirements and changing circumstances.				
3a-5	Consider and discuss fundamental issues relating to the overall functioning of the CEP in light of the aims of the Environmental Protocol and the tasks of the CEP described in Art. 12 of the Protocol.				

CEP Five-year Work Plan

1. Environmental Pressure Priorities

1a. Introduction of non-native species & wildlife disease
Context: *Antarctica's biodiversity and its intrinsic values are potentially at risk from the introduction of non-native species, derived from a range of sources including human activities. Whilst guidance has been developed to minimise the risk of unintentionally introducing plants and invertebrates to the terrestrial environment, less attention has been given to marine non-native species (NNS) risks and microorganisms. Because of steadily growing human activities in the Antarctic Treaty area and progressing climate change, the risk of non-native organisms arriving and establishing is likely to increase. Further, the highly pathogenic avian influenza (HPAI) is a new threat to the area which deserves special attention and response measures. Regionality: This issue is of continent-wide importance, but particularly where human activities move between local and biogeographic regions such as in the Antarctic Peninsula region where human activity is increasing and climate is changing rapidly.*
Interlinks with: Climate Change Implications for the Environment; Tourism and NGO activities; Monitoring and state of the environment reporting; Biodiversity knowledge; Implementing and improving the EIA provisions of Annex I; Operating and further elaborating the Antarctic Protected Area system
Objective: Promote prevention measures. Facilitate monitoring of and surveillance for NNS and wildlife disease, particularly in high-risk areas, and ensure that – also through CEP actions – operators have enough information and tools to prevent and respond to NNS and wildlife disease.
Priority Actions 1. Develop rapid response mechanisms and strategy for use in the instance of NNS and wildlife disease outbreaks. 2. Identify areas at high risk of wildlife disease and develop a monitoring program for such areas. 3. Identify biosecurity measures to prevent intra-continental species introductions. **Regular Actions**: • Review the progress and contents of the CEP Non-native Species Manual (5 years). • Review reports on implementation and effectiveness of biosecurity measures and the NNS manual (as appropriate). • Review updates on status of known and new established non-native species (as appropriate). • Consider the current threat caused by the highly pathogenic avian influenza (HPAI) (annually).

1b. Impacts of tourism and NGO activities and implications of growth and diversification

Context: *Tourism and non-governmental activities in the Antarctic have grown steadily since they began in the 1950s. The numbers of tourists and tour operators have increased as has the number and geographic spread of sites being visited. The range of activities being undertaken has also diversified. It is recognised that tourism has the potential to result in impacts on the environmental, intrinsic, wilderness, aesthetic, and scientific values of Antarctica. Unforeseen cumulative impacts may also arise. Future development of Antarctic tourism and potential management responses need to be considered in light of the associated environmental implications, also in the context of other pressures being faced in the region, such as climate change. Regionality: This issue is particularly important in the Antarctic Peninsula region, ie. that area of Antarctica where human activity, including tourism, is most intense and growing/expanding and where the climate is changing rapidly. It is also important to maintain awareness of development in land-based tourism.*

Interlinks with:

Introduction of non-native species & wildlife disease; Climate Change Implications for the Environment; Repair and Remediation of Environmental Damage; Pollution; Monitoring and state of the environment reporting; EIA provisions; Biodiversity knowledge; Operating and further elaborating the Antarctic Protected Area system

Objective: Facilitate research and monitoring to understand the impacts of tourism and non-governmental activities, seen also in light of other environmental impacts and activities. Through CEP actions provide tools and guidance to avoid or minimize environmental impacts.

Priority Actions:

1. Develop mechanism enabling rapid considerations of and changes to existing Visitor Site Guidelines when immediate action is required for site management due to particular and urgent environmental concerns.
2. Develop tools and guidance – in addition to Visitor Site Guidelines – to avoid or minimize environmental impacts of tourism and NGO activities.
3. Discuss and prepare a framework for an environmental monitoring programme to assess the impacts of tourism and NGO activities that will also consider the potential for using sensitivity and carrying capacity to reduce impacts (relevant to action 2a-1).
4. Develop a framework for pre-assessment of new, novel or particularly concerning activities (also listed as action 2d-4).
5. Advance recommendations from ship-borne tourism ATME (2010) and the CEP tourism study (2012).

Regular Actions:

- Regular review of all existing Visitor Site Guidelines to ensure that they are accurate and up to date, including precautionary updates where appropriate (5 years).
- Regular review of the General Guidelines for Visitors to the Antarctic in collaboration with COMNAP, IAATO and other relevant expert organisations.
- Proactively monitor tourism trends (in collaboration with IAATO and the Secretariat) in order to identify and advise the ATCM on the need for additional management measures.

1c. Climate Change Implications for the Environment
Context: *Observations, modelling and global assessments describe significant changes in Antarctic physical and living systems, both marine and terrestrial. Changes in the Antarctic environments and dependent and associated ecosystems are linked to and influence climate change drivers globally. While climate change has global impacts and will contribute to ecosystem disruption and loss of biodiversity beyond the Antarctic region, the impacts on the Antarctic environment itself are also of substantial concern. Climate change may benefit some Antarctic species in the short-term, for example, by expanding the size of ice-free areas available for colonisation, or with warmer waters increasing biological productivity in the ocean. However, the loss of habitat for some species, the threat of non-native species establishing and outcompeting native species, the increasing exposure to re-released contaminants due to melting ice and the loss of natural values are some of the potential negative implications of climate change. Regionality: This issue is of continent-wide importance, although there are substantial variations in the degree of change and associated consequences.*
Interlinks with: Introduction of non-native species & wildlife disease; Monitoring and state of the environment reporting; Biodiversity knowledge; Repair or remediation of environmental damage; Operating and further elaborating the Antarctic Protected Area system; improving the EIA provisions of Annex I; Long-range and local pollution
Objective: To support efforts to monitor, mitigate, prepare for, adapt and build resilience to the environmental impacts of a changing climate and the associated implications for the governance and management of Antarctica through the implementation of the Climate Change Response Work Programme (CCRWP).
Priority Actions: 1. Implement the Climate Change Response Work Programme, keep it updated and review and revise in light of relevant input and discussions. **Regular Actions:** • Consider subsidiary group report, including CCRWP updates (annually).

1d. Long-range and local pollution
Context: *Antarctica is one of the cleanest, least polluted places on Earth. However, there is growing evidence that Antarctica is increasingly exposed to chemical stressors, both long-range transport of chemical contaminants and pollutants and local discharges. Some of these chemicals have been detected in the Antarctic environment and can accumulate in the Antarctic biota. Microplastic pollution has also been found in Antarctica, but the presence and effects of microplastics within food webs are still little understood. Similarly, the extent and effects of globally transported pollutants in Antarctica are poorly understood. Regionality: This issue is of continent-wide importance.*
Interlinks with: Climate Change Implications for the Environment; Repair or remediation of environmental damage; Facilitating monitoring and state of the environment reporting
Objective: Facilitate initiatives to systematically monitor and track long-range and local pollution and enable Parties to respond appropriately, including communication to/with relevant local and global organizations. Furthermore, provide guidance and tools to monitor, exchange data, reduce and respond to local and global pollution (primarily chemical and plastic pollution).
Priority Actions: **1.** Develop a framework for systematic, standardised and comparable sampling and data collection of pollution in the Antarctic as per Resolution 5 (2019). **2.** Identify appropriate mechanisms for updates on status and trends of pollutants in Antarctica, including a database to share and store information. **3.** Assess the need for guidance /regional plan on avoiding pollution. **Regular Actions:** • Review of the Clean-Up Manual to consider and include local pollution information (as appropriate).

2. Management Response Priorities

2a. Facilitating monitoring and state of the environment reporting

Context: *In order to meet the overarching objectives of the Protocol on Environmental Protection to the Antarctic Treaty (the Environmental Protocol) to protect the Antarctic environment it is helpful and necessary to develop relevant management actions. These may include actions to understand and report on if and how the Antarctic environment, on a continental, regional and local scale is changing, including understanding how human activities contribute to those changes. Environmental monitoring is fundamental to assessing and understanding change on all scales. Regionality: This issue is of continent-wide importance.*

Interlinks with:

Climate change implications; Biodiversity knowledge; Tourism and NGO activities; Repair or remediation of environmental damage; Long-range and local pollution; Operating and further elaborating the Antarctic Protected Area system

Objective: Encourage and facilitate coordinated and systematic monitoring efforts to understand the pressure on and state of the Antarctic environment. Enable reporting on state and trends for key environmental values in Antarctica.

Priority Actions:

1. Consider objectives for environmental monitoring needed to fulfil the requirement of the Environmental Protocol and develop an initial framework of parameters that based on environmental values and cumulative impact, would require monitoring to meet those objectives.
2. Identify existing monitoring activities and data available to undertake and report on an initial gap analysis between the existing monitoring portfolio and what is required.
3. Consider and facilitate the development of possible mechanisms to facilitate access to monitoring data in collaboration with SCAR, COMNAP, CCAMLR (CEMP) and other relevant expert organisations.
4. Develop a dashboard system or other appropriate mechanism enabling future periodic summary of monitoring activities in order to derive effective measures.

2b. Considering marine spatial protection and management
Context: *The biological and physical processes of the marine and terrestrial environments in the Antarctic Treaty Area are closely connected. Therefore, it is necessary to consider ocean-land connectivity to address protection and management needs. The Environmental Protocol aims to protect the Antarctic environment and associated and dependent ecosystems, which clearly link the continent and the surrounding ocean. While CCAMLR is responsible for marine spatial protection and management under the CAMLR Convention, the ATCM can take decisions within its competence with regard to marine spatial protection and management in accordance with the Antarctic Treaty and the Protocol. Regionality: This issue is of continent-wide importance.*
Interlinks with: Implementing a systematic approach to the protected areas system; Climate Change Implications for the Environment; Biodiversity knowledge; Monitoring and state of the environment reporting; Long-range and local pollution; Operating and further elaborating the Antarctic Protected Area system; Implementing and improving the EIA provisions of Annex I; Non-native Species and Diseases
Objective: Facilitate monitoring, protection and management of marine environmental values in i.a. marine ecosystems, species, processes and areas within the framework of the provisions of the Environmental Protocol.
Priority Actions: 1. Identify needs for spatial marine protection and management measures. 2. Consider connectivity between land and ocean, and complementary actions that could be taken by Parties with respect to MPAs, incl. providing advice relating to Resolution 5 (2017). 3. Consider approaches to managing threats to the marine environment (e.g. pollution, wastewater discharge, etc.). 4. Consider how the protected areas system could be used to address the protection of terrestrial and marine environments from activities not covered by CCAMLR. **Regular Actions:** • Maintain dialogue (or sharing of information) with SC-CAMLR on complementary actions within the competence of the ATCM (Resolution 5 (2017)) (continuously). • Hold joint CEP/SC-CAMLR workshops to progress spatial protection and management (c. 5 years).

2c. Operating and further elaborating the Antarctic Protected Area system
Context: *Annex V to the Environmental Protocol establishes a framework for designating Antarctic Specially Protected Areas (ASPAs) and Antarctic Specially Managed Areas (ASMAs). These areas are intended to support the objective of protecting comprehensively the Antarctic environment. Important work has been done to underpin the development of a representative series of ASPAs, including spatial analyses to identify distinct 'Environmental Domains' and 'Antarctic Conservation Biogeographic Regions'. The Antarctic Treaty Parties have agreed that these spatial frameworks are useful references to guide the designation of ASPAs within a systematic environmental-geographic framework, and the Committee for Environmental Protection (CEP) has recognised the need for a more systematic approach to the development of the protected area system. Regionality: This issue is of continent-wide importance.*
Interlinks with: Climate change implications, Tourism and NGO activities, Biodiversity knowledge; State of the environment and marine spatial protection; Implementing and improving the EIA provisions of Annex I
Objective: Assess the effectiveness of the current series of ASPAs with regard to the provisions of Article 3.2 of Annex V and provide advice on the further elaboration of the series of protected areas within a systematic environmental-geographical framework, as well as the managed areas in accordance with Article 4 of Annex V.
Priority Actions: 1. Undertake work to advance actions agreed by the Committee from discussions on the protected areas workshop (2019) as presented in the final report of CEP XXII (para 182). 2. Develop criteria for assessing the suitability of bird colonies for ASPA designation, including to identify what constitutes 'major colonies of breeding birds' as set out in Article 3.2(c) of Annex V to the Environmental Protocol, and identify IBAs that meet those criteria. (CEP XX report, paragraph 157). 3. Assess the extent to which type locality of species are or should be represented within the series of ASPAs (CEP XXIX report, paragraph 160). 4. Consider criteria for prioritising areas requiring protection based on risk. 5. Consider further mechanisms for protection of outstanding geological values. **Regular Actions:** • Review of ASPA/ASMA management plans, on the basis of the input from the Subsidiary Group on Management Plans, and proposed new locations (annually). • Consider the report of the SGMP (annually). • Maintain and update Protected Area guidance material (continuously).

2d. Implementing and improving the EIA process

Context: *The Environmental Protocol requires an EIA to be undertaken prior to an activity occurring in the Antarctic Treaty Area, and applies to almost all scientific, logistical and non-governmental activities that occur in the region. The EIA process is a key tool in helping to meet the Parties' commitment to comprehensively protect the Antarctic environment. The real benefit is the contribution it can make to planning an activity. Building EIA concepts into the processes and procedures for organising an activity from the very beginning increases the rigour of the planning process and greatly improves the identification of alternative, more environmentally friendly options. Increasing pressures on the Antarctic environment (through for example climate change and expanding human activity) means that the management benefits of the EIA tool will be increasingly important. It is therefore important to continue to review and, where appropriate, improve the effectiveness of the Antarctic EIA system.*

Interlinks with:

Climate Change Implications for the Environment; Tourism and NGO activities; Biodiversity knowledge; Facilitating monitoring and state of the environment reporting

Objective: Ensure clear guidance to all those responsible for activities in the Antarctic Treaty Area on conducting appropriate assessments of the activities. Assist through guidance material Parties in assessing, authorizing and permitting activities on basis of EIAs. Allow for a continuous improvement of the EIA process, where appropriate, including EIA follow-up and associated monitoring activities to assess the effectiveness of mitigation and management measures.

Priority Actions:

1. Develop guidelines for assessing cumulative impacts.
2. Develop guidance on how to undertake an environmental baseline condition survey.
3. Progress recommendations from the EIA assessment of effectiveness report (CEP XXIV, para 73).
4. Develop a framework for pre-assessment relating to new, novel or particularly concerning activities (also listed as action 1b-3).

Regular Actions:

- Review draft CEEs (as required).
- Review EIA guidelines and consider wider policy advising ATCM on updating, strengthening or otherwise improving existing rules and measures (5 years).

2e. Increasing the understanding of Antarctic biodiversity
Context: *Antarctica's biodiversity faces multiple threats. Fundamental knowledge about the environment is required in order to understand changes, impacts, risks, which species are found where, what are their dynamics, etc. While significant advances have been made in recent years, Antarctica's biological and ecological domains remain, to a large extent, unexplored. This hampers the development and implementation of effective management actions to protect biodiversity. At the same time, in accordance with the Environmental Protocol, management action should be considered on basis of the best scientific and technical advice available in keeping with the precautionary approach.* *Regionality: This issue is of continent-wide importance.*
Interlinks with: Climate change implications; Monitoring and state of the environment reporting; Operating and further elaborating the Antarctic Protected Area system; EIA provisions; Introduction of non-native species & wildlife disease; Tourism & NGO activities
Objective: Keep up to date on status and trends in biodiversity as well as the threats it is faced with and implement and inform relevant management actions.
Priority Actions: 1. Consider status and threats to Antarctic biodiversity to inform management/protection of Antarctic biodiversity. 2. CEP to review further scientific advice on anthropogenic impacts on wildlife, and on basis of this consider any need for further management actions or measures. 3. Consider the risks for disease when developing biodiversity protocols or tools. **Regular Actions**: • Consider the conservation status of Antarctic species at risk due to climate change (in line with CCRWP action).

2f. Repair and Remediation of Environmental Damage
Context: *Environmental damage in Antarctica might occur as the result of chemical, physical or biological processes resulting from human activities in the region. Furthermore, it might occur as a result of one-off or irregular activities, emergency situations as well as situations in which the environment has been impacted or degraded over longer periods of time. For example, chemical impacts might arise from pollution events, such as the critical failure of a fuel tank; a coastal shipping disaster, or the slow degradation of abandoned bases; leaking fuel tanks, or presence of waste dumps. Physical impacts might arise from regular foot and vehicle traffic causing tracking, or damage to vegetation, as well as from the establishment and ongoing operation of Antarctic stations and bases. Biological impacts might arise through the introduction and establishment of non-native species (cf. 1a.). The environmental and geographic characteristics of Antarctica means that response actions and approaches used elsewhere may need to be adapted, while taking into account the high standards of environmental protection in Antarctica relative to many other parts of the world. Regionality: This issue is of continent-wide importance, wherever there have been or are human activities ongoing in both marine and terrestrial environments.*
Interlinks with: Long-range and local pollution; Climate Change Implications for the Environment; Facilitating monitoring and state of the environment reporting; Introduction of non-native species & wildlife disease
Objective: Facilitate actions to identify, respond to, repair and remediate environmental damage in Antarctica. Furthermore, assess whether all actions that should have been taken with respect to repair and remediation have been taken and promote actions where they still may be required.
Priority Actions: 1. Develop an inventory of past sites of activities. 2. Develop an action plan with guidance and priority ranking to implement remediation where needed. 3. Develop a rapid response mechanism to respond to new or emerging issues. **Regular Actions:** • Review of the Clean-Up Manual and include new tools as appropriate. Members to work on the development of new techniques or guidelines (5 years) • Exchange of information on experience with repair and remediation (as appropriate)

2g. Designating and managing Historic Sites and Monuments
Context: *Human presence in Antarctica is, seen in the global context, extremely short. Since the first sighting of the continent in 1820, the extent to which humans have left their mark here is relatively limited. In such a context, the limited historical evidence of a connection between man and land becomes extremely visible and special. Parties therefore have given full recognition to the historic sites, structures and objects as part of humankind's cultural heritage. The Environmental Protocol makes the Historic Sites and Monuments (HSM) list the key mechanism for the protection of historic values in Antarctica.*
Interlinks with: Tourism and NGO activities; Climate Change Implications for the Environment; Operating and further elaborating the Antarctic Protected Area system; Facilitating monitoring and state of the environment reporting
Objective: Provide Parties with guidance and support in assessing and managing heritage.
Priority Actions: 1. Develop criteria for maintenance and management of HSMs, especially in the context of climate change and its impact on the environment, structure and/or objects. 2. Implement a regular review process of HSMs for effectiveness of management/conservation plans (if relevant) with regard to climate change and its impacts on the special values and potential clean-up. 3. Further develop criteria for Conservation Management Plans for historic sites, structure and/or objects.

3. Operational Priorities

3a. Effective Operation of the CEP and Strategic Planning
Context: *The CEP was established under the Environmental Protocol to advise the ATCM on matters relating to the protection of the Antarctic environment. After more than 25 years of work, the Committee has consolidated itself as a highly relevant and important component of the Antarctic Treaty system. The CEP agenda is normally full and broad and the Committee is in many ways "the workhorse of the ATCM". Focus on strategic planning provides for a focus of CEP activities on the environmental issues requiring the greatest attention.*
Interlinks with:
Objective: Ensure that the CEP systematically works to provide advice in implementing the objectives of the Environmental Protocol to the ATCM in a prioritized, strategic and efficient manner, facilitating broader participation by Members in the work of the Committee.
Priority Actions: 1. Use the 5YWP actively to frame the CEP meetings. 2. Consider opportunities for enhancing the working relationship between the CEP and the ATCM. 3. Consider opportunities for enhancing broader participation by Members in the work of the Committee. 4. Implement a regular review of priorities based on ATCM requirements and changing circumstances. 5. Consider and discuss fundamental issues relating to the overall functioning of the CEP in light of the aims of the Environmental Protocol and the tasks of the CEP described in Art. 12 of the Protocol. **Regular Actions:** • Keep the five-year work plan updated (annually).

Appendix 2

Climate Change Response Work Programme

CCRWP Vision: Taking into account the conclusions and recommendations from the ATME on Climate Change in 2010, the CCRWP provides a mechanism for identifying and revising goals and specific actions by the CEP to support efforts within the Antarctic Treaty System to prepare for, and build resilience to, the environmental impacts of a changing climate and the associated implications for the governance and management of Antarctica.

Climate related issue	Gaps/needs	Response area	Action/Task	Priority	Who	IP	CEP 2025	IP	CEP 2026	IP	CEP 2027	IP	CEP 2028	IP	CEP 2029
1) Enhanced potential for non-native species (NNS) introduction establishment	• Framework for surveillance for non-native species establishments in marine, terrestrial and freshwater environment • Response strategy for suspected NNS introductions • Assessment of whether existing regimes for preventing NNS introductions and transfer are sufficient. Analyze management tools applied in other areas.	Management	a. Continue to develop the NNS manual consistent with Resolution 6 (2011), ensuring climate change impacts are included, specifically in the • Development of surveillance approaches (p. 21) • Response strategy (p. 22) • EIA guidelines to include NNS (p. 18)	1.3	CEP / Parties	Parties to undertake preparatory work relevant to discussions on the development of NNS surveillance and response strategy Parties to consider implementation of the guidelines contained in the revised NNS manual in planning and conducting their activities	Initiate ISW[1] to develop a NNS surveillance and response strategy, including identification of highest risk habitats / bioregions Consider education initiatives around the risk from non-natives	ISW	Receive report of ISW and take action accordingly						Ensure climate change implications are sufficiently considered and appropriately incorporated in specific guidelines to reduce non-native species release with wastewater discharge Ensure climate change implications are sufficiently considered and appropriately incorporated in review of NNS manual

[1] ISW = Intersessional work (could be ICG, workshop, interested Members, etc.).

Climate related issue	Gaps/needs	Response area	Action/Task	Priority	Who	IP	CEP 2025	IP	CEP 2026	IP	CEP 2027	IP	CEP 2028	IP	CEP 2029
			b. Review of IMO biofouling guidelines to check adequacy for Southern Ocean and vessels moving from region to region	2.6	Interested Parties, Experts and Observers				Ensure climate change implications are sufficiently considered and appropriately incorporated in discussions relating to biofouling in accordance with 5-year work plan.						
	• Improved understanding of risks associated with relocation of native terrestrial species • Assessment and mapping of Antarctic habitats at risk of invasion • Assessment of risks of introducing non-native marine species • Techniques for eradication and control	Manageme nt / Research	c. Undertake a risk assessment: identification of native species at risk of relocation, and pathways for intra-continental transfer, including developing regional maps / descriptions of habitats at risk of invasion	1.2	CEP, Interested Parties, Experts and Observers	ISW	Receive report of ISW and take action accordingly								
			d. Undertake a risk assessment: identification of marine habitats at risk of invasion and pathways for introduction	1.8	CEP, Interested Parties, Experts and Observers					Parties to undertake preparatory work ahead of discussions on assessing the risks of marine NNS introductions.	Initiate ISW to assess risk of marine NNS introductions.	IS W	Receive report of ISW and take action accordingly	IS W	
			e. Progress actions identified under "Response" in NNS	1.6	NAPs, SCAR				Ensure climate change implications are sufficiently considered and appropriately incorporated in						

Climate related issue	Gaps/needs	Response area	Action/Task	Priority	Who	IP	CEP 2025	IP	CEP 2026	IP	CEP 2027	IP	CEP 2028	IP	CEP 2029
			manual (p. 22-23)						non-native species response strategy.						
	• Ongoing surveillance programme to identify status of NNS in light of climate change	Monitoring	f. Implement marine and terrestrial monitoring in accordance with established surveillance framework (pt. a) once developed	1.9	NAPs, SCAR	Parties to identify existing research projects relevant to surveillance and bring information to CEP 2025	Consideration of information provided by Parties (see 1a above).				Members to report on measures taken to implement surveillance and response actions		Members to report on measures taken to implement surveillance and response actions		
2) Change to the terrestrial (incl. aquatic) biotic and abiotic environment due to climate change	• Understanding how terrestrial and freshwater biota will respond to a changing climate and the impacts of these changes • Understanding as to how the abiotic terrestrial environment will change and the impacts of these changes	Research	a. Support and undertake research to improve understanding of current and future change and to inform response	1.9	NAPs, SCAR	SCAR to assimilate current major research initiatives relevant to terrestrial and freshwater environmental change.	Ongoing. Update reports to be provided, including through the Portal.		Ongoing. Update reports to be provided, including through the Portal.		Ongoing. Update reports to be provided, including through the Portal.		Ongoing. Update reports to be provided, including through the Portal.		
			b. Support and undertake long term monitoring of change, including collaborative efforts (e.g. ANTOS).	1.8	NAPs, SCAR	SCAR to develop advisory to CEP on relevance of ANTOS findings / outcomes to CEP's management interests.	Consider questions relating to access of data for the CEP		Consider obvious gaps in monitoring network and encourage initiation where such gaps exist						

Climate related issue	Gaps/needs	Response area	Action/Task	Priority	Who	IP	CEP 2025	IP	CEP 2026	IP	CEP 2027	IP	CEP 2028	IP	CEP 2029
			c. Continue to develop biogeographic tools (EDA and ACBR) to provide a sound basis for informing Antarctic area protection and management at regional and continental scales in light of climate change, including identifying the need to set aside reference areas for future research and identifying areas resilient to climate change	2.1	Initiated by interested Parties and CEP		Parties to provide update reports on research and management efforts to apply biogeographic tools.		Plan for a joint SCAR/CEP workshop on Antarctic biogeography, including to: identify practical management applications of biogeographic tools and future research needs	Joint SCAR/CEP workshop on Antarctic biogeography	Consider report from joint SCAR/CEP workshop on Antarctic biogeography				
			d. Identify and prioritize Antarctic biogeographic regions most vulnerable to climate change	1.6	Initiated by interested Parties and CEP		Parties to provide updates on research undertaken or planned to identify climate change vulnerable biogeographic regions.								

Climate related issue	Gaps/needs	Response area	Action/Task	Priority	Who	IP	CEP 2025	IP	CEP 2026	IP	CEP 2027	IP	CEP 2028	IP	CEP 2029
		Management	e. Review and revise where necessary existing management tools to consider if they afford the best practical adaptation measure to areas at risk from climate change	1.9	CEP								Parties to provide information on experiences of implementing climate considerations in the EIA process.		
			f. Holistic review of existing Protected Areas network and the process for designation of such areas to ensure they take into account climate change impacts and consider how we might respond.	1.8	CEP	SGMP ASMA work Initiate work on developing guidelines/criteria for delisting of protected areas due to ia. climate change	SGMP work on ASMA guidelines (cf. SGMP work plan) considers and incorporates appropriately the implication of climate change		Plan for intersessional workshop on a review of the protected areas system	WS[2]	Review the outcomes to the Protected Areas Workshop.				

[2] Workshop

Climate related issue	Gaps/needs	Response area	Action/Task	Priority	Who	IP	CEP 2025	IP	CEP 2026	IP	CEP 2027	IP	CEP 2028	IP	CEP 2029
			g. Initiate action with the aim to protect representative areas of each biogeographic region and areas likely to provide refuges to species and ecosystems at risk	2.3	CEP				Provide a status report to the ATCM on the status of the Antarctic Protected Areas network						
3) Change to marine near-shore abiotic and biotic environment (excluding OA)[3]	• Understanding, and have the ability to predict, near-shore marine changes and impacts of the change • Have a broader understanding of what monitoring data will be required to assess climate driven changes to the marine environment	Research	a. Encourage research by national programmes and SCAR and seek state of knowledge updates from SCAR on climate impacts on marine biota	2.0	NAPs, SCAR	SCAR to assimilate current research initiatives relevant to marine environmental change.	Ongoing. Update reports to be provided, incl. through the Portal.		Ongoing. Update reports to be provided, incl. through the Portal.		Ongoing. Update reports to be provided, incl. through the Portal.		Ongoing. Update reports to be provided, incl. through the Portal.		
			b. Support and undertake collaborative long-term monitoring of change (eg. SOOS, ANTOS) and seek regular state of knowledge reports from such programmes	2.0	NAPs, SCAR	SCAR to assimilate overview of how existing research programmes (such as SOOS and ANTOS) can contribute to CEP's management interests. CEP Chair to write to Steering Committees of relevant international research	Ongoing. Update reports to be provided, incl. through the Portal.		Ongoing. Update reports to be provided, incl. through the Portal.		Ongoing. Update reports to be provided, incl. through the Portal.		Ongoing. Update reports to be provided, incl. through the Portal.		

[3] Noting the importance of CCAMLR consideration of climate change issues in the Southern Ocean

Climate related issue	Gaps/needs	Response area	Action/Task	Priority	Who	IP	CEP 2025	IP	CEP 2026	IP	CEP 2027	IP	CEP 2028	IP	CEP 2029
						programmes (e.g. ICED) to request regular update reports.									
		Manageme nt	c. Review and revise where necessary existing management tools to consider if they afford the best practical adaptation measure to species or geographic areas at risk from climate change in SO	2.0	CEP										
			d. Continue to work with CCAMLR to identify the process for defining reference areas for future research	2.5	CEP, SCAR, SC-CAMLR										
			e. Maintain regular dialogue (or sharing of information) with SC-CAMLR on Climate Change and the Southern Ocean in particular on actions being taken	1.5	CEP, CCAMLR										Hold workshop as noted in CEP 5- year work plan
4) Ecosystem change due to ocean acidification	• Understanding of the impact of OA to marine biota and ecosystems	Research	a. As required, encourage further research and assessment on impact of OA informed by the SCAR report	1.9	NAPs, SCAR		Ongoing. Update reports to be provided, incl. through the Portal.		Ongoing. Update reports to be provided, incl. through the Portal.		Ongoing. Update reports to be provided, incl. through the Portal.		Ongoing. Update reports to be provided, incl. through the Portal.		

Climate related issue	Gaps/needs	Response area	Action/Task	Priority	Who	IP	CEP 2025	IP	CEP 2026	IP	CEP 2027	IP	CEP 2028	IP	CEP 2029
		Management	b. Consider forthcoming SCAR report on OA and act accordingly (understanding some actions may be best advanced by ATCM)	1.6	CEP, CCAMLR[4]										
			c. Review and revise where necessary existing relevant management tools to consider if they afford the best practical adaptation measure to species or geographic areas at risk from ocean acidification	2.4	CEP, CCAMLR[3]										
5) Climate change impact to the built (human) environment resulting in impacts on natural and heritage values	• Understanding how the abiotic terrestrial environment will change and how this might impact result in impacts on environmental or heritage values • Understanding of effects of climate change on contaminated sites and implications for species/ecosystems (eg. whether climate change will increase mobilization and exposure of species/ecosystems	Research	a. National operators to assess risk of change in climate (eg. permafrost) to their infrastructure and environmental consequences	3.0	NAPs, COMNAP				Encourage COMNAP to assess risk of climate change to NAP infrastructure				Receive report from COMNAP and take action accordingly		
			b. Assess risk of changes in climate change to HSM/heritage ASPA	2.9	Proponents and interested Parties								Initiate risk assessment for HSMs		

[4] Including in context of proposed joint workshop (pt. 3e)

Climate related issue	Gaps/needs	Response area	Action/Task	Priority	Who	IP	CEP 2025	IP	CEP 2026	IP	CEP 2027	IP	CEP 2028	IP	CEP 2029
	to contaminants and understanding how species/ecosystems will respond to exposure to such contaminants) • Understanding what conservation/remedial interventions might be applicable to counteract these impacts		c. Identify and specify research needs and communicate them to the research community	3.3	CEP										
		Management	d. Update the EIA guidelines to take into account the impacts of cc, eg ensuring proposed long term facilities are suitably resilient to cc and will not have an impact on species or habitats at risk.	1.9	CEP										
			e. Further development of the Clean Up Manual (ref. Resolution 2 (2013))	2.0	CEP		Ensure clean up manual revisions (referred to in 5 year plan) consider implications of climate change								
			f. Encourage national programmes to assess which sites of their past activities (not yet cleaned up or remediated) are more likely to be more affected by climate change in order to prioritize their work.	2.3	NAPs		Members to provide a status report to CEP on which sites of their past activities (not yet cleaned up or remediated) are more likely to be affected by climate change and plans to clean up or remediate those sites		Ongoing		Ongoing		Ongoing		

Climate related issue	Gaps/needs	Response area	Action/Task	Priority	Who	IP	CEP 2025	IP	CEP 2026	IP	CEP 2027	IP	CEP 2028	IP	CEP 2029
6. Marine and terrestrial species at risk due to climate change	• Understand population status, trends, vulnerability and distribution of *key* Antarctic species • Improved understanding of effect on climate on species at risk, including critical thresholds that would give irreversible impacts • Framework for monitoring to ensure the effects on *key* species are identified • Understand relationship between species and climate change impacts in important locations/areas	Research	a. Encourage research by national programmes, SCAR and SC-CCAMLR, eg. through programmes such as AntEco and AntERA, and CCAMLR Ecosystem Monitoring Program (CEMP)	1.6	NAPs, SCAR, SC-CCAMLR	SCAR to assimilate overview of how existing research programmes (such as AntERA and AntECO) can contribute to CEP's management interests.									
		Management	b. Consider if and how the IUCN red list criteria can be applied on a regional basis for the Antarctic in the context of climate change[5]	2.4	SCAR		Facilitate a programme of work with SCAR, SC-CAMLR, ACAP and IUCN to: 1. Initiate a programme to provide regular update reports on the status of Antarctic species		Facilitate a programme of work with SCAR, SC-CAMLR, ACAP and IUCN to: 1. Progress assessments on Antarctic species not yet assessed 2. Develop an approach to applying the Red List criteria on a regional basis in Antarctica						
			c. Begin a rolling programme of status assessments for Antarctic species focusing particularly on those species not currently assessed in	1.7	CEP, SCAR, ACAP		See 6 a above						Provide update report to ATCM on status, trends and vulnerability of Antarctic species		

[5] Note that the IUCN criteria cover many aspects besides climate change, and does not necessarily identify the effects solely due to climate change. The benefit of using IUCN criteria in our response to climate change will be assessed prior to its use.

Climate related issue	Gaps/needs	Response area	Action/Task	Priority	Who	IP	CEP 2025	IP	CEP 2026	IP	CEP 2027	IP	CEP 2028	IP	CEP 2029
			the IUCN Red List												
			d. Review and revise where necessary existing management tools, to consider if they afford the best practical adaptation measure to species at risk of climate change	1.6	CEP CCAMLR consid.		See 6 a above								
			e. Where necessary develop management actions to maintain or improve the conservation status of species threatened by climate change, eg. through SPS action plans.	2.0	CEP, SCAR CCAMLR consid.		Ongoing		Ongoing		Ongoing				
7. Marine, terrestrial and freshwater habitats at risk due to climate change	• Understand habitat status, trends, vulnerability and distribution • Improved understanding of the effects of	Research	a. Encourage research by national programmes, SCAR and SC-CCAMLR	2.4	NAPs, SCAR, SC-CCAMLR		Ongoing. Update reports to be provided, incl. through the Portal		Ongoing. Update reports to be provided, incl. through the Portal		Ongoing. Update reports to be provided, incl. through the Portal		Ongoing. Update reports to be provided, incl. through the Portal		

Climate related issue	Gaps/needs	Response area	Action/Task	Priority	Who	IP	CEP 2025	IP	CEP 2026	IP	CEP 2027	IP	CEP 2028	IP	CEP 2029
	climate change on habitat, eg. sea ice extent and duration, snow cover, ground moisture, microclimate, changing melt flows and consequences to lake systems • Improved understanding of potential expansion of human presence in Antarctica as a result of changes resulting from climate change through e.g. changes in sea ice distribution; collapse of ice shelves; expansion of ice-free area.	Manageme nt	b. Review and revise where necessary existing management tools to consider if they afford the best practical adaptation measure to habitats at risk of climate change. c. Assess vulnerabilities in space and time, exposed by changing sea-ice extent in the Antarctic Peninsula region and on this basis consider potential management implications for this region, noting that it experiences high and increasing levels of human activity.	2.3	CEP CCAMLR consid.										

Appendix 3

Preliminary Agenda for CEP 27 (2025)

1) Opening of the Meeting
2) Adoption of the Agenda
3) Strategic Discussions on the Future Work of the CEP
4) Operation of the CEP
5) Cooperation with other Organisations
6) Repair and Remediation of Environment Damage
7) Climate Change Implications for the Environment:
    a. Strategic Approach
    b. Implementation and Review of the Climate Change Response Work Programme
8) Environmental Impact Assessment (EIA):
    a. Draft Comprehensive Environmental Evaluations
    b. Other EIA Matters
9) Area Protection and Management Plans:
    a. Management Plans
    b. Historic Sites and Monuments
    c. Site Guidelines
    d. Marine Spatial Protection and Management
    e. Other Annex V Matters
10) Conservation of Antarctic Flora and Fauna:
    a. Quarantine and Non-native Species
    b. Specially Protected Species
    c. Other Annex II Matters
11) Environmental Monitoring and Reporting
12) Inspection Reports
13) General Matters
14) Election of Officers
15) Preparation for the Next Meeting
16) Adoption of the Report
17) Closing of the Meeting

3. Appendices

Preliminary Agenda for ATCM 47, Working Groups and Allocation of Items

Plenary

1) Opening of the Meeting
2) Election of Officers and Creation of Working Groups
3) Adoption of the Agenda, Allocation of Items to Working Groups and Consideration of the Multi-year Strategic Work Plan
4) Operation of the Antarctic Treaty System: Reports by Parties, Observers and Experts
5) Report of the Committee for Environmental Protection
6) Operation of the Antarctic Treaty System:
    a. Request from Canada to become a Consultative Party
    b. Request from Belarus to become a Consultative Party

Working Group 1: Policy, Legal, Institutional

6) Operation of the Antarctic Treaty System:
    c. General matters
7) Operation of the Antarctic Treaty System: Matters related to the Secretariat
8) Liability
9) Biological Prospecting in Antarctica
10) Exchange of Information
11) Education Issues
12) Multi-year Strategic Work Plan
    a. Policy, Legal and Institutional priorities

Working Group 2: Science, Operations, Tourism

12) Multi-year Strategic Work Plan
    b. Science, Operations and Tourism priorities
13) Safety and Operations in Antarctica
14) Inspections under the Antarctic Treaty and Environment Protocol
15) Science issues, future science challenges, scientific cooperation and facilitation
16) Implications of Climate Change for Management of the Antarctic Treaty Area
17) Tourism and Non-governmental Activities in the Antarctic Treaty Area, including Competent Authorities Issues

Special Working Group 3: Development of a Tourism Framework

18) Development of a Tourism Framework

Plenary

19) Preparation of the 48th Meeting
20) Any other Business
21) Adoption of the Final Report
22) Close of the Meeting

46th ANTARCTIC TREATY CONSULTATIVE MEETING May 20 to 30, 2024 | KOCHI-INDIA

HOST COUNTRY COMMUNIQUÉ

May 30, 2024

India hosted the 46th Antarctic Treaty Consultative Meeting (ATCM-46) and the 26th Committee for Environmental Protection (CEP-26) from May 20 to 30, 2024, in Kochi, Kerala. Organized by the Ministry of Earth Sciences through the National Centre for Polar and Ocean Research (NCPOR), the meetings included in-person and virtual attendance. A total of 404 delegates were registered for the 46th ATCM of which 328 attended in person and 76 attended virtually.

Ambassador Pankaj Saran chaired the ATCM, while Dr. Anoop Tiwari and Dr. Heike Herata chaired the CEP meeting. ATCM Working Group 2 was co-chaired by Dr Phil Tracey and Ms Sonia Ramos Garcia, and Working Group 1 was chaired by Mr Ted Kill. Dr Vijay Kumar acted as the Head of the Host Country Secretariat (HCS) and Dr Rahul Mohan as the Deputy Head of the HCS.

The event was officially opened by Mr. Kiren Rijiju, Union Cabinet Minister of Earth Sciences and was joined by Mr. Pavan Kapoor, Secretary (West) of the Ministry of External Affairs, and Dr. Shailesh Nayak, former Secretary of the Ministry of Earth Sciences. They emphasized India's commitment to Antarctic treaty, scientific research, climate change studies, and international cooperation. Mr Kiren Rijiju expressed India's honour to host the 46th ATCM and contribute to the global dialogue on peace, science, and environmental stewardship in Antarctica for preserving the most pristine wilderness on the planet. Mr Pavan Kapoor expressed the need to advance scientific knowledge to find solutions to climate change and global warming focused on polar ecosystems and India's readiness to collaborate in Antarctic affairs. Dr Shailesh Nayak discussed three major climate-change issues pertaining to Antarctica: polar ice melting and sea level rise, regional warming and ocean acidification.

The SCAR lecture as part of the Plenary, delivered by Dr. Sheeba Chenoli, highlighted the teleconnections between tropical regions and Antarctic region.

Key discussions at the ATCM included the operation of the Antarctic Treaty System, liability, biological prospecting, exchange of information, education issues, multi-year strategic work plan, safety, inspections, science issues, future science challenges, scientific cooperation, climate change implications, and tourism management. Agreements were reached on several important matters.

The Parties emphasised the importance of education and outreach activities as an essential element of cooperation enshrined in the Antarctic Treaty and the Environmental Protocol.

A significant outcome was the adoption of a decision on development of an ambitious, comprehensive, flexible and dynamic framework for regulating tourism and non-governmental activities in Antarctica. Parties also discussed consultative status requests from Canada and

Belarus, but no consensus was reached.

The CEP meeting, during May 20 to 24, addressed a range of issues and contributed to the implementation of the Environmental Protocol in Antarctica. The Committee agreed to prioritise further work on: the management implications of sea ice change; enhancing environmental impact assessment of major activities; protecting the emperor penguin; and developing an international framework for environmental monitoring in Antarctica. Following the advice of the CEP, the Parties adopted 17 revised and new management plans for ASPAs (Antarctic Specially Protected Areas) and several modifications /additions to the list of Historic and Monument Sites (HSMs). The ATCM also encouraged efforts to increase renewable energy use, and to ensure robust implementation of biosecurity measures to minimise the risks of Highly Pathogenic Avian Influenza (HPAI). The CEP elected a new Chair, Ms Ceisha Poirot from New Zealand.

The Host Country Secretariat through the National Centre for Polar and Ocean Research (NCPOR), Goa, conducted several side events to mark the ATCM-46 and CEP-26. It organised a seminar entitled 'Changing Antarctic and Challenges Ahead' jointly with the Korean Polar Research Institute and Polar Cooperation Research Centre, Kobe University on May 20, 2024 comprising of two panel discussions themed 'Challenges in Antarctic governance' and 'Shared responsibilities and commitments for Antarctic future'. A specially customised Mystamp with the ATCM-46 logo was released in collaboration with India Post. A mural themed 'Species-rich Antarctica' designed by school children, aimed at enhancing awareness of Antarctica amongst the young minds was unveiled in collaboration with Germany, ASOC and its partners. A panel discussion on 'Antarctic Synergy: Driving Scientific Progress through Diplomacy, fostering Cooperation through Research' was organised as an outreach effort for the college students from Kochi, Kerala.

The 46th Antarctic Treaty Consultative Meeting was held with an overarching theme of "Vasudhaiva Kutumbakam" a Sanskrit phrase which means one Earth, one family, one future. This resonates deeply with the Antarctic Treaty System – promoting peace, scientific cooperation, and preservation of Antarctica for mankind.

The Parties expressed their gratitude to India and their appreciation for the excellent hospitality and facilities provided for the Meeting.

The next ATCM (ATCM 47) will be hosted by Italy in 2025.

PART II

Measures, Decisions and Resolutions

1. Measures

Measure 1 (2024)

Antarctic Specially Protected Area No 116 (New College Valley, Caughley Beach, Cape Bird, Ross Island): Revised Management Plan

The Representatives,

Recalling Articles 3, 5 and 6 of Annex V to the Protocol on Environmental Protection to the Antarctic Treaty providing for the designation of Antarctic Specially Protected Areas ("ASPA") and approval of Management Plans for those Areas;

Recalling

- Recommendation XIII-8 (1985), which designated Caughley Beach as Site of Special Scientific Interest ("SSSI") No 10 and annexed a Management Plan for the Site;
- Recommendation XIII-12 (1985), which designated New College Valley as Specially Protected Area ("SPA") No 20;
- Recommendation XVI-7 (1991), which extended the expiry date of SSSI 10;
- Recommendation XVII-2 (1992), which annexed a Management Plan for SPA 20;
- Measure 1 (2000), which expanded SPA 20 to incorporate Caughley Beach, annexed a revised Management Plan for the Area, and provided that thereupon SSSI 10 shall cease to exist;
- Decision 1 (2002), which renamed and renumbered SPA 20 as ASPA 116;
- Measures 1 (2006), 1 (2011) and 1 (2016), which adopted revised Management Plans for ASPA 116;

Recalling that Recommendation XIII-8 (1985) was designated as no longer current by Measure 13 (2014);

Recalling that Recommendation XIII-12 (1985) was designated as no longer current by Decision 1 (2011);

Recalling that Recommendation XVI-7 (1991) did not become effective and was designated as no longer current by Decision 1 (2011);

Recalling that Recommendation XVII-2 (1992) did not become effective and was withdrawn by Measure 1 (2010);

Recalling that Measure 1 (2000) did not become effective and was withdrawn by Decision 3 (2017);

Noting that the Committee for Environmental Protection ("CEP") has endorsed a revised Management Plan for ASPA 116;

Desiring to replace the existing Management Plan for ASPA 116 with the revised Management Plan;

Recommend to their Governments the following Measure for approval in accordance with paragraph 1 of Article 6 of Annex V to the Protocol on Environmental Protection to the Antarctic Treaty:

That:

1. the revised Management Plan for Antarctic Specially Protected Area No 116 (New College Valley, Caughley Beach, Cape Bird, Ross Island), which is annexed to this Measure, be approved; and

2. the Management Plan for Antarctic Specially Protected Area No 116 annexed to Measure 1 (2016) be revoked.

Measure 2 (2024)

Antarctic Specially Protected Area No 128 (Western shore of Admiralty Bay, King George Island, South Shetland Islands): Revised Management Plan

The Representatives,

Recalling Articles 3, 5 and 6 of Annex V to the Protocol on Environmental Protection to the Antarctic Treaty providing for the designation of Antarctic Specially Protected Areas ("ASPA") and approval of Management Plans for those Areas;

Recalling

- Recommendation X-5 (1979), which designated the Western shore of Admiralty Bay, King George Island as Site of Special Scientific Interest ("SSSI") No 8 and annexed a Management Plan for the Site;
- Recommendations XII-5 (1983), XIII-7 (1985) and Resolution 7 (1995), which extended the expiry date for SSSI 8;
- Measure 1 (2000), which adopted a revised Management Plan for SSSI 8;
- Decision 1 (2002), which renamed and renumbered SSSI 8 as ASPA 128;
- Measure 2 (2006), which designated Admiralty Bay, King George Island as Antarctic Specially Managed Area ("ASMA") No 1, within which ASPA 128 is located;
- Measures 14 (2014) and 1 (2023), which adopted revised Management Plans for ASMA 1;
- Measures 4 (2014) and 2 (2019), which adopted revised Management Plans for ASPA 128;

Recalling that Recommendations X-5 (1979), XII-5 (1983), XIII-7 (1985) and Resolution 7 (1995) were designated as no longer current by Decision 1 (2011);

Recalling that Measure 1 (2000) did not become effective and was withdrawn by Decision 3 (2017);

Noting that the Committee for Environmental Protection ("CEP") has endorsed a revised Management Plan for ASPA 128;

Desiring to replace the existing Management Plan for ASPA 128 with the revised Management Plan;

Recommend to their Governments the following Measure for approval in accordance with paragraph 1 of Article 6 of Annex V to the Protocol on Environmental Protection to the Antarctic Treaty:

That:

1. the revised Management Plan for Antarctic Specially Protected Area No 128 (Western shore of Admiralty Bay, King George Island, South Shetland Islands), which is annexed to this Measure, be approved; and

2. the Management Plan for Antarctic Specially Protected Area No 128 annexed to Measure 2 (2019) be revoked.

Measure 3 (2024)

Antarctic Specially Protected Area No 135 (North-east Bailey Peninsula, Budd Coast, Wilkes Land): Revised Management Plan

The Representatives,

Recalling Articles 3, 5 and 6 of Annex V to the Protocol on Environmental Protection to the Antarctic Treaty providing for the designation of Antarctic Specially Protected Areas ("ASPA") and approval of Management Plans for those Areas;

Recalling

- Recommendation XIII-8 (1985), which designated North-east Bailey Peninsula, Budd Coast, Wilkes Land as Site of Special Scientific Interest ("SSSI") No 16 and annexed a Management Plan for the Site;
- Resolution 7 (1995) and Measure 2 (2000), which extended the expiry date of SSSI 16;
- Decision 1 (2002), which renamed and renumbered SSSI 16 as ASPA 135;
- Measures 2 (2003), 8 (2008) and 6 (2013), which adopted revised Management Plans for ASPA 135;

Recalling that Recommendation XIII-8 (1995) was designated as no longer current by Measure 13 (2014);

Recalling that Resolution 7 (1995) was designated as no longer current by Decision 1 (2011);

Recalling that Measure 2 (2000) did not become effective and was withdrawn by Measure 5 (2009);

Recalling that the Committee for Environmental Protection ("CEP") XXII (2019) reviewed and continued without changes the Management Plan for ASPA 135, which is annexed to Measure 6 (2013);

Noting that the CEP has endorsed a revised Management Plan for ASPA 135;

Desiring to replace the existing Management Plan for ASPA 135 with the revised Management Plan;

Recommend to their Governments the following Measure for approval in accordance with paragraph 1 of Article 6 of Annex V to the Protocol on Environmental Protection to the Antarctic Treaty:

That:

1. the revised Management Plan for Antarctic Specially Protected Area No 135 (North-east Bailey Peninsula, Budd Coast, Wilkes Land), which is annexed to this Measure, be approved; and
2. the Management Plan for Antarctic Specially Protected Area No 135 annexed to Measure 6 (2013) be revoked.

Measure 4 (2024)

Antarctic Specially Protected Area No 136 (Clark Peninsula, Budd Coast, Wilkes Land, East Antarctica): Revised Management Plan

The Representatives,

Recalling Articles 3, 5 and 6 of Annex V to the Protocol on Environmental Protection to the Antarctic Treaty providing for the designation of Antarctic Specially Protected Areas ("ASPA") and approval of Management Plans for those Areas;

Recalling

- Recommendation XIII-8 (1985), which designated Clark Peninsula, Budd Coast, Wilkes Land as Site of Special Scientific Interest ("SSSI") No 17 and annexed a Management Plan for the Site;
- Resolution 7 (1995), which extended the expiry date of SSSI 17;
- Measure 1 (2000), which adopted a revised Management Plan for SSSI 17;
- Decision 1 (2002), which renamed and renumbered SSSI 17 as ASPA 136;
- Measures 1 (2006), 7 (2009) and 5 (2014), which adopted revised Management Plans for ASPA 136;

Recalling that Recommendation XIII-8 was designated as no longer current by Measure 13 (2014).

Recalling that Resolution 7 (1995) was designated as no longer current by Decision 1 (2011);

Recalling that Measure 1 (2000) did not become effective and was withdrawn by Decision 3 (2017);

Recalling that the Committee for Environmental Protection ("CEP") XXII (2019) reviewed and continued without changes the Management Plan for ASPA 136, which is annexed to Measure 5 (2014);

Noting that the CEP has endorsed a revised Management Plan for ASPA 136;

Desiring to replace the existing Management Plan for ASPA 136 with the revised Management Plan;

Recommend to their Governments the following Measure for approval in accordance with paragraph 1 of Article 6 of Annex V to the Protocol on Environmental Protection to the Antarctic Treaty:

That:

1. the revised Management Plan for Antarctic Specially Protected Area No 136 (Clark Peninsula, Budd Coast, Wilkes Land, East Antarctica), which is annexed to this Measure, be approved; and
2. the Management Plan for Antarctic Specially Protected Area No 136 annexed to Measure 5 (2014) be revoked.

Measure 5 (2024)

Antarctic Specially Protected Area No 137 (Northwest White Island, McMurdo Sound): Revised Management Plan

The Representatives,

Recalling Articles 3, 5 and 6 of Annex V to the Protocol on Environmental Protection to the Antarctic Treaty providing for the designation of Antarctic Specially Protected Areas ("ASPA") and approval of Management Plans for those Areas;

Recalling

- Recommendation XIII-8 (1985), which designated Northwest White Island, McMurdo Sound as Site of Special Scientific Interest ("SSSI") No 18 and annexed a Management Plan for the Site;
- Recommendation XVI-7 (1991) and Measure 3 (2001), which extended the expiry date of SSSI 18;
- Decision 1 (2002), which renamed and renumbered SSSI 18 as ASPA 137;
- Measures 1 (2002), 9 (2008), 7 (2013) and 7 (2023), which adopted revised Management Plans for ASPA 137;

Recalling that Recommendation XIII-8 was designated as no longer current by Measure 13 (2014);

Recalling that Recommendation XVI-7 (1991) did not become effective and was designated as no longer current by Decision 1 (2011);

Recalling that Measure 3 (2001) did not become effective and was withdrawn by Measure 4 (2011);

Recalling that the Committee for Environmental Protection ("CEP") XXI (2018) reviewed and continued without changes the Management Plan for ASPA 137, which is annexed to Measure 7 (2013);

Noting that the CEP has endorsed a revised Management Plan for ASPA 137;

Desiring to replace the existing Management Plan for ASPA 137 with the revised Management Plan;

Recommend to their Governments the following Measure for approval in accordance with paragraph 1 of Article 6 of Annex V to the Protocol on Environmental Protection to the Antarctic Treaty:

That:

1. the revised Management Plan for Antarctic Specially Protected Area No 137 (Northwest White Island, McMurdo Sound), which is annexed to this Measure, be approved; and
2. the Management Plan for Antarctic Specially Protected Area No 137 annexed to Measure 7 (2023) be revoked.

Measure 6 (2024)

Antarctic Specially Protected Area No 141 (Yukidori Valley, Langhovde, Lützow-Holm Bay): Revised Management Plan

The Representatives,

Recalling Articles 3, 5 and 6 of Annex V to the Protocol on Environmental Protection to the Antarctic Treaty providing for the designation of Antarctic Specially Protected Areas ("ASPA") and approval of Management Plans for those Areas;

Recalling

- Recommendation XIV-5 (1987), which designated Yukidori Valley, Langhovde, Lützow-Holm Bay as Site of Special Scientific Interest ("SSSI") No 22 and annexed a Management Plan for the Site;
- Recommendation XVI-7 (1991), which extended the expiry date of SSSI 22;
- Measure 1 (2000), which adopted a revised Management Plan for SSSI 22;
- Decision 1 (2002), which renamed and renumbered SSSI 22 as ASPA 141;
- Measures 7 (2014) and 3 (2019), which adopted revised Management Plans for ASPA 141;

Recalling that Recommendation XIV-5 (1987) was designated as no longer current by Measure 13 (2014);

Recalling that Recommendation XVI-7 (1991) did not become effective and was designated as no longer current by Decision 1 (2011);

Recalling that Measure 1 (2000) did not become effective and was withdrawn by Decision 3 (2017);

Noting that the Committee for Environmental Protection ("CEP") has endorsed a revised Management Plan for ASPA 141;

Desiring to replace the existing Management Plan for ASPA 141 with the revised Management Plan;

Recommend to their Governments the following Measure for approval in accordance with paragraph 1 of Article 6 of Annex V to the Protocol on Environmental Protection to the Antarctic Treaty:

That:

1. the revised Management Plan for Antarctic Specially Protected Area No 141 (Yukidori Valley, Langhovde, Lützow-Holm Bay), which is annexed to this Measure, be approved; and

2. the Management Plan for Antarctic Specially Protected Area No 141 annexed to Measure 3 (2019) be revoked.

Measure 7 (2024)

Antarctic Specially Protected Area No 142 (Svarthamaren): Revised Management Plan

The Representatives,

Recalling Articles 3, 5 and 6 of Annex V to the Protocol on Environmental Protection to the Antarctic Treaty providing for the designation of Antarctic Specially Protected Areas ("ASPA") and approval of Management Plans for those Areas;

Recalling

- Recommendation XIV-5 (1987), which designated Svarthamaren as Site of Special Scientific Interest ("SSSI") No 23 and annexed a Management Plan for the Site;
- Resolution 3 (1996), which extended the expiry date of SSSI 23;
- Measure 1 (1999), which adopted a revised Management Plan for SSSI 23;
- Decision 1 (2002), which renamed and renumbered SSSI 23 as ASPA 142;
- Measures 2 (2004), 8 (2009), 8 (2014) and 4 (2019), which adopted revised Management Plans for ASPA 142;

Recalling that Recommendation XIV-5 was designated as no longer current by Measure 13 (2014);

Recalling that Resolution 3 (1996) was designated as no longer current by Decision 1 (2011);

Recalling that Measure 1 (1999) did not become effective and was withdrawn by Measure 8 (2009);

Noting that the Committee for Environmental Protection ("CEP") has endorsed a revised Management Plan for ASPA 142;

Desiring to replace the existing Management Plan for ASPA 142 with the revised Management Plan;

Recommend to their Governments the following Measure for approval in accordance with paragraph 1 of Article 6 of Annex V to the Protocol on Environmental Protection to the Antarctic Treaty:

That:

1. the revised Management Plan for Antarctic Specially Protected Area No 142 (Svarthamaren), which is annexed to this Measure, be approved; and

2. the Management Plan for Antarctic Specially Protected Area No 142 annexed to Measure 4 (2019) be revoked.

Measure 8 (2024)

Antarctic Specially Protected Area No 151 (Lions Rump, King George Island, South Shetland Islands): Revised Management Plan

The Representatives,

Recalling Articles 3, 5 and 6 of Annex V to the Protocol on Environmental Protection to the Antarctic Treaty providing for the designation of Antarctic Specially Protected Areas ("ASPA") and approval of Management Plans for those Areas;

Recalling

- Recommendation XVI-2 (1991), which designated Lions Rump, King George Island, South Shetland Islands as Site of Special Scientific Interest ("SSSI") No 34 and annexed a Management Plan for the Site;
- Measure 1 (2000), which annexed a revised Management Plan for SSSI 34;
- Decision 1 (2002), which renamed and renumbered SSSI 34 as ASPA 151;
- Measures 11 (2013) and 5 (2019), which adopted revised Management Plans for ASPA 151;

Recalling that Measure 1 (2000) did not become effective and was withdrawn by Decision 3 (2017);

Noting that the Committee for Environmental Protection ("CEP") has endorsed a revised Management Plan for ASPA 151;

Desiring to replace the existing Management Plan for ASPA 151 with the revised Management Plan;

Recommend to their Governments the following Measure for approval in accordance with paragraph 1 of Article 6 of Annex V to the Protocol on Environmental Protection to the Antarctic Treaty:

That:

1. the revised Management Plan for Antarctic Specially Protected Area No 151 (Lions Rump, King George Island, South Shetland Islands), which is annexed to this Measure, be approved; and
2. the Management Plan for Antarctic Specially Protected Area No 151 annexed to Measure 5 (2019) be revoked.

Measure 9 (2024)

Antarctic Specially Protected Area No 154 (Botany Bay, Cape Geology, Victoria Land): Revised Management Plan

The Representatives,

Recalling Articles 3, 5 and 6 of Annex V to the Protocol on Environmental Protection to the Antarctic Treaty providing for the designation of Antarctic Specially Protected Areas ("ASPA") and approval of Management Plans for those Areas;

Recalling

- Measure 3 (1997), which designated Botany Bay, Cape Geology, Victoria Land as Site of Special Scientific Interest ("SSSI") No 37 and adopted a Management Plan for the Site;
- Decision 1 (2002), which renamed and renumbered SSSI 37 as ASPA 154;
- Measures 2 (2003), 11 (2008), 12 (2013) and 6 (2019), which adopted revised Management Plans for ASPA 154;

Recalling that Measure 3 (1997) did not become effective and was withdrawn by Measure 6 (2011);

Noting that the Committee for Environmental Protection ("CEP") has endorsed a revised Management Plan for ASPA 154;

Desiring to replace the existing Management Plan for ASPA 154 with the revised Management Plan;

Recommend to their Governments the following Measure for approval in accordance with paragraph 1 of Article 6 of Annex V to the Protocol on Environmental Protection to the Antarctic Treaty:

That:

1. the revised Management Plan for Antarctic Specially Protected Area No 154 (Botany Bay, Cape Geology, Victoria Land), which is annexed to this Measure, be approved; and

2. the Management Plan for Antarctic Specially Protected Area No 154 annexed to Measure 6 (2019) be revoked.

Measure 10 (2024)

Antarctic Specially Protected Area No 160 (Frazier Islands, Windmill Islands, Wilkes Land, East Antarctica): Revised Management Plan

The Representatives,

Recalling Articles 3, 5 and 6 of Annex V to the Protocol on Environmental Protection to the Antarctic Treaty providing for the designation of Antarctic Specially Protected Areas ("ASPA") and approval of Management Plans for those Areas;

Recalling

- Measure 2 (2003), which designated Frazier Islands, Windmill Islands, Wilkes Land, East Antarctica as ASPA 160 and adopted a Management Plan for the Area;
- Measures 13 (2008) and 14 (2013), which adopted revised Management Plans for ASPA 160;

Recalling that the Committee for Environmental Protection ("CEP") XXII (2019) reviewed and continued without changes the Management Plan for ASPA 160, which is annexed to Measure 14 (2013);

Noting that the CEP has endorsed a revised Management Plan for ASPA 160;

Desiring to replace the existing Management Plan for ASPA 160 with the revised Management Plan;

Recommend to their Governments the following Measure for approval in accordance with paragraph 1 of Article 6 of Annex V to the Protocol on Environmental Protection to the Antarctic Treaty:

That:

1. the revised Management Plan for Antarctic Specially Protected Area No 160 (Frazier Islands, Windmill Islands, Wilkes Land, East Antarctica), which is annexed to this Measure, be approved; and

2. the Management Plan for Antarctic Specially Protected Area No 160 annexed to Measure 14 (2013) be revoked.

Measure 11 (2024)

Antarctic Specially Protected Area No 161 (Terra Nova Bay, Ross Sea): Revised Management Plan

The Representatives,

Recalling Articles 3, 5 and 6 of Annex V to the Protocol on Environmental Protection to the Antarctic Treaty providing for the designation of Antarctic Specially Protected Areas ("ASPA") and approval of Management Plans for those Areas;

Recalling

- Measure 2 (2003), which designated Terra Nova Bay, Ross Sea as ASPA 161 and adopted a Management Plan for the Area;
- Measures 14 (2008), 15 (2013) and 7 (2019), which adopted revised Management Plans for ASPA 161;

Noting that the Committee for Environmental Protection ("CEP") has endorsed a revised Management Plan for ASPA 161;

Desiring to replace the existing Management Plan for ASPA 161 with the revised Management Plan;

Recommend to their Governments the following Measure for approval in accordance with paragraph 1 of Article 6 of Annex V to the Protocol on Environmental Protection to the Antarctic Treaty:

That:

1. the revised Management Plan for Antarctic Specially Protected Area No 161 (Terra Nova Bay, Ross Sea), which is annexed to this Measure, be approved; and

2. the Management Plan for Antarctic Specially Protected Area No 161 annexed to Measure 7 (2019) be revoked.

Measure 12 (2024)

Antarctic Specially Protected Area No 171 (Narębski Point, Barton Peninsula, King George Island): Revised Management Plan

The Representatives,

Recalling Articles 3, 5 and 6 of Annex V to the Protocol on Environmental Protection to the Antarctic Treaty providing for the designation of Antarctic Specially Protected Areas ("ASPA") and approval of Management Plans for those Areas;

Recalling

- Measure 13 (2009), which designated Narębski Point, Barton Peninsula, King George Island as ASPA 171 and adopted a Management Plan for the Area;
- Measures 11 (2014) and 8 (2019), which adopted revised Management Plans for ASPA 171;

Noting that the Committee for Environmental Protection ("CEP") has endorsed a revised Management Plan for ASPA 171;

Desiring to replace the existing Management Plan for ASPA 171 with the revised Management Plan;

Recommend to their Governments the following Measure for approval in accordance with paragraph 1 of Article 6 of Annex V to the Protocol on Environmental Protection to the Antarctic Treaty:

That:

1. the revised Management Plan for Antarctic Specially Protected Area No 171 (Narębski Point, Barton Peninsula, King George Island), which is annexed to this Measure, be approved; and

2. the Management Plan for Antarctic Specially Protected Area No 171 annexed to Measure 8 (2019) be revoked.

Measure 13 (2024)

Antarctic Specially Protected Area No 173 (Cape Washington and Silverfish Bay, Terra Nova Bay, Ross Sea): Revised Management Plan

The Representatives,

Recalling Articles 3, 5 and 6 of Annex V to the Protocol on Environmental Protection to the Antarctic Treaty providing for the designation of Antarctic Specially Protected Areas ("ASPA") and approval of Management Plans for those Areas;

Recalling

- Measure 17 (2013), which designated Cape Washington and Silverfish Bay, Terra Nova Bay, Ross Sea as ASPA 173 and adopted a Management Plan for the Area;
- Measure 9 (2019), which adopted a revised Management Plans for ASPA 173;

Noting the approval of the Commission for the Conservation of Antarctic Marine Living Resources ("CCAMLR"), at its thirty-first meeting, of the draft Management Plan for the ASPA at Cape Washington and Silverfish Bay, Terra Nova Bay, Ross Sea;

Noting that the Committee for Environmental Protection ("CEP") has endorsed a revised Management Plan for ASPA 173;

Desiring to replace the existing Management Plan for ASPA 173 with the revised Management Plan;

Recommend to their Governments the following Measure for approval in accordance with paragraph 1 of Article 6 of Annex V to the Protocol on Environmental Protection to the Antarctic Treaty:

That:

1. the revised Management Plan for Antarctic Specially Protected Area No 173 (Cape Washington and Silverfish Bay, Terra Nova Bay, Ross Sea), which is annexed to this Measure, be approved; and

2. the Management Plan for Antarctic Specially Protected Area No 173 annexed to Measure 9 (2019) be revoked.

Measure 14 (2024)

Antarctic Specially Protected Area No 175 (High Altitude Geothermal sites of the Ross Sea region): Revised Management Plan

The Representatives,

Recalling Articles 3, 5 and 6 of Annex V to the Protocol on Environmental Protection to the Antarctic Treaty providing for the designation of Antarctic Specially Protected Areas ("ASPA") and approval of Management Plans for those Areas;

Recalling

- Recommendation XIV-5 (1987), which designated the Summit of Mount Melbourne, Victoria Land as Site of Special Scientific Interest ("SSSI") No 24, and annexed a Management Plan for the Site;
- Resolution 3 (1996) and Measure 2 (2000), which extended the expiry dates for SSSI 24;
- Recommendation XVI-8 (1991), which designated Cryptogam Ridge, located within SSSI 24, as Specially Protected Area ("SPA") No 22, and annexed a Management Plan for the Area;
- Recommendation XIII-8 (1985), which designated Tramway Ridge as SSSI 11, and Measures 2 (1995) and 3 (1997), which adopted revised Management Plans for the Site;
- Decision 1 (2002), which renamed and renumbered SSSI 24 and SPA 22 as merged ASPA 118 (Summit of Mount Melbourne, Victoria Land), and renamed and renumbered SSSI 11 as ASPA 130;
- Measures 2 (2003) and 5 (2008), which adopted revised Management Plans for ASPA 118;
- Measure 1 (2002), which adopted a revised Management Plan for ASPA 130;
- Measure 13 (2014), which merged ASPAs 118 and 130 as ASPA 175 (High Altitude Geothermal sites of the Ross Sea region), and adopted a Management Plan for the Area;

Recalling that Resolution 3 (1996) was designated as no longer current by Decision 1 (2011);

Recalling that Measure 2 (2000) did not become effective and was withdrawn by Measure 5 (2009);

Recalling that Recommendation XVI-8 (1991) and Measure 2 (1995) did not become effective and were designated as no longer current by Decision 1 (2011);

Recalling that Measure 3 (1997) did not become effective and was withdrawn by Measure 6 (2011);

Noting that the Committee for Environmental Protection ("CEP") has endorsed a revised Management Plan for ASPA 175;

Desiring to replace the existing Management Plan for ASPA 175 with the revised Management Plan;

Recommend to their Governments the following Measure for approval in accordance with paragraph 1 of Article 6 of Annex V to the Protocol on Environmental Protection to the Antarctic Treaty:

That:

1. the revised Management Plan for Antarctic Specially Protected Area No 175 (High Altitude Geothermal sites of the Ross Sea region), which is annexed to this Measure, be approved; and

2. the Management Plan for Antarctic Specially Protected Area No 175 annexed to Measure 13 (2014) be revoked.

Measure 15 (2024)

Antarctic Specially Protected Area No 180 (Danger Islands Archipelago, North-eastern Antarctic Peninsula): Management Plan

The Representatives,

Recalling Articles 3, 5 and 6 of Annex V to the Protocol on Environmental Protection to the Antarctic Treaty providing for the designation of Antarctic Specially Protected Areas ("ASPA") and approval of Management Plans for those Areas;

Noting that the Committee for Environmental Protection ("CEP") has endorsed a Management Plan for ASPA 180;

Recognising that this area supports outstanding environmental, scientific, historic, aesthetic or wilderness values, or ongoing or planned scientific research, and would benefit from special protection;

Desiring to designate Danger Islands Archipelago, North-eastern Antarctic Peninsula as ASPA 180 and to approve the Management Plan for this Area;

Recommend to their Governments the following Measure for approval in accordance with paragraph 1 of Article 6 of Annex V to the Protocol on Environmental Protection to the Antarctic Treaty:

That:

1. Danger Islands Archipelago, North-eastern Antarctic Peninsula be designated as Antarctic Specially Protected Area No 180; and

2. the Management Plan, which is annexed to this Measure, be approved.

Measure 16 (2024)

Antarctic Specially Protected Area No 181 (Farrier Col, Horseshoe Island, Marguerite Bay): Management Plan

The Representatives,

Recalling Articles 3, 5 and 6 of Annex V to the Protocol on Environmental Protection to the Antarctic Treaty providing for the designation of Antarctic Specially Protected Areas ("ASPA") and approval of Management Plans for those Areas;

Noting that the Committee for Environmental Protection ("CEP") has endorsed a Management Plan for ASPA 181;

Recognising that this area supports outstanding environmental, scientific, historic, aesthetic or wilderness values, or ongoing or planned scientific research, and would benefit from special protection;

Desiring to designate Farrier Col, Horseshoe Island, Marguerite Bay as ASPA 181 and to approve the Management Plan for this Area;

Recommend to their Governments the following Measure for approval in accordance with paragraph 1 of Article 6 of Annex V to the Protocol on Environmental Protection to the Antarctic Treaty:

That:

1. Farrier Col, Horseshoe Island, Marguerite Bay be designated as Antarctic Specially Protected Area No 181; and

2. the Management Plan, which is annexed to this Measure, be approved.

Measure 17 (2024)

Antarctic Specially Protected Area No 182 (Western Bransfield Strait and Eastern Dallmann Bay): Management Plan

The Representatives,

Recalling Articles 3, 5 and 6 of Annex V to the Protocol on Environmental Protection to the Antarctic Treaty providing for the designation of Antarctic Specially Protected Areas ("ASPA") and approval of Management Plans for those Areas;

Recalling

- Recommendation XVI-3 (1991), which designated Western Bransfield Strait, off Low Island, South Shetland Islands, as Site of Special Scientific Interest ("SSSI") No 35 and annexed a Management Plan for the Site;
- Measure 3 (2001), which extended the expiry date of SSSI 35;
- Decision 1 (2002), which renamed and renumbered SSSI 35 as ASPA 152;
- Measures 2 (2003), 10 (2009) and 9 (2015), which adopted revised Management Plans for ASPA 152;
- Recommendation XVI-3 (1991), which designated East Dallmann Bay, off Brabant Island as SSSI 36 and annexed a Management Plan for the Site;
- Measure 3 (2001), which extended the expiry date of SSSI 36;
- Decision 1 (2002), which renamed and renumbered SSSI 36 as ASPA 153;
- Measures 2 (2003), 11 (2009) and 10 (2015), which adopted revised Management Plans for ASPA 153;

Recalling that Recommendation XVI-3 (1991) did become effective and was withdrawn by Measure 10 (2009);

Recalling that Measure 3 (2001) did not enter into effect and was withdrawn by Measure 4 (2011);

Noting that the Committee for Environmental Protection ("CEP") has endorsed a new ASPA at Western Bransfield Strait and Eastern Dallmann Bay, incorporating ASPAs 152 and 153, and has endorsed the Management Plan annexed to this Measure;

Recognising that this area supports outstanding environmental, scientific, historic, aesthetic or wilderness values, or ongoing planned scientific research, and would benefit from special protection;

Desiring to designate Western Bransfield Strait and Eastern Dallmann Bay as ASPA 182, incorporating ASPAs 152 and 153, and to approve the Management Plan for this Area;

Recommend to their Governments the following Measure for approval in accordance with paragraph 1 of Article 6 of Annex V to the Protocol on Environmental Protection to the Antarctic Treaty:

That:

1. Western Bransfield Strait and Eastern Dallmann Bay be designated as Antarctic Specially Protected Area No 182;

2. the Management Plan, which is annexed to this Measure, be approved;

3. the Management Plan for Antarctic Specially Protected Area No 152, annexed to Measure 9 (2015), and the Management Plan for Antarctic Specially Protected Area No 153, annexed to Measure 10 (2015), be revoked; and

4. Antarctic Specially Protected Areas No 152 and No 153 shall not be used as future designations.

Measure 18 (2024)

Revised List of Antarctic Historic Sites and Monuments: new Historic Sites and Monuments No 96 and updating information for Historic Sites and Monuments No 93, 63, 75, and 24

The Representatives,

Recalling the requirements of Article 8 of Annex V to the Protocol on Environmental Protection to the Antarctic Treaty to maintain a list of current Historic Sites and Monuments ("HSM") and that such sites "shall not be damaged, removed or destroyed";

Recalling

- Resolution 3 (2009), which recommended that Parties use the Guidelines for the designation and protection of Historic Sites and Monuments;
- Resolution 2 (2018), which recommended that Parties use the Guidelines for the assessment and management of Heritage in Antarctica;
- Recommendation VII-9, which added Amundsen's Cairn to the "List of Historic Monuments Identified and Described by the Proposing Government or Governments";
- Measure 4 (1995), which added Base Y on Horseshoe Island, Marguerite Bay, western Graham Land to the list of HSM;
- Measure 1 (2001), which added 'A' Hut of Scott Base, Ross Island to the list of HSM;
- Measure 12 (2019), which added the wreck of the *Endurance* to the list of HSM, and Measure 18 (2022), which amended HSM 93;
- Decision 1 (2019), which added new information fields to the List of HSM;
- Decision 1 (2021), which sets out the information contained in fields that continue to be a formal part of the List of HSM and that changes to these fields would require adoption through a Measure;
- Measure 23 (2021), which adopted the reformatted List of HSM;

Desiring to update the descriptions of Historic Sites and Monuments numbers 93, 63, 75 and 24;

Desiring to add a Commemorative plaque commemorating the first visit to the Lake Untersee area to the list as HSM 96;

Recommend to their Governments the following Measure for approval in accordance with paragraph 2 of Article 8 of Annex V to the Protocol on Environmental Protection to the Antarctic Treaty:

That:

1. the information in the List of Historic Sites and Monuments for HSM 93, be amended as below:

   Description: Wreck of the vessel *Endurance*, including all artefacts contained within or formerly contained within the ship, which may be lying on the seabed in or near the wreck within a 1500m radius. This includes all fixtures and fittings associated with the ship, including the ship's wheel, bell, etc. The designation also includes all items of personal possessions left on the ship by the ship's company at the time of its sinking.

2. the information in the List of HSM for HSM 63, be amended as below:

   Description: 'Base Y' on Horseshoe Island, Marguerite Bay, western Graham Land. Noteworthy as a relatively unaltered and completely equipped British scientific base of the late 1950s. 'Blaiklock', the refuge hut located on Blaiklock Island at 67° 32' 31.7768'' S, 67° 11' 50.6349'' W, is considered an integral part of the base.
   Management tools: Visitor Site Guidelines – 24. Horseshoe Island. A Conservation Management Plan has been prepared.
   Physical features of the environment and cultural and local context: The site located on a small isthmus on Sally Cove consists of the original main building, a weather balloon shed, dog pens, emergency store, plus a refuge on Blaiklock Island some 20 miles north. There are two masts on high points near the main building, and two small wooden boats in a small cove to the north. Inside, the station contains almost all of its original contents, fixtures and fittings, including kitchen utensils, stocks of food and fuel, workshop tools, radio equipment, and a diesel generator. The excellent condition and completeness of both the buildings and artefacts are of considerable historical significance; together they provide a very special time-capsule of British life and science in the Antarctic during the late 1950s. Historic former science and sledging station now managed by the UK Antarctic Heritage Trust as a heritage site. www.ukaht.org. The site has a comprehensive conservation management plan and is actively conserved by a professional conservation team.

3. the information in the List of HSM for HSM 75, be amended as below:

   Name: Hillary's TAE/IGY Hut 'A', Geomagnetic Huts 'G' and 'H' – Scott Base, Ross Island
   Description: Hut A of Scott Base, being the only existing Trans Antarctic Expedition 1956/1957 building in Antarctica sited at Pram Point, Ross Island, Ross Sea Region, Antarctica. Huts G and H are both original buildings from the International Geophysical Year. They remain in the original sites as built in 1957, to the north-west of Hut A. Their physical positions are inextricably linked to a continuous record of scientific observations of the earth's magnetism, unbroken since 1957. They were prefabricated buildings, designed specially for Antarctic conditions and without ferrous components of any sort, thereby enabling their use for geomagnetic purposes.
   Type: Station and huts
   Conservation status: Following major conservation work by the New Zealand-based Antarctic Heritage Trust 2016-17, Hut A is structurally sound and weathertight and artefact collection has been conserved. Annual monitoring and maintenance ensure ongoing stability of this building.
   Conservation works have yet to be carried out on Huts G and H. The buildings are structurally sound and serviceable, showing the wear and tear expected for buildings some 65 years old. The New Zealand-based Antarctic Heritage Trust intend to carry out asbestos removal and conservation works on the buildings in the coming years.
   Description of the historical context: These buildings represent the beginnings of the New Zealand Antarctic programme in 1957, the base from which Sir Edmund Hillary mounted his traverse to the South Pole by tractor, in support of the Trans Antarctic Expedition. The geomagnetic huts were the hub of the contribution from NZ scientists to the International Geophysical Year (1957-58) and constitute an important site in the history of science on the Antarctic continent; they have provided a continuous international record of scientific observations of the earth's magnetism, unbroken between 1957-2023.
   The huts are closely associated with a number of scientists from 1957–58 to the present

day; Dr Trevor Hatherton's name in particular is well known and highly regarded internationally in the annals of Antarctic science.
Applicable criteria in accordance with Resolution 3 (2009):
a) a particular event of importance in the history of science or exploration of Antarctica occurred at the place
b) a particular association with a person who played an important role in the history of science or exploration of Antarctica
d) representative of, or forms part of, some wide-ranging activity that has been important in the development and knowledge of Antarctica
e) particular technical, historical, cultural or architectural value in its materials, design or method of construction
Management tools: Conservation Management Plan, Code of Conduct, Hut guide system, Briefing to all Scott Base arrivals, Historic Sites and Monuments in the Ross Sea Region poster displayed at stations in the region.

Physical features of the environment and cultural and local context: The huts are in the immediate vicinity of Scott Base. Hut A is frequently visited by local base staff from Scott Base and McMurdo, and by seasonal tourist visits. Hut A is kept heated and well maintained. Huts G and H are both still on their original sites, as built in 1957, to the north-west of Hut A.

4. the information in the List of HSM for HSM 24, be amended as below:

   Description: Rock cairn, known as 'Amundsen's cairn', in Queen Maud Range, erected by Roald Amundsen on 6 January 1912 on a peak Amundsen named Bettytoppen, on his way back to Framheim from the South Pole.
   Location: 85°10'23,8"S 163°36'5,9"W
   Conservation status: The cairn remains intact. There is a paraffin tank inside the cairn, which is in good condition. A tin box containing two notes which was originally placed in the cairn by Amundsen, has long since been removed. A plaque commemorating Amundsen's expedition is placed at the base of the cairn.

5. the following be added to the List of HSM as below:

   No: 96
   Name: Commemorative plaque commemorating the first visit to the Lake Untersee area.
   Description: A brass plaque measuring 220 mm × 120 mm, 4 mm thick, with the names of five members of the 14th Soviet Antarctic Expedition who visited the area in 1969, mounted on an aluminium pipe set on a rocky surface.
   Location: 71° 20' 25.0" S, 13° 27' 00" E
   Proposing Party: Russian Federation
   Party undertaking management: Russian Federation
   Type: Commemorative plaque
   Conservation status: In good condition
   Description of the historical context: At the beginning of 1969, the first visit to Lake Untersee took place. Members of the geological and geophysical team of the 14th Soviet Antarctic Expedition (14 SAE) conducted the first ground survey of the area, which included glaciological, geomorphological, ornithological and hydrological observations, depth measurements and water sampling, collection of materials on moraine deposits and seabed sediments. The first description of the lake area showed its uniqueness and promise for further research and also served as the basis for subsequent expeditions to this area.
   Applicable criteria in accordance with Resolution 3 (2009): a) a particular event of importance in the history of science or exploration of Antarctica occurred at the place.

Management tools: Management activities do not require a formal management plan. Observation and necessary actions to maintain the HSM in proper condition will be carried out during scientific expeditions in this area.

Physical features of the environment and cultural and local context: The plaque is mounted on an aluminium pipe installed on a rocky surface, on the top of a ridge extending north-south, at its southernmost point, directly above the slope towards the lake.

6. the Secretariat of the Antarctic Treaty be requested to update the list annexed to Measure 23 (2021) and make it available on its website.

2. Decisions

Decision 1 (2024)

Notification by the Consultative Parties regarding the list of observers under Article VII of the Antarctic Treaty and Article 14 of the Protocol on Environmental Protection to the Antarctic Treaty through the Secretariat of the Antarctic Treaty

The Representatives,

Recalling that Article VII (1) of the Antarctic Treaty ("the Treaty") and Article 14 of the Protocol on Environmental Protection to the Antarctic Treaty ("the Protocol") provide that the Consultative Parties to the Antarctic Treaty shall inform the other Consultative Parties regarding the designation of observers to carry out inspections;

Taking into account that, since the entry into force of the Treaty and since the subsequent creation of the Secretariat of the Antarctic Treaty ("the Secretariat"), new and more efficient ways of submitting and exchanging information have been developed, such as circulars that the Secretariat sends to Contracting Parties by email;

Recalling in this regard Article 2.2 (c) of Measure 1 (2003), which provides that the Secretariat shall facilitate and coordinate communications and exchange of information amongst Parties on all exchanges required under the Treaty and the Protocol;

Considering that the preservation and distribution of information constitutes one of the main functions of the Secretariat;

Seeking to give as much certainty as possible to the start and termination dates of the designated observer's appointment, in order to always keep the current list of observers updated;

Decide that:

1. communication through the Secretariat of the Antarctic Treaty of the appointment of designated observers is considered an appropriate form of communication, in accordance with Article VII (1) of the Antarctic Treaty and Article 14 of the Protocol on Environmental Protection to the Antarctic Treaty;

2. in addition, this information may, but need not, also be communicated to each of the Consultative Parties via traditional diplomatic channels;

3. once such information has been received, the Secretariat will immediately notify all Consultative Parties via a circular sent through email;

4. the Secretariat will include all information provided in the communications identified in paragraph 1 of this Decision in the restricted access area of its website;

5. the communication of the appointment of designated observers will include both the start and termination date of their appointment;

6. in the absence of specification of the termination date, the termination date will be 3 years after the date of appointment;

7. should a designated observer's appointment cease before the termination date communicated for their appointment or before the date indicated in paragraph 6 of this Decision, the Party will communicate this development to the Secretariat of the Antarctic Treaty in order to keep the current list updated; and

8. Decision 2 (2019) be revoked.

Decision 2 (2024)

Revised Rules of Procedure for the Antarctic Treaty Consultative Meeting

The Representatives,

Recalling Decision 2 (2016) Revised Rules of Procedure for the Antarctic Treaty Consultative Meeting;

Recalling that, at Antarctic Treaty Consultative Meeting ("ATCM") XLV (2023), the Secretariat of the Antarctic Treaty ("the Secretariat") was tasked to review, within existing resources, all relevant Antarctic Treaty documents pertaining to current and future cooperation, to provide options for potential adoption by the ATCM that would ensure gender-neutral language across these documents;

Noting that the Secretariat has reviewed the current Rules of Procedure for the ATCM and has prepared draft Revised Rules of Procedure for the ATCM, in each of the official languages of the Antarctic Treaty, to address inconsistencies identified with the United Nations Guidelines for gender-inclusive language ("UN Guidelines");

Desiring to replace, at this time, only the current English language version of the Rules of Procedure for the ATCM;

Further desiring to submit the French, Russian and Spanish versions of the draft Revised Rules of Procedure for the ATCM for proof-reading to ensure that the substance of their current provisions has not been altered;

Recognising the need to provide guidance to the Secretariat concerning its editorial procedures in respect of gender-inclusive language;

Decide:

1. that the Revised Rules of Procedure for the Antarctic Treaty Consultative Meeting annexed to this Decision replace the Revised Rules of Procedure for the Antarctic Treaty Consultative Meeting (2016) in the English language only;

2. to request the Secretariat to send the French, Russian and Spanish versions of the draft Revised Rules of Procedure for the ATCM for proof-reading to be presented for consideration to the 47th Antarctic Treaty Consultative Meeting;

3. that the Secretariat will take into account the UN Guidelines in its standard editorial procedures; and

4. that the Secretariat will include a link to the UN Guidelines in the online guidance it provides on the preparation of documents, as a resource for delegates.

Revised Rules of Procedure for the Antarctic Treaty Consultative Meeting (2024)

1. Meetings held pursuant to Article IX of the Antarctic Treaty shall be known as Antarctic Treaty Consultative Meetings. Contracting Parties entitled to participate in those Meetings shall be referred to as "Consultative Parties"; other Contracting Parties which may have been invited to attend those Meetings shall be referred to as "non-Consultative Parties". The Executive Secretary of the Secretariat of the Antarctic Treaty shall be referred to as the "Executive Secretary".

2. The Representatives of the Commission for the Conservation of Antarctic Marine Living Resources, the Scientific Committee on Antarctic Research and the Council of Managers of National Antarctic Programs, invited to attend those Meetings in accordance with Rule 31, shall be referred to as "Observers".

Representation

3. Each Consultative Party shall be represented by a delegation composed of a Representative and such Alternate Representatives, Advisers and other persons as each State may deem necessary. Each non-Consultative Party which has been invited to attend a Consultative Meeting shall be represented by a delegation composed of a Representative and such other persons as it may deem necessary within such numerical limit as may from time to time be determined by the Host Government in consultation with the Consultative Parties. The Commission for the Conservation of Antarctic Marine Living Resources, the Scientific Committee on Antarctic Research and the Council of Managers of National Antarctic Programs shall be represented by their respective Chair or President, or other persons appointed to this end. The names of members of delegations and of the observers shall be communicated to the Host Government prior to the opening of the Meeting.

4. The order of precedence of the delegations shall be in accordance with the alphabet in the language of the Host Government, all delegations of non-Consultative Parties following after those of Consultative Parties, and all delegations of observers following after non-Consultative Parties.

Officers

5. A Representative of the Host Government shall be the Temporary Chair of the Meeting and shall preside until the Meeting elects a Chair.

6. At its inaugural session, a Chair from one of the Consultative Parties shall be elected. The other Representatives of Consultative Parties shall serve as Vice-Chairs of the Meeting in order of precedence. The Chair normally shall preside at all plenary sessions. If the Chair is absent from any session or part thereof, the Vice-Chairs, rotating on the basis of the order of precedence as established by Rule 4, shall preside during each such session.

Secretariat

7. The Executive Secretary shall act as Secretary to the Meeting. The Executive Secretary shall be responsible, with the assistance of the Host Government, for providing secretariat

services for the meeting, as provided in Article 2 of Measure 1 (2003), as provisionally applied by Decision 2 (2003) until Measure 1 becomes effective.

Sessions

8. The opening plenary session shall be held in public, other sessions shall be held in private, unless the Meeting shall determine otherwise.

Committees and Working Groups

9. The Meeting, to facilitate its work, may establish such committees as it may deem necessary for the performance of its functions, defining their terms of reference.

10. The committees shall operate under the Rules of Procedure of the Meeting, except where they are inapplicable.

11. Working Groups may be established by the Meeting, or its committees to deal with various agenda items. The Meeting will determine the provisional arrangements for Working Groups at the end of each Consultative Meeting, when it approves the preliminary agenda for the subsequent Meeting (under Rule 36). These arrangements will include:

    a. the establishment of Working Group(s) for the subsequent Meeting;

    b. the appointment of Working Group Chair(s); and

    c. the allocation of agenda items to each Working Group.

    Where the Meeting decides that a Working Group should be continued for more than one year, the Chair(s) of those Working Group(s) may be appointed for a period of one or two consecutive Meetings in the first instance. Working Group Chairs may subsequently be appointed for further terms of one or two years, but will not serve for more than four consecutive years in the same Working Group.

    Should the Meeting be unable to appoint a Working Group Chair(s) for the subsequent Meeting, a Chair(s) shall be appointed at the beginning of the subsequent Meeting.

Conduct of Business

12. A quorum shall be constituted by two-thirds of the Representatives of Consultative Parties participating in the Meeting.

13. The Chair shall exercise the powers of the office in accordance with customary practice. The Chair shall see to the observance of the Rules of Procedure and the maintenance of proper order. The Chair, in the exercise of office functions, remains under the authority of the Meeting.

14. Subject to Rule 28, no Representative may address the Meeting without having previously obtained the permission of the Chair and the Chair shall call upon speakers in the order in which they signify their desire to speak. The Chair may call speakers to order if their remarks are not relevant to the subject under discussion.

15. During the discussion of any matter, a Representative of a Consultative Party may rise to a point of order and the point of order shall be decided immediately by the Chair in

accordance with the Rules of Procedure. A Representative of a Consultative Party may appeal against the ruling of the Chair. The appeal shall be put to a vote immediately, and the Chair's ruling shall stand unless over-ruled by a majority of the Representatives of Consultative Parties present and voting. A Representative of a Consultative Party rising to a point of order shall not speak on the substance of the matter under discussion.

16. The Meeting may limit the time to be allotted to speakers, and the number of times they may speak on any subject. When the debate is thus limited and Representatives have spoken their allotted time, the Chair shall call them to order without delay.

17. During the discussion of any matter, a Representative of a Consultative Party may move the adjournment of the debate on the item under discussion. In addition to the proposer of the motion, Representatives of two Consultative Parties may speak in favour of, and two against, the motion, after which the motion shall be put to the vote immediately. The Chair may limit the time to be allowed to speakers under this Rule.

18. A Representative of a Consultative Party may at any time move the closure of the debate in the item under discussion, whether or not any other Representatives have signified their wish to speak. Permission to speak on the closure of the debate shall be accorded only to Representatives of two Consultative Parties opposing the closure, after which the motion shall be put to the vote immediately. If the Meeting is in favour of the closure, the Chair shall declare the closure of the debate. The Chair may limit the time to be allowed to speakers under this Rule. (This Rule shall not apply to debate in committees.)

19. During the discussion of any matter, a Representative of a Consultative Party may move the suspension or adjournment of the Meeting. Such motions shall not be debated, but shall be put to the vote immediately. The Chair may limit the time to be allowed to the speaker moving the suspension or adjournment of the Meeting.

20. Subject to Rule 15, the following motions shall have precedence in the following order over all other proposals or motions before the Meeting:

    a) to suspend the Meeting;

    b) to adjourn the Meeting;

    c) to adjourn the debate on the item under discussion;

    d) for the closure of the debate on the item under discussion.

21. Decisions of the Meeting on all matters of procedure shall be taken by a majority of the Representatives of Consultative Parties participating in the Meeting, each of whom shall have one vote.

Languages

22. English, French, Russian and Spanish shall be the official languages of the Meeting.

23. Any Representative may speak in a language other than the official languages. However, in such cases speakers shall provide for interpretation into one of the official languages.

Measures, Decisions, and Resolutions and Final Report

24. Without prejudice to Rule 21, Measures, Decisions and Resolutions, as referred to in Decision 1 (1995), shall be adopted by the Representatives of all Consultative Parties present and will thereafter be subject to the provisions of Decision 1 (1995).

25. The final report shall also contain a brief account of the proceedings of the Meeting. It will be approved by a majority of the Representatives of Consultative Parties present and shall be transmitted by the Executive Secretary to Governments of all Consultative and non-Consultative Parties which have been invited to take part in the Meeting for their consideration.

26. Notwithstanding Rule 25, the Executive Secretary, immediately following the closure of the Consultative Meeting, shall notify all Consultative Parties of all Measures, Decisions and Resolutions taken and send them authenticated copies of the definitive texts in an appropriate language of the Meeting. In respect to a Measure adopted under the procedures of Article 6 or 8 of Annex V of the Protocol, the respective notification shall also include the time period for approval of that Measure.

Non-Consultative Parties

27. Representatives of non-Consultative Parties, if invited to attend a Consultative Meeting, may be present at:

    a) all plenary sessions of the Meeting; and

    b) all formal Committees or Working Groups, comprising all Consultative Parties, unless a Representative of a Consultative Party requests otherwise in any particular case.

28. The relevant Chair may invite Representatives of non-Consultative Parties to address the Meeting, Committee or Working group which they are attending, unless a Representative of a Consultative Party requests otherwise. The Chair shall at any time give priority to Representatives of Consultative Parties who signify their desire to speak and may, in inviting Representatives of non-Consultative Parties to address the Meeting, limit the time to be allotted to each speaker and the number of times they may speak on any subject.

29. Non-Consultative Parties are not entitled to participate in the taking of decisions.

30.

    a) Non-Consultative Parties may submit documents to the Secretariat for distribution to the Meeting as information documents. Such documents shall be relevant to matters under Committee consideration at the Meeting.

    b) Unless a Representative of a Consultative Party requests otherwise such documents shall be available only in the language or languages in which they were submitted.

Antarctic Treaty System Observers

31. The observers referred to in Rule 2 shall attend the Meetings for the specific purpose of reporting on:

    a) in the case of the Commission for the Conservation of Antarctic Marine Living Resources, developments in its area of competence.

    b) in the case of the Scientific Committee on Antarctic Research:

i) the general proceedings of SCAR;

ii) matters within the competence of SCAR under the Convention for the Conservation of Antarctic Seals;

iii) such publications and reports as may have been published or prepared in accordance with Recommendations IX-19 and VI-9 respectively.

c) in the case of the Council of Managers of National Antarctic Programs, the activities within its area of competence.

32. Observers may be present at:

a) the plenary sessions of the Meeting at which the respective Report is considered;

b) formal committees or working groups, comprising all Contracting Parties at which the respective Report is considered, unless a Representative of a Consultative Party requests otherwise in any particular case.

33. Following the presentation of the pertinent Report, the relevant Chair may invite the observer to address the Meeting at which it is being considered once again, unless a Representative of a Consultative Party requests otherwise. The Chair may allot a time limit for such interventions.

34. Observers are not entitled to participate in the taking of decisions.

35. Observers may submit their Report and/or documents relevant to matters contained therein to the Secretariat, for distribution to the Meeting as working papers.

Agenda for Consultative Meetings

36. At the end of each Consultative Meeting, the Host Government of that Meeting shall prepare a preliminary agenda for the next Consultative Meeting. If approved by the Meeting, the preliminary agenda for the next Meeting shall be annexed to the Final Report of the Meeting.

37. Any Contracting Party may propose supplementary items for the preliminary agenda by informing the Host Government for the forthcoming Consultative Meeting no later than 180 days before the beginning of the Meeting; each proposal shall be accompanied by an explanatory memorandum. The Host Government shall draw the attention of all Contracting Parties to this Rule no later than 210 days before the Meeting.

38. The Host Government shall prepare a provisional agenda for the Consultative Meeting. The provisional agenda shall contain:

a) all items on the preliminary agenda decided in accordance with Rule 36; and

b) all items the inclusion of which has been requested by a Contracting Party pursuant to Rule 37.

Not later than 120 days before the Meeting, the Host Government shall transmit to all the Contracting Parties the provisional agenda, together with explanatory memoranda and any other papers related thereto.

Experts from International Organisations

39. At the end of each Consultative Meeting, the Meeting shall decide which international organisations having a scientific or technical interest in Antarctica shall be invited to designate an expert to attend the forthcoming Meeting in order to assist it in its substantive work.

40. Any Contracting Party may thereafter propose that an invitation be extended to other international organisations having a scientific or technical interest in Antarctica to assist the Meeting in its substantive work; each such proposal shall be submitted to the Host Government for that Meeting not later than 180 days before the beginning of the Meeting and shall be accompanied by a memorandum setting out the basis for the proposal.

41. The Host Government shall transmit these proposals to all Contracting Parties in accordance with the procedure in Rule 38. Any Consultative Party which wishes to object to a proposal shall do so not less than 90 days before the Meeting.

42. Unless such an objection has been received, the Host Government shall extend invitations to international organisations identified in accordance with Rules 39 and 40 and shall request each international organisation to communicate the name of the designated expert to the Host Government prior to the opening of the Meeting. All such experts may attend the Meeting during consideration of all items, except for those items relating to the operation of the Antarctic Treaty System which are identified by the previous Meeting or upon adoption of the agenda.

43. The relevant Chair, with the agreement of all the Consultative Parties, may invite experts to address the meeting they are attending. The Chair shall at any time give priority to Representatives of Consultative Parties or non-Consultative Parties or Observers referred to in Rule 31 who signify their desire to speak, and may in inviting experts to address the Meeting limit the time to be allotted to them and the number of times they may speak on any subject.

44. Experts are not entitled to participate in the taking of decisions.

45.
    a) Experts may, in respect of the relevant agenda item, submit documents to the Secretariat for distribution to the Meeting as information documents.

    b) Unless a Representative of a Consultative Party requests otherwise, such documents shall be available only in the language or languages in which they were submitted.

Intersessional Consultations

46. Intersessionally, the Executive Secretary shall, within the competence established under Measure 1 (2003) and associated instruments that govern the operation of the Secretariat, consult the Consultative Parties, when legally required to do so under relevant instruments of the ATCM and when the exigencies of the circumstances require action to be taken before the opening of the next ATCM, using the following procedure:

    a) Each Consultative Party shall keep the Executive Secretary advised on an ongoing basis of its Representative and any Alternate Representatives, who shall have authority to speak for their Consultative Party for the purposes of intersessional consultations.

b) The Executive Secretary shall maintain a list of the Representatives and Alternate Representatives and ensure that it remains current.

c) When intersessional consultations are required, the Executive Secretary shall transmit the relevant information and any proposed action to all Consultative Parties through their Representatives and any Alternate Representatives designated under paragraph (a) above, indicating an appropriate date by which responses are requested.

d) The Executive Secretary shall ensure that all Consultative Parties acknowledge the receipt of such transmission.

e) Each Consultative Party shall consider the matter and communicate its reply, if any, to the Executive Secretary through its Representative or an Alternate Representative by the specified date.

f) The Executive Secretary after informing the Consultative Parties of the result of the consultations, may proceed to take the proposed action if no Consultative Party has objected.

g) The Executive Secretary shall keep a record of the intersessional consultations, including results of those intersessional consultations and actions taken and shall reflect these results and actions in the Secretariat report to the ATCM for its review.

47. Intersessionally, when a request for information about the activities of the ATCM is received from an international organisation having a scientific or technical interest in Antarctica, the Executive Secretary shall coordinate a response, using the following procedure:

a) The Executive Secretary shall transmit the request and a first draft response to all Consultative Parties through their Representatives and any Alternate Representatives designated under Rule 46 (a), proposing to answer the request, and including an appropriate date by which Consultative Parties should either (1) indicate that it would not be appropriate to answer, or (2) provide comments to the first draft response. The date shall give a reasonable amount of time to provide comments, taking into account any deadlines set by the initial requests for information. If a Consultative Party indicates that a response would not be appropriate, the Executive Secretary shall send only a formal response, acknowledging the request without going into the substance of the matter.

b) If there is no objection to proceeding and if comments are provided before the date specified in the transmission referred to in paragraph (a) above, the Executive Secretary shall revise the response in light of the comments and transmit the revised response to all Consultative Parties, including an appropriate date by which reactions are requested.

c) If any further comments are provided before the date specified in the transmission referred to in paragraph (b) above, the Executive Secretary shall repeat the procedure referred to in paragraph (b) above until no further comments are provided.

d) If no comments are provided before the date specified in a transmission referred to in paragraph (a), (b) or (c) above, the Executive Secretary shall circulate a final version and shall request both an active digital "read"-confirmation and an active digital "accept"-confirmation from each Consultative Party, suggesting a date by which the "accept"-confirmation should be received. The Executive Secretary shall keep the Consultative Parties informed about the progress of received confirmations. After receipt of "accept"-confirmations from all Consultative Parties the Executive

Secretary shall sign and send the response to the international organisation concerned, on behalf of all Consultative Parties, and shall provide a copy of the signed response to all Consultative Parties.

e) Any Consultative Party may, at any stage of this process, ask for more time for consideration.

f) Any Consultative Party may, at any stage of this process, indicate that it would not be appropriate to respond to the request. In this case the Executive Secretary shall send only a formal response, acknowledging the request without going into the substance of the matter.

Meeting Documents

48. Working Papers shall refer to papers submitted by Consultative Parties that require discussion and action at a Meeting and papers submitted by Observers referred to in Rule 2.

49. Secretariat Papers shall refer to papers prepared by the Secretariat pursuant to a mandate established at a Meeting, or which would, in the view of the Executive Secretary, help inform the Meeting or assist in its operation.

50. Information Papers shall refer to:

- Papers submitted by Consultative Parties or Observers that provide information in support of a Working Paper or that are relevant to discussions at a Meeting;
- Papers submitted by Non-Consultative Parties that are relevant to discussions at a Meeting; and
- Papers submitted by Experts that are relevant to discussions at a Meeting.

51. Background Papers shall refer to papers submitted by any participant that will not be introduced in a Meeting, but that are submitted for the purpose of formally providing information.

52. Procedures for the submission, translation and distribution of documents are annexed to these Rules of Procedure.

Amendments

53. These Rules of Procedure may be amended by a two-thirds majority of the Representatives of Consultative Parties participating in the Meeting. This Rule shall not apply to Rules 24, 27, 29, 34, 39-42, 44, and 46, amendments of which shall require the approval of the Representatives of all Consultative Parties present at the Meeting.

Annex

Procedures for the Submission, Translation and Distribution of Documents for the ATCM and the CEP

1. These procedures apply to the submission, translation and distribution of official papers for the Antarctic Treaty Consultative Meeting (ATCM) and for the Committee for Environmental Protection (CEP) as defined in their respective Rules of Procedure. These papers consist of Working Papers, Secretariat Papers, Information Papers and Background Papers.
2. Papers that are submitted to both the ATCM and the CEP should indicate, where feasible, what portions or elements of the paper should, in the opinion of the submitter, be discussed in each forum.
3. Documents to be translated are Working Papers, Secretariat Papers, reports submitted to the ATCM by ATCM Observers and invited Experts according to the provisions of Recommendation XIII-2, reports submitted to the ATCM in relation to Article III-2 of the Antarctic Treaty, and Information Papers that a Consultative Party requests be translated. Background Papers will not be translated.
4. Papers that are to be translated, with the exception of the reports of Intersessional Contact Groups (ICG) convened by the ATCM or CEP, Chair Reports from Antarctic Treaty Meetings of Experts, and the Secretariat's Report and Programme, should not exceed 1500 words. When calculating the length of a paper, proposed Measures, Decisions and Resolutions and their attachments are not included.
5. Papers that are to be translated should be received by the Secretariat no later than 45 days before the Consultative Meeting. If any such paper is submitted later than 45 days before the Consultative Meeting, it may only be considered if no Consultative Party objects.
6. The Secretariat should receive Information Papers for which no translation has been requested and Background Papers that participants wish to be listed in the Final Report no later than 30 days before the Meeting.
7. The Secretariat will indicate on each document submitted by a Contracting Party, an Observer, or an Expert the date it was submitted.
8. When a revised version of a Paper made after its initial submission is resubmitted to the Secretariat for translation, the revised text should indicate clearly the amendments that have been incorporated.
9. The Papers should be transmitted to the Secretariat by electronic means and will be uploaded to the ATCM Home Page established by the Secretariat. Working Papers received before the 45 day limit should be uploaded as soon as possible and in any case not later than 30 days before the Meeting. Papers will be uploaded initially to the password protected portion of the website, and moved to the non-password protected part once the Meeting has concluded.
10. Parties may agree to present any paper for which a translation has not been requested to the Secretariat during the Meeting for translation.
11. No paper submitted to the ATCM should be used as the basis for discussion at the ATCM or at the CEP unless it has been translated into the four official languages.
12. Within three months of the end of the Consultative Meeting, the Secretariat will post on the ATCM Home Page a preliminary version of the Final Report of the Meeting in the four

official languages. This version of the report shall be clearly marked "PRELIMINARY" and shall indicate that it is subject to final formatting, editing, and publishing processes.

13. Within six months of the end of the Consultative Meeting, the Secretariat will circulate to Parties and also post on the ATCM Home Page the Final Report of that Meeting in the four official languages.

Decision 3 (2024)

Secretariat Report, Programme and Budget

The Representatives,

Recalling Measure 1 (2003) on the establishment of the Secretariat of the Antarctic Treaty ("the Secretariat");

Bearing in mind the Financial Regulations for the Secretariat of the Antarctic Treaty ("the Financial Regulations") annexed to Decision 4 (2003) and amended by Decision 6 (2005);

Decide:

1. to approve the audited Financial Report for 2022/23 annexed to this Decision (Annex 1);

2. to take note of the Secretariat Report 2023/24, which includes the Provisional Financial Report for 2023/24, annexed to this Decision (Annex 2);

3. to take note of the Five Year Forward Budget Profile 2025/26-2029/30 and approve the Secretariat Programme 2024/25, including the Budget for 2024/25 and the Forecast Budget 2025/26, annexed to this Decision (Annex 3);

4. to direct the Secretariat to establish a Special Fund in accordance with the provisions of Regulation 6.2(d) of the Financial Regulations, to be used to fund activities in support of the development of a consistent and comprehensive framework for the regulation of tourism and other non-governmental activities in Antarctica, and to receive voluntary contributions in accordance with the provision of Regulation 7.4 of the Financial Regulations for that purpose;

5. to direct the Secretariat to establish a Special Fund in accordance with the provisions of Regulation 6.2 (d) of the Financial Regulations, to be used to defray the cost of a joint CEP/SC-CAMLR Workshop to be conducted in the week before the CEP 27 meeting in 2025, and to receive voluntary contributions in accordance with the provision of Regulation 7.4 of the Financial Regulations for that purpose; and

6. to authorise the transfer of up to US$ 20 000 to the Special Fund referred in operative paragraph 5 from the surplus accumulated in the General Fund; and to request that the Executive Secretary of the Secretariat open at the Antarctic Treaty Consultative Meeting Forum a topic to report to the Consultative Parties on financial issues.

ANNEX I

Opinion of the Auditor

Secretary
of the Secretariat of the Antarctic Treaty
Maipú 757, 4th floor
CUIT (Tax No.) 30-70892567-1
Re: ATCM 46 - CEP 26 Antarctic Treaty Consultative Meeting, 2024 - Kochi, India.

1. Report on the Financial Statements

We have audited the attached Financial Statements of the Secretariat of the Antarctic Treaty, which include the following: Statement of Income and Expenditure, Statement of Financial Position, Statement of Changes in Net Assets, Statement of Cash Flow and Explanatory Notes for the financial year started 1 April 2022 and ended 31 March 2023.

2. Management Responsibility for Financial Statements

The Secretariat of the Antarctic Treaty, constituted under Argentine Law No. 25.888, of 14 May 2004, is responsible for the preparation and reasonable presentation of the attached financial statements according to accounting methods based on cash movements in accordance with International Accounting Standards and the specific Standards for Antarctic Treaty Consultative Meetings. Such responsibility includes: designing, implementing and maintaining internal controls for the preparation and presentation of the Financial Statements such that they are free of misstatements, due to error or fraud, selecting and implementing appropriate accounting policies, and preparing accounting estimates which are reasonable under the circumstances.

3. Auditor's Responsibility

Our responsibility is to express our opinion on these Financial Statements based on our audit.

The audit was conducted in accordance with International Auditing Standards and the Annex to Decision 3 (2012) of the XXXI Antarctic Treaty Consultative Meeting, which describes the tasks to be carried out by the external auditor.

These standards require compliance with ethical requirements, and planning and execution of the audit so as to provide reasonable assurance that the Financial Statements are free of material misstatements.

An audit includes the execution of procedures in order to obtain evidence of the amounts and the exposure reflected in the Financial Statements. The procedures selected depend on the auditor's judgement, including an assessment of the risks of material misstatement in the Financial Statements.

In conducting such a risk assessment, the auditor considers the internal control relevant to the preparation and reasonable presentation of the Financial Statements by the organisation, in order to design suitable procedures that are appropriate to the circumstances.

An audit also includes an assessment of appropriateness of the accounting principles used, an opinion on whether the accounting estimates made by the Secretariat are reasonable, as well as an assessment of the general presentation of the Financial Statements.

We believe that the audited evidence we have obtained is sufficient and appropriate to provide a basis for our opinion as auditors.

4. Opinion

In our opinion, the attached Financial Statements of the Secretariat of the Antarctic Treaty corresponding to the financial period ending 31 March 2023 have been prepared, in all material aspects, in accordance with International Accounting Standards, the specific standards for Antarctic Treaty Consultative Meetings, and methods of accounting based on cash flow.

5. Other Matters

The information contained in Note 1 to the attached Financial Statements indicates that they have been prepared by the Secretariat of the Antarctic Treaty following the guidelines established in the Financial Regulations annexed to Decision 4 (2003), in accordance with the International Financial Reporting Standards (IFRS) of the International Accounting Standards Board, which differ in certain aspects related to valuation and presentation from the professional accounting standards in force in the Autonomous City of Buenos Aires, Argentina.

In addition, the information mentioned in the preceding paragraph reflects the currency conversion differences generated over a financial year in a context of strong devaluation of the legal tender of the Argentine Republic.

6. Additional information required by law

Pursuant to the analysis described in point 3, I report that the above-mentioned Financial Statements are based on accounting records that are not transcribed into books in accordance with current Argentine standards.

We also report that, according to the accounting entries at 31 March 2023, the liabilities accrued in favour of the Argentine Integrated Pension System (SIPA) in Argentine pesos and pursuant to settlements made by the Secretariat amounted to ARS 2 466 680.61 (USD 11 446.31), there being no debt due and payable in Argentine pesos at that date.

It is worth noting that labour relations are governed by Secretariat of the Antarctic Treaty Staff Regulations.

Autonomous City of Buenos Aires, 3 April 2024

SINDICATURA GENERAL DE LA NACIÓN
(GENERAL OFFICE OF THE COMPTROLLER)
C.P.C.E.C.A.B.A. T°1 - F°2

Ariel Maximiliano Bozzano
Certified Public Accountant (U.B.A.)
C.P.C.E.C.A.B.A. T° 379 F° 44

Annex I - Final Report for 2022/23

1. Income and Expenditure Statement for all funds for the financial year started 1 April 2022 and ended 31 March 2023, compared with the previous financial year.

		Budget	
INCOME	**31/3/2022**	**31/3/2023**	**31/3/2023**
Contributions (Note 10)	1 378 097	1 378 097	1 378 097
General Fund (Note 1.11)	-	-	-
Other income (Note 2)	975	-	2 485
Total income	1 379 072	1 378 097	1 380 582
EXPENDITURE			
Salaries and wages	707 463	748 087	742 146
Translation and interpretation services	240 184	310 000	322 460
Travel and accommodation	26 532	108 500	105 599
Information technology	45 873	52 000	48 499
Printing, editing and copying	12 517	14 500	10 192
General services	34 206	47 418	45 024
Communications	16 543	18 000	17 092
Office expenses	14 618	16 000	15 157
Administration	6 228	8 200	6 111
Representation expenses	770	4 000	1 485
Financing (Note 9)	19 104	21 800	58 791
Total expenditure	1 124 040	1 348 505	1 372 556
ALLOCATION OF FUNDS			
Staff termination fund	26 768	29 592	29 592
Staff replacement fund	-	-	-
Operating fund	-	-	-
Translation contingency fund	-	-	-
Total allocation of funds	26 768	29 592	29 592
Total expenditure and allocations	1 150 808	1 378 097	1 402 148
Surplus (Deficit) for the period	228 264	0 00	(21 566)

This statement must be read in conjunction with the accompanying Notes 1 to 10

Annex I - Final Report for 2022/23

2. Statement of Financial Position at 31 March 2023 and comparison with the previous financial year.

	31/3/2022	31/3/2023
ASSETS		
Current assets		
Cash and cash equivalents (Note 3)	2 131 016	1 952 036
Contributions due (Note 10)	141 963	181 983
Other receivables (Note 4)	1 122	-
Other current assets (Note 5)	49 953	119 812
Total current assets	2 324 055	2 253 831
Non-current assets		
Fixed assets (Notes 1.3 and 6)	89 722	91 076
Total non-current assets	89 722	91 076
Total Assets	2 413 777	2 344 907
LIABILITIES		
Current liabilities		
Accounts payable (Note 7)	29 232	127 918
Contributions received in advance (Note 10)	660 495	534 769
Special voluntary fund for specific purposes (Note 1.9)	24 171	-
Remuneration and contributions payable (Note 8)	32 611	35 571
Total current liabilities	746 509	698 258
Non-current liabilities		
Staff termination fund (Note 1.4)	96 897	126 489
Staff replacement fund (Note 1.5)	50 000	50 000
Translation contingency fund (Note 1.6)	30 000	30 000
Involuntary separation from service fund (Note 1.7)	80 291	81 495
Fixed assets replacement fund (Note 1.8)	23 426	24 780
Total non-current liabilities	280 614	312 764
Total Liabilities	1 027 123	1 011 022
NET ASSETS	1 386 655	1 333 885

This statement must be read in conjunction with the accompanying Notes 1 to 10

Annex I - Final Report for 2022/23

3. **Statement of Changes in Net Assets as of 31 March 2023 and comparison with the previous period.**

Represented by	**Net assets 31/3/2022**	**Income**	**Expenditure and Appropriations**	**Other income**	**Net assets 31/3/2023**
General fund	1 156 703	1 378 097	(1 402 148)	2 485	1 135 137
- for staff appraisal					-
- to cover translation contingency fund					(30 000)
- to set up an involuntary separation from service fund					(1 204)
Operating fund (Note 1.9)	229 952				229 952
Net assets	1 386 655				1 333 885

This statement must be read in conjunction with the accompanying Notes 1 to 10

Annex I - Final Report for 2022/23

4 Statement of cash flows for the financial year started on 1 April 2022 and ended on 31 March 2023, compared with the previous financial year.

Variations in cash and cash equivalents	31/3/2022		31/3/2023	
Cash and cash equivalents at year-start	1 541 947		2 131 016	
Cash and cash equivalents at year-end	2 131 016		1 952 036	
Net increase in cash and cash equivalents		589 069		(178 980)
Causes of the variations in cash and cash equivalents				
Operating activities				
Contributions received	977 611		677 583	
Payment of remunerations and salaries	(707 064)		(740 354)	
Payment of translation services	(233 224)		(257 041)	
Payment of travel, accommodation, etc.	(21 731)		(114 129)	
Payment of printing, editing and copying services	(12 517)		(12 399)	
Payment of general services	(27 721)		(17 664)	
Other payments to suppliers	(85 316)		(84 181)	
Net cash and cash equivalent flow from operating activities		(109 964)		(548 185)
Investment activities				
Purchase of fixed assets	(1 983)		(14 158)	
Net cash and cash equivalent flow from investment activities		(1 983)		(14 158)
Financing activities				
Contributions received in advance	660 495		534 769	
Payment of severance and replacement expenses	-		-	
Preparation for ATCM	-		-	
Translation costs	-		(30 000)	
Collection pt. 5.6 Staff Regulations	208 453		152 432	
Payment pt. 5.6 Staff Regulations	(170 370)		(175 132)	
Net change in rentals	15 200		(43 477)	
Net movement AFIP (Argentine revenue service)	17. 445		(12 150)	
Sundry income / (expenditure)	975		2 485	
Net cash and cash equivalent flow from financing activities		732 198		428 927
Foreign currency activities				
Net loss	(31 182)		(45 564)	
Net cash and cash equivalent flow from foreign currency activities		(31 182)		(45 564)
Net increase in cash and cash equivalents		589 070		(178 980)

This statement must be read in conjunction with the accompanying Notes 1 to 10

Notes to the Financial Statements at 31 March 2022 and 2023

1 BASIS FOR PREPARATION OF THE FINANCIAL STATEMENTS

These financial statements are expressed in US dollars, in compliance with the guidelines established in the Financial Regulations, Annex to Decision 4 (2003). These statements were prepared in accordance with the International Financial Reporting Standards (IFRS) of the International Accounting Standards Board (IASB). The accounting method used is accrual-based.

1.1 Historical Cost

The financial statements have been prepared under the historical cost convention, unless indicated otherwise.

1.2 Office

The office of the Secretariat is provided by the Ministry of Foreign Affairs, International Trade and Religious Affairs of the Argentine Republic. Its use is free of rent and common expenses.

1.3 Fixed assets

All items are valued at historical cost, less accumulated depreciation. Depreciation is calculated on a straight-line basis at annual rates appropriate to extinguish their values at the end of their estimated useful life. The aggregate residual value of fixed assets does not exceed their economic use value.

1.4 Staff termination fund

In accordance with Article 10.4 of the Staff Regulations, the fund shall be sufficiently funded to compensate executive staff members at a rate of one month basic pay for each year of service.

1.5 Staff replacement fund

The fund is used to cover the travel costs of the Secretariat's executive staff to and from the headquarters of the Secretariat.

1.6 Translation contingency fund

In accordance with Decision 4 (2009), the Fund was set up to cover translation expenses, which may be caused by the unforeseen increase in the volume of documents submitted to the ATCM for translation. During the financial year ended 31 March 2023, this fund was used to the extent of 30 000 and it was also increased by 30 000 from the General Fund.

1.7 Involuntary separation from service fund

Compliant with Article 10.5 of the Secretariat of the Antarctic Treaty Staff Regulations for general services staff.

1.8 Fixed assets replacement fund

In accordance with the IAS, assets whose useful life exceeds one financial year must be disclosed as an asset in the Statement of Financial Position. Up to March 2010, the balancing entry was an adjustment to the General Fund. With effect from April 2010 the balancing entry corresponding to these assets is shown in liabilities under this item.

1.9 Operating fund

In accordance with Financial Regulation Article 6.2 (a), this must not exceed one-sixth (1/6) of the budget for the current financial year. In the current financial year, this fund was unallocated.

1.10 Special voluntary fund for specific purposes

Pt (82) of the XXXV ATCM Final Report, to receive voluntary contributions by the parties. The Voluntary Fund is money to meet the payment of rent and common expenses for the financial year.

1.11 General fund

This Fund was set up to account for the Secretariat's income and expenditure.

Notes to the Financial Statements at 31 March 2022 and 2023

		31/3/2022	31/3/2023
2 Other Income			
Interest earned		-	-
Discounts obtained		975	2.485
	Total	975	2.485
3 Cash and cash equivalents			
Cash in U.S. dollars		1 480	1 274
Cash in Argentine pesos		159	16
Banco de la Nación Argentina - Special account in U.S. dollars		2 116 254	66 704
Banco de la Nación Argentina - Current account in Argentine pesos		13 123	1 884 042
Investments		-	-
	Total	2 131 016	1 952 036
4 Other receivables			
Staff regulations pt. 5.6		1 122	-
5 Other current assets			
Advance payments		18 178	94 557
VAT receivable		27 500	24 824
Other expenses to be recovered		4 275	430
	Total	49 953	119 812
6 Fixed assets			
Books and subscriptions		17 341	18 136
Office equipment		40 227	40 227
Furniture		52 436	52 436
Computer hardware and software		150 937	164 300
	Total original cost	260 940	275 098
Accumulated depreciation		(171 218)	(184 021)
	Total	89 722	91 076
7 Accounts payable			
Commercial suppliers		3 503	19 446
Accrued expenditure		25 742	108 471
Other		(13)	-
	Total	29 232	127 918
8 Remuneration and contributions payable			
Remuneration		9 900	11 692
Contributions		22 711	23 878
	Total	32 611	35 571
9 Financing			
Exchange rate difference due to payments		13 328	9 144
Exchange rate difference disbursement Argentina		2 056	34 822
Exchange rate difference VAT refund		3 720	14 826
	Total	19 104	58 792

Notes to the Financial Statements at 31 March 2022 and 2023

10 Contributions due and paid in advance at the beginning of the financial year, committed and collected during the financial year and due and received in advance at the close of the financial year.

Contributions Parties	Due at 31/3/2022	Paid in advance at 31/3/2022	Com-mitted	Received during the financial year	Due at 31/3/2023	Paid in advance at 31/3/2023
Argentina			60 347	60 347		
Australia		60.335	60 347	60 335		60 323
Belgium		40.009	40 021			
Brazil	55.822		40 021		95 843	
Bulgaria			33 923	33 923		
Chile	46.119		46 119	92 238		
China			46 119	46 119		
Czech Republic			40 021	80 042		40 021
Ecuador			33 923	33 923		
Finland			40 021	40 021		
France		60.347	60 347	60 347		60 347
Germany			52 216	52 216		
India			46 119	46 119		
Italy		52.216	52 216	52 216		52 216
Japan			60 347	60 347		
Norway		60.327	60 347	60 367		60 347
New Zealand		60.322	60 347	60 372		60 347
Netherlands		46.119	46 119	46 119		46 119
Peru		33.965	33 923	34 313		34 355
Poland		40.021	40 021			
Republic of Korea		40.021	40 021			
Russian Federation			46 119		46 119	
Spain			46 119	46 119		
South Africa		46.119	46 119			
Sweden			46 119	46 119		
United Kingdom		60.347	60 347	60 347		60 347
Ukraine			40 021		40 021	
United States		60.347	60 347	60 347		60 347
Uruguay	40.021		40 021	80 042		
Total	141 962	660 495	1 378 097	1 212 336	181 983	534 769

Albert Lluberas Bonaba
Executive Secretary

Gabriela A. Russo
Financial Manager

Provisional Financial Report FY 2023/24

APPROPRIATION LINES	Audited Statement 2022/23	Budget 2023/24	Prov Statement 2023/24
INCOME			
Contributions pledged	$ 1 378 097	$ 1 378 097	$ 1 378 099
Voluntary contributions	$ -	$ -	$ -
Other income	$ 4 053	$ 6 500	$ 7 052
Total Income	**$ 1 382 150**	**$ 1 384 597**	**$ 1 385 151**
EXPENSES			
SALARIES			
Executive staff	$ 313 326	$ 328 898	$ 329 146
General staff	$ 406 124	$ 420 371	$ 427 310
ATCM support staff	$ 13 616	$ 14 900	$ 15 730
Trainee	$ -	$ 600	$ -
Overtime	$ 9 081	$ 10 000	$ 10 742
Total Salaries	$ 742 147	$ 774 769	$ 782 928
TRANSLATION AND INTERPRETATION			
Translation and Interpretation	$ 322 460	$ 313 500	$ 341 795
TRAVEL			
Travel, lodging, allowance, misc.	$ 105 599	$ 106 900	$ 108 626
INFORMATION TECHNOLOGY			
Hardware	$ 13 090	$ 11 000	$ 12 904
Software	$ 3 052	$ 3 500	$ 3 756
Development	$ 24 107	$ 25 500	$ 17 138
Hardware & software maintenance	$ 3 371	$ 3 500	$ 4 144
Support	$ 4 880	$ 7 000	$ 4 095
Total Information Technology	$ 48 500	$ 50 500	$ 42 038
PRINTING, EDITING & COPYING			
Final Report	$ 8 727	$ 10 000	$ 11 709
Other publications	$ 1 465	$ 2 500	$ 4 245
Total Printing Editing & Copying	$ 10 192	$ 12 500	$ 15 954
GENERAL SERVICES			
Legal advice & counselling	$ 4 416	$ 3 000	$ 2 591
Payroll services	$ 8 315	$ 8 400	$ 5 726
External audit	$ 11 428	$ 11 428	$ 11 428
Cleaning, maintenance & security	$ 7 528	$ 8 000	$ 3 911
Training	$ 3 330	$ 6 000	$ 4 626
Banking	$ 9 268	$ 8 000	$ 11 003
Rental of equipment	$ 740	$ 1 000	$ 791
Total General Services	$ 45 025	$ 45 828	$ 40 076
COMMUNICATION			
Telephone	$ 4 317	$ 3 500	$ 3 814
Internet	$ 5 584	$ 4 500	$ 8 228
Web hosting	$ 6 468	$ 8 500	$ 3 435
Postage	$ 723	$ 700	$ 634
Total Communication	$ 17 092	$ 17 200	$ 16 112

		Audited Statement 2022/23		Budget 2023/24		Prov Statement 2023/24
OFFICE						
Stationery & consumables	$	2 975	$	3 000	$	2 219
Books & subscriptions	$	795	$	1 000	$	546
Insurance	$	5 223	$	3 300	$	3 548
Furniture	$	2 128	$	1 500	$	109
Office equipment	$	241	$	3 000	$	1 365
Office improvement	$	3 796	$	4 000	$	1 279
Total Office	$	15 158	$	15 800	$	9 066
ADMINISTRATIVE						
Office supplies	$	748	$	2 000	$	1 151
Local transport	$	34	$	700	$	38
Miscellaneous	$	2 907	$	2 700	$	2 485
Utilities	$	2 416	$	2 500	$	2 520
Total Administrative	$	6 105	$	7 900	$	6 194
REPRESENTATION						
Representation	$	1 485	$	4 000	$	1 453
FINANCING						
Expenditures exchange (gain)/loss	$	9 144	$	16 000	$	13 613
Host Country Payments exchange (gain)/loss	$	34 822	$	6 500	$	51 930
VAT Refunds net (gain)/loss	$	16 394	$	7 500	$	21 041
Total Financing (gain)/loss	$	60 360	$	30 000	$	86 584
SUBTOTAL EXPENSES	**$**	**1 374 123**	**$**	**1 378 897**	**$**	**1 450 825**
FUND APPROPRIATIONS						
Working Capital Fund	$	-	$	-	$	-
Staff Replacement Fund	$	-	$	-	$	-
Staff Termination Fund	$	29 592	$	33 620	$	33 696
Involuntary Separation from Service	$	-	$	-	$	-
Translation Contingency Fund	$	-	$	-	$	-
Total Fund Appropriation	$	29 592	$	33 620	$	33 696
TOTAL EXPENSES & APPROPRIATIONS	**$**	**1 403 715**	**$**	**1 412 517**	**$**	**1 484 521**
Surplus / (Deficit) for the period	**$**	**(21 565)**	**$**	**(27 920)**	**$**	**(99 370)**

FUND ACTIVITY

	Audited Statement 2022/23	Net Movements 2023/24	Prov Statement 2023/24

GENERAL FUND

	Audited Statement 2022/23	Net Movements 2023/24	Prov Statement 2023/24
Audited start balance	$ 1 103 934		
To Involuntary Separation from Service Fund		$ (2 363)	
To Translation Contingency Fund		$ (37 880)	
Surplus/(Deficit) for the current period		$ (99 370)	
Provisional end balance			**$ 964 321**

WORKING CAPITAL FUND

	Audited Statement 2022/23	Net Movements 2023/24	Prov Statement 2023/24
Audited start balance	$ 229 952		
Provisional end balance		$ -	**$ 229 952**

STAFF REPLACEMENT FUND (1)

	Audited Statement 2022/23	Net Movements 2023/24	Prov Statement 2023/24
Audited start balance	$ 50 000		
Provisional end balance		$ -	**$ 50 000**

STAFF TERMINATION FUND (2)

	Audited Statement 2022/23	Net Movements 2023/24	Prov Statement 2023/24
Audited start balance	$ 126 489		
Appropriation in the current period		$ 33 696	
Provisional end balance			**$ 160 185**

INVOLUNTARY SEPARATION FROM SERVICE (3)

	Audited Statement 2022/23	Net Movements 2023/24	Prov Statement 2023/24
Audited start balance	$ 81 495		
From General Fund		$ 2 363	
Provisional end balance			**$ 83 858**

TRANSLATION CONTINGENCY FUND (4)

	Audited Statement 2022/23	Net Movements 2023/24	Prov Statement 2023/24
Audited start balance	$ 30 000		
Translation of CEE Petrel final documents		$ (17 880)	
From General Fund		$ 37 880	
Provisional end balance			**$ 50 000**

FINANCIAL REGULATION 6.3

	Audited Statement 2022/23	Net Movements 2023/24	Prov Statement 2023/24
General Fund	$ 1 103 934	$ (139 613)	$ 964 321
Unpaid Contributions (5)	$ (181 983)		$ (178 675)
Cash Surplus	**$ 921 951**		**$ 812 657**

Notes

1) Decision 1 (2006)
2) Decision 1 (2006)
3) Decision 3 (2019)
4) Decision 4 (2009) and Decision 2 (2023)
5) Unpaid contributions as of 31 March 2023 and 31 March 2024

Secretariat Programme 2024/2025

Summary

This document outlines the proposed plans for the Secretariat's activities for the intersessional period 2024/25. It focuses on the Secretariat's regular activities and on other additional activities aimed to enhance the ATS services and products offered to Parties. Financial information for this period is also included.

Introduction

This work programme outlines the activities proposed for the Secretariat in the Financial Year 2024/25 (from 1 April 2024 to 31 March 2025).

The programme focuses on the Secretariat's regular activities, such as the preparation of ATCM 47, the publication of Reports, tasks assigned to the Secretariat under Measure 1 (2003), and the various tasks requested by the latest ATCMs. It also covers other additional activities proposed to enhance the ATS services and products offered to Parties.

The programme and the accompanying budget figures for 2024/25 are based on the Forecast Budget for the Financial Year 2024/2025 approved in Decision 2 (2023).

Support for intersessional activities

During recent years, both the ATCM and the CEP have produced a substantial amount of intersessional work, mainly through Intersessional Contact Groups (ICGs) and informal discussion forums. The Secretariat will continue to provide support to these discussions, issue regular reminders of discussions in progress, and regularly provide detailed updates on the status of these discussions on the forum. The Secretariat will maintain close contact with ATCM Working Group Chairs to assist in the preparation of the next meeting.

Concerning the CEP, the Secretariat will continue to work with the CEP Chair and the conveners of the Subsidiary Group on Climate Change Response (SGCCR) and the Subsidiary Group on Management Plans (SGMP). The Secretariat will also maintain regular communication with the CEP Chair to facilitate the intersessional work of the CEP and prepare for the next meeting.

Planned support for ATCM 47 (2025) and ATCM 48 (2026)

The Government of Italy and the Secretariat of the Antarctic Treaty will jointly organise ATCM 47 and CEP 27, which will take place in 2025. The responsibilities of the Host Country Secretariat and the Antarctic Treaty Secretariat are described in the Organisational Manual, updated annually by the Antarctic Treaty Secretariat. The main tasks of the Secretariat at the meeting are document management, supervision of technical services, organisation of translation and interpretation services, assistance to Chairs and support for the compilation and publication of the Final Report. The Host Country Secretariat is responsible for the organisation of the venue, the provision of technical services, the contracting of rapporteur services and the social functions.

The translation and interpretation services comprise the translation of documents before, during and after the meeting, and interpretation during sessions. The Secretariat will also organise the note-taking services during the meeting and is responsible for the compilation and editing of the reports of the ATCM and CEP Meeting. The Secretariat will also establish a section of its website to make documents and other relevant materials available for delegates and to provide online registration to the meeting.

The Secretariat will also continue to assist the Government of Japan concerning the organisation of ATCM 48 (2026), including issues such as office and meeting room layouts and capacity, IT and audio-visual support and planning of events.

Coordination and contact

In addition to maintaining regular contact via email and telephone with the Parties and international institutions of the Antarctic Treaty system, attendance at meetings is an important tool for maintaining coordination and communication. Therefore, the Executive Secretary will attend the CCAMLR-43 meeting in Hobart in October 2024 and the SCAR Delegates meeting in Chile in July 2024, and the Executive Secretary and Deputy Executive Secretary will participate in the COMNAP Annual General Meeting 36 in Buenos Aires in August 2024.

Website and Web-based Services

Development of the Secretariat website

Based on user feedback, the Secretariat will make improvements to the meeting page tools such as the comments and notification systems. The development of an Antarctic Treaty application to be used on mobile devices before and during meetings will be evaluated in this period.

Databases and Maps

Antarctic Treaty database

The Secretariat will continue the process of refinement of the categories and topics currently used to classify ATCM measures in the Antarctic Treaty database to facilitate the search and filtering of measures. As indicated in the Secretariat Report 2023/2024, the work carried out in the "Tourism" category during the past year will be expanded to other subjects. The Secretariat stands ready to receive comments and suggestions on this initiative and will inform Parties on the progress of these initiatives during the intersessional period.

Mapping tools

The Secretariat will continue to explore the possible uses of the existing web-based geographical information platform for representing a variety of georeferenced content already existing in its databases or that could result from new information exchange requirements. In connection with this, the development of a new map displaying science activities is planned.

The Electronic Information Exchange System (EIES)

As usual, the Secretariat will continue to assist Parties in posting their information exchange materials, send periodic reminders to encourage compliance, and process information uploaded using the File Upload functionality. In addition, the Secretariat plans to produce new video tutorials and add tools to facilitate the follow-up of the uploading process to the EIES.

Improvements to summarized reports will be implemented to allow the retrieval of information on the total number of visitors to Antarctica per season, and on the location and status of all Antarctic stations and refuges, as reported by Parties through the EIES.

Training activities

Upon request, the Secretariat will continue to perform in-person and virtual training sessions with Party delegates and EIES operators to support their use of the EIES, explain new features and exchange views on how to continually enhance the system.

Also upon request, the Secretariat will continue to offer training activities at the ATS Headquarters on issues related to the Antarctic Treaty Consultative Meetings, based on the draft training programme attached as Annex 5 to the Secretariat Report 2023-24, submitted as SP 4 to ATCM 46. Parties are invited to contact the Secretariat to coordinate these activities for the intersessional period 2024/25. In relation to this, the Secretariat considers that the organization of the 2024 SCAR and COMNAP annual delegates' meeting in Chile and Argentina, respectively, presents a good opportunity for Parties to consider offering these activities to their representatives.

To allow for broader participation, the Secretariat also plans to prepare a summarized, virtual presentation on the topics covered in the draft training programme described above to be offered to all interested Parties in a webinar format via Zoom meeting. Details on this initiative will be circulated to Parties during 2024.

Final Reports and other Publications

ATCM Final Report and CEP Report

For ATCM 46 in Kochi, the Secretariat has prepared for the timely translation in the four Treaty languages of the CEP Chair's non-paper on the CEP advice to the ATCM. After the meeting, the Secretariat will translate, publish and distribute the ATCM 46 Final Report and its Annexes in the four Treaty languages according to the Procedures for the Submission, Translation and Distribution of Documents for the ATCM and the CEP Meeting, and other requirements established by the ATCM (ATCM XXXII Final Report, para. 72).

The Final Report will be available on the Secretariat's website and hard copies will be distributed by courier and diplomatic channels. Delegations wishing to receive only digital versions are invited to communicate their preference to the Secretariat at their earliest convenience. Hard copies will also be available for purchase through online retailers. The Secretariat will adjust its internal procedures to continue to improve the editorial quality of the report, including pre-meeting and post-meeting document formatting.

Other documents and publications

If new rules are adopted, the Secretariat will publish an updated edition of the *Rules of Procedure of the Antarctic Treaty Consultative Meeting and the Committee for Environmental Protection* in the four Treaty languages. This book would be available on the Secretariat website and hard copies would also be available from online retailers worldwide. The Secretariat is ready to produce a new edition of the *Compilation of Key Documents of the Antarctic Treaty System* in the four Treaty languages, if needed.

Documentation and Public Information

Documents of the ATCM

In order to complete the Meeting Documents database, the Secretariat will contact the Parties that organised Consultative Meetings and other Meetings for which Final Reports and meeting papers are still missing.

The Secretariat will make available on its website additional documents arising from ATCM 46, including reports from ATCM Observers and Experts and other documents, in line with the provisions established by the ATCM (ATCM XXXII Final Report, para. 72).

Editorial Guidelines

The Secretariat will continually update its editorial guidelines, with the aim of standardising the work of rapporteurs, translators, proofreaders and Secretariat staff. The Secretariat will update its web-based technical glossary (lexicon) for internal use, to improve consistency in the translation of ATCM documents.

Image Bank

The Secretariat is planning to present a new platform for the current image bank, to provide a renewed visual aspect and new tools for searching, selecting and downloading photographic material. The Secretariat will keep Parties updated on this initiative during the intersessional period.

The Secretariat reiterates its invitation to Parties, Observers and Experts to provide the Secretariat with original photographic material to be published in the image bank under a Creative Commons license. Photographs corresponding to Antarctic Treaty Meetings held before the establishment of the Secretariat, as well as those related to fieldwork carried out by Parties in Antarctica in pursuit of compliance with the regulations established by the ATCM and the CEP, such as inspection activities, will be particularly appreciated. The Tools for Delegates section of the Secretariat website offers delegates a form for submitting photographic material.

Likewise, the Secretariat would appreciate receiving videos related to the Consultative Meetings, such as the presentation videos displayed each year by the host country of the following meeting during the closing plenary session.

Personnel

On 1 April 2024, the Secretariat staff consisted of the following personnel:

Position	Since	Rank	Step	Term
Executive staff				
Executive Secretary	1-09-2017	E1	7	31-08-2025
Deputy Executive Secretary	1-08-2019	E3	4	31-07-2027
General staff				
Information Officer	1-11-2004	G1	6	
Support Officer (part-time)	1-02-2020	G2	4	
Editor	1-02-2006	G2	6	
Accountant	1-04-2023	G3	2	
IT Specialist	1-02-2019	G3	5	
Communications Specialist (part-time)	1-10-2010	G4	6	
Office Manager	15-11-2012	G4	6	
Cleaning Assistant (part-time)	1-07-2015	G7	6	

No changes are foreseen in the General staff positions of the Secretariat for this period.

For this reporting period with the Secretariat programme starting on 1st April, as already informed at the last ATCM in 2023, Parties may decide on an updated procedure for the Call for Selection of a new Executive Secretary to be carried out during ATCM 46 in 2024 and ATCM 47 in 2025, when the selection will be made. The Secretariat has provided the Host Country and State Depositary with the relevant references and previously used forms, and for the needed consideration and update, resulting in their presentation of a WP (WP 17) to propose a Decision to be adopted by the Parties.

Financial Matters

The Budget for the Financial Year 2024/25 and the Forecast Budget for the Financial Year 2025/26 are included in Appendix 1.

Draft Budget for the Financial Year 2024/25

Allocation to the appropriation lines follows closely the proposed forecast from last year. Only smaller adjustments to the foreseen expenses in the Financial Year 2024/25 have been introduced to reflect rising costs in US Dollars both locally and internationally, and the possible impact of further devaluations in the Financing line.

The cost of living continued to rise sharply in Argentina in the year 2023. The inflation rate (Índice de Precios al Consumidor) for 2023 published by INDEC (Instituto Nacional de Estadística y Censos de la República Argentina) was 211%. Until November 2023, this was only partially compensated by a rise of the US Dollar against the Argentine Peso of 118%; however, in December 2023 the newly elected government devaluated the Peso by an additional 51%.

The first quarter of 2024 has shown even higher inflation, surpassing 50% for that period alone, with a virtually fixed exchange rate. Therefore, considering the unpredictability of the situation in terms of cost of living in Argentina, the Executive Secretary proposes a rise of salaries of the Secretariat Staff of 2,9%, in line with average world inflation.

The proposed salary scale is provided in Appendix 3.

Despite the impact of these factors, due to conservative and precautionary management, the budget estimates a deficit of 89 922 USD, which would be covered by the existing surplus in the General Fund.

Quarterly reports of budget implementation will be provided to the Parties in accordance with Decision 2 (2023).

Funds

Working Capital Fund

According to Financial Regulation 6.2 (a), the Working Capital Fund must be maintained at 1/6 of the Secretariat's budget (currently 229 952 USD).

Staff Termination Fund

The Staff Termination Fund will be credited with 36 491 USD in accordance with Staff Regulation 10.4 (see Appendix 1).

Forecast Budget for the Financial Year 2025/26

It is expected that most of the regular activities of the Secretariat will continue in the Financial Year 2025/26 including meetings in person in 2025 in Italy and therefore, unless the programme undergoes major changes, no major change in appropriation lines is foreseen.

However, as income would remain stable while minor rise adjustments in USD for local costs in Argentina and moderate global inflation are expected to continue, the Forecast Budget for this period is expected to show a deficit of 91 972 USD which would be covered by accumulated surplus in the General Fund.

The contributions for the Financial Year 2025/26 will not rise. Appendix 2 shows the contribution scale for the Financial Year 2025/26.

Five-Year Forward Budget profile 2025/26 - 2029/30

Under reasonable assumptions the budget profile allows a zero-nominal increase in contributions, which has remained unchanged since 2014, until 2029/30. However, it is possible that at some point during this five-year period, changes in local and global conditions create the need to discuss a possible rise in contributions, or a revision of the category of each Party in the contribution scale to offset larger deficits, as explained in SP 6 *Five-Year Budget Profile* presented separately.

Budget FY 2024/25 and Forecast FY 2025/26

APPROPRIATION LINES	Prov Statement 2023/24	Forecast 2024/25	Budget 2024/25	Forecast 2025/26
INCOME				
Contributions pledged	$ 1 378 099	$ 1 378 097	$ 1 378 097	$ 1 378 097
Voluntary contributions	$ -	$ -	$ -	$ -
Other income	$ 7 052	$ 6 000	$ 6 000	$ 6 000
Total Income	**$ 1 385 151**	**$ 1 384 097**	**$ 1 384 097**	**$ 1 384 097**
EXPENSES				
SALARIES				
Executive staff	$ 329 146	$ 332 909	$ 343 600	$ 335 000
General staff	$ 427 310	$ 399 974	$ 413 400	$ 418 000
ATCM support staff	$ 15 730	$ 16 000	$ 15 000	$ 15 500
Trainee	$ -	$ 1 200	$ 600	$ 1 200
Overtime	$ 10 742	$ 10 500	$ 10 500	$ 11 000
Total Salaries	**$ 782 928**	**$ 760 583**	**$ 783 100**	**$ 780 700**
TRANSLATION AND INTERPRETATION				
Translation and Interpretation	**$ 341 795**	**$ 325 000**	**$ 335 000**	**$ 335 000**
TRAVEL				
Travel, lodging, allowance, misc.	**$ 108 626**	**$ 114 000**	**$ 114 000**	**$ 115 000**
INFORMATION TECHNOLOGY				
Hardware	$ 12 904	$ 11 000	$ 11 500	$ 12 000
Software	$ 3 756	$ 3 500	$ 4 000	$ 4 500
Development	$ 17 138	$ 26 500	$ 26 000	$ 27 000
Hardware & software maintenance	$ 4 144	$ 3 500	$ 4 000	$ 4 500
Support	$ 4 095	$ 7 500	$ 7 000	$ 7 500
Total Information Technology	**$ 42 038**	**$ 52 000**	**$ 52 500**	**$ 55 500**
PRINTING, EDITING & COPYING				
Final Report	$ 11 709	$ 11 000	$ 11 500	$ 11 500
Other publications	$ 4 245	$ 3 000	$ 3 000	$ 3 000
Total Printing Editing & Copying	**$ 15 954**	**$ 14 000**	**$ 14 500**	**$ 14 500**
GENERAL SERVICES				
Legal advice & counselling	$ 2 591	$ 3 500	$ 3 000	$ 3 500
Payroll services	$ 5 726	$ 8 400	$ 8 000	$ 8 000
External audit	$ 11 428	$ 11 428	$ 11 428	$ 11 900
Cleaning, maintenance & security	$ 3 911	$ 8 000	$ 7 500	$ 8 000
Training	$ 4 626	$ 7 000	$ 6 000	$ 7 000
Banking	$ 11 003	$ 8 500	$ 10 500	$ 11 000
Rental of equipment	$ 791	$ 1 000	$ 1 000	$ 1 000
Total General Services	**$ 40 076**	**$ 47 828**	**$ 47 428**	**$ 50 400**
COMMUNICATION				
Telephone	$ 3 814	$ 4 000	$ 4 500	$ 5 000
Internet	$ 8 228	$ 5 000	$ 7 000	$ 7 000
Web hosting	$ 3 435	$ 9 000	$ 7 000	$ 9 500
Postage	$ 634	$ 700	$ 1 000	$ 1 000
Total Communication	**$ 16 112**	**$ 18 700**	**$ 19 500**	**$ 22 500**

	Prov Statement 2023/24	Forecast 2024/25	Budget 2024/25	Forecast 2025/26
OFFICE				
Stationery & consumables	$ 2 219	$ 3 300	$ 3 300	$ 3 500
Books & subscriptions	$ 546	$ 1 000	$ 1 000	$ 1 000
Insurance	$ 3 548	$ 3 700	$ 4 000	$ 4 500
Furniture	$ 109	$ 2 000	$ 2 000	$ 2 000
Office equipment	$ 1 365	$ 3 500	$ 3 000	$ 3 000
Office improvement	$ 1 279	$ 4 000	$ 4 000	$ 4 500
Total Office	**$ 9 066**	**$ 17 500**	**$ 17 300**	**$ 18 500**
ADMINISTRATIVE				
Office supplies	$ 1 151	$ 2 500	$ 2 000	$ 2 000
Local transport	$ 38	$ 800	$ 500	$ 500
Miscellaneous	$ 2 485	$ 3 200	$ 3 200	$ 3 200
Utilities	$ 2 520	$ 3 000	$ 4 500	$ 5 000
Total Administrative	**$ 6 194**	**$ 9 500**	**$ 10 200**	**$ 10 700**
REPRESENTATION				
Representation	**$ 1 453**	**$ 4 000**	**$ 4 000**	**$ 4 000**
FINANCING				
Expenditures exchange (gain)/loss	$ 13 613	$ 15 000	$ 17 000	$ 17 000
Host Country Payments exchange (gain)/lo:	$ 51 930	$ 5 000	$ 12 000	$ 12 000
VAT Refunds net (gain)/loss	$ 21 041	$ 7 500	$ 11 000	$ 11 000
Total Financing (gain)/loss	**$ 86 584**	**$ 27 500**	**$ 40 000**	**$ 40 000**
SUBTOTAL EXPENSES	**$ 1 450 825**	**$ 1 390 611**	**$ 1 437 528**	**$ 1 446 800**
FUND APPROPRIATIONS				
Working Capital Fund	$ -	$ -	$ -	$ -
Staff Replacement Fund	$ -	$ -	$ -	$ -
Staff Termination Fund	$ 33 696	$ 36 491	$ 36 491	$ 29 269
Involuntary Separation from Service	$ -	$ -	$ -	$ -
Translation Contingency Fund	$ -	$ -	$ -	$ -
Total Fund Appropriation	**$ 33 696**	**$ 36 491**	**$ 36 491**	**$ 29 269**
TOTAL EXPENSES & APPROPRIATIONS	**$ 1 484 521**	**$ 1 427 102**	**$ 1 474 019**	**$ 1 476 069**
Surplus / (Deficit) for the period	**$ (99 370)**	**$ (43 005)**	**$ (89 922)**	**$ (91 972)**

FUND BALANCE

	Prov Statement 2023/24	Forecast 2024/25	Budget 2024/25	Forecast 2025/26
Working Capital Fund	$ 229 952	$ 229 952	$ 229 952	$ 229 952
Staff Replacement Fund	$ 50 000	$ 50 000	$ 50 000	$ 50 000
Staff Termination Fund	$ 160 185	$ 196 601	$ 196 601	$ 88 908
Involuntary Separation from Service	$ 83 858	$ 86 290	$ 86 290	$ 86 290
Translation Contingency Fund	$ 50 000	$ 30 000	$ 50 000	$ 50 000

Contribution Scale FY 2025/26

Party	Cat.	Mult.	Variable	Fixed	Total
Argentina	A	3,6	$ 36 587	$ 23 760	$ 60 347
Australia	A	3,6	$ 36 587	$ 23 760	$ 60 347
Belgium	D	1,6	$ 16 261	$ 23 760	$ 40 021
Brazil	D	1,6	$ 16 261	$ 23 760	$ 40 021
Bulgaria	E	1	$ 10 163	$ 23 760	$ 33 923
Chile	C	2,2	$ 22 359	$ 23 760	$ 46 119
China	C	2,2	$ 22 359	$ 23 760	$ 46 119
Czech Republic	D	1,6	$ 16 261	$ 23 760	$ 40 021
Ecuador	E	1	$ 10 163	$ 23 760	$ 33 923
Finland	D	1,6	$ 16 261	$ 23 760	$ 40 021
France	A	3,6	$ 36 587	$ 23 760	$ 60 347
Germany	B	2,8	$ 28 456	$ 23 760	$ 52 217
India	C	2,2	$ 22 359	$ 23 760	$ 46 119
Italy	B	2,8	$ 28 456	$ 23 760	$ 52 217
Japan	A	3,6	$ 36 587	$ 23 760	$ 60 347
Republic of Korea	D	1,6	$ 16 261	$ 23 760	$ 40 021
Netherlands	C	2,2	$ 22 359	$ 23 760	$ 46 119
New Zealand	A	3,6	$ 36 587	$ 23 760	$ 60 347
Norway	A	3,6	$ 36 587	$ 23 760	$ 60 347
Peru	E	1	$ 10 163	$ 23 760	$ 33 923
Poland	D	1,6	$ 16 261	$ 23 760	$ 40 021
Russian Federation	C	2,2	$ 22 359	$ 23 760	$ 46 119
South Africa	C	2,2	$ 22 359	$ 23 760	$ 46 119
Spain	C	2,2	$ 22 359	$ 23 760	$ 46 119
Sweden	C	2,2	$ 22 359	$ 23 760	$ 46 119
Ukraine	D	1,6	$ 16 261	$ 23 760	$ 40 021
United Kingdom	A	3,6	$ 36 587	$ 23 760	$ 60 347
United States	A	3,6	$ 36 587	$ 23 760	$ 60 347
Uruguay	D	1,6	$ 16 261	$ 23 760	$ 40 021

Total Pledged	**$ 1 378 097**

Salary Scale FY 2024/25

Schedule A

SALARY SCALE FOR THE EXECUTIVE STAFF

(United States Dollar)

2024/25		STEPS														
Level		I	II	III	IV	V	VI	VII	VIII	IX	X	XI	XII	XIII	XIV	XV
E1	A	$ 145 413	$ 148 117	$ 150 824	$ 153 530	$ 156 236	$ 158 940	$ 161 646	$ 164 353							
E1	B	$ 181 765	$ 185 147	$ 188 529	$ 191 913	$ 195 295	$ 198 676	$ 202 058	$ 205 442							
E2	A	$ 122 446	$ 124 749	$ 127 052	$ 129 353	$ 131 655	$ 133 956	$ 136 257	$ 138 560	$ 140 863	$ 143 165	$ 145 466	$ 145 727	$ 147 999		
E2	B	$ 153 057	$ 155 935	$ 158 815	$ 161 691	$ 164 568	$ 167 444	$ 170 321	$ 173 200	$ 176 080	$ 178 955	$ 181 833	$ 182 159	$ 184 999		
E3	A	$ 102 107	$ 104 326	$ 106 548	$ 108 769	$ 110 992	$ 113 213	$ 115 434	$ 117 656	$ 119 876	$ 122 097	$ 124 319	$ 125 651	$ 126 983	$ 129 174	$ 131 364
E3	B	$ 127 632	$ 130 408	$ 133 186	$ 135 963	$ 138 740	$ 141 515	$ 144 293	$ 147 071	$ 149 845	$ 152 621	$ 155 399	$ 157 063	$ 158 728	$ 161 469	$ 164 205
E4	A	$ 84 666	$ 86 722	$ 88 782	$ 90 834	$ 92 894	$ 94 948	$ 97 002	$ 99 062	$ 101 120	$ 103 174	$ 105 232	$ 105 805	$ 107 833	$ 109 861	$ 111 889
E4	B	$ 105 833	$ 108 403	$ 110 979	$ 113 543	$ 116 118	$ 118 687	$ 121 252	$ 123 826	$ 126 399	$ 128 966	$ 131 539	$ 132 255	$ 134 791	$ 137 326	$ 139 862
E5	A	$ 70 196	$ 72 037	$ 73 875	$ 75 717	$ 77 554	$ 79 392	$ 81 234	$ 83 068	$ 84 911	$ 86 751	$ 88 586	$ 89 182			
E5	B	$ 87 745	$ 90 047	$ 92 345	$ 94 645	$ 96 943	$ 99 242	$ 101 542	$ 103 836	$ 106 138	$ 108 438	$ 110 734	$ 111 477			
E6	A	$ 55 570	$ 57 337	$ 59 104	$ 60 874	$ 62 639	$ 64 406	$ 66 176	$ 67 943	$ 69 709	$ 70 784	$ 71 478				
E6	B	$ 69 461	$ 71 672	$ 73 878	$ 76 091	$ 78 299	$ 80 508	$ 82 721	$ 84 929	$ 87 137	$ 88 480	$ 89 347				

Note: Row B is the base salary (shown in Row A) with an additional 25% for salary on-costs (retirement fund and insurance premiums, installation and repatriation grants, education allowances etc.) and is the total salary entitlement for executive staff in accordance with regulation 5.1.

Schedule B

SALARY SCALE FOR THE GENERAL STAFF

(United States Dollar)

		STEPS														
Level		I	II	III	IV	V	VI	VII	VIII	IX	X	XI	XII	XIII	XIV	XV
G1		$ 69 629	$ 72 877	$ 76 127	$ 79 375	$ 82 760	$ 86 290									
G2		$ 58 024	$ 60 731	$ 63 438	$ 66 145	$ 68 968	$ 71 909									
G3		$ 48 352	$ 50 607	$ 52 865	$ 55 120	$ 57 473	$ 59 926									
G4		$ 40 295	$ 42 175	$ 44 055	$ 45 935	$ 47 894	$ 49 938									
G5		$ 33 287	$ 34 841	$ 36 394	$ 37 948	$ 39 569	$ 41 260									
G6		$ 27 285	$ 28 557	$ 29 830	$ 31 104	$ 32 432	$ 33 816									
G7		$ 14 750	$ 15 387	$ 16 026	$ 16 664	$ 17 329	$ 18 024									

Decision 4 (2024)

Multi-year Strategic Work Plan for the Antarctic Treaty Consultative Meeting

The Representatives,

Reaffirming the values, objectives and principles contained in the Antarctic Treaty and its Protocol on Environmental Protection;

Recalling Decision 3 (2012) on the Multi-year Strategic Work Plan ("the Plan") and its principles;

Bearing in mind that the Plan is complementary to the agenda of the Antarctic Treaty Consultative Meeting ("ATCM") and that the Parties and other ATCM participants are encouraged to contribute as usual to other matters on the ATCM agenda;

Decide:

1. to adopt the Plan annexed to this Decision; and

2. that the Plan annexed to Decision 5 (2023) is no longer current.

ATCM Multi-year Strategic Work Plan

	Priority	ATCM 46 (2024)	Intersessional	ATCM 47 (2025)	Intersessional	ATCM 48 (2026)	Intersessional	ATCM 49 (2027)
1.	Consider coordinated outreach to non-party states whose nationals or assets are active in Antarctica and states that are Antarctic Treaty Parties but not yet to the Protocol	ATCM to identify and reach out to non-party states whose nationals are active in Antarctica	Coordination to be considered within competent authority online forum	ATCM to identify and reach out to non-party states whose nationals are active in Antarctica	Coordination to be considered within competent authority online forum	ATCM to identify and reach out to non-party states whose nationals are active in Antarctica	Coordination to be considered within competent authority online forum	ATCM to identify and reach out to non-party states whose nationals are active in Antarctica
2.	Contribute to nationally and internationally coordinated education and outreach activities from an Antarctic Treaty perspective	WG1 to consider the report of the ICG on Education and Outreach	ICG on Education and Outreach	WG1 to consider the report of the ICG on Education and Outreach	ICG on Education and Outreach	WG1 to consider Education and Outreach	ICG on Education and Outreach	WG1 to consider Education and Outreach
3.	Share and discuss strategic science priorities in order to identify and pursue opportunities for collaboration as well as capacity building in science, particularly in relation to climate change	Parties to consider to assess progress against the recommendations and priority actions identified by the 2022 ACCE Decadal Synopsis and the 2023 joint CEP/ATCM session on climate change	Parties to upload information in the EIES relating to scientific cooperation in all research projects.	Parties to provide specific information on how to engage in international scientific initiatives, particularly in relation to climate change		Parties to continue providing specific information on how to engage in international scientific initiatives, particularly in relation to climate change		
4.	To bring Annex VI into force and to continue to gather information on repair and remediation of environmental damage and other	ATCM to evaluate progress made towards Annex VI becoming effective in accordance with Article IX of the		ATCM to evaluate progress made towards Annex VI becoming effective in		ATCM to evaluate progress made towards Annex VI becoming effective in		ATCM to evaluate progress made towards Annex VI becoming

	Priority	ATCM 46 (2024)	Intersessional	ATCM 47 (2025)	Intersessional	ATCM 48 (2026)	Intersessional	ATCM 49 (2027)
	relevant issues to inform future negotiations on liability	Antarctic Treaty, and what action may be necessary and appropriate to encourage Parties to approve Annex VI in a timely manner		accordance with Article IX of the Antarctic Treaty, and what action may be necessary and appropriate to encourage Parties to approve Annex VI in a timely manner		accordance with Article IX of the Antarctic Treaty, and what action may be necessary and appropriate to encourage Parties to approve Annex VI in a timely manner		effective in accordance with Article IX of the Antarctic Treaty, and what action may be necessary and appropriate to encourage Parties to approve Annex VI in a timely manner
5.	Assess the progress of the CEP on its ongoing work to review best practices and to improve existing tools and develop further tools for environmental protection, including environmental impact assessment procedures	WG 1 to consider advice of the CEP and discuss the policy considerations of the review of Environmental Impact Assessment (EIA)		WG 1 to consider advice of the CEP and discuss the policy considerations of the review of Environmental Impact Assessment (EIA)		WG 1 to consider advice of the CEP and discuss the policy considerations of the review of Environmental Impact Assessment (EIA)		WG 1 to consider advice of the CEP and discuss the policy considerations of the review of Environmental Impact Assessment (EIA)
6.	Promoting decarbonization and increase of energy efficiency in Antarctic operations to advance on the implementation of Resolution 4 (2022)	Parties to share information on their experiences on Infrastructure vulnerability, Biosecurity protocols, ways to increase energy efficiency and waste and		Parties to share information on their projects to decarbonize and increase energy efficiency in Antarctic operations		Parties to continue sharing information on their projects to decarbonize and increase energy efficiency in Antarctic operations		

	Priority	ATCM 46 (2024)	Intersessional	ATCM 47 (2025)	Intersessional	ATCM 48 (2026)	Intersessional	ATCM 49 (2027)
		emissions reductions						
7.	Modernisation of Antarctic Stations in context of climate change	ATS to provide a summary of documents submitted on the modernisation of Antarctic stations from 2016 to 2023 Parties to continue sharing information on modernisation of Antarctic stations Parties to assess the performance of this priority	Parties through their National Antarctic Programmes to engage in discussions on modernisation and potential risks in the context of climate change during next COMNAP meeting	Consider advice from Parties and COMNAP on infrastructure modernisation and potential risks in the context of climate change		Parties to assess the performance of this priority		
8.	Contribute to strengthening the consistent implementation of the Polar Code	Parties to continue sharing documents on the national experiences at implementing the Polar Code Parties to submit papers on how they promote implementation of the Polar Code to different stakeholders in their national maritime clusters.		Parties to continue sharing documents on national experiences and best practices on implementing the IMO Polar Code in the Antarctic Treaty area Parties to submit papers on how they promote the harmonized implementation of		Parties to assess the progress of this priority		

	Priority	ATCM 46 (2024)	Intersessional	ATCM 47 (2025)	Intersessional	ATCM 48 (2026)	Intersessional	ATCM 49 (2027)
		Parties to discuss possible ways to cooperate with the Arctic Council States and other major Flag States for sharing information and best practices in implementing the Polar Code.		the Polar Code to stakeholders in their national maritime clusters				
9.	Promote enhancement of hydrographic surveying in Antarctica	Parties to inform their geographical priorities to map unchartered areas Parties, IAATO and IHO to report on progress in hydrographical products Parties to assess progress on this priority	ATS to liaise with IHO to invite them to provide feedback in ATCM 47	Parties to consider IHO advice Parties to assess the progress on this priority		Parties to assess the progress of this priority		
10.	Develop a strategic approach to the management of Antarctic tourism to ensure it is conducted in a safe and environmentally responsible way	Review progress on implementation and entry into force of Measure 4 (2004) and Measure 15 (2009)	Interested Parties, in consultation with the Secretariat, to consider proposals for changes to the information exchange	Review progress on implementation and entry into force of Measure 4 (2004) and Measure 15 (2009) and invite				

	Priority	ATCM 46 (2024)	Intersessional	ATCM 47 (2025)	Intersessional	ATCM 48 (2026)	Intersessional	ATCM 49 (2027)
			requirements and the EIES to share information on separately authorized tourist and other non-governmental activities, linkages between such activities, and information on science activities.	Parties to provide any relevant updates Parties are invited to report on implementation of tourism-related ATCM Resolutions				
			ICG on the development of a framework for the regulation of tourism and other non-governmental activities in Antarctica, including on-line workshops Workshop on the Development of a framework for the regulation of tourism and other non-governmental activities in	Special Working Group on the development of a framework for the regulation of tourism and other non-governmental activities in Antarctica				

	Priority	ATCM 46 (2024)	Intersessional	ATCM 47 (2025)	Intersessional	ATCM 48 (2026)	Intersessional	ATCM 49 (2027)
			Antarctica prior to and in conjunction with ATCM 47					
11.	Enhancing compliance with ATCM regulations relating to non-governmental activities including tourism activities	Parties will approve a best practice guide on how to gather and share evidence of suspected non-compliance	Request feedback on utility of guide	Further enhance the guide				
12.	Address equality, diversity and inclusion issues, by promoting full participation of underrepresented groups in Antarctic science and operations activities across all Antarctic issues, including science, operations, policy and law	Parties, Observers and Experts to share information on their plans and policies on these issues		Parties, Observers and Experts to share information on their plans and policies on these issues Parties to assess progress on this priority Consider the elaboration of a comprehensive policy on equality, diversity and inclusion in the Antarctic community		The Parties, Observers and Experts that have not shared information on their plans and policies on these issues yet are invited to present them. Consider the elaboration of a comprehensive policy on equality, diversity and inclusion in the Antarctic community		

	Priority	ATCM 46 (2024)	Intersessional	ATCM 47 (2025)	Intersessional	ATCM 48 (2026)	Intersessional	ATCM 49 (2027)
13.	Strengthen coordination on the management of hazardous natural events in Antarctic facilities	Parties to continue exchanging plans to manage hazardous natural events in Antarctic facilities Parties to discuss where to consider these plans Invite COMNAP to report on the work of its Technical Collaboration Group		Parties to discuss how/where to report these plans (e.g. EIES) Parties to assess progress on this priority				
14.	Continue work on addressing the heightened risks that highly pathogenic avian influenza presents in Antarctica		ICG on biosecurity protocols	Parties to consider any updated work and advice from Parties, Observers and Experts on managing risk Parties to consider report of ICG on biosecurity protocols		Parties to consider any updated work and advice from Parties, Observers and Experts on managing risk		

Note: The ATCM Working Groups mentioned above are not permanent but are established by consensus at the end of each Antarctic Treaty Consultative Meeting.

Decision 5 (2024)

Development of a Framework for the Regulation of Tourism and Other Non-Governmental Activities in Antarctica

The Representatives,

Affirming the determination of the Antarctic Treaty Consultative Meeting ("ATCM") to continue to manage and regulate tourism and other non-governmental activities in the Antarctic Treaty area in accordance with the values, objectives and principles of the Antarctic Treaty and its Protocol on Environmental Protection ("the Protocol");

Acknowledging the longstanding efforts of the ATCM to manage Antarctic tourism and other non-governmental activities, including the adoption of specific Measures, Decisions and Resolutions in support of the management of these activities;

Recalling Resolution 7 (2009) *General Principles of Antarctic Tourism* through which the ATCM articulated general principles to be used to inform and guide further work in managing Antarctic tourism activities;

Recognising the potential of properly managed tourism to enhance public appreciation of the intrinsic values of Antarctica;

Concerned by the actual and potential impacts of the recent large increase in visitation and diversification of tourism and other non-governmental activities in the Antarctic Treaty area;

Desiring to that end to continue to draw upon the best scientific and technical advice available, including relevant data, consistent with Article 10 of the Protocol;

Reaffirming their commitment to the comprehensive protection of the Antarctic environment and dependent and associated ecosystems and the protection of Antarctica as a natural reserve, devoted to peace and science;

Reaffirming that protection of the environment is essential, and precaution is to be applied to preserve Antarctica for present and future generations;

Committed to ensuring that all activities undertaken in the Antarctic Treaty area are conducted as safely as possible;

Recalling that ATCM XLV initiated a dedicated process to develop a comprehensive and consistent framework for the regulation of tourism and other non-governmental activities in the Antarctic Treaty area (Decision 6 (2023));

Determined to take urgent, ambitious and comprehensive action, including with respect to the potential of broad and cumulative effects on the Antarctic environment of all human activities;

Aiming at developing such a framework in an expeditious manner;

Decide:

1. to develop a comprehensive and consistent framework for the regulation of Antarctic tourism and other non-governmental activities;

2. that the development of such a framework continues to be discussed in a special Working Group of the ATCM, taking into account:
   - best practices and examples developed by the ATCM;
   - the relevance of existing practices and examples, including those developed by the International Association of Antarctica Tour Operators ("IAATO"), and from around the world;
   - existing requirements for information exchange under Decision 4 (2023) and any need to revise them;
   - information exchanged through the Electronic Information Exchange System;
   - results of monitoring and observation programmes;
   - the implementation of the precautionary approach;

3. that the framework:
   - be ambitious, comprehensive, dynamic and flexible;
   - builds upon the specific Measures, Decisions and Resolutions in support of the management of tourism and other non-governmental activities as well as their implementation;
   - addresses the orderly, coordinated and predictable conduct of tourism and other non-governmental activities, and does not undermine the objectives of governmental activities;
   - addresses all aspects of tourism and other non-governmental activities, including but not limited to tourism's relationship with the protection of the environment, scientific research, and the preservation of human life and safety;
   - will be developed from discussions of the topics listed in the Annex with a view to addressing them in the framework; and

4. that the dedicated process referred to in Decision 6 (2023) is to be completed as soon as possible, noting that the 50th ATCM is expected to be held in 2028, and:
   - will include intersessional work in the form of an ATCM intersessional contact group, convened by the Chair of the special Working Group, including online workshops as appropriate, taking into account different time zones;
   - may, subject to available resources, include intersessional work in the form of:
     - in-person workshops enabling virtual attendance;
     - Meetings of Experts and/or Special ATCMs as agreed by the ATCM.

List of Topics

Building block 1: Managing growth

- Numbers (visitors, ships, aircraft, operators, etc.)
- Timing (length of season)
- Sites (number, types, location, regions, sensitivity, unvisited, protection of) and spatial management, on the basis of site and regional Antarctic scale considerations
- Infrastructure

Building block 2: Managing diversification

- Activities
- Transportation modes
- Actors (e.g., independent actors with no link to State Party/responsible government entity)

Building block 3: Monitoring

- Monitoring, including environmental monitoring (e.g. data collection, management, access and use)
- Observation, inspection and supervision
- Funding
- Coordination
- Responsibilities
- Reporting

Building block 4: Compliance and Enforcement

- Identification of causes of non-compliance, including reporting
- Addressing cases of non-compliance
- Observation, inspection and supervision

Building block 5: Governance

- Leadership role of the ATCM
- Advice from the CEP
- Cooperation and coordination, including between National competent authorities
- Addressing National competent authorities shopping, including relevant issues of national legislation
- In-field coordination
- Independent data management and information and reporting
- Exchange of information
- Fees
- Safety (ship safety, air safety, liability, insurance, emergency response, search and rescue, contingency planning, etc.)

- Liability
- Activities of state/non-state hybrid nature
- Not undermining the objectives of governmental activities
- Accreditation of operators
- Harmonisation of authorisation processes
- Institutional arrangements
- Addressing clear state responsibility for all tourist and other non-governmental activities

Building block 6: General Topics

- Objectives
- Scope
- Definitions
- Precaution
- Environment (consequences to, state of, cumulative effects of all kinds of anthropogenic activities, etc.)
- Assessment methodologies
- Primacy of scientific research in relation to all tourism and other non-governmental activities
- Addressing the status of science activities associated with tourism and other non-governmental activities
- Protection of values
- Relationship to existing rules and instruments (of the ATS)
- Incorporation of existing Resolutions, guidelines, regulations, practices, as appropriate
- Avoidance or mitigation of non-climatic stressors to the environment
- Adaptive governance (flexibility; futureproofing)
- Public education and awareness

3. Resolutions

Resolution 1 (2024)

Revised Guide to the Preparation of Management Plans for Antarctic Specially Protected Areas

The Representatives,

Recalling the requirements under Article 5 of Annex V to the Protocol on Environmental Protection to the Antarctic Treaty ("the Protocol") to prepare and revise Management Plans for Antarctic Specially Protected Areas;

Recalling also the Action within the Committee for Environmental Protection ("CEP") Climate Change Response Work Programme to 'Review and revise where necessary existing management tools to consider if they afford the best practical adaptation measure to areas at risk from climate change';

Noting that under Resolution 2 (2011), the Antarctic Treaty Consultative Meeting ("ATCM") adopted a revised version of the Guide to the Preparation of Management Plans for Antarctic Specially Protected Areas ("the Guide");

Desiring to update the Guide to reflect current best practice in the preparation of Management Plans for Antarctic Specially Protected Areas, including with regard to climate change;

Considering the revision of the Guide by the CEP and its Subsidiary Group on Management Plans;

Recommend that:

1. the Guide to the Preparation of Management Plans for Antarctic Specially Protected Areas annexed to this Resolution replace the Guide adopted by Resolution 2 (2011) and be used by those engaged in the preparation or revision of Management Plans;

2. the Antarctic Treaty Secretariat post the text of Resolution 2 (2011) on its website in a way that makes clear that it is no longer current; and

3. the Antarctic Treaty Secretariat make Appendix 2 of this Guide available as a stand-alone document on its website.

Guide to the Preparation of Management Plans for Antarctic Specially Protected Areas

Background

Purpose of the Guide

In 1991 the Antarctic Treaty Consultative Parties (ATCPs) adopted the Protocol on Environmental Protection to the Antarctic Treaty (Environmental Protocol) to ensure comprehensive environmental protection in Antarctica. The Environmental Protocol designates the whole of Antarctica as "a natural reserve" devoted to peace and science.

Annex V to the Environmental Protocol, adopted subsequently at ATCM XVI under Recommendation XVI-10, provides a legal framework for the establishment of specially protected and managed areas within the overall "natural reserve". The text of Annex V is available on the ATS website at http://www.ats.aq/documents/recatt/Att004_e.pdf.

Annex V specifies that any area in the Antarctic Treaty area, including any marine area, may be designated as an Antarctic Specially Protected Area (ASPA) to protect outstanding environmental, scientific, historic, aesthetic or wilderness values, any combination of those values, or ongoing or planned scientific research (Article 3, Annex V).

The Annex further specifies that any Party to the Antarctic Treaty, the Committee for Environmental Protection (CEP), the Scientific Committee on Antarctic Research (SCAR) or the Commission for the Conservation of Antarctic Marine Living Resources (CCAMLR) may propose an area for designation as an Antarctic Specially Protected Area by submitting a proposed Management Plan to the Antarctic Treaty Consultative Meeting (Article 5, Annex V).

The original version of this Guide, adopted by the Parties as an appendix to Resolution 2 (1998), was revised in 2011 (Resolution 2 (2011)) and again in 2024, including to further incorporate climate change considerations (Resolution 1 (2024)). The Guide has been developed in order to assist any proponent in the process of proposing an Antarctic Specially Protected Area, with the following concrete aims:

- to assist Parties in their efforts to prepare Management Plans for proposed Antarctic Specially Protected Areas (ASPA) as required by the Protocol (Article 5, Annex V);
- to provide a framework which, when followed, enables Management Plans to meet the requirements of the Protocol;
- to help achieve clear content, clarity, consistency (with other Management Plans) and effectiveness to expedite their review, adoption and implementation; and
- where appropriate, assist proponents to give consideration to the possible implications of climate change for the Area and proposed activities within it.

It is important to note that this guide is intended as no more than an aide-mémoire to the production of Management Plans for ASPAs. It has no legal status. Anyone intending to prepare a Management Plan should examine the provisions of Annex V to the Protocol carefully and seek advice from their national authority at an early stage.

Protected areas network

Annex V obliges Parties to seek to identify, within a *systematic environmental-geographical framework*, and to include in the series of Antarctic Specially Protected Areas:

- areas kept inviolate from human interference so that future comparisons may be possible with localities that have been affected by human activities;
- representative examples of major terrestrial, including glacial and aquatic, ecosystems and marine ecosystems;

- areas with important or unusual assemblages of species, including major colonies of breeding native birds or mammals;
- the type locality or only known habitat of any species;
- areas of particular interest to ongoing or planned scientific research;
- examples of outstanding geological, glaciological or geomorphological features;
- areas of outstanding aesthetic and wilderness value;
- sites or monuments of recognized historic value; and
- such other areas as may be appropriate to protect the outstanding environmental, scientific, historic, aesthetic or wilderness values, any combination of those values, or ongoing or planned scientific research.

This provision of the Environmental Protocol provides the essential framework for an *Antarctic protected areas network*. The operationalization of what this framework entails has, however, been debated since the adoption of Annex V.

A number of analyses and evaluations of representation of the nine categories listed in Article 3.2 of Annex V have been conducted since the adoption of Annex V. First through a SCAR/IUCN Workshop on Protected Areas in 1992, then in two Protected Area workshops held in conjunction with CEP I and II in 1998 and 1999. In an analysis presented to CEP VIII in 2005 (ATCM XXVIII - WP 11) it was noted that:

- there is an uneven distribution of ASPAs amongst the categories set out in Article 3.2 of Annex V, which is simply a product of history, in that a series of ad hoc designations have been made over time, rather than a systematic selection of sites within an overarching strategy or framework.
- in the absence of such a framework there is no means for assessing whether the current distribution is appropriate or not.
- in the absence of a holistic approach to management of the protected areas system (along the lines of a strategic environmental geographic framework as provided for in Article 3.2 of Annex V), the distribution of sites can be no more than simply noted.

More recently, a joint SCAR/CEP Workshop on Further Developing the Antarctic Protected Area System was held in 2019. Based on the outcomes of this workshop, CEP XXII forwarded a report to the ATCM advising on the state of the protected area system (*Report on the State of the Antarctic Protected Area System* - Attachment A to ATCM XLII - WP 70).

The understanding of the term systematic environmental-geographic framework has evolved over time. However, the Environmental Domains Analysis prepared and presented in its final version to the CEP by New Zealand in 2005 constitutes the basis for our latest understanding of the concept. The Environmental Domains Analysis provides a classification of areas providing a data-derived, spatially explicit delineation of environmental variables in Antarctica, to be used for *inter alia* identification of priority sites for protection. The Domains Analysis provides a tool for a holistic and strategic designation of ASPAs, rather than assessing sites on their individual merits in isolation of other factors.

The ATCM has concurred that the Environmental Domains Analysis for the Antarctic Continent be used consistently and in conjunction with other tools agreed within the Antarctic Treaty System as a dynamic model for the identification of areas that could be designated as Antarctic Specially Protected Areas within the systematic environmental-geographical framework referred to in Article 3.2 of Annex V to the Protocol (Resolution 3 (2008)).

The Environmental Domains Analysis provides a useful and important measure of environmental variation across Antarctica that, in terms of the ice-free domains, can be considered essential as a first order assessment of likely systematic variation in biodiversity. For meaningful analysis at the finer spatial scales typically used in protected area designation, the EDA must nevertheless be supplemented with biodiversity data, which not only reflect current conditions but, importantly, historical processes that cannot in many instances be captured by modern environmental data.

In a further development, the ice-free areas of the Antarctic continent and close lying islands within the Antarctic Treaty area were classified into 16 biologically distinct Antarctic Conservation Biogeographic Regions (ACBRs), based on analyses of spatially explicit biodiversity data available from the Scientific Committee on Antarctic Research (SCAR) Biodiversity Database. The ATCM recommended that the Antarctic Conservation Biogeographic Regions be used in conjunction with the Environmental Domains Analysis and other tools agreed within the Antarctic Treaty system to support activities relevant to the interests of the Parties, including as a dynamic model for the identification of areas that could be designated as Antarctic Specially Protected Areas within the systematic environmental-geographic framework referred to in Article 3.2 of Annex V to the Environmental Protocol (Resolution 3 (2017)).

In 2015, the ATCM recognised BirdLife International's extensive global network of Important Bird Areas (IBAs), which includes 205 IBAs within the Treaty Area (Resolution 5 (2015)) (see Attachment to ATCM XXXVIII - IP 27). The ATCM recommended that the Committee for Environmental Protection provide an update to the ATCM on the extent to which these IBAs are, or should be, represented within the series of ASPAs, in particular those areas that might qualify as "major colonies of breeding native birds". Proponents may wish to consult the subsequent update report (available as Attachment A to ATCM XL - IP 16).

In 2022, the CEP agreed to encouraged Members to consider the protection of the type localities for Antarctic species, as listed in Annex V Article 3.2(d), and draw on the research presented in ATCM XLIV - WP 20, as well as other relevant tools, when: reviewing management plans for existing ASPAs; planning, assessing and conducting activities; and considering the designation of new ASPAs within a systematic environmental-geographic framework.

Identifying areas for protection

The designation of an area as a protected area provides the area with a higher level of protection beyond that achieved by other forms of planning and management measures under the Protocol in order to achieve specific protection aims and objectives.

When seeking to assess whether an area in fact needs such protection, it is necessary to be clear as to what values the area would aim to protect and as to the actual need to protect these values beyond the general protection provided by the Environmental Protocol. The CEP has adopted guidelines for implementation of the Framework for Protected Areas set forth in Article 3, Annex V to the Environmental Protocol that will assist any proponent in the process of such an evaluation. In such a process it would also need to consider how the designation of an ASPA would complement the existing protected areas network within the systematic environmental-geographical framework provided by the Environmental Domains Analysis, Antarctic Conservation Biogeographic Regions, Important Bird Areas and other relevant data available. Ensuring a thorough and in-depth analysis along these lines will indicate to the proponent whether designation of the area as a protected area is in fact required.

Proponents may also seek to identify values to be protected in areas that are subject to the impact of climate change with a view to mitigate or adapt to the climate impact through the management of human activities, and also consider whether climate change may have particular value for scientific research in the area.

Only when a candidate area has been through such an overall assessment is it correct to initiate the process of developing a Management Plan for the area, in line with the guidance provided by this document.

Relevant guidance material

- Annex V to the Environmental Protocol (http://www.ats.aq/documents/recatt/Att004_e.pdf)

- Guidelines for implementation of the Framework for Protected Areas set forth in Article 3, Annex V of the Environmental Protocol (http://www.ats.aq/documents/recatt/Att081_e.pdf)
- Environmental Domains Analysis (http://www.ats.aq/documents/recatt/Att408_e.pdf)
- Antarctic Conservation Biogeographic Regions (https://documents.ats.aq/recatt/att628_e.pdf)
- SCAR - Antarctic Climate Change and the Environment Reports (https://scar.org/library-data/scar-library/acce?lowbandwidth=0)
- Antarctic Environments Portal: Information Summaries (https://environments.aq)

Format of Management Plans for ASPAs

Article 5 of Annex V specifies matters that each ASPA Management Plan should address. The following sections of this Guide provide guidance in addressing those requirements (summarised in Table 1).

The CEP has highlighted the benefits of promoting consistency between protected area Management Plans. The Template for Antarctic Specially Protected Area Management Plans presented at Appendix 3 is intended as a standard framework into which proponents can insert content specific to the area in question when preparing a new or revised ASPA Management Plan.

The template includes cross-reference to the relevant sections of this Guide. References to the Guide are provided in *italicised text* and should be deleted from the Management Plan.

The template is formatted in accordance with the *Manual for the submission of documents to the Antarctic Treaty Consultative Meeting and the Committee for Environmental Protection* prepared by the Secretariat of the Antarctic Treaty. Proponents should consult the Manual for guidance on specific formatting issues, such as for tables and figures incorporated in a Management Plan.

Management plan section / section of Guide	**Article 5 reference**
Introduction	
1. Description of values to be protected	3a
2. Aims and objectives	3b
3. Management activities	3c
4. Period of designation	3d
5. Maps	3g
6. Description of the Area	3 e (i - iv)
6(v) Special zones within the Area	3f
7. Terms and conditions for entry Permits	3 i (i - x)
8. Supporting documentation	3h

Table 1. Headings used in this Guide cross-referenced to Article 5 of Annex V

Guidance for the content of Management Plans

Since the development of Management Plans for ASPAs is an evolving process, preparers of Management Plans should be aware of current best practice and are strongly urged to consult examples agreed at past ATCMs. The current Management Plan for each ASPA can be accessed from the Protected Areas database on the website of the Secretariat of the Antarctic Treaty, at https://www.ats.aq/devph/en/apa-database.

The template at Appendix 3 includes suggested standard wording for some sections. The availability of suggested standard wording is not intended to discourage proponents from developing and implementing site-specific or creative and innovative approaches to area protection and management. Suggested wording that relates directly to requirements arising from the Environmental Protocol is identified with an asterisk (*). As appropriate, the suggested wording should be utilised, modified, or replaced with alternative text that adequately reflects site-specific considerations for the Area in question.

A Management Plan should provide sufficient details about the special features of the Area and any requirements for access and management to ensure that individuals planning to visit the Area and national authorities responsible for issuing permits are able to do so in a manner consistent with the purpose for designation. It should clearly identify why the Area is designated, and what additional measures (beyond the general provisions of the Environmental Protocol and Annexes) apply to the Area as a result. The following sections provide guidance to proponents on the content addressed under each standard Management Plan heading.

Introduction

An introduction to the Management Plan is not a stated requirement of Article 5 of Annex V, but can provide a useful overview. Information might include a summary of the important features of the Area, its history (e.g. initial designation, modifications, earlier Management Plans), the scientific research and other activities that have been carried out there.

Reasons why special protection is deemed necessary or desirable should also be stated in the Management Plan, preferably in the introduction. In this respect, the *Guidelines for implementation of the Framework for Protected Areas set forth in Article 3, Annex V of the Environmental Protocol* appended to Resolution 1 (2000) (http://www.ats.aq/documents/recatt/Att081_e.pdf) are a useful reference.

The CEP has agreed that Management Plans should include a clear statement about the primary reason for the Area's designation[1]. It is useful to include such a statement in the Introduction to the Management Plan, which serves as a summary of the Management Plan, as well as in the following section describing the values to be protected.

The CEP has also encouraged proponents to describe how the Area complements the Antarctic protected areas system as a whole[2]. For this purpose it should *inter alia* refer to the Environmental Domains Analysis of Antarctica (http://www.ats.aq/documents/recatt/Att408_e.pdf), appended to Resolution 3 (2008), the Antarctic Conservation Biogeographic Regions, appended to Resolution 3 (2017), the list of Important Bird Areas (IBAs) and to the existing suite of ASPAs. If applicable, the Introduction might also usefully describe how the Area complements others in the local vicinity or region.

As appropriate, when discussing why special protection is deemed necessary, the introduction may usefully summarise how climate change has/is expected to have implications for the values of the Area.

---

[1] CEP VIII Final Report, paragraph 187.
[2] CEP VIII Final Report, paragraph 187.

1. Description of values to be protected

Article 3 of Annex V to the Environmental Protocol states that any area, including any marine area, may be designated as an ASPA so as to protect outstanding environmental, scientific, historic, aesthetic or wilderness values and sets out a series of such values which ATCPs shall seek to incorporate into ASPAs.

In considering any new proposal for an ASPA, thought needs to be given as to how protected area status would address the values identified in Article 3 of Annex V, and whether such values are already adequately represented by protected areas in Antarctica.

This section should include a statement about the primary reason for designation but should also describe the full range of reasons for the Area's designation. The description of the value or values of the Area should state, clearly and in detail, why it is that the site deserves special protection and how ASPA designation will strengthen protection measures. This may include a description of the actual or potential risks the values are facing. For example, if the designation of the Area is intended to prevent interference with ongoing or planned scientific investigations this section should describe the nature and value of this research.

The Antarctic environment is subject not only to natural variability in factors such as climate, ice extent and the density and spatial extent of biological populations, but also the effects of rapid regional climate change (particularly in the Antarctic Peninsula region). Therefore this section could also, where relevant, give a description of the potential environmental changes faced by the Area in light of such rapid change (e.g. potential thinning of glaciers; rapid retreat of ice-shelves and exposure of new ice-free terrain; impacts on sea ice-dependent penguin species by ocean warming and declining sea ice extent; the likelihood/risk of establishment of non-native species or natural colonists originating from more northerly (and therefore less climatically severe) latitudes etc.)

In cases where the intent is to protect the value of sites as reference areas or controls for long-term environmental monitoring programmes, the particular characteristics of the Area relevant to long-term monitoring should be described. In cases where ASPA designation is being conferred to protect historic, geological, aesthetic, wilderness or other values, those values should be described in this section.

In all cases the description of values should provide sufficient detail to enable readers to understand precisely what the ASPA designation is intended to protect. It should not provide a full description of the Area, which is presented in Section 6.

2. Aims and objectives

This section should establish what is intended to be achieved by the Management Plan and how the Plan will address protection of the values described above. For example, the aims of the Plan might highlight an intention to:

- avoid certain specified changes to the Area;
- prevent any human interference with specified features or activities in the Area;
- allow only certain types of research, management, or other activities that would not interfere with the reason for the site's designation;
- minimize, to the maximum extent practicable, the introduction of non-native species, which could compromise the environmental and scientific values of an area; or
- maximise the resilience of the identified key values (Section 1) in the Area to climate change, by managing human activities in the Area.

It is important to note that the description of values and the objectives will be used by the national permitting authority to help decide activities that can, and cannot, be authorised to be conducted in the Area. Consequently, the values to be protected and the objectives of the plan must be described specifically, not generally.

3. Management activities

Management activities outlined in this section should relate to the aims of the Management Plan and to the objectives for which the Area was designated.

There should be a clear indication of what is prohibited, what should be avoided or prevented as well as what is allowed. The Plan should make it clear when permitted activities can take place. For example, some activities may only be allowed during periods that do not coincide with the breeding season of sensitive species.

This section should describe such actions as will be taken to protect the particular values of the Area (e.g. installation and maintenance of scientific instruments, establishment of marked routes or landing sites, erection of signs indicating that the site is an ASPA and that entry is prohibited except in accordance with a permit issued by an appropriate national authority, removal of abandoned equipment or materials). If the management activities require cooperative action by two or more Parties conducting or supporting research in the Area, the arrangements for carrying out the required activities should be jointly developed and described in the Management Plan.

It is important to remember, and to note in the Management Plan, that active management may require an environmental impact assessment, which should be undertaken in accordance with the requirements of Annex I to the Environmental Protocol.

If no special management activities are required, this section of the Plan should state, "None required".

4. Period of designation

Designation of an ASPA is for an indefinite period unless the Management Plan provides otherwise. It is a requirement under Article 6.3 of Annex V that a review of the Management Plan is initiated at least every five years, and updated as necessary.

If the intent is to provide protection for a finite period, while a particular study or other activity is conducted, an expiry date should be included in this section.

5. Maps

Maps are a critical component of any Management Plan and should be clear and sufficiently detailed. If the Area is particularly large, then a number of maps that vary in scale may be appropriate, but the minimum is likely to be two: one showing the general region in which the Area is situated, as well as the position of all nearby protected areas; and a second map illustrating the details of the Area itself.

It is essential that the maps clearly indicate the boundary of the Protected Area, as described under section 6.1 below.

Guidelines for maps are given in Appendix 1 together with a checklist of features to be considered for inclusion.

6. Description of the Area

This section requires an accurate description of the Area, and where appropriate its surroundings, to ensure that individuals planning a visit and national authorities responsible for issuing permits are sufficiently appraised of the special features of the Area.

It is important that this section describes adequately those features of the Area that are being protected, thus alerting users of the Management Plan to features of particular sensitivity. This section should preferably not duplicate the description of the values of the Area.

The section is divided into five subsections:

6(i) Geographical co-ordinates, boundary markers and natural features

The boundary of the Area should be delineated unambiguously and the important features clearly described, as the boundary delineation will form the basis of legal enforcement. The boundary of the Area should be carefully selected and described. It is preferable to describe a boundary that is identifiable at all times of the year. This is often difficult due to snow cover in winter, but at least in summer it should be possible for any visitor to determine the limits of the Area. For Areas near to sites frequented by tourists this is especially important. It is best to choose static boundary markers such as exposed rock features. Features that might be expected to vary in location throughout the year or during the five-year review period of the Management Plan, such as the edges of snow fields or wildlife colonies, are unlikely to be suitable. In some instances it may be advisable to install boundary markers where natural features are not sufficient.

Consideration should be given to the likely future impacts of climate change when determining or reviewing the boundaries of the Protected Area. Particular thought should be given to the designation of boundaries using features other than ice-free ground. For example, future climate change induced glacial retreat, ice shelf collapse and lake level change will have an impact on ASPAs whose boundary definitions follow these features.

Geographical co-ordinates included in the boundary description should be as accurate as possible. They should be given as latitude and longitude in degrees, minutes and seconds. If possible, reference should be made to published maps or charts to allow the Area boundaries to be delineated on the map. The survey and mapping methods employed should be stated, if possible, along with the name of the agency producing the maps or charts referred to.

The importance of Global Navigation Satellite Systems (GNSS) (e.g., GPS, GLONASS, Galileo and BeiDou) for fixing positions cannot be overstated. The opportunity to revise the plan for each ASPA is an opportunity to use GNSS, to provide accurate locational information on boundaries. It is strongly recommended that plans are not submitted without such information. If possible, an electronic record of boundary positions should be provided to the Antarctic Treaty Secretariat (e.g., as a shapefile).

When describing the physical features of the Area, only place names formally approved by a Consultative Party and included in the SCAR Composite Gazetteer of Antarctica should be used (http://data.aad.gov.au/aadc/gaz/scar/). All names referred to in the text of the Plan should be shown on the maps. If a new place name is needed, approval will be required by the appropriate national committee and the place name submitted for inclusion in the SCAR Composite Gazetteer of Antarctica before using the new name on any maps and before submitting the plan.

The description of the natural features of the Area should include descriptions of the local topography such as permanent snow/ice fields, the presence of any water bodies (lakes, streams, pools) and a brief summary of the local geology and geomorphology. An accurate, brief description of the biological features of the Area is also useful including notes on major plant communities, microbial mats, bird and seal colonies and numbers of individuals or breeding pairs of birds. As appropriate, the section might also usefully include (i) a description of documented climate change impacts on the Area and (ii) details of any climate change predictions relevant to the Area.

If the Area contains a marine component the management plan may need to be submitted to CCAMLR for consideration – see the section below on 'Approval process for ASPA Management Plans'.

6(ii) Access to the Area

This subsection should include descriptions of preferred access routes to the Area by land, sea or air. These should be clearly defined to prevent confusion and suitable alternatives provided if the preferred route is unavailable.

All access routes as well as marine anchorages and helicopter landing areas should be described and clearly marked on the accompanying map of the Area. Helicopter landing areas should usually be located well outside the ASPA boundary to ensure minimum interference with the integrity of the Area.

The subsection should also describe preferred walking and, when permitted, vehicle routes within the Area.

When preparing this section of the management plan, consideration should be given to_how management arrangements for access to the Area by land, sea and/or air may need to be practically addressed according to the changing environmental conditions (e.g., changes to sea ice duration and extent, wind speed and direction, location and size of ice-free areas, and the presence and distribution of wildlife when possible).

6(iii) Location of structures within and adjacent to the Area

It is necessary to describe and accurately locate all structures within or adjacent to the Area. These include, for example, boundary markers, sign boards, cairns, field huts, depots and research facilities. Where possible, the date the structures were erected and the country to whom they belong should be recorded, as well as the details of any HSMs in the area. If applicable, the timing of the planned removal of any structures should also be noted (e.g., in the case of temporary scientific or other installations).

6(iv) Location of other protected areas in the vicinity

There is no specific radius to be used when describing other protected areas 'in the vicinity', but a distance of approximately 50 km has been used in many plans adopted so far. All such protected areas (i.e., ASPAs, ASMAs, HSMs, CCAS Seal Reserves, CCAMLR CEMP sites, etc.) in the vicinity should be given by name and, where appropriate, number. The coordinates and approximate distance and direction from the Area in question should also be provided.

6(v) Special zones within the Area

Article 5.3(f) of Annex V allows for the identification of zones within ASPAs and ASMAs "*in which activities are to be prohibited, restricted, or managed for the purpose of achieving the aims and objectives...*" of the management plan.

Those preparing management plans should consider whether the objectives of the plan could be achieved more effectively by designating one or more zones. Clearly demarcated zones help provide clear information to site visitors on where, when and why special management conditions apply. They can be useful to communicate the goals and requirements of management in a clear and simple manner. For example, special zones might include bird colonies to which access is restricted during the breeding season, or sites where scientific experiments should not be disturbed.

In order to help achieve greater consistency in the application of the zoning tool in Antarctica, a standard set of commonly used zones that should meet management needs in most situations has been identified and defined (Table 2).

As is the case with all guidelines, there may arise instances where exceptions are both needed and desirable. When this is the case, those preparing management plans might consider the application of alternative zones. It is important to keep in mind, however, that management plans should aim to use zones that are as simple and consistent as possible across all sites within Antarctica. This will help to ensure that plan conditions are understandable and easy to follow, and thereby assist in the practical protection and management of these special areas.

If no zones are designated within the Area, this should be specifically stated in the Management Plan.

Table 2. Zoning Guidelines for ASPAs

Zone	Specific Zone Objectives
Facilities Zone	To ensure that science support facilities and related human activities within the Area are contained and managed within designated areas

Access Zone	To provide guidance for approach and/or landing of aircraft, boats, vehicles or pedestrians accessing the Area and by doing so protect areas with sensitive assemblages of species or scientific equipment etc. and/or provide for safety
Historic Zone	To ensure that those who enter the Area are aware of the areas or features within that are sites, buildings and/or artefacts of historic importance and to manage them appropriately
Scientific Zone	To ensure that those who enter the Area are aware of the areas within that are sites of current or long-term scientific investigation or have sensitive scientific equipment installed
Restricted Zone	To restrict access into a particular part of the Area and/or activities within it for a range of management or scientific reasons, e.g. owing to special scientific or ecological values, because of sensitivity, presence of hazards, or to restrict emissions or constructions at a particular site. Access into Restricted Zones should normally be for compelling reasons that cannot be served elsewhere within the Area
Prohibited Zone	To prohibit access into a particular part of the ASPA until such time it is agreed by the ATCM (and not individual Parties) that the management plan should be changed to allow access

7. Terms and conditions for entry permits

7(i) General permit conditions

Article 3.4 of Annex V to the Environmental Protocol specifies that entry into ASPAs is prohibited except in accordance with a permit issued by an appropriate national authority.

The Management Plan should set out the conditions under which a permit might be issued. When drafting Management Plans, authors should be aware that the authorities appointed to issue permits for entry into ASPAs will use the contents of this section to determine whether, and under what conditions, permits may be issued.

Article 7.3 of Annex V to the Environmental Protocol directs that each Party must require the permit holder to carry a copy of the permit whilst in the ASPA. This section of the Management Plan should note that all permits should contain a condition requiring the permit holder to carry a copy of the permit whilst in the ASPA.

Article 5 of Annex V sets out 10 separate issues that need to be addressed when considering the terms and conditions that might be attached to permits. These are set out below:

7(ii) Access to, and movement within or over, the Area

This section of the Management Plan should set out restrictions on the means of transport, points of access, routes and movement within the Area. It should also address the direction of approach for aircraft and the minimum height for overflying the Area. Such information should state the type of aircraft (e.g. fixed or rotary wing) on which the restrictions are based, that should be included as conditions of permits that are issued.

Where appropriate, the Management Plan should make reference to relevant guidelines adopted by the CEP, such as the *Guidelines for the Operation of Aircraft near Concentrations of Birds* (http://www.ats.aq/documents/recatt/Att224_e.pdf) appended to Resolution 2 (2004) and the Environmental Guidelines for Operation of Remotely Piloted Aircraft Systems (RPAS) in Antarctica (v. 1.1) appended to Resolution 4 (2018).

When preparing this section of the management plan, consideration should be given to how management arrangements for access to and movement within or over the Areas by land, sea and/or air may need to be practically addressed according to changing environmental conditions. As described in subsection *6(ii) Access to the Area*, changes resulting from climate change may relate to e.g. sea ice duration and extent, wind speed and direction, sea level change, location and size of ice-free areas, the presence and distribution of wildlife, permafrost melting, soft ground presence.

7(iii) Activities which may be conducted in the Area

This should detail what may be undertaken within the protected area and the conditions under which such activities are allowed. For example, to avoid interference with wildlife, only certain types of activity might be permitted.

If the Management Plan proposes that active management within the Area may be necessary in the future, this should also be listed here.

7(iv) Installation, modification, or removal of structures

It is useful to identify what, if any, structures are permitted within the Area. For example, certain scientific research equipment, markers or other structures might be allowed to be installed within the Area.

To assist with tracking the purpose of such structures, the Management Plan should explain how structures are to be identifiable. General and/or specific guidance on relevant considerations to minimise the adverse effects of installations on the values of the Area may also be useful.

If any existing structures are present (e.g. refuges) the Management Plan should also indicate action which might be authorised to modify or remove the structures. Alternatively, if no structures are to be permitted within the Area the Management Plan should make this clear.

When preparing this section of the management plan, consideration should be given to the implications of climate change for the suitability/location of new structures and whether existing structures may need to be removed, modified or relocated (e.g., due to changes in active layer permafrost depth, levels of snow accumulation, distribution of wildlife or accessibility).

7(v) Location of field camps

It is likely that field camps would not usually be permitted within the boundaries of the Area. However, it may be permissible under certain conditions such as overriding reasons of safety. If so the conditions under which field camps may be permitted should be stated. It is possible that field camps would only be acceptable in certain parts of the Area. Such campsites should be identified and recorded on the supporting maps.

In instances where relatively permanent field camps are permitted, the management plan should consider the vulnerability of the chosen camp sites towards climate change, (eg. changing solid ice, changes in the streams/rivers courses, transformation of solid ground into soft unsafe ground, flooding possibility, and others).

7(vi) Restrictions on materials and organisms which may be brought into the Area

This section should set out prohibitions and give guidance on the management of any materials that are to be used or stored in the Area.

There is a complete prohibition on the deliberate introduction of non-native species and diseases to the Antarctic Treaty area under Article 4 of Annex II to the Environmental Protocol, except in accordance with a separate permit issued under the Authority provided for in Annex II. Article 4 also states that (i) precautions are taken within the Treaty area to prevent accidental introductions of microorganisms, (ii) appropriate efforts are made to ensure poultry and avian products are free from contamination by diseases, (iii) deliberate introduction of non-sterile soil is prohibited and (iv) the unintentional importation of non-sterile soil is minimized to the maximum extent practicable. Therefore, recommended measures to reduce the risk of non-native species introductions applied throughout Antarctica should also apply to the Protected

Area. Proponents may consider measures to address the risk of non-native species introductions, noting that climate change may increase the likelihood of the establishment of any non-native species arriving in some Areas. In accordance with the key guiding principles of 'Prevention', 'Surveillance' and 'Response', described in the CEP Non-native Species Manual (Resolution 4 (2016); latest update of the Manual: paragraph 193 CEP XXII Report (2019)), the management plan should, as appropriate, include provisions relating to the cleaning of camping equipment, scientific equipment, vehicles and personal footwear and clothing to remove propagules before entering the ASPA. SCAR's 'Environmental code of conduct for terrestrial scientific field research in Antarctica' (Resolution 5 (2018)) and 'Code of Conduct for Activity within Terrestrial Geothermal Environments in Antarctica' (Resolution 3 (2016)) may provide some useful biosecurity recommendations.

Careful consideration should be given to the risk of introducing non-native species to the Protected Area on or via foodstuffs or associated containers and packaging. Non-sterile soil, plant propagules, eggs and live insects could be introduced in association with fresh fruits and vegetables, while bird or marine mammal pathogens may be introduced to the Area via poultry products. The Management Plan may state that such products should not be permitted in the area or specify measures to minimize the risk of pathogen release to the environment.

In some instances, special precautions may need to be taken to prevent the introduction of non-native species. If, for example, the Area has been designated for its special microbial communities, it may be necessary to require more stringent biosecurity precautions to minimize shedding of human commensal microorganisms and redistribution of other environmental microorganism from outside the Area. The use of sterile protective over-clothing and thoroughly cleaned footwear may be appropriate.

It may be necessary, for example, to bring some chemicals into the Area for research or management purposes. If so guidance should be provided as to how they must be stored, handled and removed. It may also be necessary to bring food and fuel into the Area, and guidance about the use, storage and removal of such materials should be given. Radio isotope and/or stable isotopes should only be released into the environment within the ASPA after careful consideration of the long-term impacts of such activities on the future environmental and scientific values of the Area.

7(vii) Taking of, or harmful interference with, native flora and fauna

This is prohibited under Article 3 of Annex II to the Environmental Protocol except in accordance with a permit issued under the provisions of Annex II; this should be stated in all permits authorising this activity in the Area. The requirements under Article 3 of Annex II must be adhered to, and commonly applied guidelines such as the SCAR Code of Conduct for the Use of Animals for Scientific Purposes in Antarctica (Resolution 4 (2019)) may be presented as the minimum standard.

7(viii) The collection or removal of materials not brought into the Area by the permit holder

It may be permissible to remove from the Area materials such as beach litter, dead or pathological fauna or flora or abandoned relics and artefacts from previous activities. What items or samples can be removed by the permit holder should be clearly stated.

7(ix) Disposal of waste

Annex III to the Environmental Protocol deals with the management of wastes in Antarctica. This section of the plan should specify requirements for the disposal of wastes that should be included as conditions of permits. The requirements set out in Annex III must be used as the minimum standards for waste disposal in an ASPA.

As a general rule all wastes, including all human wastes, generated by visitors to an ASPA should be removed from the Area. Exceptions, which must accord with the provisions of the Environmental Protocol, should be identified as appropriate in this section of the Management Plan. In particular, consideration should be given to the likely impacts of sewage waste disposal on birds and marine mammals within the Area.

7(x) Measures that may be necessary to continue to meet the aims of the Management Plan

When appropriate this section should establish the conditions under which the issue of a permit may be necessary so as to ensure continued protection of the Area. For example, it may be necessary to issue permits to allow for monitoring of the Area; to allow for repair or re-placement of boundary markers and signs; or to allow for some active management as set out in section 3 above.

When preparing this section of the management plan, consideration should be given to management activities that may assist to understand or address the implications of climate change for the Area (e.g., visits to review management arrangements or to undertake long-term monitoring of environmental change).

Where a management plan provides that, for exceptional reasons, non-native species are introduced in accordance with a separate permit, this section should discuss the need for measures to contain the non-native species and contingency procedures to be followed should the non-native species be released unintentionally into the environment. For example, it might specify that adequate biosecurity materials should be taken into the field work location to fulfil the requirements of the biosecurity plan, and personnel undertaking the work should be trained in their use.

In Protected Areas where non-native species are known to have become established, the Management Plan may outline measures to minimize further distribution of the species or its propagules to other locations, particularly taking into account the likelihood of species establishment and dispersion due to climate change.

7(xi) Requirements for reports

This section should describe the requirement for reports that should be included as a condition in permits issued by an appropriate national authority. It should, as appropriate, specify the information that should be included in reports. An ASPA visit report form is presented in Appendix 2 of this guide and is available for download from the ATS website www.ats.aq.

It may be useful to give a deadline by which time reports of a visit to the Area must be made (e.g. within six months). To address instances where the Area may be visited by groups authorised by Parties other than the Party that proposed the Management Plan, it may be useful to indicate that visit reports should be exchanged to assist in managing the Area and reviewing the Management Plan.

Many reporting requirements will be generally applicable, but in some cases it may be appropriate to specify particular information that will be of assistance in managing the Area. For example, for Areas designated to protect bird colonies it may be appropriate to request visiting groups undertaking surveys to report detailed information on census data, and locations of any new colonies or nests not previously recorded.

8. Supporting documentation

This section should refer to any additional documents that may be relevant. These may include any scientific reports or papers describing the values of the Area in greater detail, although as a general rule the various components of the Area and the intended management activities should be explained in the various sections of the Management Plan itself. Any such papers or supporting documents should be fully cited.

Approval process for ASPA Management Plans

Article 5 of Annex V provides that any Party, the CEP, SCAR or CCAMLR may submit a draft Management Plan for consideration by the ATCM. In practice, draft Management Plans are generally submitted by one or more Parties to the CEP for consideration.

The process by which Management Plans are handled from drafting through to acceptance is summarised by the flow chart in Figure 1. This is based on the requirements of Article 6 of

Annex V, the Guidelines for CEP Consideration of New and Revised Draft ASPA and ASMA Management Plans (Annex 1 of Appendix 3 to the CEP XI Final Report), and other related guidelines.

The approval process for an ASPA Management Plan has many critical stages, which can take a long time to complete. However, these stages are necessary as an ASPA Management Plan requires the agreement of all Antarctic Treaty Consultative Parties at an ATCM.

Preparing the draft Management Plan

In the initial stages of drafting the Management Plan, it is recommended that widespread consultation, both nationally and internationally, is undertaken on the scientific, environmental and logistical elements of the Plan as appropriate. This will aid the passage of the Plan through the more formal process at the ATCM.

Proponents of new Areas are strongly encouraged to consider relevant guidelines and references that will assist in assessing, selecting, defining and proposing areas that might require greater protection through designation as an ASPA, including:

- *Guidelines for Implementation of the Framework for Protected Areas set forth in Article 3, Annex V of the Environmental Protocol* – Resolution 1 (2000).
- *Environmental Domains Analysis for the Antarctic continent* – Resolution 3 (2008).
- Important Bird Areas in Antarctica – Resolution 5 (2015).
- *Revised Antarctic Conservation Biogeographic Regions* – Resolution 3 (2017).

When considering the designation of a new ASPA, proponents are encouraged to inform the CEP at an early stage (e.g. even before detailing a Management Plan for the area) so that proposals can be discussed in the context of the protected areas system as a whole. Proponents are encouraged to use the Guidelines: A prior assessment process for the designation of ASPA and ASMAs (Appendix 4, CEP XX Final Report). A template is provided in the Guidelines to provide a practical and non-mandatory means of facilitating provision of information consistent with the prior assessment guidelines.

Sometimes a proposal for a new ASPA requires the de-listing of previously agreed ASPAs. Under such circumstances, proponents are encouraged to consult the *Guidelines for de-designation of ASPAs* (Appendix 3, CEP XXIII Final Report).

When revising an existing Management Plan, it may be informative to use the *Checklist to assist in the inspection of Antarctic Specially Protected Areas and Antarctic Specially Managed Areas* (Resolution 4 (2008)) as a tool to identify necessary changes and improvements.

Submitting the draft Management Plan for consideration

The draft Management Plan should be submitted to the CEP, as an attachment to a Working Paper prepared in accordance with the *Revised Guide to the presentation of Working Papers containing proposals for Antarctic Specially Protected Areas, Antarctic Specially Managed Areas or Historic Sites and Monuments* – Resolution 2 (2021).

If the Area contains a marine component that meets the criteria outlined in Decision 9 (2005) *Marine protected areas and other areas of interest to CCAMLR*, the draft Management Plan should also be submitted to CCAMLR for consideration. The proponents should make arrangements to ensure that any feedback from CCAMLR (which holds its annual meetings in October/November) is available before the proposal is considered by the CEP.

Consideration by the CEP and ATCM

The CEP will consider the Management Plan, if appropriate taking into account any comments from CCAMLR. The CEP may refer the Management Plan to the ATCM for consideration and adoption, or to the Subsidiary Group on Management Plans (SGMP) for intersessional review.

In accordance with its Terms of Reference (see Appendix 1 to the CEP XIII Final Report), the SGMP will consider each draft Management Plan referred to it, advise the proponent(s) on recommended changes, consider any revised version of the Management Plan prepared during the intersessional period, and report to the CEP on its review. The revised Management Plan and the CEP's report would then be considered by the CEP meeting and, if agreed, referred to the ATCM for consideration and adoption.

If the ATCM agrees on the Management Plan a Measure is adopted in accordance with Article IX(1) of the Antarctic Treaty. Unless the Measure specifies otherwise, the Plan is deemed to have been approved 90 days after the close of the ATCM at which it was adopted, unless one or more of the Consultative Parties notifies the Depository within that time-period that it wishes to have an extension of that period or is unable to approve the Measure.

Review and revision of Management Plans

A review of the Management Plan shall be initiated every five years in accordance with Article 6.3 of Annex V to the Environmental Protocol and updated as required. Updated Management Plans then follow the same course of agreement as before.

When undertaking Management Plan reviews, thought should be given to the need for further or continued site protection of species whose abundance or range has increased substantially. Thought should also be given to whether new climate change and impact knowledge/research have relevance for the management arrangements. If site protection is deemed potentially unnecessary in an area where a protected species is no longer present and/or the environmental or scientific values for which the area was designated no longer apply, proponents are encouraged to consult the *Guidelines for de-designation of ASPAs* (Appendix 3, CEP XXIII Final Report).

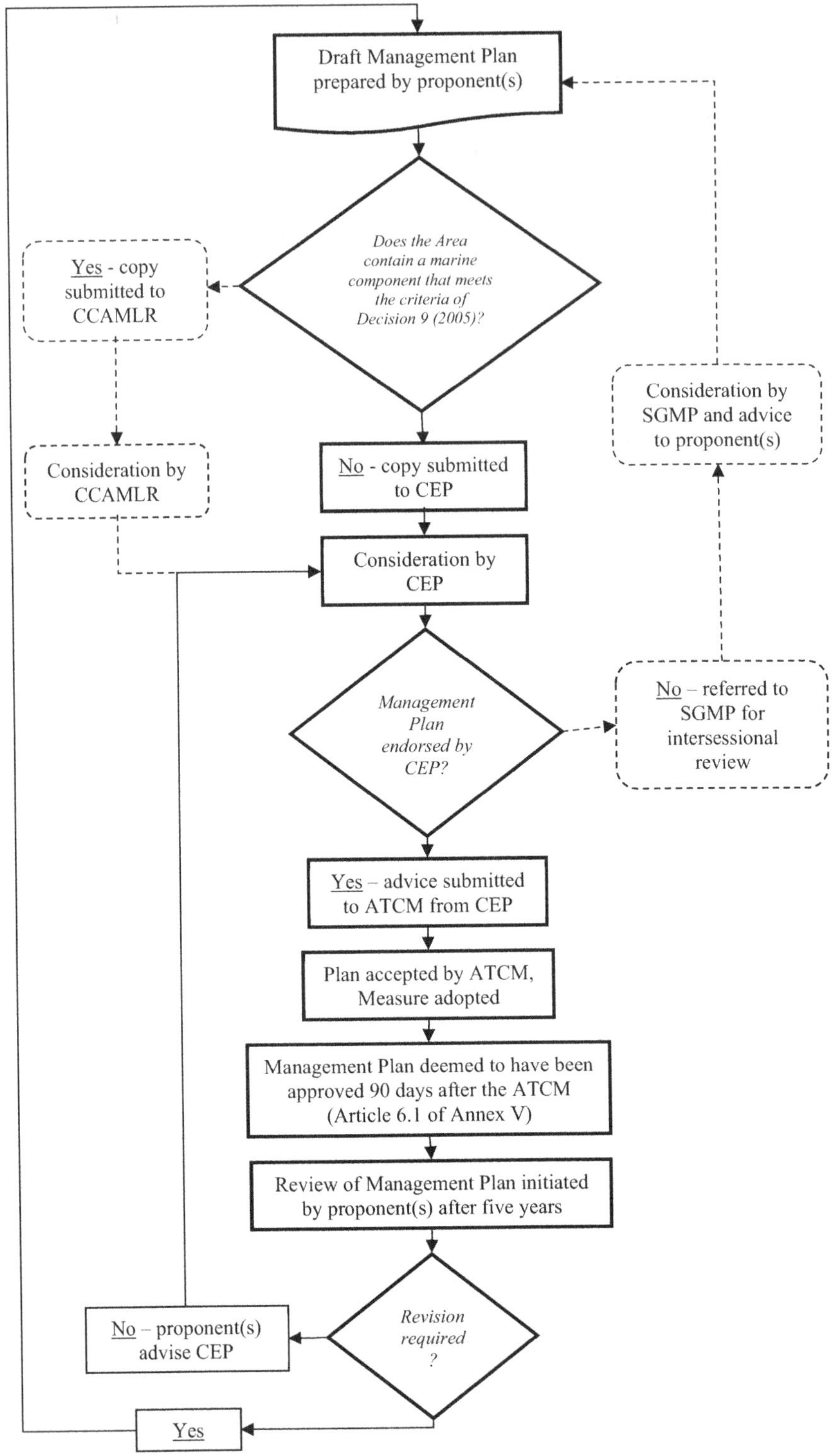
Draft Management Plan prepared by proponent(s)
Does the Area contain a marine component that meets the criteria of Decision 9 (2005)?
Yes - copy submitted to CCAMLR
Consideration by CCAMLR
No - copy submitted to CEP
Consideration by CEP
Management Plan endorsed by CEP?
No – referred to SGMP for intersessional review
Consideration by SGMP and advice to proponent(s)
Yes – advice submitted to ATCM from CEP
Plan accepted by ATCM, Measure adopted
Management Plan deemed to have been approved 90 days after the ATCM (Article 6.1 of Annex V)
Review of Management Plan initiated by proponent(s) after five years
Revision required ?
No – proponent(s) advise CEP
Yes

Figure 1. Flow chart showing the approval process for ASPA Management Plans. Prior to the submission of a draft ASPA Management Plan to CEP, the proponents are encouraged to submit to the CEP, as an attachment to a Working Paper, a completed prior-assessment template, as provided in Guidelines: A prior assessment process for the designation of ASPA and ASMAs (Appendix 4, CEP XX Final Report)

Appendix 1. Guidance notes for producing maps for inclusion in Management Plans

Management Plans should include a general location map to show the position of the Area and the location of any other protected areas in the vicinity, and at least one detailed map of the site showing those features essential for meeting the Management Plan objectives.

1) Each map should include lines of latitude and longitude as well as having a scale bar. Avoid statements of scale (e.g. 1:50000) because enlargement/reduction renders such statements useless. The map projection and horizontal and vertical datums used should be indicated.
2) It is important to use up-to-date coastline data that include features such as ice shelves, ice tongues and glaciers. Ice recession and advance continues to affect many areas with consequent changes to Area boundaries. If an ice feature is used as a boundary the date of the source from which the data was acquired (e.g. survey or satellite image) should be shown.
3) Maps should show the following features: any specified routes; any special zones (e.g., Prohibited or Restricted Zones); boat and/or helicopter landing sites and access points; camp-sites; installations and huts; major animal concentrations and breeding sites; any extensive areas of vegetation; and clear delineation between ice/snow and ice-free ground. In many instances it is useful to include a geological map of the Area. It is suggested that, in most cases, it is helpful to have contouring at an appropriate interval on all maps of the Area. But contouring should not be so close as to obscure other features or symbols on the map.
4) Contours should be included on maps at an interval appropriate to the scale of the map.
5) Be aware when preparing the map that it will be reduced to about 150 x 200 mm size to fit into the ATCM official report. This is of importance in selecting the size of symbols, the closeness of contouring and the use of shading. Reproduction is always monochrome so do not use colours to distinguish features in the original. There may well be other versions of an Area map available but, as far as the legal status of the Management Plan is concerned, it is the version published with the Final Report of the Antarctic Treaty Consultative Meeting that is the definitive version which will be included in national legislation.
6) If the Area will require evaluation by CCAMLR, then the location of nearby CEMP sites should be indicated. CCAMLR has requested that the location of bird and seal colonies and the access routes from the sea should be indicated on a map, wherever possible.
7) Other figures can assist with using the Management Plan in the field:
    - For photographs, good contrast prints are essential for adequate reproduction. Screening or digitising of photograph will improve reproduction when the plan is photocopied. If an image such as an aerial photograph or satellite image is used in the map, then the source and date of acquisition of the image should be stated.
    - Some Management Plans have already used 3-dimensional terrain models, which again can provide important locational information when approaching an Area, especially by helicopter. Such drawings need careful design if they are not to become confusing when reduced.

A checklist of features to be considered for inclusion on maps

1. Essential features

1.1 Title
1.2 Latitude and longitude
1.3 Scale bar with numerical scale
1.4 Comprehensive legend
1.5 Adequate and approved place names
1.6 Map projection and spheroid modification
1.7 North arrow
1.8 Contour interval
1.9 If image data are included, then date of image collection

2. Essential topographical features

2.1 Coastline, rock and ice
2.2 Peaks and ridge lines
2.3 Ice margins and other glacial features
2.4 Contours (labelled as necessary) survey points and spot heights

3. Natural Features

3.1 Lakes, ponds, streams
3.2 Moraines, screes, cliffs, beaches
3.3 Beach areas
3.4 Vegetation
3.5 Bird and seal colonies

4. Anthropogenic Features

4.1 Station
4.2 Field huts, refuges
4.3 Campsites
4.4 Roads and vehicle tracks, footpaths
4.5 Landing areas for fixed wing aeroplanes and helicopters
4.6 Wharf, jetties
4.7 Power supplies, cables
4.8 Aerials, Antennae
4.9 Fuel storage areas
4.10 Water reservoirs and pipes
4.11 Emergency caches
4.12 Markers, signs
4.13 Historic sites or artefacts, archaeological sites
4.14 Scientific installations or sampling areas
4.15 Site contamination or modification

5. Boundaries

5.1 Boundary of Area
5.2 Boundaries of special zones or areas. Boundaries of the contained protected area
5.3 Boundary signs and markers (including cairns)
5.4 Boat/aircraft approach routes
5.5 Navigation markers or beacons
5.6 Survey points and markers

The same approach is obviously required of any inset maps.

At the conclusion of drafting, a check should be made on cartographic quality to ensure:

- Balance between the elements.
- Appropriate shading to enhance features, but which will not be confusing when photocopied and where degree of shading should reflect importance.
- Correct and appropriate text with no features overlap.
- An appropriate legend using SCAR approved map symbols, wherever possible.
- White text appropriately shadowed on all image data.

Appendix 2. Antarctic Specially Protected Area (ASPA) visit report form

1) ASPA number:
2) ASPA name:
3) Permit number:
4) Permit period From: To:
5) National authority issuing Permit:
6) Date Report filed:
7) Contact details for Principal Permit Holder: Name: Job Title or Position: Phone number: Email:
8) Number of people Permitted to enter the Area: That actually entered the Area:
9) List of all persons who entered the Area under the current Permit:
10) Objectives of the visit to the Area under the current Permit:
11) Date(s) and duration of visit(s) under the current Permit:
12) Mode of transport to/from and within the Area:
13) Summary of activities conducted in the Area:
14) Descriptions and locations of samples collected (type, quantity, and details of any Permits for sample collection):
15) Descriptions and locations of markers, instrumentation or equipment installed or removed, or any material released into the environment (noting how new installations are intended to remain in the Area):
16) Measures taken during this visit to ensure compliance with the Management Plan:
17) On an attached photocopy of the map of the Area, please show (as applicable): camp site location(s), land/sea/air movements or routes, sampling sites, installations, deliberate release of materials, any impacts, and features of special significance not previously recorded. GPS coordinates should be provided for such locations wherever possible:
18) Any other comment or information, such as: • Observations of human effects on the Area, distinguishing between those resulting from the visit and those due to previous visitors:

- Evaluation of whether the values for which the Area was designated are being adequately protected:
- Features of special significance that have not been previously recorded for the Area:
- Recommendations on further management measures needed to protect the values of the Area, including location and appraisal of condition of structures, markers, etc.:
- Any departures from the provisions of the Management Plan during this visit, noting dates, magnitudes and locations:

Appendix 3. Template for Antarctic Specially Protected Area Management Plans

Management Plan for Antarctic Specially Protected Area No. [XXX]

[INSERT NAME OF PROTECTED AREA]

Introduction

The Guide to the Preparation of Management Plans for Antarctic Specially Protected Areas (the Guide) provides guidance for this section of Management Plans. No suggested standard wording is provided here because the content of this section will be specific to the Area in question.

[Site-specific content should be inserted here]

1. Description of values to be protected

Section 1 of the Guide provides guidance for this section of Management Plans. No suggested standard wording is provided here because the content of this section will be specific to the Area in question.

[Site-specific content should be inserted here]

2. Aims and objectives

Many existing Management Plans share similar aims and objectives. A pool of suggested standard wording has been developed and can be used, amended or deleted as appropriate for the Area in question (see below). Proponents are encouraged to identify site-specific aims and objectives, and should consider the guidance for this section of Management Plans given in Section 2 of the Guide.

Management of [insert name of Area] aims to:

- avoid degradation of, or substantial risk to, the values of the Area by preventing unnecessary human disturbance to the Area;
- avoid degradation of, or substantial risk to, the values of the Area by preventing unnecessary human disturbance to the Area, its features and artefacts through managed access to [insert specific hut here];
- allow scientific research in the Area provided it is for compelling reasons which cannot be served elsewhere and which will not jeopardize the natural ecological system in that Area;
- prevent or minimise the introduction to the Area of alien plants, animals and microbes;
- minimise the possibility of the introduction of pathogens which may cause disease in fauna populations within the Area;
- preserve [a part of] the natural ecosystem of the Area as a reference area for future comparative studies;
- maintain the historic values of the Area through planned conservation and archaeological work programmes;
- [further site-specific content should be inserted here]

In the case of Areas to which educational and outreach visits are permitted, the following text might be considered:

- allow activities in the Area for educational and outreach purposes, provided that such activities are for compelling reasons which cannot be served elsewhere and which will not jeopardise the natural ecological system in that Area;
- [further site-specific content should be inserted here]

3. Management activities

Many existing Management Plans share similar wording in this section. A pool of suggested standard wording has been developed and can be used, amended or deleted as appropriate for the Area in question (see below). Proponents are encouraged to identify site-specific management activities and should consider the guidance for this section of Management Plans given in Section 3 of the Guide.

None required.

[Insert type of information] on the location of the Area [stating special restrictions that apply] shall be displayed prominently, and a copy of this Management Plan shall be made available, at [insert location of information].

Copies of this Management Plan [and informative material] shall be made available to vessels [and aircraft] [insert: travelling/planning to visit/visiting/operating in] the vicinity of the Area.

Signs illustrating the location and boundaries, with clear statements of entry restrictions, shall be placed at appropriate locations on the boundary of the Area [and Restricted Zone] to help avoid inadvertent entry.

Markers, signs or other structures (e.g., fences, cairns) erected within the Area for scientific or management purposes shall be secured and maintained in good condition and removed when no longer required.

In accordance with the requirements of Annex III to the Protocol on Environmental Protection to the Antarctic Treaty, abandoned equipment or materials shall be removed to the maximum extent possible provided doing so does not adversely impact the environment and the values of the Area.*

The Area shall be visited as necessary[, and no less than once every five years,] to assess whether it continues to serve the purposes for which it was designated and to ensure that management [and maintenance] activities are adequate.

Visits shall be permitted as necessary in order to facilitate the study and monitoring of anthropogenic changes that could affect the protected values in the Area, in particular, [insert specific activity]. Impact study and monitoring should be conducted, to the maximum extent possible, by non-invasive methods.

National Antarctic Programmes operating in the Area shall consult together with a view to ensuring the above management activities are implemented.

The Management Plan shall be reviewed no less than once every five years and updated as required.*

Personnel [national programme staff, field expeditions, tourists and pilots] in the vicinity of, accessing or flying over the Area shall be specifically instructed, by their national programme [or appropriate national authority] as to the provisions and contents of the Management Plan.

All pilots operating in the region shall be informed of the location, boundaries and restrictions applying to entry and over-flight in the Area.

[Further site-specific content should be inserted here]

4. Period of designation

Many existing Management Plans share similar wording in this section. Suggested wording has been developed and can be utilised as appropriate (see below) Section 4 of the Guide provides guidance for this section of Management Plans.

Designated for an indefinite period. / Designated for a [x] year period.

5. Maps

Section 5 of the Guide provides guidance for this section of Management Plans. Guidance for producing the maps themselves is given in Appendix 1 of the Guide. No suggested standard wording is provided here because the content of this section will be specific to the Area in question. However, proponents could utilise the following suggested format:

- [Map X, Title of Map X
- Map Y, Title of Map Y
- Map Z, Title of Map Z]

6. Description of the Area

Section 6 of the Guide provides general guidance for this section of Management Plans. Content should be inserted under the following sub-section headings.

6(i) Geographical co-ordinates, boundary markers and natural features

Section 6(i) of the Guide provides guidance for this section of Management Plans. No suggested standard wording is provided here because the content of this section will be specific to the Area in question.

[Site-specific content should be inserted here]

6(ii) Access to the Area

Section 6(ii) of the Guide provides guidance for this section of Management Plans. No suggested standard wording is provided here because the content of this section will be specific to the Area in question.

[Site-specific content should be inserted here]

6(iii) Location of structures within and adjacent to the Area

Section 6(iii) of the Guide provides guidance for this section of Management Plans. No suggested standard wording is provided here because the content of this section will be specific to the Area in question.

[Site-specific content should be inserted here]

6(iv) Location of other protected areas in the vicinity

Section 6(iii) of the Guide provides guidance for this section of Management Plans. No suggested standard wording is provided here because the content of this section will be specific to the Area in question. However, proponents could utilise the following suggested format (e.g. ASPA 167, Hawker Island, 68°35'S, 77°50'E, 22 km to the north-east):

[Other protected areas in the vicinity include (see Map XX):

- ASPA XXX, Name of Protected Area, latitude, longitude, XX km to the [direction]
- ASPA YYY, Name of Protected Area, latitude, longitude, XX km to the [direction]
- etc]

6(v) Special zones within the Area

Section 6(v) of the Guide provides guidance for this section of Management Plans, if any such zones are present. If there are no special zones, the following standard wording could be used. No other suggested standard wording is provided here because the content of this section will be specific to the Area in question.

There are no special zones within the Area. / [Site-specific content should be inserted here]

7. *Terms and conditions for entry permits*

7(i) General permit conditions

Many existing Management Plans share similar wording in this section. A pool of suggested standard wording has been developed and can be used, amended or deleted as appropriate for the Area in question (see below). Proponents are encouraged to identify site-specific permit conditions, and should consider the guidance for this section of Management Plans given in Section 7(i) of the Guide.

Entry into the Area is prohibited except in accordance with a Permit issued by an appropriate national authority. Conditions for issuing a Permit to enter the Area are that:*

- it is issued for compelling scientific reasons which cannot be served elsewhere, or for reasons essential to the management of the Area;
- the actions permitted are in accordance with this Management Plan;*
- the activities permitted will give due consideration via the environmental impact assessment process to the continued protection of the [environmental, scientific, historic, aesthetic or wilderness] values of the Area;
- the Permit shall be issued for a finite period;
- the Permit shall be carried when in the Area;*
- [further site-specific content should be inserted here]

In the case of Areas to which educational and outreach visits are permitted, the following text might be considered:

- it is issued for compelling scientific, educational or outreach reasons which cannot be served elsewhere, or for reasons essential to the management of the Area;
- [further site-specific content should be inserted here]

7(ii) Access to, and movement within or over, the Area

Many existing Management Plans share similar wording in this section. A pool of suggested standard wording has been developed and can be used, amended or deleted as appropriate for the Area in question (see below). Proponents are encouraged to identify site-specific content, and should consider the guidance for this section of Management Plans given in Section 7(ii) of the Guide.

Vehicles are prohibited within the Area and all movement within the Area should be on foot.

Vehicle use in the Area should be kept to a minimum.

The operation of aircraft over the Area should be carried out, as a minimum requirement, in compliance with the 'Guidelines for the Operation of Aircraft near Concentrations of Birds' contained in Resolution 2 (2004).

The operation of Remotely Piloted Aircraft Systems (RPAS) over the Area should be carried out, as a minimum requirement, in compliance with the 'Environmental Guidelines for Operation of Remotely Piloted Aircraft Systems (RPAS) in Antarctica (v 1.1) contained in Resolution 4 (2018).

Pedestrian traffic should be kept to the minimum necessary to undertake permitted activities and every reasonable effort should be made to minimise trampling effects.

Movement within the Area by foot should be on designated tracks only.

Where no routes are identified, pedestrian traffic should be kept to the minimum necessary to undertake permitted activities and every reasonable effort should be made to minimise trampling effects.

Visitors should avoid areas of visible vegetation and care should be exercised walking in areas of moist ground, particularly the stream course beds, where foot traffic can easily damage sensitive soils, plant and algal communities, and degrade water quality.

[Further site-specific content should be inserted here]

7(iii) Activities which may be conducted within the Area

Many existing Management Plans share similar wording in this section. A pool of suggested standard wording has been developed and can be used, amended or deleted as appropriate for the Area in question (see below). Proponents are encouraged to identify site-specific content, and should consider the guidance for this section of Management Plans given in Section 7(iii) of the Guide.

Activities which may be conducted within the Area include:

- compelling scientific research which cannot be undertaken elsewhere;
- sampling, which should be the minimum required for approved research programmes;
- conservation and maintenance;
- essential management activities, including monitoring;
- operational activities in support of scientific research or management within or beyond the Area, including visits to assess the effectiveness of the Management Plan and management activities;
- [further site-specific content, including any requirements for active management within the site which may be necessary in the future, should be added here]

In the case of Areas to which tourist visits are permitted (e.g. Historic Sites and Monuments designated as ASPAs) or to which educational and outreach visits are permitted, the following text might be considered:

- tourist visits;
- activities for educational and outreach purposes;
- [further site-specific content should be inserted here]

7(iv) Installation, modification, or removal of structures

Many existing Management Plans share similar wording in this section. A pool of suggested standard wording has been developed and can be used, amended or deleted as appropriate for the Area in question (see below). Proponents are encouraged to identify site-specific content, and should consider the guidance for this section of Management Plans given in Section 7(iv) of the Guide.

No [new] structures are to be erected within the Area, or scientific equipment installed, except for compelling scientific or management reasons and for a pre-established period, as specified in a permit.

Permanent structures or installations are prohibited [with the exception of permanent survey markers and boundary signs].

No [new] structures are to be erected within the Area, or scientific equipment installed.

All markers, structures or scientific equipment installed in the Area must be clearly identified by country, name of the principal investigator or agency, year of installation and date of expected removal.

All such items should be free of organisms, propagules (e.g. seeds, eggs) and non-sterile soil, and be made of materials that can withstand the environmental conditions and pose minimal risk of contamination of the Area.

Installation (including site selection), maintenance, modification or removal of structures and equipment shall be undertaken in a manner that minimises disturbance to the values of the Area.

Existing structures must not be removed, except in accordance with a permit.

Structures and installations must be removed when they are no longer required, or on the expiry of the permit, whichever is the earlier.

Removal of specific structures or equipment for which the permit has expired shall be [the responsibility of the authority which granted the original permit and shall be] a condition of the Permit.

[Further site-specific content should be inserted here]

7(v) Location of field camps

In most cases the content of this section will be specific to the Area in question. Proponents are encouraged to identify site-specific content, and should consider the guidance for this section of Management Plans given in Section 7(v) of the Guide. In the case of Areas where camping is prohibited, or where there are existing campsites, the following text might be considered:

Camping is prohibited within the Area.

Existing camp sites should be used where practicable.

[Further site-specific content should be inserted here]

7(vi) Restrictions on materials and organisms which may be brought into the Area

Many existing Management Plans share similar wording in this section. A pool of suggested standard wording has been developed and can be used, amended or deleted as appropriate for the Area in question (see below). Proponents are encouraged to identify site-specific content, and should consider the guidance for this section of Management Plans given in Section 7(vi) of the Guide.

In addition to the requirements of the Protocol on Environmental Protection to the Antarctic Treaty, restrictions on materials and organisms which may be brought into the Area are:

- the deliberate introduction of animals, plant material, micro-organisms and non-sterile soil into the Area shall not be permitted. Precautions shall be taken to prevent the accidental introduction of animals, plant material, micro-organisms and non-sterile soil from other biologically distinct regions (within or beyond the Antarctic Treaty area).* Site-specific bio-security measures are listed below:
    - [site-specific measures should be inserted here];
- fuel or other chemicals shall not be stored in the Area unless specifically authorised by Permit condition. They shall be stored and handled in a way that minimises the risk of their accidental introduction into the environment;
- materials introduced into the Area shall be for a stated period only and shall be removed by the end of that stated period;
- [further site-specific conditions should be inserted here]

7(vii) Taking of, or harmful interference with, native flora and fauna

Many existing Management Plans share similar wording in this section. A pool of suggested standard wording has been developed and can be used, amended or deleted as appropriate for the Area in question (see below). Proponents are encouraged to identify site-specific content, and should consider the guidance for this section of Management Plans given in Section 7(vii) of the Guide.

Taking of, or harmful interference with, native flora and fauna is prohibited, except in accordance with a permit issued in accordance with Annex II to the Protocol on Environmental Protection to the Antarctic Treaty.*

Where taking or harmful interference with animals is involved this should, as a minimum standard, be in accordance with the SCAR Code of Conduct for the Use of Animals for Scientific Purposes in Antarctica.

[Further site-specific content should be inserted here]

7(viii) The collection or removal of materials not brought into the Area by the permit holder

Many existing Management Plans share similar wording in this section. A pool of suggested standard wording has been developed and can be used, amended or deleted as appropriate for the Area in question (see below). Proponents are encouraged to identify site-specific content, and should consider the guidance for this section of Management Plans given in Section 7(viii) of the Guide.

Unless specifically authorized by permit, visitors to the Area are prohibited from interfering with or from handling, taking or damaging any designated historic site or monument, or any anthropogenic material meeting the criteria in Resolution 5 (2001). Similarly, relocation or removal of artefacts for the purposes of preservation, protection or to re-establish historical accuracy is allowable only by permit. Any new or newly identified anthropogenic materials found should be notified to the appropriate national authority.

Other material of human origin likely to compromise the values of the Area, and which was not brought into the Area by the Permit Holder or otherwise authorised, may be removed from the Area unless the environmental impact of the removal is likely to be greater than leaving the material *in situ*: if this is the case the appropriate national authority must be notified and approval obtained.

[Further site-specific content should be inserted here]

7(ix) Disposal of waste

Many existing Management Plans share similar wording in this section. A pool of suggested standard wording has been developed and can be used, amended or deleted as appropriate for the Area in question (see below). Proponents are encouraged to identify site-specific content, and should consider the guidance for this section of Management Plans given in Section 7(ix) of the Guide.

All wastes, including all human wastes, shall be removed from the Area.

All wastes, other than human wastes, shall be removed from the Area. [Although removal from the Area is preferable, human wastes may be disposed of into the sea]

Waste generated as a consequence of the activities developed in the Area shall be temporarily stored (insert site specific location details) in such a way as to prevent their dispersal into the environment and removed when activities have been concluded.

[Further site-specific content should be inserted here]

7(x) Measures that may be necessary to continue to meet the aims of the Management Plan

Many existing Management Plans share similar wording in this section. A pool of suggested standard wording has been developed and can be used, amended or deleted as appropriate for the Area in question (see below). Proponents are encouraged to identify site-specific content and should consider the guidance for this section of Management Plans given in Section 7(x) of the Guide.

Permits may be granted to enter the Area to:

- carry out monitoring and Area inspection activities, which may involve the collection of a small number of samples or data for analysis or review;
- erect or maintain signposts, structures or scientific equipment;
- carry out protective measures;
- [further site-specific content should be inserted here]

Any specific sites of long-term monitoring shall be appropriately marked on site and on maps of the Area. A GNSS position should be obtained for lodgement with the Antarctic Data Directory System through the appropriate national authority.

To help maintain the ecological and scientific values of the Area visitors shall take special precautions against introductions. Of particular concern are microbial, animal or vegetation introductions sourced from soils from other Antarctic sites, including stations, or from regions outside Antarctica. To the maximum extent practicable, visitors shall ensure that footwear, clothing and any equipment – particularly camping and sampling equipment – is thoroughly cleaned before entering the Area.

To avoid interference with long-term research and monitoring activities or duplication of effort, persons planning new projects within the Area should consult with established programmes and/or appropriate national authorities.

[Further site-specific content should be inserted here]

7(xi) Requirements for reports

Many existing Management Plans share similar wording in this section. A pool of suggested standard wording has been developed and can be used, amended or deleted as appropriate for the Area in question (see below). Proponents are encouraged to identify site-specific content, and should consider the guidance for this section of Management Plans given in Section 7(xi) of the Guide.

The principal permit holder for each visit to the Area shall submit a report to the appropriate national authority as soon as practicable, and no later than six months after the visit has been completed.*

Such reports should include, as appropriate, the information identified in the visit report form contained in the Guide to the Preparation of Management Plans for Antarctic Specially Protected Areas. If appropriate, the national authority should also forward a copy of the visit report to the Party that proposed the Management Plan, to assist in managing the Area and reviewing the Management Plan.

Parties should, wherever possible, deposit originals or copies of such original visit reports in a publicly accessible archive to maintain a record of usage, for the purpose of any review of the Management Plan and in organising the scientific use of the Area.

[Further site-specific content should be inserted here]

8. Supporting documentation

Section 8 of the Guide provides guidance for this section of Management Plans. No suggested standard wording is provided here because the content of this section will be specific to the Area in question.

[Site-specific content should be inserted here]

Resolution 2 (2024)

General Guidelines for Visitors to the Antarctic

The Representatives,

Recalling Recommendation XVIII-1 (1994), which annexed the Guidance for those organising and conducting tourism and non-governmental activities in the Antarctic and Resolution 3 (2011), which annexed General Guidelines for Visitors to the Antarctic ("General Guidelines");

Recalling Resolution 4 (2021), which annexed updated General Guidelines;

Recalling that, at Antarctic Treaty Consultative Meeting ("ATCM") XLV (2023), the Secretariat of the Antarctic Treaty ("the Secretariat") was tasked to review, within existing resources, all relevant Antarctic Treaty documents pertaining to current and future cooperation, to provide options for potential adoption by the ATCM that would ensure gender-neutral language across these documents;

Noting that the Secretariat has reviewed the General Guidelines and has prepared draft revised General Guidelines, in each of the official languages of the Antarctic Treaty, to address identified inconsistencies with the United Nations Guidelines for gender-inclusive language ("UN Guidelines");

Desiring to replace, at this time, only the current English language version of the General Guidelines;

Further desiring to submit the French, Russian and Spanish versions of the draft revised General Guidelines for proof-reading to ensure that the substance of their current provisions has not been altered;

Recommend that their Governments:

1. request the Secretariat to replace the English language version of the General Guidelines currently on its website with the revised version annexed to this Resolution; and

2. request the Secretariat to send the French, Russian and Spanish versions of the draft revised General Guidelines for proofreading to be presented for consideration to the 47th Antarctic Treaty Consultative Meeting.

General Guidelines for Visitors to the Antarctic

The General Guidelines apply to all visitors and all activities in the Antarctic Treaty area[1]. All visits to Antarctica should be conducted in accordance with the Antarctic Treaty, its Protocol on Environmental Protection, and relevant Measures, Decisions and Resolutions adopted at Antarctic Treaty Consultative Meetings (ATCMs). All activities must be subject to an Environmental Impact Assessment and must have prior approval/permission or meet all the requirements of the relevant National Competent Authority.

These Guidelines provide general guidance for visiting any location, with the aim of ensuring that visits do not have adverse impacts on the Antarctic environment, including wildlife and ecosystems, or on its scientific, wilderness and aesthetic values. ATCM Site Guidelines for Visitors provide additional site-specific advice for some locations. Guidelines concerning particular risks such as aircraft use, or avoiding the introduction of non-native species may also apply.

Consult these Guidelines before you visit Antarctica and plan how to minimise your impact. If you are part of a guided visitor group, abide by these guidelines, pay attention to your guides, and follow their instructions. If you are the organiser of your own visit or the visit of a group and respective activities, you are responsible for abiding by these guidelines. You are also responsible for identifying the features of the sites you visit that may be vulnerable to visitor impacts, and for complying with any specific requirements related to protected areas, Historic Sites and Monuments, activities or risks. Specific requirements can be included within ATCM Site Guidelines, Antarctic Specially Protected Area (ASPA) and Antarctic Specially Managed Area (ASMA) management plans, or station visit guidelines.

PROTECT ANTARCTIC WILDLIFE

WILDLIFE	• The taking of, or harmful interference with, Antarctic wildlife is prohibited. • When in the vicinity of wildlife – either on land or at sea, move or manoeuvre slowly and carefully and keep noise to a minimum. • Maintain an appropriate distance from wildlife to avoid disturbance. While in many cases a greater distance may be necessary, in general keep at least 5m from wildlife on land. Abide by any guidance on distances in species- or site-specific guidelines. • Always give animals the right of way and do not block their access routes between the sea and land, nesting places or other destinations. • Animals may alter their behaviour if disturbed. Observe wildlife behaviour. If wildlife changes its behaviour (standing when it was sitting, moving its head around alerted, start vocalising when it was silent, etc.) stop moving, or slowly increase your distance. • Stay outside the margins of a colony and observe from a safe distance. Animals are particularly sensitive to disturbance when they are breeding (including nesting) or moulting. • Every situation is different. Consider the topography and the individual circumstances of the site, as these may have an impact on the vulnerability of wildlife to disturbance. • Watch your steps for eggs, chicks or nest materials of skuas, penguins or petrels.

[1] It is acknowledged that exceptions to the application of elements of these guidelines may be made for scientific and official governmental activities if the realization of these activities so require and if prior approval has been given by the National Competent Authority and the activity meets all requirements of the relevant national authority.

	• Unpiloted aerial vehicles must not be used in the vicinity of wildlife. • Do not feed wildlife or leave food or scraps lying around.
VEGETATION	• Vegetation, including mosses and lichens, is fragile and very slow growing. Do not walk, drive or land on any moss beds or lichen covered rocks, in order to avoid damage. • When travelling on foot, stay on established tracks whenever possible to minimise disturbance or damage to the soil and vegetated surfaces. Where a track does not exist, choose your route carefully, taking the most direct route while avoiding vegetation, fragile terrain, scree slopes, and wildlife.
INTRODUCTION OF NON-NATIVE SPECIES AND PATHOGENS	• Do not introduce any plants or animals into the Antarctic. • In order to prevent the introduction of non-native species and disease, carefully wash boots and clean all equipment including clothes, bags, tripods, tents and walking sticks before bringing them to Antarctica. Pay particular attention to boot treads, velcro fastenings and pockets which could contain soil or seeds. Vehicles and aircraft should also be cleaned. • In order to prevent the transfer of non-native species and disease between locations in Antarctica ensure all clothing, boots and equipment are cleaned thoroughly before moving between sites and regions.

RESPECT PROTECTED AREAS AND STRUCTURES

ANTARCTIC SPECIALLY MANAGED AREAS (ASMAs) AND ANTARCTIC SPECIALLY PROTECTED AREAS (ASPAs)	• Activities in ASPA and ASMAs must comply with the provisions of the relevant Management Plan and abide by any restrictions regarding the conduct of activities in these areas. • A permit from a National Competent Authority is required for entry into any ASPA. Carry the permit and obey any permit conditions at all times while visiting an ASPA. • Check the locations and boundaries of ASPAs and ASMAs in advance and refer to the provisions of their Management Plans (all can be found at the Antarctic Treaty Secretariat website (www.ats.aq)).
HISTORIC SITES AND MONUMENTS (HSMs) AND OTHER STRUCTURES	• Some historic huts have been designated as ASPAs and require a permit to visit. Visits must follow the provisions laid out in the respective management plan. • Historic huts and structures can, in some cases, be visited for touristic, recreational and educational purposes. Visitors should not use them for other purposes except in emergency circumstances. • Do not damage, remove, destroy or change any historic site, monument, or artefact, or other building or emergency refuge (whether occupied or unoccupied). • Consult relevant ATCM Site Guidelines for Visitors for specific rules concerning historic sites, monuments, items or buildings and other structures in the vicinity. • Before entering any historic structure, clean your boots of snow and grit and remove snow and water from clothes, as these can cause damage to structures or artefacts. • Take care not to tread on any artefacts which may be obscured by sediments or snow when moving around historic sites.

	• If you come across an item that may be of historic value that authorities may not be aware of, do not touch or disturb it. Notify your expedition leader or NCAs. • A list of the formally designated HSMs can be found at the ATS website.

RESPECT SCIENTIFIC RESEARCH

	• Some Antarctic stations may accept visitors where prior arrangements have been made. Obtain permission before visiting Antarctic stations. • Reconfirm scheduled visits well in advance, or according to guidance provided by the manager of a station before arriving. • In addition to these general guidelines, comply with any site-specific rules or visitor guidelines in place when visiting Antarctic stations. • Do not interfere with or remove scientific equipment or markers, and do not disturb experimental study sites, field camps or stored supplies.

KEEP ANTARCTICA PRISTINE – LEAVE NO TRACE OF YOUR VISIT

WASTE	• Do not deposit any litter or garbage on land nor discard it into the sea. • No smoking except in designated areas at stations or camps, to avoid litter and risk of fire to structures. Collect ash and litter for disposal outside Antarctica. • Ensure that wastes are managed in accordance with Annexes III (waste disposal) and IV (marine pollution) to the Protocol on Environmental Protection to the Antarctic Treaty. • Ensure that all belongings, equipment and waste are secured at all times in such a way as to prevent dispersal into the environment through high winds or wildlife foraging.
WILDERNESS VALUES	• Do not disturb or pollute lakes, streams, rivers or other water bodies (*eg*, by walking, washing yourself or your equipment, throwing stones, etc.). • Do not paint or engrave names or other graffiti on any human-created or natural surface in Antarctica. • Do not take souvenirs, whether human-created, biological or geological items, including feathers, bones, eggs, vegetation, soil, rocks, meteorites and fossils. • Place tents and equipment on snow or at previously used campsites, where possible.

BE SAFE

SAFETY PRECAUTIONS/ PREPARATIONS	• Be prepared for severe and changeable weather. Ensure that your equipment and clothing meet Antarctic standards. Remember that the Antarctic environment is inhospitable, unpredictable and potentially dangerous. • Know your capabilities, the dangers posed by the Antarctic environment, and act accordingly. Plan activities with safety in mind at all times. • Keep a larger safety distance from potentially dangerous or territorial wildlife like fur seals, both on land and at sea. Keep at least 15-25 m away where practicable. • Be careful where you walk as seals can lie camouflaged on and among rocks. Keep a safety distance from sea ice edge and be cautious when stepping over cracks in the sea ice.

	• Skuas are very territorial birds and will attack anyone approaching their nests by plummeting down on intruders. If this happens, retreat away from the point when the attack started. • Any wildlife, even penguins, can cause serious harm. Do not underestimate risks. • If you are travelling in a group, act on the guidance and instructions of your leaders. Do not stray from your group as survival in Antarctica can be a matter of minutes (especially in case of acute hypothermia). • Do not walk onto glaciers or large snow fields without proper equipment and experience. There is a real danger of falling into hidden crevasses. • Be vigilant in the vicinity of calving glaciers. Breaking pieces of ice can generate dangerous waves. • Pay special attention when climbing rocks and/or boulders, as melting permafrost with changing temperatures lead to an increased risk of avalanches. • Do not expect a rescue service. Self-sufficiency is increased and risks reduced by sound planning, quality equipment and trained personnel. • Enter emergency refuges only in case of an actual emergency. If you use equipment or food from a refuge, inform the nearest research station or the National Competent Authority that has approved/permitted the visitors activity in Antarctica once the emergency is over. • Respect any smoking restrictions. Use of combustion style lanterns and naked flames in or around historic structures is strictly discouraged. Take great care to safeguard against the danger of fire. This is a real hazard in the dry environment of Antarctica.

LANDING AND TRANSPORT REQUIREMENTS

TRANSPORT	• Do not use aircraft, vessels, small boats, hovercraft or other means of transport in ways that disturb wildlife, either at sea or on land. • Avoid flying over concentrations of birds and mammals. Follow the advice in Resolution 2 (2004) *Guidelines for the operation of aircraft near concentrations of birds in Antarctica*. • Fuelling of aircraft (fixed and rotary wing) needs to be done in a way that minimises spillage and uses suitable spill containment equipment. • Refilling of fuel tanks for small boats should take place in a way that ensures any spills can be contained, for example onboard a vessel. • Check small boats are free of any soil, plants or animals prior to the commencement of any ship-to-shore operations. • Small boats must at all times regulate their course and speed so as to minimise disturbance to wildlife and to avoid any collisions with wildlife.
SHIPS[2]	• Only one ship may visit a site at any one time. • Vessels with more than 500 passengers shall not make landings in Antarctica.
LANDING OF PASSENGERS FROM VESSELS	• A maximum of 100 passengers may be ashore from a vessel at any one time, unless site specific guidance requires fewer passengers. • During landings from vessels, maintain a 1:20 guide to passenger ratio at all sites, unless site specific advice requires more guides.

[2] A ship is defined as a vessel which carries more than 12 passengers.

Made in the USA
Monee, IL
08 November 2026

67968594R00171